RUNAWAY
SERVANTS, CONVICTS, AND APPRENTICES ADVERTISED IN THE PENNSYLVANIA GAZETTE
1728–1796

Farley Grubb PhD
Economics Department
University of Delaware

CLEARFIELD

Reprinted for Clearfield Company by
Genealogical Publishing Company
Baltimore, Maryland
2011

Copyright © 1992
Farley Grubb
All Rights Reserved.
Published by Genealogical Publishing Co., Inc.
1001 N. Calvert St., Baltimore, Md. 21202
Library of Congress Catalogue Card Number 92-73631
International Standard Book Number 0-8063-1365-X
Made in the United States of America

INTRODUCTION

Many contract workers were employed in eighteenth-century America. Most were immigrants who entered servant contracts to pay for their passage across the Atlantic. Some were British convicts transported to America and obligated to work like other contract laborers for a fixed term as a penalty for their crimes. A final group of contract workers were not newly arrived immigrants. Either they had arrived some time before entering their labor contract or were American-born. This last group entered labor contracts to gain training as apprentices, to acquire some initial payment as hired workers, or to work off jail fees.

Information on individual immigrants arriving in the mid-Atlantic region during the eighteenth century is patchy. It is limited for Irish immigrants and convicts, sketchy for English, Scottish, and Welsh immigrants and convicts, and incomplete for Germans arriving at ports other than Philadelphia. Roughly half of all immigrants arrived as contract workers, indicating that they were too poor to pay for their transatlantic passage. Poor immigrants were also less likely to leave records of their migration, such as journals, letters, diaries, estate sales, or shipping invoices. Therefore, information gleaned from sources such as newspaper advertisements for runaway contract workers can provide valuable additions to our knowledge of these immigrants. The largest group among the runaways were Irish (see the distribution reported below), which is also the group about which we know the least from other migration records. This adds to the importance of the information presented here. Finally, for genealogists and those interested in tracing their ancestors, the runaway ads are a treasure chest of details about immigrants. They identify each servant's master, location, time in America, physical features, habits, and circumstances (see the examples reported below). This is information not typically available in other immigration records. Those who locate ancestors in the list presented here are encouraged to read the complete text in the original source to take advantage of the full extent of the information in the ad.

Pennsylvania Gazette Ads for Runaways

The Pennsylvania Gazette was a weekly newspaper for which a copy of all issues, with a few exceptions, have survived from November 2, 1728 to December 14, 1796. There are a few breaks in this weekly series indicating either the paper was not published, as was the case during the Revolutionary occupation of Philadelphia, or that copies have not survived. The missing weeks are: November 7 and 14, 1765; September 17, 1777 through December 31, 1778; September 19, 1787; and September 18 through November 13, 1793. The information used here for November 28, 1728 to the end of 1789 was taken from copies of the paper reprinted by The Historical Society of Pennsylvania, The Pennsylvania Gazette, 1728-1789 (Philadelphia: Microsurance Inc., 1968), vols. 1-25, and for January 6, 1790 to December 14, 1796 from microfilm copies held at Morris Library, University of Delaware.

All issues of the paper typically had two to four pages of news, mostly up front, and two to six pages of advertisements, mostly grouped at the end of the paper. While several newspapers were published in the Delaware Valley at various times, the Pennsylvania Gazette was one of the widest circulating (see the geographic distribution of the advertisers below) and one of the longest surviving newspapers in this region during the eighteenth century. In addition to being one of the few papers for which copies of most issues are still available today, the Pennsylvania Gazette is also one of the few which always engaged in advertising and was an important source of commercial as well as political news.

The advertisements for runaway contract workers varied widely. Some were long and detailed while others were relatively short and spare. Two examples are presented below, in their entirety.

Pennsylvania Gazette, June 2, 1773

RAN AWAY on Sunday, the 30th of May last, a servant man, named BENJAMIN SMITH, a Taylor by trade, he has fair hair, and wears it tied; had on a pair of white stockings, ticking breeches, a linen shirt, ruffed at the bosom, and a half-worn wool hat. He was in company with one John Ruffel. Whoever takes up the said servant, and secures him in any of his Majesty's goals, so that his master may get him, shall have THIRTY SHILLINGS, and all reasonable charges, paid by JOHN SUMMERL, at Penn's Neck, in Salem county.

Pennsylvania Gazette, April 10, 1793
SIXTEEN DOLLARS REWARD
Ran away from the subscriber, on Sunday, the 17th of March, 1793 a Dutch Servant Man, named FRANCIS DUNNE, by trade a tallow-chandler and soap-boiler, about twenty-five years of age, five feet four inches high, of a fair complexion, straight   darkish hair, and his eyes, it is believed, are darkish; he appears somewhat smaller in every day dress than he does in Sunday cloaths; he can speak broken English, and says he can talk Low Dutch, that he is a good scholar in German, and can write some English; and pretends to be some sort of a preacher; he arrived at Philadelphia on the 9th of September, 1792, in the Ship Columbia, from Amsterdam, William Maley, master. The said servant had on, and took with him, when he went away, a large cocked hat, about half worn, a dark blue broad cloath surtout coat, basket buttons of the same colour, one olive coloured close bodied coat and waistcoat, buttons covered with the same cloth, one black sattin waistcoat, one pair of black velvet breeches, with black buttons and silk kneebands, one black satinet ditto, one pair of woolen ditto, a new pair neat's leather shoes, a square pair of silver shoe buckles, a square pair of silver knee buckles, a small stock buckle of ditto, a pair of black shoe and knee buckles, one pair of steel ditto, one white shirt without sleeves, and two half ditto, one home-spun shirt, sundry stocks and cravats, two cotton cross barred handkercheifs. It is likely he may change his name and cloaths, as he had a number with him which are not known, and he is a deceiving villain. Whoever takes up and secures the said servant in any gaol, so that his master may get him again, shall receive the above reward and all reasonable charges, paid by WILLIAM SCOTT, living in the Northern-Liberty township, near the Falls of the Schuylkill, Philadelphia county, or by THOMAS SUTTON, in Philadelphia, the corner of Front and Catherine-Streets, at No. 366. All masters of vessels are forbid to harbour or carry him off upon their peril. It is expected that he went off in company with three other German servant men, viz Andrew Bartal, Philip Bartal, and Joseph Miller, belonging to Doctor George Hunter, of Philadelphia.
Northern-Liberty township, Philadelphia county, April 10, 1793.

Data Construction

A variety of runaways were advertised in the Gazette. Along with runaway apprentices, transported convicts, and servants, there were ads for escaped wives, slaves, mulattoes, Indians, thieves and criminals, deserters from the military, bail jumpers, and jail breakers, as well as ads for horses, cattle, boats, and deranged kinsmen who had wandered away. The runaways listed in this work are restricted to civilian contract workers of European descent who were apprentices, transported convicts, or servants. Deserters, bail jumpers, criminals, slaves, mulattoes, Indians, etc. are excluded. Ads for some of these other runaways, such as slaves, have been collected elsewhere. Past efforts at extracting this kind of information have not always distinguished between contract workers and runaway thieves, bail jumpers, deserters, and jail escapees; between apprentices, convicts, immigrants under contract to pay their passage, and other servants; or between repeat ads and new escapes. Wherever possible, the information presented here makes these distinctions.

The advertisements are too long and varied to reprint in full, and the information summarized here is not a direct transcription. Only the names were directly transcribed, leaving the spelling from the Gazette intact. When the same individual appeared with different spellings, the spelling was made consistent across the ads. The same runaway ad was typically repeated in subsequent issues, usually in three to ten or more issues, and not always in consecutive issues. Only the first ad for a given runaway is reported here, and subsequent ads for the same individual are only reported if they represented a new escape and not if they were merely repeat ads for a given escape. The information is reported alphabetically by the servant's last name for the period 1728 through 1796. The information recorded for each runaway is confined to two lines each and represents the most common and quantifiable information found across the advertisements.

LINE ONE

The servant's name is listed first as spelled by the Gazette. Following a comma, information on the master is reported starting with the master's name as spelled by the Gazette. Occasionally the servant's name was not listed in the ad, and sometimes the master's name was not listed, usually with a caveat to report any information about the runaway to the printer's office. In these cases the term "No Name" is used for servants, such as "No Name Man," and the term "Unlisted Name" is used for masters. If a servant had more than one master, only one master is listed here. The next item listed is the master's county and colony (state) of residence. The colony or state is abbreviated in the standard two-letter postal code, plus EJ for East Jersey and WJ for West Jersey. While the ads frequently included township or other location descriptions, that information is not included here. Following the colony or state is the master's occupation. This category includes the term "ironworks" if the master's location included reference to an iron furnace, forge, or works. The date of the newspaper where the ad first appears is reported directly after this information on the master. Dates for all ads are known. After the date and following a comma, descriptive information on the servant is listed starting with the servant's ethnicity. Because sub-regions were only occasionally mentioned, such as Hesse, Ulster, West Country, etc., only a general ethnic designator is used, such as German, Irish, English, etc. (see the ethnic distribution reported below). In addition, because masters did not accurately distinguish between Dutch and German servants, labeling most as Dutch when the vast majority were German, all references to Dutch have been changed to German. Finally, when ethnicity was not directly mentioned, it could occasionally be inferred from other information, such as birthplace, speech dialect, port of departure, etc. Hyphenated designators are used when mixed ethnicity was indicated in the ad.

The next item is the servant's age. When an age range was listed, such as 30 to 40, the average of this range is reported. When a two-year age range was listed, such as between 18 and 19, the younger age is reported. Following the servant's age is the servant's occupation. This includes being reported as a sailor or soldier if the servant was reported as being familiar with the sea or as having been in the military, and includes occupations furnished by the masters which may only have been notional. The next item includes special information about the servant's circumstances. This shows whether the runaway had been listed as a hired worker, been purchased out of a jail, had escaped before and been advertised in the Gazette (listed as "2nd escape"), had run away before but not been advertised in the Gazette (listed as "ran before"), had a spouse or child with him, and so on. Separate escapes by runaways with the same name were in some cases multiple escapes by the same individual. Cross-checking the descriptive data in the relevant ads was used to determine these cases.

The last item on Line One is a single letter designator indicating the nature of the contract. An "A" indicates an apprentice contract. A "C" indicates that the runaway is a transported convict. An "L" indicates that the worker had arrived in America some time before entering his current labor contract from which he was running away, or that he was American-born. The absence of these letter designators indicates that the worker was not listed as a convict or an apprentice, or with enough information to be assigned an "L". Most of these workers were probably immigrants who arrived under contract to pay for their passage, though explicit information to establish that fact was seldom included in the ad. Each piece of information on Line One is separated by two spaces, except where the information was too lengthy. When a piece of information is missing, it is because it was not provided in the ad. On rare occasions, when it was clear that the same servant or master appeared more than once in the data, any inconsistent information on location and age was made consistent.

LINE TWO

Line Two is indented, with a comma and a single space between each piece of information. The first piece of information shows the amount of time that had elapsed between the initial advertisement and the date the servant ran away, usually expressed in days, as in "47 days" ago, but sometimes expressed in other units or as a general period, as in ran away in "early June." Next is the day of the week the servant ran away. In some cases this information was not directly reported in the ad, but could be calculated from the information given. By comparing dates in various ads, it is clear that the Gazette was published on Thursdays until after the Revolution, and was then published on Wednesdays. Thus, the day of the week that the servant ran away could be inferred from the date that the servant ran away and vice versa. The date when the ad was written or was placed is not reported here and was not treated as the same date as when the servant ran away.

The next item is the maximum reward offered. Sometimes masters offered a series of rewards, usually rising with the distance from their home. The reward reported here is the largest sum offered. The reward is converted into the decimal equivalent of its basic unit, i.e. dollars, pounds, pistoles, etc. When indicated in the ad, the type of pounds or dollars is listed, such as Pennsylvania, Sterling, Spanish, Continental, etc. This was seldom indicated, however. In general, pounds were most probably Pennsylvania currency and not sterling. Next is the servant's height, expressed numerically in feet and inches when so reported in the ad, such as 5'4" or 5'6-7" when a range was reported, or as short, middle, or tall when so reported in the ad. Occasionally special information about the servant is listed in parentheses after the height, such as the approximate date the servant arrived in America, the amount of time he had left to serve, if his relatives lived nearby, if he ran away from a ship, if he had been in the army or navy, if he wore an iron collar, and so on. When a piece of information is missing, it is because it was not given in the ad.

Data Summary

There are a total of 6,157 escapes, i.e. 516 apprentices, 538 convicts, and 5,103 servants. Females comprise 526 of all escapes. Deleting repeat escapes, there are a total of 5,754 different runaway individuals, i.e. 504 apprentices, 500 convicts, and 4,750 servants. All of the following calculations are out of the total number of escapes, 6,157.

The ethnic distribution is 2,449 Irish, 1,004 English, 546 German, 297 American, 163 Scots, 107 Welsh, 28 French, 6 Spanish, 3 Portuguese, 3 Swedish, 2 Danish, 2 Italian, 2 Swiss, and 1,545 with undetermined ethnicity.

The geographic distribution of master towns, counties, and colonies from which these contract workers ran away is: 246 unknown, 1 Accomack VA, 1 Albany NY, 1 Albemarle VA, 89 Anne Arundel MD, 2 Anson NC, 12 Augusta VA, 413 Baltimore MD, 1 Bedford PA, 1 Bedford VA, 7 Berkeley VA, 78 Berks PA, 5 Boston MA, 240 Bucks PA, 198 Burlington NJ, 6 Calvert MD, 7 Cape May NJ, 3 Caroline MD, 2 Caroline VA, 204 Cecil MD, 10 Charles MD, 1 Charles VA, 996 Chester PA, 2 Culpeper VA, 26 Cumberland NJ, 82 Cumberland PA, 1 Dauphin PA, 7 Delaware PA, 10 Dorchester MD, 5 Dumfries VA, 1 Dutchess NY, 12 East Jersey, 5 Essex NJ, 7 Fairfax VA, 2 Franklin PA, 56 Frederick MD, 21 Frederick VA, 6 Fredericksburg VA, 153 Gloucester NJ, 5 Gloucester VA, 24 Harford MD, 74 Hunterdon NJ, 3 Huntingdon PA, 33 Kent DE, 112 Kent MD, 2 King and Queen VA, 1 King William VA, 593 Lancaster PA, 1 Lancaster VA, 6 Loudoun VA, 1 Luzerne PA, 1 MA, 13 MD, 15 Middlesex NJ, 46 Monmouth NJ, 28 Montgomery PA, 8 Morris NJ, 328 New Castle DE, 4 New York NY, 7 NJ, 2 Norfolk VA, 24 Northampton PA, 4 Northumberland PA, 8 Northumberland VA, 16 NY, 3 Orange VA, 1 PA, 474 Philadelphia County outside the city, 929 Philadelphia City, 7 Prince George MD, 3 Prince William VA, 103 Queen Anne MD, 1 RI, 1 Richmond VA, 140 Salem NJ, 6 Somerset MD, 4 Somerset NJ, 6 Somerset PA, 10 Stafford VA, 8 Saint Mary's MD, 15 Sussex NJ, 29 Talbot MD, 2 Union NJ, 11 VA, 7 Westmoreland VA, 1 Williamsburg VA, 4 Winchester VA, 5 West Jersey, 3 Worcester MD, 89 York PA.

The yearly distribution of runaways is:

YEAR	#	YEAR	#	YEAR	#	YEAR	#	YEAR	#	YEAR	#
1728	2	1740	60	1752	164	1764	188	1776	198	1788	30
1729	18	1741	58	1753	171	1765	184	1777	43	1789	13
1730	45	1742	71	1754	183	1766	242	1778	---	1790	21
1731	32	1743	71	1755	172	1767	179	1779	13	1791	15
1732	30	1744	58	1756	97	1768	171	1780	13	1792	26
1733	19	1745	83	1757	43	1769	207	1781	10	1793	17
1734	23	1746	106	1758	44	1770	187	1782	14	1794	43
1735	16	1747	109	1759	49	1771	218	1783	36	1795	28
1736	25	1748	93	1760	85	1772	209	1784	60	1796	33
1737	40	1749	92	1761	77	1773	247	1785	71		
1738	63	1750	142	1762	116	1774	267	1786	43		
1739	56	1751	165	1763	167	1775	268	1787	18		

Acknowledgments

The students who assisted in this project were: Kyriacos Aristotelous, Duke Bowen, Kaiyuan Dai, Brint Frith, Mark Hite, Daniel Houder, Eric Jones, Paul Mas, Lizabeth Moore, Robert Prosniewski, Marc Sydnor, William Wheatley. Their contributions included gathering the initial information, coding data, cross-checking data, and proof-reading data. Anne Pfaelzer de Ortiz provided editorial assistance. Their help is greatly appreciated. I provided the final proof-reading and cross-checking of all material and am responsible for all remaining errors.

The data presented here is part of a larger research project, currently underway, on labor contract malfeasance and the experience of servants in the mid-Atlantic region between 1700 and 1820.

Farley Grubb
Newark, DE
June, 1992

SELECTED REFERENCES

Bernard Bailyn, Voyagers to the West (New York: Alfred A. Knopf, 1986).
Peter Wilson Coldham, The Complete Book of Emigrants in Bondage, 1614-1775 (Baltimore: Genealogical Publishing Co., 1988).
Peter Wilson Coldham, Emigrants from England to the American Colonies, 1773-1776 (Baltimore: Genealogical Publishing Co., 1988).
Peter Wilson Coldham, Emigrants in Chains (Baltimore: Genealogical Publishing Co., 1992).
Peter Wilson Coldham, The Complete Book of Emigrants, 1700-1750 (Baltimore: Genealogical Publishing Co., 1992).
A. Roger Ekirch, Bound for America: The Transportation of British Convicts to the Colonies, 1718-1775 (New York: Oxford University Press, 1987).
David Galenson, White Servitude in Colonial America (New York: Cambridge University Press, 1981).
Karl F. Geiser, Redemptioners and Indentured Servants in the Colony and Commonwealth of Pennsylvania (New Haven: Tuttle, Morehouse, and Taylor Co., 1901).
Farley Grubb, "The Incidence of Servitude in Trans-Atlantic Migration, 1771-1804," Explorations in Economic History, 22 (July 1985), pp. 316-39.
Farley Grubb, "Immigrant Servant Labor: Their Occupational and Geographic Distribution in the Late Eighteenth-Century Mid-Atlantic Economy," Social Science History, 9 (Summer, 1985), pp. 249-75.
Farley Grubb, "The Auction of Redemptioner Servants, Philadelphia, 1771-1804: An Economic Analysis," Journal of Economic History, 48 (Sept. 1988), pp. 583-603.
Farley Grubb, "Servant Auction Records and Immigration into the Delaware Valley, 1745-1831: The Proportion of Females among Immigrant Servants," Proceedings of the American Philosophical Society, 133 (June 1989), pp. 154-69.
Farley Grubb, "The Long-Run Trend in the Value of European Immigrant Servants, 1654-1831: New Measurements and Interpretations," Research in Economic History, 14 (1992), forthcoming.
Cheesman A. Herrick, White Servitude in Pennsylvania (Philadelphia: John Joseph McVey, 1926).
Richard B. Morris, Government and Labor in Early America (Boston: Northeastern University Press, 1981).
Sharon V. Salinger, "To Serve Well and Faithfully," Labor and Indentured Servants in Pennsylvania, 1682-1800 (New York: Cambridge University Press, 1987).
Lucy Simler, "Tenancy in Colonial Pennsylvania: The Case of Chester County," William and Mary Quarterly, 43 (1986), pp. 542-69.
Kenneth Scott and Janet R. Clark, Abstracts from the Pennsylvania Gazette, 1748-1755 (Baltimore: Genealogical Publishing Co., 1977).
Abbot Emerson Smith, Colonists in Bondage (New York: W. W. Norton, 1947).
Robert J. Steinfeld, The Invention of Free Labor (Chapel Hill, NC: University of North Carolina Press, 1991).
Billy G. Smith and Richard Wojtowicz, Blacks Who Stole Themselves: Advertisements for Runaways in the Pennsylvania Gazette, 1728-1790 (Philadelphia: University of Pennsylvania Press, 1989).
Ralph B. Strassburger and William J. Hinke, Pennsylvania German Pioneers, 3 vols. (Norristown, PA: Pennsylvania German Society, 1934).

RUNAWAY SERVANTS, CONVICTS, AND APPRENTICES ADVERTISED IN THE PENNSYLVANIA GAZETTE, 1728-1796

FORMAT: Two lines of information per runaway arranged alphabetically by the runaway's last name.

Line 1: runaway's name, master's name, master's county and colony of residence, master's occupation, date of the newspaper where the advertisement first appears, runaway's ethnicity, runaway's age, runaway's occupation (other special information), runaway's contract code.

Line 2: time between newspaper advertisement and when the worker ran away, day of the week the worker ran away, maximum reward offered, runaway's height (other special information).

William Abbot, Henry Hollingsworth Cecil MD 8/12/1772, English 22
   16 days, Tuesday, 8 dollars, 5'5",
William Abbot, Thomas Owings Baltimore MD 7/7/1773, English 23 (2nd escape)
   17 days, Monday, 5 pounds, 5'2-3",
Matthias Abel, Philip Rotman 7/5/1775, shoemaker
   1 pound, 5'3",
Barbara Abercrombie, Josiah Hibberd Chester PA 9/11/1776, Scot 27
   234 days, Saturday, 4 pounds,
Jacob Able, William Stoots Philadelphia City PA 9/4/1776, 18 tailor A
   1 dollars, 5',
Thomas Able, William Smithson Harford MD 5/3/1775, English 25
   39 days, Sunday, 3 pounds, 5'5",
Abraham Abrahams, Hugh Bowes Philadelphia City PA ship captain 7/6/1769, Irish 15
   8 days, Wednesday, 3 pounds, 5',
Mary Achison, Samuel Nuttle Philadelphia City PA mariner 8/18/1763, Irish 20
   13 days, Friday, 1.5 pounds, tall,
Charles Acres, James Smith Baltimore MD ironworks 9/26/1765, 35 C
   2 pounds, 5'8", (has been in the colonies before)
William Acton, Nathan Bewley Philadelphia PA 5/28/1752, English 35
   12 days, Saturday, 3 pounds, middle,
John Adair, James McConnell New Castle DE 1/13/1763, Irish
   5 pounds, 5'10", (arrived last fall)
William Adair, George Wells Baltimore MD 11/9/1769, Scot blacksmith
   11 days, Sunday, 5 pounds, 5'8-9",
Anne Adams, Samuel Shaw Philadelphia PA 6/6/1771, 20 hired L
   14 days, Thursday, 3 dollars,
Francis Adams, David Stewart 4/24/1755, shoemaker
   25 days, Sunday, 4 pistoles, 5'10",
George Adams, Francis Hollinshead Somerset MD sheriff 7/4/1751, 19
   8 days, Wednesday, 0.75 pounds,
George Adams, Nicholas Britton Baltimore MD 9/13/1770, English 35
   5 pounds, 5'10",
Isaac Adams, Jacob Wagner Philadelphia City PA 7/2/1772, English 20 cooper A
   9 days, Tuesday, 2 pounds, 5'6-7",
James Adams, John Adams New Castle DE 12/23/1772, Irish
   4 dollars, 5'7",
Jediah Adams, Samuel Bowker Burlington NJ 9/29/1773, 17 A
   9 days, Tuesday, 2 pounds, 5",
John Adams, John Anderson Lancaster PA 4/18/1754, Irish 22
   2 pounds, 5'10",
John Adams, William Hansell 8/10/1796, 18 blacksmith A
   38 days, Sunday, 0.005 dollars, 5'7-8",
John Adams, David Lindsatt Queen Anne's MD 9/7/1769, 24 C
   3 pounds, 5'8-9",
Lemuel Adams, Joseph Reeve Salem NJ 10/5/1791, 19
   11 days, Saturday, 6 dollars, 5'2-3",
Ralph Adams, John Meconekin Queen Anne's MD 8/31/1774, English joiner
   13 days, Friday, 20 dollars,
Samuel Adams, Daniel Hothorn Philadelphia City PA tailor 11/16/1749, Irish 17 sailor A
   4 days, Sunday, 1.5 pounds, middle,
Thomas Adams, Samuel Adams Somerset MD 7/1/1762, 19 A
   0.75 pounds, 5'8",

Scilis Adder, Benjamin Town Bucks PA 3/29/1744, baker
  2 days, Tuesday, 1.5 pounds, short,
Mary Ann Agel, Samuel Davis Burlington NJ 8/25/1763, Irish 19
  18 days, Sunday, 1 pound, short,
Barbary Ager, Robert Rutherford Hunterdon NJ 1/5/1758, Irish (female)
  19 days, Saturday, 2 pounds, middle,
Thomas Ager, Charles Howard Baltimore MD 7/7/1773, English 25 (ran before) C
  17 days, Monday, 5 pounds, 5'4-5",
Thomas Agnew, Francis Humphreys Talbot MD 8/23/1770, Irish 30 weaver
  24 days, Monday, 2 pounds,
Morris Ahiern, John Rolfe Salem NJ 11/1/1744, Irish
  4 days, Sunday, 3 pounds, tall,
David Aiken, James Graham VA 11/23/1752, Scot sailor L
  21 days, Thursday, 1 pistole,
Michael Ainsworth, John Funk Frederick VA 12/11/1755, English silversmith
  4 pistoles, middle,
William Ainsworth, William Perkins 11/20/1735, 29
  1 pound, middle,
Benjamin Alburtis, John Evans Hunterdon NJ 4/4/1751, 20 cooper A
  11 days, Sunday, 3 pounds, 5'7",
Joseph Alcott, Jonathan Brown Gloucester NJ 5/9/1781, 19 A
  2 pounds, 4'5-6",
John Alderton, William Bronson Jr New Castle DE 7/19/1775, 22 barber
  9 days, Tuesday, 6 dollars, 5', (arrived last Sept.)
Thomas Aldridge, William Roberts Anne Arundel MD 12/4/1755, English sawyer
  32 days, Sunday, 3 pistoles, middle,
Joseph Aldworth, Lydia Morgan Baltimore MD 3/28/1771, Irish 19
  23 days, Tuesday, 3 pounds, 5'8-9",
Archibald Alexander, William Seal Chester PA 8/26/1756, Irish 22 weaver
  5 days, Saturday, 2 pounds, 5'9",
Daniel Alexander, William Boyd Philadelphia PA 1/1/1754, Irish 30 barber
  111 days, Wednesday, 3 pounds, middle, (arrived 7 years ago)
Gershom Alexander, Gideon Gilpin Chester PA 5/12/1763, 13 A
  1 pound,
Robert Alexander, James Mease Philadelphia City PA 1/19/1764, Irish 17
  3 days, Monday, 6 dollars, (arrived last fall)
Robert Alexander, Joseph Penrose Philadelphia City PA 8/9/1764, Irish 17 (2nd escape)
  2 days, Tuesday, 3 pounds, short,
Robert Alexander, Lawrence Shinney Philadelphia City PA 8/8/1765, Irish 18 (3rd escape)
  9 days, Tuesday, 2 pounds, 5',
Robert Alexander, Lawrence Shinney Philadelphia City PA 6/18/1767, Irish 19 (4th escape)
  11 days, Sunday, 0.5 pounds, 5'5",
Robert Alexander, William Hembel 4/6/1785, Irish 19
  9 days, Monday, 8 dollars,
Timothy Alexander, James Bayard Cecil MD 5/3/1744, English 35 shoemaker
  14 days, Thursday, 2 pounds,
Samuel Alison, Joseph Dixon Chester PA 10/26/1752, Irish 30 soldier
  3 days, Monday, 2 pounds, 5'8",
James Allcorn, Jacob Houseman Salem NJ 5/8/1776, American 17 L
  13 days, Friday, 5 dollars, short,
William Allcut, Israel Robeson Berks PA 7/16/1761, 15
  14 days, Thursday, 1.5 pounds,
William Allcut, Israel Robeson Berks PA 9/22/1763, 17 (2nd escape)
  19 days, Saturday, 3 pounds, 5'8",
William Allcut, Joseph Kirk Chester PA 5/8/1766, 20 (3rd escape)
  14 days, Thursday, 3 pounds, 5'8",
Aaron Allen, Joseph Scull Philadelphia City PA 8/24/1749, American 17 L
  5 days, Saturday, 1 pound,
Aaron Allen, Joshua Wood New Castle DE 4/5/1750, American 17 (2nd escape) L
  1.5 pounds, 5',
Aaron Allen, Andrew Sinnickson Salem NJ 6/26/1755, American 22 (3rd escape) L
  17 days, Monday, 2 pounds, middle,
James Allen, Isaac Janney Cecil MD 4/25/1754, Irish 24
  7 days, Thursday, 3 pounds, short,
James Allen, Thomas Water Frederick MD ironworks 9/8/1763, English 30 cooper
  5 pounds, 5'7",

John Allen, David Jarrett Chester PA 10/15/1794, 16 A
  6 days, Thursday, 6 dollars, 5'1-2",
Jonathan Allen, Abraham Darlington Chester PA 6/21/1775, Scot 21
  11 days, Sunday, 8 dollars, 5'9",
Joseph Allen, James Smith Philadelphia City PA brassfounder 8/1/1754, English 38 founder
  3 days, Monday, 2 pounds, 5'5",
Mary Allen, Joseph Park Chester PA 7/10/1776, English gaol sale L
  22 days, Wednesday, 4 dollars,
Patrick Allen, Richard Jarrard Philadelphia PA wheelwright 7/1/1742, Irish 30 joiner
  4 days, Sunday, 1 pound, middle,
Thomas Allen, Enoch Pearson Frederick VA 3/4/1756, Irish barber
  30 days, Tuesday, 3 pistoles, 5'2",
Samuel Allison, David English New Castle DE 11/15/1753, 35
  8 days, Wednesday, 3 pounds,
Elizabeth Allmark, John Buckley New Castle DE 4/9/1761, English 19
  8 days, Wednesday, 1 pound, middle,
Elizabeth Allmark, Robert Whitehall Lancaster PA 1/13/1763, English 21 (2nd escape)
  4 dollars,
Samuel Allsworth, Samuel Poole Anne Arundel MD 5/31/1770, 22 gunstocker C
  62 days, Friday, 20 dollars, 5'6-7",
Mary Aloan, David Niven New Castle DE 4/20/1738, Irish 26
  37 days, Tuesday, 2 pounds,
Katherine Alrig, John Biddle Philadelphia City PA 11/27/1760, German 16
  15 days, Wednesday, 3 pounds, short,
William Alton, James Chalmers New Castle DE 2/15/1738, English brickmaker
  2 pounds, short,
Matthias Ambruster, Obadiah Elliot New Castle DE 8/13/1752, German 36
  5 days, Saturday, 2 pounds, 5'6",
John Ancell, Thomas Colgate Baltimore MD 8/21/1766, English 30 C
  11 days, Sunday, 3 pounds, 5'6-7",
Alexander Anderson, John Henderson Philadelphia City PA nailmaker 11/10/1790, 19 nailmaker A
  63 days, Wednesday, 5 dollars, 5'4",
Barbara Anderson, William Simonds Chester PA 7/19/1764, Irish 20
  9 days, Tuesday, 1.5 pounds, (relatives live nearby)
James Anderson, John McDonogh York PA 12/28/1769, Irish
  17 days, Monday, 3 pounds, 5'7-8",
James Anderson, Sachevera Wood Philadelphia City PA 6/16/1763, tailor A
  235 days, Sunday, 5 pounds, (relatives live nearby)
James Anderson, Captain Crymer Baltimore MD ship captain 8/18/1763, English 32 C
  10 days, Monday, 1 pistole, 5'5",
John Anderson, Benedict Calvert Anne Arundel MD 6/24/1756, English brickmaker C
  18 days, Sunday, 40 pistoles, 5'10",
John Anderson, Francis Leech Lancaster PA 7/9/1752, Irish 20 hired L
  3 pounds, 5'8",
Joseph Anderson, Thomas Ennalls Dorchester MD 12/15/1773, Irish 30 schoolmaster
  10 dollars, 5'10",
Katherine Anderson, Martin Bickham Gloucester NJ 7/7/1748, Irish 23
  2 days, Tuesday, 3 pounds, middle,
Robert Anderson, Lewis Williams Philadelphia PA 8/13/1741, 30
  1 days, Wednesday, 1.5 pounds, middle,
Thomas Anderson, George Bard Lancaster PA 5/25/1769, Irish 19
  9 days, Tuesday, 3 pounds, 5'4",
William Anderson, John Trimble New Castle DE 1/22/1741, Irish 18 tailor
  4 days, Sunday, 1 pound, middle,
William Anderson, Alexander Craig Chester PA 4/16/1747, Irish 24 tailor (2nd escape)
  8 days, Wednesday, 2 pounds,
William Anderson, Alexander Craig Chester PA 11/12/1747, Irish 24 tailor (3rd escape)
  101 days, Monday, 1 pound,
William Anderson, John Carwood 11/17/1773, 21 ropemaker
  16 days, Tuesday, 2 pounds, 5'2-3",
Richard Andrew, Jacob McCombs New Castle DE 11/28/1771, Irish 19
  29 days, Wednesday, 8 dollars, 5'8-9",
Joseph Andrews, John Ensor Jr Baltimore MD 4/25/1765, Italian 27 C
  10 pounds, 5'8",
William Daniel Angess, John Francis 5/7/1772, English 25 C
  142 days, Sunday, 10 pounds, 5',

James Angus, Joseph McCulloch Philadelphia City PA 10/25/1775, Irish 18
    124 days, Saturday, 1 pound, 5'6-7", (lately arrived)
Thomas Anslow, James James New Castle DE 3/28/1751, German 25
    24 days, Monday, 3 pounds, 5'8",
Nathaniel Anster, Isaac Wayne Chester PA 12/25/1766, Irish 25
    4 days, Sunday, 1 pound, 5'6",
Nathaniel Anster, Isaac Wayne Chester PA 11/12/1767, Irish 26 (2nd escape)
    18 days, Sunday, 2 pounds, 5'6", (arrived 1 year ago)
Nathaniel Anster, Isaac Wayne Chester PA 6/6/1771, Irish 30 (3rd escape)
    4 days, Sunday, 8 dollars, 5'7", (arrived 4 years ago)
Nathaniel Anster, Isaac Wayne Chester PA 9/26/1771, Irish 30 (4th escape)
    14 days, Thursday, 1 pound, 5'7",
Nathaniel Anster, John Chambers Burlington NJ 4/19/1775, Irish 34 (5th escape)
    9 days, Tuesday, 1.5 pounds,
John Apperley, Philemon Thomas Queen Anne's MD 8/21/1755,
    1 pound,
James Wenman Appleton, Jonathan Davies Charles MD 11/27/1740, 19
    106 days, Wednesday, 7 pounds, short,
William Archdeacon, William Dimitt Baltimore MD 9/2/1742, 49 C
    32 days, Sunday, 3 PA pounds, tall,
John Archeacon, John Cottringer Philadelphia City PA 5/7/1772, Irish tailor
    15 days, Wednesday, 3 pounds, 5'4-5",
Benjamin Archer, William Lux Baltimore MD 5/3/1764, English 22 hatter C
    11 days, Sunday, 7.5 pounds,
Stephen Archer, John Rittinger Philadelphia PA 7/26/1775, English
    11 days, Sunday, 4 dollars, 5'5", (arrived in 1773)
William Archer, Matthias Graff Lancaster PA hatter 7/13/1769, Irish 22 L
    about 5 months ago, 3 pounds, 5'7",
George Armstong, William Jones Baltimore MD 9/1/1773, English 30 C
    22 days, Wednesday, 4 pounds, 5'5",
Eleanor Armstrong, William Evitt Philadelphia City PA 4/2/1772, Irish 26
    166 days, Friday, 6 dollars, 5'4", (arrived last June)
Mary Armstrong, John Rees Kent DE 7/12/1759,
    2 pounds, 5'2",
Mary Armstrong, Jacob Mytinger Philadelphia City PA 11/16/1785, Irish 14
    16 days, Monday, 6 dollars, short, (arrived 14 months ago)
Robert Armstrong, Adin Pancoast Frederick MD 7/14/1773, English 21 C
    18 days, Sunday, 10 pounds, 5'8-9",
Thomas Armstrong, Amos Garrett Lancaster PA ironworks 9/20/1753, Irish 26
    5 days, Saturday, 4 pistoles, 5'8",
Shelly Arnett, Shepard Kollock Philadelphia PA 5/1/1782, 19 (male) A
    7 days, Wednesday, 8 dollars, 5'6",
Valentine Arnold, Owen Jones Philadelphia City PA baker 6/18/1752, German 18 baker
    8 days, Wednesday, 3 pounds, short,
Jonathan Arnott, Samuel Osbourne Philadelphia City PA 2/12/1754, English 17
    2 days, Tuesday, 1.1 pounds,
Robert Ascot, James Haldane Philadelphia City PA 9/10/1767, English 23 coppersmith
    11 days, Sunday, 2 pounds, 5'1",
Betty Ashburn, Adam Williams Philadelphia PA 7/20/1758, Irish 50
    9 days, Tuesday, 1 pound,
Margaret Ashcroft, James Porter Chester PA blacksmith 9/26/1754, English 18
    7 days, Thursday, 1 pound, short,
Joseph Asheton, Henry Weston Philadelphia City PA 7/26/1786, 18 A
    10 days, Sunday, 1 dollar, 5'9",
Thomas Ashford, D. Dulany Talbot MD 10/30/1746, C
    90 days, Friday, 10 pounds, 5'10",
Patrick Ashley, James Crawford Lancaster PA 10/12/1769, 19
    2 pounds, 5'5",
Benjamin Ashton, Matthias Keen Philadelphia PA 11/21/1751, 20
    26 days, Saturday, 2 pounds, 5'10",
Richard Ashton, Thomas Dunning Philadelphia City PA 9/19/1734, 25
    4 days, Sunday, 5 pounds,
George Astins, Douglas Campbell Chester PA 3/13/1753, Irish 21
    15 days, Wednesday, 2 pounds, short,
Charlotte Ann Aston, George Evans Philadelphia PA 6/21/1764, English 16
    4 days, Sunday, 1.5 pounds, middle,

Charlotte Ann Aston, James Hamer Philadelphia PA 2/7/1765, English 17 (2nd escape)
 9 days, Tuesday, 3 dollars,
George Aston, Robert Boyle Chester PA tanner 8/23/1750, Irish 20
 3 pistoles, 5'6",
Thomas Atchison, Valentine Himes Chester PA 11/2/1785, Irish 22
 3 days, Sunday, 8 dollars, 5'7-8",
Anne Atkins, Nicholas Coues Bucks PA 8/16/1753, 22
 11 days, Sunday, 1.5 pounds, middle,
John Atkins, William Steward Kent MD 6/25/1752, English butcher C
 2 pounds, 6',
Samuel Atkins, Moses Brinton Lancaster PA 11/6/1766, Irish 22
 4 days, Sunday, 1.5 pounds, short, (lately arrived)
Samuel Atkins, Moses Brinton Lancaster PA 10/8/1767, Irish 23 (2nd escape)
 11 days, Sunday, 2 pounds, 5'3", (arrived last fall)
Thomas Atkison, James Scott Lancaster PA 6/1/1774, Irish 25
 16 days, Tuesday, 4 dollars,
Francis Atterbury, Thomas Shephard Philadelphia PA 8/28/1746, English 27
 15 days, Wednesday, 1.5 pounds, middle,
William Attwood, Henry Williams Queen Anne's MD 6/27/1754, English 19
 8 days, Wednesday, 2.5 pounds,
William Attwood, Samuel Parker 5/1/1776, 35 brassfounder
 14 days, Thursday, 1.5 pounds, 5'4",
John Bacchus, George Hooke York PA 5/16/1751, German
 24 days, Monday, 4 pounds, 6',
John Badger, Benjamin Chew 6/12/1776, English 19
 7 days, Thursday, 3 pounds, 5'3-4",
Thomas Badley, Alexis Lemmon Baltimore MD ironworks 9/5/1771, 50 C
 10 days, Monday, 3 pounds, 5'6-7",
Charles Badmin, William Hasleton Philadelphia City PA 12/3/1747, 17 A
 1 pound, short,
Andreas Bafeener, Joseph Gray Philadelphia City PA 11/16/1733, German 25
 4 days, Sunday, 2 pounds, tall,
Thomas Bagg, Blakesten Ingledeau Philadelphia City PA butcher 5/19/1737, Irish 30
 11 days, Sunday, 3 pounds, middle,
John Bagnall, William Hill Baltimore MD 9/1/1773, English 21 C
 22 days, Wednesday, 4 pounds, 5'9-10",
Thomas Bahn, William Dewees Jr Lancaster PA ironworks 9/14/1774, 26
 3 days, Monday, 4 dollars, 5'6",
John Bailey, John Elder Lancaster PA 11/20/1755, Irish 23
 41 days, Friday, 2 pounds, 5'7",
William Bailey, John Shaw NY merchant 12/14/1774,
 5'7",
Mary Baily, George Liggett Chester PA 12/1/1773, Irish
 10 days, Monday, 4 dollars,
Peter Bair, Conrad Leatherman York PA 5/15/1776, 16 shoemaker A
 9 days, Tuesday, 4 dollars,
Catherine Baker, Enoch Story Philadelphia City PA 1/1/1761, German 14
 9 days, Tuesday, 3 pounds, short,
Hubberd Baker, Philip Jackson Luzerne PA 3/16/1796, 19 A
 22 days, Tuesday, 0.06 dollars, 6',
Hugh Baker, Robert Lewis Jr Philadelphia City PA 10/11/1770, Irish 19 (2nd escape)
 4 days, Sunday, 5 pounds, 5'8",
Hugh Baker, Robert Lewis Jr Philadelphia City PA 5/24/1770, Irish 19
 4 days, Sunday, 5 pounds, 5'8",
Isaac Baker, Thomas Pim Chester PA 10/7/1772, English 17
 8 days, Wednesday, 2 pounds,
James Baker, William Waugh York PA 9/8/1773, Irish 22
 15 days, Wednesday, 2.5 pounds, 5'10",
John Baker, Thomas Laycock Chester PA 8/11/1784, Irish
 6 days, Thursday, 4 dollars, 6',
John Baker, John Grattan Augusta VA merchant 5/28/1772, English 20 C
 46 days, Sunday, 5 pounds, 5'8",
John Baker, Charles Ridgely Jr Baltimore MD ironworks 4/17/1760, English blacksmith C
 10 days, Monday, 5 pistoles, short,
Mary Baker, Andrew McGill Baltimore MD 7/9/1752,
 17 days, Monday, 1 pound,

Samuel Baker, Thomas Reed   Chester PA 3/14/1765, American 18 A
   9 days, Tuesday, 2 pounds, 5',
Thomas Baker, Richard Tighman Earle Queen Anne's MD 8/18/1757, bricklayer C
   18 days, Sunday, 3 pounds, 5'9",
William Baker, Edward Hanson Baltimore MD 11/9/1769, Irish
   11 days, Sunday, 5 pounds, 5'7",
William Baker, William Pennell Chester PA 7/17/1776, English
   68 days, Saturday, 2.5 pounds,
John Bakera, Andrew Beyer Philadelphia PA 5/14/1761, German 18
   7 days, Thursday, 5 pounds, 5'5",
Daniel Baldrige, John King Philadelphia City PA 12/2/1762, Scot (took wife and 2 children)
   60 days, Sunday, 5 pounds, 5'8",
Joseph Balford, Amos Austin Burlington NJ 8/18/1737, Irish 19
   10 days, Monday, 5 pounds,
Albinus Ball, Robert Adair Chester PA 9/7/1758, English 25 tanner
   11 days, Sunday, 2 pounds, 6', (was in the navy)
Christiana Ball, Henry Neill Philadelphia City PA 7/7/1773, English 20
   3 pounds,
Catherine Ball, Henry Neill Philadelphia City PA 8/4/1773, English 21 (2nd escape)
   3 pounds, (lately arrived)
Philip Balthasar, Richard Potter 2/5/1794, German 22 tailor
   23 days, Monday, 15 dollars, 5'7", (lately arrived)
William Bamber, John De Nyce Philadelphia City PA 10/31/1751, Irish barber
   1 pound, tall,
George Bamford, Jacob Shearer Philadelphia PA 4/1/1795, 18 farmer A
   10 days, Sunday, 12 dollars,
Edward Banbury, Stephen Burrows Hunterdon NJ 5/26/1743, 40 blacksmith
   10 days, Monday, 2 pounds,
Nathaniel Banester, William Jarret Philadelphia PA 6/19/1776, 17
   4 days, Sunday, 6 dollars, 5'4",
Elizabeth Barber, Thomas Godfrey Philadelphia City PA glazier 5/19/1737, English 21
   2 days, Tuesday, 1 pound, middle,
John Barber, Brittingham Dickerson Baltimore MD 11/9/1769, English sawyer
   11 days, Sunday, 5 pounds, 5'9-10",
William Barcley, James Kelso Baltimore MD 5/25/1774, 30 plaisterer L
   9 days, Tuesday, 10 pounds, 5'3-4", (arrived 13 years ago)
Charles Barker, Samuel Meredith Chester PA ironworks 5/21/1747, Irish
   34 days, Friday, 5 pounds,
John Barker, Richard Waln Jr Philadelphia PA 6/10/1742, English 18
   5 days, Saturday, 2 pounds, short,
John Barker, George Hoffnaels Lancaster PA 7/28/1768, 25 (ran before)
   4 dollars, 5'7",
William Barker, Edward Bosman Baltimore MD 8/23/1770, English 40 C
   8 days, Wednesday, 1 pound, 5'8",
George Barkley, William Thompson Baltimore MD 11/16/1743, Irish 26 tailor
   7 days, Thursday, 10 pounds, middle,
James Barkley, Joseph Crean Lancaster PA 8/6/1767,
   18 days, Sunday, 1.5 pounds, 5'11",
James Barkley, John Bull Philadelphia PA 3/16/1774, American 18 L
   9 days, Tuesday, 1.5 pounds, 5'8-9",
John Barkman, David Williamson Middlesex NJ 7/5/1764, German
   3 pounds,
Thomas Barlo, Richard Dennis New Castle DE 2/11/1752, American 21 A
   8 days, Wednesday, 5 pounds, 5'8",
John Barlow, Samuel Dick Salem NJ 11/28/1771, English 35
   16 months ago, 4 pounds, 5'9",
James Barly, John Keppler Philadelphia PA 3/10/1747, Irish 17
   12 days, Saturday, 3 pounds, middle,
Elizabeth Barnes, William Herring Philadelphia PA 1/9/1766, American 16 L
   5 days, Saturday, 0.75 pounds,
Elizabeth Barnes, Joseph Dutton New Castle DE 1/21/1768, American 18 (2nd escape) L
   1 pound,
Margaret Barnes, John Longdale Norfolk VA 1/5/1748, English breeches-maker
   93 days, Sunday, 1 pound, short,
Martha Barnes, David Heldreth Monmouth NJ 7/24/1735, 36
   24 days, Monday, 1 pound,

Jacob Barnet, Michael Cougler miller 11/14/1751, German
    9 days, Tuesday, 3 pounds, 5'6",
Levy Barnett, Jeremiah Sheredine Baltimore MD ironworks 11/20/1766, English 22 C
    8 days, Wednesday, 5 pounds, (arrived 12 months age)
Levy Barnett, Thomas Harrison Anne Arundel MD ironworks 6/18/1767, English 23 (2nd escape) C
    early June, 3 pounds, 5'8",
William C Barnett, James Boyd Frederick VA 4/12/1739, English wigmaker C
    47 days, Saturday, 2 pistols,
Matthew Barnhill, Henry Timanus Montgomery PA 4/22/1795, 18 shoemaker A
    10 days, Sunday, 30 dollars, 5', (has 2 years 7 months left to serve)
John Barnickle, Henry William Stiegal Lancaster PA glassmaker 4/27/1774, German
    15 days, Wednesday, 4 dollars, 5'3-4",
Isaac Barono, Abraham Wood Bucks PA 4/23/1730, French 25
    4 days, Sunday, 3 pounds, short,
Michael Barratt, John Nicholson Salem NJ 4/5/1764, 27 soldier
    11 days, Sunday, 2 pounds, 5'8",
Robert Barre, George Randell Lancaster PA 5/2/1771, Scot 23 nailer
    last Easter, 3 pounds,
John Barret, Thomas Robbins Philadelphia City PA blockmaker 3/14/1765, 16 A
    10 days, Monday, 1.5 pounds, 4',
Richard Barret, Nathaniel Grubb Chester PA 7/21/1737, Irish 20
    2 days, Tuesday, 2 pounds, tall,
Absalom Barrett, John Steelman Cape May NJ 8/3/1769, American 18 L
    10 days, Monday, 5 pounds, 5'6",
Richard Barrett, John Bordley Kent MD 8/27/1752, Irish 55 carpenter
    2.5 pounds, 6', (former soldier)
Lotts Barris, Theophilus Gardner Philadelphia City PA 3/27/1760, Irish 20 (female)
    6 days, Friday, 2 pounds, 5'8", (arrived August 1758)
Bartholomew Barron, John Anderson Cecil MD 3/22/1764, Irish 30
    7 days, Thursday, 2 pounds, 5'9",
Silvester Barron, David Cumming 9/22/1773, Irish 20 coppersmith
    21 days, Thursday, 6 dollars, 5'6",
Patrick Barros, John Davis Cumberland PA 2/5/1776, Irish
    22 days, Wednesday, 4 dollars, 5'6",
John Barrot, Jacob Bell Philadelphia City PA shoemaker 12/13/1775, 19 shoemaker A
    11 days, Sunday, 4 dollars, 5'6-7",
George Barrow, Humphrey Smith Philadelphia City PA 7/18/1765, English 19 wool comber
    42 days, Thursday, 5 pounds, 5'4",
Peter Barrs, Samuel Leonard Monmouth NJ 7/24/1755, French
    3 pounds, 5'6",
George Barry, John Lewis Gloucester VA 6/15/1738, 16 barber C
    51 days, Tuesday, 1 pistole, (arrived last March)
Michael Barry, Francis Pearson Chester PA 12/30/1742, Irish 24 weaver
    11 days, Sunday, 1.5 pounds, middle,
Robert Barry, William Woodcock New Castle DE 2/25/1755, Irish
    30 days, Tuesday, 2 pounds, 5'5",
Andrew Bartel, Michael Christman Berks PA 4/25/1765, German 27
    10 days, Monday, 3 pounds, 5'6",
Mrs. Bartel, Michael Christman Berks PA 4/25/1765, German 24 (has small child)
    10 days, Monday, 3 pounds, (wife to Andrew Bartel)
Adam Bartlemey, John Potts 6/17/1756, German carpenter
    8 days, Wednesday, 1.5 pounds, tall,
John Bartlett, Oliver Hastings Kent MD 6/6/1771, English 43 tinker C
    16 days, Tuesday, 4 pounds,
James Bartley, Amos Williams Chester PA 3/3/1773, 23 L
    16 days, Tuesday, 8 dollars, 5'10",
Hans Henry Bartram, Joseph Larkin Chester PA 6/5/1776, German 19
    3 days, Monday, 5 dollars, 5'7",
Frederick Basermain, Daniel Stonemats Philadelphia City PA 9/13/1775, German 19 cooper
    3 days, Monday, 8 dollars, 5'6",
John Christopher Basier, Benjamin Archer Burlington NJ blacksmith 10/28/1772, German 20
    3 dollars, 5'6-7",
John Christopher Basier, Emanuel Grubb New Castle DE 3/23/1774, German 21 (2nd escape)
    10 days, Monday, 5 pounds, 5'9",
Benjamin Bassweil, Michael Bishop Philadelphia PA 7/7/1779, English
    100 dollars, 5'4-5",

Samuel Bateman, Henry Vanbebber New Castle DE 5/13/1762, English soldier L
    9 days, Tuesday, 3 pounds,
Robert Baterby, John Ramsay Lancaster PA 12/17/1767, Irish 19 weaver
    15 days, Wednesday, 3 pounds, 5'5",
John Bates, Jonathan Wainwright Philadelphia City PA 7/24/1776, English 27
    4 days, Sunday, 5 pounds, 5'6-7",
George Bath, Edward Matthews Philadelphia City PA 1/22/1756, English
    25 days, Sunday, 3 pounds, 5'9",
John Bath, Josiah Clapham Frederick MD 10/16/1766, Scot weaver C
    mid-Aug., 5 pounds, 5'6",
John Batt, Valentine Larsch Baltimore MD 10/2/1760, 50 skins-dresser C
    6 pounds, 5'8",
Robert Batterbee, John Ramsey Lancaster PA 6/30/1768, Irish 19 weaver (ran before)
    16 days, Tuesday, 3 pounds, 5'4-5",
John Batterfly, Henry Snodderly Lancaster PA 3/13/1776, Irish 26
    29 days, Wednesday, 5 dollars, 5'3-4",
Bartholomew Baum, Peter Hassenclever EJ ironworks 6/12/1766, German miner
    14 days, Thursday, 5 pounds, (under a 3 year 4 month contract, imported)
John Bauman, George Levers Northampton PA 11/16/1785, German 30 hatter L
    22 days, Tuesday, 2 pounds, 5'5-6",
Isaac Baxter, Adam Hoops Bucks PA 6/21/1770, Irish 19 netmaker
    5'10",
John Beady, Walter Thetford New Castle DE 2/13/1750, Irish
    1 pound, short,
George Beans, Norris Carr Bucks PA 7/5/1770, 16 tailor A
    46 days, Sunday, 0.25 pounds, (has served one year to the tailor's trade)
Hugh Beaty, James Gilchrist Lancaster PA 8/9/1753, 16
    13 days, Friday, 2 pounds,
Jacob Beaver, George Palsgrove Philadelphia PA 11/30/1774, German 22
    22 days, Wednesday, 6 dollars, 4'10",
Jacob Beaver, Henry Jacobie Northampton PA 6/21/1775, German 23 (2nd escape)
    22 days, Wednesday, 8 dollars, 5'1",
Peter Beaver, Jacob Paul 2/18/1762, German-American 25 L
    9 days, Tuesday, 3 pounds,
Henricus Becker, George G Woelpper Philadelphia City PA 6/15/1796, German 24 butcher
    3 days, Sunday, 30 dollars, 5'4-5",
John Ludwig Becker, Godfrey King York PA 9/20/1775, German 20
    50 days, Wednesday, 1 pound, 5'6",
John Beddall, Ruth Harlen Chester PA 8/18/1743,
    4 days, Sunday, 1 pound, short,
Richard Beddes, Thomas Rees Lancaster PA 9/13/1739, 17
    7 days, Thursday, 3 pounds,
Rebecca Beech, Casper Snevely Lancaster PA 8/26/1772, English 19
    16 days, Tuesday, 4 pounds, (lately arrived)
John Beeten, Joseph Brown Lancaster PA 11/29/1775, 20 carpenter A
    11 days, Sunday, 8 dollars, 5'6-7",
Henry Begdriff, John Chandler Chester PA 11/20/1760, German 20
    16 days, Tuesday, 2 pounds, 5'7",
James Bell, Edenezor Call Philadelphia City PA chaise-maker 12/15/1763, Irish 22 harnessmaker
    11 days, Sunday, 3 pounds, 5'6",
James Bell, John Withy Chester PA 2/14/1765, Irish 24 harnessmaker (2nd escape)
    17 days, Monday, 2 pounds, 5'6",
James Bell, Samuel Hanson Charles MD 11/16/1774, English 40 miner
    3 pounds, (arrived last Sept.)
John Bell, Joseph Gray Philadelphia City PA 3/28/1749, Swedish-American 33 L
    3 pounds, short,
Cassius Belliger, Israel Pemberton Philadelphia City PA 10/15/1767, English 19
    10 days, Monday, 10 pounds,
Joseph Belong, George Steuart Anne Arundel MD 7/27/1774, English 35 joiner C
    47 days, Saturday, 5 pounds,
Christopher Bench, Jeremiah Smith Salem NJ 7/18/1765, 18
    1.5 pounds,
Lawrence Bench, John James Salem NJ 6/23/1790,
    7 days, Wednesday, 5 pounds, 6',
Robert Bencroft, Philip Weathrall Cecil MD 12/7/1769, Irish 22 stone-mason
    11 days, Sunday, 6 dollars, 5'10", (arrived last Sept.)

John Benn, Alexander Hunt Chester PA 10/19/1738, Irish 20
    4 days, Sunday, 1 pound, short,
George Bennet, Lewis Wilmin Lancaster PA 11/3/1768, 24 A
    25 days, Sunday, 2 pounds, 5'5",
John Bennet, Mary Wilson Queen Anne's MD 4/21/1737, English 25 butcher
    8 days, Wednesday, 3 pounds,
John Bennet, George Falkar Philadelphia City PA 8/14/1782, 16 cordwainer A
    2 dollars, 4'9-10",
Margaret Bennet, John Read New Castle DE 9/23/1762, Irish
    21 days, Thursday, 2 pounds,
Thomas Bennet, James Clark Middlesex NJ 11/16/1749, English 40
    6 days, Friday, 2 pounds, middle,
Thomas Bennet, John Murray Baltimore MD 10/6/1768, 33
    10 days, Monday, 2 pounds, 5'6-7",
James Bennett, Henry Meve Chester PA 1/6/1773, English 20
    31 days, Monday, 5 pounds, 5'10", (convicted of felony last term)
John Bennett, Charles Miller New Castle DE 8/14/1746, American 19 brassfounder A
    5 pounds,
Benjamin Benson, Daniel Livergood Berks PA 5/8/1782, 19 joiner A
    6 pounds, 6',
Richard Benson, John McFaden Philadelphia PA 10/26/1769, weaver
    13 days, Friday, 1.5 pounds, 5'8",
Thomas Benson, George Brown Baltimore MD 7/11/1745, English
    4 pounds, tall,
Thomas Bentley, James Smith Lancaster PA 6/30/1748, American L
    15 days, Wednesday, 4 pounds, short,
Thomas Bently, Henry Smith Philadelphia PA 2/27/1734, 18
    15 days, Wednesday, 3 pounds,
Thomas Berady, Simon Souder Cumberland NJ 4/27/1785, Irish
    15 days, Tuesday, 3 pounds,
John Bergenhoose, Joseph Johnson Philadelphia PA 4/24/1776, American 20 L
    10 days, Monday, 5'9",
Henry Berger, William Clarke Hunterdon NJ 11/11/1772, German 27
    5 pounds, 5'9-10",
Conrad Bernard, Aaron Matson Chester PA 11/9/1774, German 24
    15 days, Wednesday, 4 pounds, 5'6", (arrived 3 weeks ago)
Christina Bernhard, Michael Bens Lancaster PA 4/10/1755, German 20
    9 days, Tuesday, 5 pounds,
Jacob Bernhard, Michael Bens Lancaster PA 4/10/1755, German
    9 days, Tuesday, 5 pounds, 6',
John Justes Bernsheuer, John Rup Philadelphia City PA 12/5/1771, German 25 shoemaker
    4 days, Sunday, 6 pounds, 5'9", (arrived last July)
Francis Berrara, Joseph Bell Burlington NJ ironworks 7/5/1775, Spanish 30
    10 days, Monday, 5 dollars, 6'2",
Francis Berrara, Joseph Cox Burlington NJ ironworks 7/10/1776, Spanish 31 (2nd escape)
    17 days, Monday, 5 dollars, 6'2",
Benjamin Berry, Samuel Eves New Castle DE sadler 5/14/1730,
    9 days, Tuesday, 1 pound, middle,
Benjamin Berry, Samuel Eves New Castle DE sadler 1/26/1731, (2nd escape)
    14 days, Thursday, 3 pounds, middle,
Benjamin Berry, Samuel Eves New Castle DE sadler 3/4/1731, (3rd escape)
    10 days, Monday, 1 pound, middle,
Benjamin Berry, Samuel Eves New Castle DE sadler 5/20/1731, (4th escape)
    16 days, Tuesday, 1 pound,
Garrat Berry, Andrew Gardiner Salem NJ 12/14/1742, Irish 30
    37 days, Tuesday, 1 pound, middle,
John Berry, Robert Hays Lancaster PA 7/28/1768, Irish 25
    6 days, Friday, 3 pounds, short, (arrived this summer)
Michael Berry, Thomas Sugar Philadelphia City PA carpenter 2/7/1740, Irish carpenter
    2 pounds,
Engel Bertelosen, James Brown Gloucester NJ 7/24/1776, German 29
    9 days, Tuesday, 3 dollars, 5'7-8",
Andrew Bertle, Joseph Johnson Philadelphia PA 5/23/1771, German shoemaker
    4 days, Sunday, 8 dollars, 5'6", (arrived 10 months ago)
Christian Beryon, David Cooper Gloucester NJ 6/28/1775, German 28
    16 days, Tuesday, 6 dollars, middle,

James Bethell, Benjamin Everett Kent MD 1/29/1754, English 19
    8 days, Wednesday, 3 pounds, short,
Hugh Betty, William Littler Chester PA 12/25/1755,
    6 days, Friday, 1 pound, 5',
Thomas Bevan, James Miller Prince George MD 11/29/1770, 25
    3 days, Monday, 3 pounds, 5'4-5",
Frederick Beyerlein, Lewis Stroak Philadelphia PA tanner 10/2/1776, 19
    4 pounds,
John Beyrot, Bynkdict Eichelman Lancaster PA 8/29/1771, German 21
    3 months ago, 3 pounds, 5'7",
Thomas Bibbling, Camaliel Butler Anne Arundel MD 4/25/1751, English 30 bricklayer
    2.5 pistoles,
John Lawrence Bicking, Tench Coxe Philadelphia City PA 6/8/1785, German 30 baker
    4 days, Saturday, 8 dollars, 5'9", (arrived last fall)
Patrick Bickum, David Clayton Salem NJ 6/25/1772, Scot 23
    1.5 pounds, 5'8",
James Biddle, Thomas Hart Philadelphia City PA bricklayer 10/14/1731, chimneysweep
    4 days, Sunday, 1 pound, middle,
John Bernard Biederey, Marcus Kull Philadelphia City PA baker 4/26/1744, German 20
    3 pounds, tall,
John Biffey, Edward Stevenson Frederick MD 3/12/1772, 22
    4 pounds, 5'6-7",
James Bigley, Jonathan Willis Chester PA 4/21/1748, Irish 18
    3 days, Monday, 2 pounds, tall,
John Billon, James Clark Richmond VA 5/30/1765, English 30 C
    5 pounds, 5'6",
Henry Bimpson, George Crow New Castle DE 9/28/1752, English 30 clockmaker
    9 days, Tuesday, 5 pounds, 5'8",
John Bingley, Charles Lawrence 4/14/1768, English 19 carpenter A
    18 days, Sunday, 5 pounds, 5'6",
Bartholomew Bird, John Senhouse Anne Arundel MD 3/6/1740, 26 shoemaker C
    5 Maryland pounds, middle,
Israel Bird, Eleazer Twining Bucks PA 9/29/1768, English
    4 days, Sunday, 1.5 pound, 5'8-9",
Samuel Bird, John Davis Philadelphia City PA 7/12/1775, English 20 upholsterer
    15 days, Wednesday, 3 pounds, 5'8",
William Bird, James Lawrie Monmouth NJ 2/20/1772, 21
    4 days, Sunday, 4 dollars, 5'4",
Patrick Birds, John Patton Berks PA ironworks 8/4/1784, Irish 24 blacksmith
    10 days, Sunday, 16 dollars, 5'9", (lately arrived)
John Birk, Richard Graham Dumfies VA 5/3/1759, Irish C
    26 days, Saturday, 5 pounds, 5'8",
John Michael Bischoff, Philip Steffan Chester PA 9/19/1765, German 21
    11 days, Sunday, 5 pounds,
Andrew Bishop, Going Lamphier Fairfax VA 6/20/1765, Irish 22
    20 days, Friday, 3 pounds, 5'8",
James Bishop, Robert Thornburgh Cumberland PA ironworks 6/6/1765, English 28 soldier L
    10 pounds, 5'8",
Joseph Bishop, Michael Scheimer Chester PA 2/13/1766, German 21
    10 days, Monday, 5 pounds, middle,
Joseph Bishop, Solomon Miller 8/31/1785, German 40
    17 days, Sunday, 8 dollars, 5'6",
Joseph Bishop, Turbutt Benton Sr Queen Anne's MD 9/7/1769, 23 C
    3 pounds, 5'7-8",
Charles Black, Alexander Miller New Castle DE 3/14/1765, Irish 25
    6 days, Friday, 3 pounds, (arrived a few weeks ago)
Charles Black, Alexander Miller New Castle DE 8/15/1765, Irish 25 (2nd escape)
    4 days, Sunday, 2.5 pounds, 5'5-6",
George Black, Robert Smith Bucks PA 4/1/1756, German 18
    8 days, Wednesday, 2.5 pounds, 5'6",
John Black, John Reedle Philadelphia City PA 5/16/1771, Scot 23 tailor
    33 days, Saturday, 2 pounds,
Patrick Black, Robert McGraw Lancaster PA 2/27/1766, 25
    3 pounds, 5'7",
Thomas Black, Richard Osburn Loudoun VA 9/7/1774, Irish C
    4 pounds, 5'6",

James Blackaler, Thomas Stevenson Hunterdon NJ 6/29/1774, English 20
    14 days, Thursday, 4 dollars, 5'4", (arrived last fall)
Francis Blackburn, Charles Beatty Frederick MD fuller 9/22/1768, Scot 22 fuller L
    10 days, Monday, 6 pounds,
John Blackell, John Footman Baltimore MD 10/18/1770, English 26 C
    101 days, Monday, 1 pound, 6',
Henry Blackenborn, Jacob Umeneetter Bucks PA 6/19/1766, German 21 miller
    12 days, Saturday, 5 pounds, 5'5",
William Blackmore, Isaac Harris Salem NJ 7/31/1776, English
    10 days, Monday, 8 dollars, 5'7-8",
Samuel Blair, Joseph Smith Baltimore MD ironworks 1/15/1756, ship carpenter
    21 days, Thursday, 2 pistols,
William Blake, Jacob Chandler Hunterdon NJ 10/19/1752, tailor
    5 days, Saturday, 1 pound,
William Blake, Peter Hunter Baltimore MD 7/7/1768, English 35 shoemaker C
    11 days, Sunday, 5 pounds, 5'9",
William Blake, Peter Hunter Baltimore MD 7/26/1770, English 37 shoemaker C
    16 days, Tuesday, 5 pounds, 5'10",
Henry Blakeley, John McMakin Bucks PA 6/10/1742, Irish 17
    25 days, Sunday, 2 pounds, 5'4",
John Blakely, John Solors Jr 7/24/1755, Irish coachmaker C
    5 pounds, middle,
William Blamey, John King New Castle DE 12/28/1769, American 17 L
    2 pounds, 5'6-7",
John Blamy, John Jones Philadelphia City PA cooper 8/25/1763,
    9 days, Tuesday, 1.5 pounds, 4'10",
William Blanklett, William Smithson Harford MD 5/3/1775, English 27
    39 days, Sunday, 3 pounds, 5'4",
Henry Block, Michael Dotterer Philadelphia PA 8/16/1770, German
    4 days, Sunday, 1 pound, 5',
Richard Block, John Way New Castle DE 3/31/1768, Irish 21
    19 days, Saturday, 10 dollars, 5'8-9",
John Blowden, Arthur Wells Philadelphia City PA 3/11/1731, 23 shoemaker (ran before)
    1 day, Wednesday, 2 pounds, middle,
John Blowden, William Smith Philadelphia City PA shoemaker 3/22/1733, 25 shoemaker (2nd esc)
    11 days, Sunday, 5 pounds,
John Blowden, William Smith Philadelphia City PA shoemaker 10/11/1733, 25 shoemaker (3rd esc)
    3 pounds,
John Blowden, James Norrel Berks PA 11/20/1735, 27 shoemaker hired (4th escape) L
    11 days, Sunday, 3 pounds,
William Blows, John Hirst Bucks PA 4/20/1749, English 28 L
    4 days, Sunday, 5 pounds,
James Bluet, George Marclay Philadelphia City PA 7/11/1787, 17 cordwainer A
    7 days, Wednesday, 0.05 pounds, 5'4",
William Blumefield, Patrick Renalds Burlington NJ 5/16/1751, English 35 carpenter gaol sale L
    2 pistols, 5'10",
Samuel Boardman, John Cresson 11/18/1762, 19 (2nd escape) A
    4 days, Sunday, 2 pounds, 5'10",
Samuel Boardman, John Cresson 9/9/1762, 19 A
    4 days, Sunday, 2 pounds, 5'8",
William Boat, John Baldwin Bucks PA 7/7/1748, Irish 20 shoemaker
    4 days, Sunday, 2 pounds,
Hans Boch, Thomas Hall Chester PA 2/25/1755, German
    9 days, Tuesday, 2 pounds, 5'9",
Robert Bockford, William Coppuck Burlington NJ 7/11/1765, 20
    1 pound, 5'8-9",
Unity Boddin, Abraham Carpenter Philadelphia City PA 12/29/1757, maid
    11 days, Sunday, 1.5 pounds, (arrived last summer)
John Boddiscurts, Joseph Lynn Philadelphia City PA shipwright 1/17/1738, shipwright
    3 pounds, middle,
Henry Conrad Bogar, Thomas Bull Bucks PA ironworks 7/21/1773, German 24 smith
    10 days, Monday, 6 dollars, 5'7-8", (arrived last May)
William Hampton Boggs, Isaac FitzRandolph Philadelphia City PA 9/27/1780, 16 shoemaker A
    2 days, Monday, 20 continental dollars,
John Bohannon, George Heppler Montgomery PA 7/12/1786, Irish 22
    18 days, Saturday, 8 dollars, 5'9", (lately arrived)

John Boling, Mahlon Wright Burlington NJ 7/7/1773, English 21
   9 days, Tuesday, 3 pounds, 5'7-8",
John Bolivant, James Lemmon Harford MD 10/19/1774, Irish 24
   8 dollars, 6',
Judith Bolton, Elizabeth Robertson Philadelphia City PA 3/12/1767,
   12 days, Saturday, 1 pound, short, (has been many years with the army)
William Bolton, David Caldwell Bucks PA 6/1/1774, English 15
   12 days, Saturday, 2 pounds, 5',
James Bond, Joseph Lynn Philadelphia City PA shipwright 6/15/1738, English sawyer
   2 pounds,
Elizabeth Bone, Abraham Wayne Philadelphia City PA 1/13/1773, German 21
   7 days, Thursday, 8 dollars,
William Bone, William Dimitt Baltimore MD 9/2/1742, 19 C
   32 days, Sunday, 3 PA pounds,
Robert Bools, Patrick Rock Harford MD 5/1/1776, English 28 C
   260 days, Tuesday, 20 dollars, 5'7-8",
William Boon, Thomas Tyson Philadelphia PA 11/3/1773, English 23 nailer
   8 dollars, 5'10",
William Boon, Thomas Tyson Philadelphia PA 7/19/1775, English 25 nailer (2nd escape)
   16 days, Tuesday, 6 dollars, 5'8-9",
Thomas Booth, Thomas Edwards Lancaster PA 9/2/1736, Irish 21
   2 pounds, short,
Matthias Borell, Henry Emig Bucks PA 10/13/1773, German 26
   17 days, Monday, 5 pounds,
Justus Bornschier, John Roop Philadelphia City PA 11/24/1773, German shoemaker
   31 days, Monday, 3 pounds, 5'7-8",
William Borrow, William Dockery Queen Anne's MD 11/8/1759, English 21 C
   59 days, Monday, 2 pounds, 5'8",
James Borson, John Drummond Kent MD 7/9/1741, Scot
   one month ago, 2 pounds, short,
Edward Bosden, John Vansant Kent MD 7/27/1769, English
   17 days, Monday, 10 dollars, 5'6-7",
Carolina Bosinger, Arthur Broades Philadelphia PA 8/4/1779, German 30
   22 days, Tuesday, 20 dollars, (arrived some years ago)
William Bostock, James Wallace Anne Arundel MD ironworks 9/12/1765, English 30 weaver C
   25 days, Sunday, 5 pounds, 5'4", (arrived Aug. 1764)
Thomas Boswell, Hugh Coulter Philadelphia City PA 4/28/1748, sailor L
   8 days, Wednesday, 5 pistoles,
John Bottin, Edward Norwood Baltimore MD 11/21/1771, 25 C
   26 days, Saturday, 3 pounds, 5'8",
James Boucher, Samuel Evans Chester PA 11/3/1748, Irish 18 shoemaker
   3 days, Monday, 2 pounds, middle,
James Boucher, John Leake Philadelphia PA 9/7/1749, Irish 19 shoemaker (2nd escape)
   3 days, Monday, 1.5 pounds, middle,
James Boucher, John Lettimore New Castle DE 1/21/1752, Irish 21 shoemaker (3rd escape) L
   6 days, Friday, 5 pounds, middle,
John Boudenhaken, Matthias Kiger Salem NJ 10/6/1757, German 35
   9 days, Tuesday, 3 pounds, short,
John Bourk, John Farrail Albany NY 9/8/1757, 20
   5 pistoles, 5'2",
Richard Bourk, Didymus Lewis Chester PA 5/3/1775, Irish sailor
   5 days, Saturday, 4 dollars, 5'6-7", (use to the sea)
James Bourne, Captain Hinton Philadelphia City PA ship captain 11/21/1751, Irish weaver
   1 pound, short, (ran from ship)
John Bourne, Henry Mitchell Bucks PA 1/31/1749, Irish 20
   8 days, Wednesday, 2 pounds, short,
Patrick Bourne, Andrew Zelefio Cecil MD 6/5/1740, Irish
   10 days, Monday, 1.5 pounds, middle,
John Bous, Christopher Yeakle Philadelphia PA 2/2/1780, 17 A
   about 604 days,
Samuel Bowden, Jacob Van Bidder Cecil MD 10/17/1754, English painter
   11 days, Sunday, 3 pounds, 5'8", (use to the sea)
Michael Bowdle, John Scholey Burlington NJ 5/31/1744, Irish 20
   4 days, Sunday, short,
Henry Bowen, James Sharples Chester PA 4/5/1739, 17
   33 days, Saturday, 1 pound, short,

Owen Bowen, John Kille 1/12/1774, American 27 L
16 days, Tuesday, 3 pounds, 5'10-11",
Patrick Bowen, Jacob Lemmon Baltimore MD 11/17/1784, Irish 20 weaver
5 pounds, 5'5", (lately arrived)
Richard Bowen, Samuel Worthington Philadelphia PA 4/30/1730, 22
5 days, Saturday, 2.5 pounds,
William Bowen, George Matthew Philadelphia City PA ship captain 10/3/1751, Welsh 22 tailor
5 days, Saturday, 2 pounds, 5'8", (ran from ship)
Cornelius Bower, Thomas Potts Sr Philadelphia City PA 11/3/1748, 30
11 days, Sunday, 3 pounds, 5'10", (has been several years out privateering)
John Bower, Jacob Keyser Philadelphia City PA 7/2/1761, 17 tailor
1 pound, 5',
Thomas Bowling, Riginald Graham Baltimore MD 11/25/1772, Irish 25 C
19 days, Saturday, 10 pounds, 5'10-11", (arrived 12 months ago)
John Bowls, Joseph Decow Hunterdon NJ 1/18/1739, shoemaker
25 days, Sunday, 1.5 pounds, middle,
Thomas Bowman, John Lee Webster Baltimore MD 3/5/1767, English gardener
13 days, Friday,
Jeff Box, Thomas Dockery Queen Anne's MD 1/2/1766, American 18 A
10 days, Monday, 2 pounds,
No Name Boy, Zachariah Robbins Monmouth NJ 10/13/1743, 17 shoemaker
14 days, Thursday, 3 pounds,
No Name Boy, John Patton Cecil MD 3/18/1731, Irish 16
4 days, Sunday, 1 pound,
No Name Boy, Thomas McCool Baltimore MD 10/30/1760, 13 tailor
1 pound,
No Name Boy, Sarah McDowell Chester PA 4/11/1771, 16
last mid-May, 8 dollars,
No Name Boy, Mary Miller Lancaster PA 2/5/1777, Irish 16
76 days, Friday, 1 pound,
No Name Boy, James Cummings Chester PA 10/23/1776, Scot 23
13 days, Friday, 8 dollars,
No Name Boy, Philip Wescot Cumberland NJ 10/14/1795, 17
29 days, Tuesday, 8 dollars,
No Name Boy, Thomas Robinson New Castle DE 11/27/1766, Swedish 19 shoemaker A
5 days, Saturday, 8 dollars, 5'8",
No Name Boy, Nathan Newlin Chester PA 11/21/1771, 18 cooper A
8 days, Wednesday, 1 pound, 5'4",
John Boyce, Stephen Onion Baltimore MD ironworks 6/27/1751, 25
11 days, Sunday, 3 pounds, short, (use to the sea)
Joseph Boyce, Caleb Evans Philadelphia City PA blacksmith 3/6/1753, 19 A
5'9",
Andrew Boyd, Alexander Brown Salem NJ 6/21/1770, Irish 20
2 pounds, 5'4-5",
Ann Boyd, Redmond Cunningham Philadelphia City PA 3/3/1742, Irish 22
0 days, Thursday, 1.5 pounds, tall, (ran from ship)
Elizabeth Boyd, Francis Pearson Chester PA 10/28/1762, 18
30 days, Tuesday, 1.5 pounds,
James Boyd, Rowland Evans Philadelphia PA 7/11/1771, Irish 20
11 days, Sunday, 3 pounds, 5'8-9",
Philemon Boyd, John Everley Philadelphia PA 11/9/1774, Irish 19 weaver
10 days, Monday, 4 dollars, 5'7-8",
John Gabriel Boyer, Henry Lisle Philadelphia City PA 7/6/1774, German 18
3 days, Monday, 2.5 pounds, short,
Michael Boyl, John McClean New Castle DE 5/9/1765, 20 blacksmith A
11 days, Sunday, 3 pounds,
Daniel Boyle, Samuel Marshall Chester PA 9/13/1775, Irish
3 days, Monday, 6 dollars, 5'5",
James Boyle, Samuel Pritchard VA sheriff 11/16/1752,
122 days, Friday, 3 pistoles,
James Boyle, Isham Randolph Philadelphia City PA ship captain 4/16/1748, sailor L
2 pounds, 5'9",
John Boyle, William R Atlee Chester PA 6/10/1795, Irish 15
8 days, Tuesday, 10 dollars, 5'6",
Patrick Boyle, William Lavell Talbot MD 8/23/1775, Irish tailor
10 days, Monday, 2 pounds, 6',

William Boyle, Edward Wilmer Cecil MD 7/31/1760, English 26 fuller C
    35 days, Thursday, 2 pistoles, 5'10",
Nancy Boylen, Thomas Jones Bucks PA 12/3/1767, gaol sale L
    1.5 pounds, middle,
Patrick Boylen, Benjamin Marpole Chester PA 8/31/1785, Irish 18
    10 days, Sunday, 2.5 pounds, 5'5-6",
James Brabens, William Edwards Baltimore MD 11/23/1769, C
    23 days, Tuesday, 5 pounds,
Robert Brabner, Joseph Darlington Chester PA 5/6/1762, Irish 19 A
    2 pounds, 5'8",
Thomas Bradbury, James Baxter Cecil MD ironworks 1/6/1737, English C
    18 days, Sunday, 3 pounds,
Hugh Bradford, John Inskape Burlington NJ 3/8/1748, Irish
    2 pounds, middle,
Joseph Bradford, Alexander Baird Kent MD 4/25/1754, Irish 23 C
    11 days, Sunday, 1.5 pounds, 6',
Darby Bradley, Edward Woodward Chester PA 5/14/1741, Irish 18
    3 days, Monday, 2 pounds, middle,
Hugh Bradley, George Moore Lancaster PA 6/25/1767, Irish
    13 days, Friday, 2 pounds, 5',
John Bradley, Thomas Potts NJ ironworks 4/13/1774, Irish 47
    24 days, Monday, 3 pounds, short,
Patrick Bradley, Samuel Kennedy Chester PA doctor 3/12/1772, Irish 32
    3 days, Monday, 1.5 pounds, 5'3",
Thomas Bradley, Henry Harson Bucks PA 9/10/1767, Irish
    2 pounds, 5'10",
Edward Bradshaw, Robert Anson Cecil MD 4/8/1756, clerk C
    1.5 pounds,
Thomas Bradshaw, Daniel Coate Burlington NJ 8/24/1774, 18 A
    1 pounds, 5'3",
Daniel Brady, William Hudson Philadelphia PA tanner 1/20/1747, Irish 20
    2 days, Tuesday, 2 pounds, 5'10",
Mary Brady, Alexander Poe Lancaster PA 11/22/1753, Irish
    1.5 pounds,
Michael Brady, William Tucker Hunterdon NJ 3/23/1769, Irish 19 shoemaker
    5 days, Saturday, 3 pounds, 5'4",
Richard Brady, Joshua Baker Lancaster PA 6/29/1738, Irish 22 miller
    16 days, Tuesday, 1.5 pounds,
John Brag, Joseph Pemberton Jr Philadelphia City PA grazier 6/7/1775, English brickmaker
    11 days, Sunday, 6 dollars, 5'9-10",
John Bragan, Jacob Rubely Lancaster PA 10/24/1754, Irish 25
    25 days, Sunday, 3 pounds, 4'8",
William Brambel, John Vernor Lancaster PA 8/27/1752, English 30
    16 days, Tuesday, 3 pounds,
Elizabeth Branet, John Pinkerton Philadelphia City PA 3/30/1774, German
    5 days, Saturday, 4 dollars,
Andrew Brann, Alexander Johnson New Castle DE 9/1/1763, Irish 20 weaver
    27 days, Friday, 3 pounds, 5'8",
Patty Brannas, George Leib Philadelphia PA tanner 2/5/1777, German 25
    30 days, Tuesday, 3 dollars,
Michael Brannen, Daniel Britt New Castle DE 7/25/1751, Irish 20
    6 days, Friday, 5 pounds, middle,
William Brannen, Hugh Donally Berks PA 6/1/1774, Irish 26
    21 days, Thursday, 2 pounds, 5'4",
James Brannon, Jacob Giles Baltimore MD 10/25/1753, Irish 20 schoolmaster
    11 days, Sunday, 5 pounds,
Bartholomew Branon, John Keer Lancaster PA 11/22/1770, Irish 21 tailor
    15 days, Wednesday, 3 dollars, 6',
Patrick Breasland, James Cooper Gloucester NJ 5/3/1764, 18
    7 days, Thursday, 2 pounds, 5'7",
Gasper Breemar, Aquilla Hall Baltimore MD 2/25/1768, German
    61 days, Saturday, 5 pounds, 6', (arrived in 1764)
Hans Hendriat Christian Bremer, Samuel Clement Gloucester NJ 9/11/1776, German 19
    4 dollars, 5'5-6",
Christopher Brett, William Gibson Lancaster PA 12/10/1761, gaol sale L
    18 days, Sunday, 1.5 pounds,

Edward Brewer, William Kelly NY 11/4/1756, Irish house carpenter
    5 pounds, 5'4",
Henry Brewer, Nicholas Parker Bucks PA 4/23/1730, Irish 30
    4 days, Sunday, 3 pounds, middle,
Daniel Brian, Caleb Ranstead Philadelphia City PA 9/23/1731, Irish 18
    4 days, Sunday, 1.5 pounds, short,
Daniel Brian, Garret Boone Philadelphia PA 3/28/1765, Irish soldier
    5 pounds, 5'8",
John Brian, Robert Cumming Frederick MD 7/25/1771, Irish 30 baker
    3 pounds, 5'6-7",
Mary Brian, John Firth Salem NJ 2/11/1768, Irish 18
    11 days, Sunday, 3 pounds, middle,
Frederick Brick, William Hembel Philadelphia City PA tailor 8/3/1774, German 27 tailor
    3 days, Monday, 10 pounds, 5', (arrived last fall)
Frederick Brick, William Hembel Philadelphia City PA tailor 3/27/1776, German 29 tailor (2nd esc)
    15 days, Wednesday, 5 pounds,
Magdalene Brick, William Hembel Philadelphia City PA tailor 3/27/1776, German
    15 days, Wednesday, 5 pounds, (wife to Frederick Brick, has a 6 month old child)
John Bridwell, Daniel Goodman Philadelphia City PA baker 5/30/1754, English 40 baker
    11 days, Sunday, 2 pounds,
Daniel Brien, Francis Crostigin Middlesex NJ 9/22/1743, Irish 18
    7 days, Thursday, 2 pounds, middle,
Mary Brighten, John Jenkins Lancaster PA 5/21/1783, 17
    0.03 pounds,
John Brine, George Weaver Lancaster PA 5/5/1773, Irish 19
    7 days, Thursday, 3 pounds, 5'6",
Alice Briscoe, Edmund Beach Philadelphia City PA 9/6/1759, Welsh 25
    13 days, Friday, 2 pounds, 5',
Joseph Brit, Jacob Walker Chester PA 4/13/1785, Irish 20
    3 days, Sunday, 5 dollars, 5'7",
Daniel Britt, John Grant New Castle DE 1/16/1766, American 14 tailor A
    16 days, Tuesday, 0.05 pounds,
Patrick Britt, Charles Mothesby Baltimore MD 9/15/1763, Irish 45
    32 days, Sunday, 2 pounds, 5',
Pettit Brittin, John Gordon Philadelphia City PA 10/14/1795, 20 A
    73 days, Sunday, 8 dollars, 5'9-10", (relatives live nearby)
John Brixey, Francis Dudley Burlington NJ 3/15/1775, English 20
    3 days, Monday, 5 pounds, 6',
James Broadly, Robert Bridges 7/16/1788, Irish 18
    5 days, Friday, 0.05 pounds,
James Broady, Daniel Turner Cecil MD 6/23/1768, Irish 30
    227 days, Sunday, 6 pounds, 6'2",
Darby Broderick, Samuel Wright Burlington NJ 1/13/1729, Irish
    about 323 days, 3 pounds, middle,
John Broderick, Jacob Keyser Philadelphia City PA 7/9/1767, Irish tailor
    5'3",
Rudolph Brokehouse, Alexander Lewis Chester PA 9/5/1771, German 30 soldier L
    4 dollars, 5'10",
Eustatlus Broker, Robert Lewis New Castle DE 10/9/1755, English
    6 days, Friday, 1 pound, 5'10",
Frederick Broner, John Rup Philadelphia City PA 4/6/1774, German shoemaker
    4 days, Sunday, 5 pounds, 5'2",
John Bronon, Thomas Lewis Chester PA 7/27/1749, Irish 23 tanner
    3 pounds,
Patrick Bronon, Joseph Bosley Jr Baltimore MD 8/28/1766, Irish 18 C
    23 days, Tuesday, 8 dollars, 5'2",
Rudolph Brookhouse, Josiah Allen Chester PA 9/9/1772, German 35 soldier L
    11 days, Sunday, 4 dollars, 5'8-9",
Sarah Brookman, Thomas Pierce Philadelphia City PA 3/31/1743, 20
    (no other information)
Ann Brooks, Daniel Gest Chester PA 6/26/1760, English 23
    30 days, Tuesday, 1.5 pounds, short,
George Brooks, William Bird Philadelphia PA 7/18/1751, English 25
    5 days, Saturday, 1.5 pounds, short, (lately arrived)
James Brooks, Samuel Galloway Anne Arundel MD 7/6/1774, painter
    19 days, Saturday, 4 pounds, 5'9",

James Brooks, George Culin Chester PA 1/9/1766, American L
    13 days, Friday, 2 pounds, 5'4-5",
John Brooks, Alexander Crukshank Philadelphia City PA shoemaker 6/5/1746, Irish shoemaker
    1.5 pounds, short,
John Brooks, Jacob Giles Baltimore MD 11/21/1751, English 28 butcher
    23 days, Tuesday, 7 pounds, short, (arrived last June)
Philip Brooks, John Ogden Chester PA 9/18/1776, English 17
    10 days, Monday, 6 dollars, 5'6",
Richard Brooks, John Hackett Union NJ ironworks 9/27/1764, English 25 carter
    16 days, Tuesday, 3 pistoles, 5'3",
William Brooks, Jeremiah Sheredine Baltimore MD ironworks 7/7/1763, English 30 C
    10 days, Monday, 5 pounds, 5'8",
Leonard Broom, James Vaux Philadelphia PA 5/26/1773, English 33 gardener
    3 days, Monday, 3 pounds, 5'6",
Daniel Brothers, John Hughes Philadelphia PA 6/30/1743, Irish 19
    2 pounds, middle,
Ann Broughton, George Ross Lancaster PA 1/30/1766, American L
    16 days, Tuesday, 1.5 pounds, 5'4-5",
David Brown, Nathan Folwell Burlington NJ 9/22/1763, Irish weaver
    5 days, Saturday, 2 pounds, (arrived 8 weeks ago)
Dennis Brown, Mary Cannan 5/8/1766, Irish tailor
    8 dollars, 5'3-4",
James Brown, Curtis Grubb Lancaster PA ironworks 7/9/1767, English 20
    7 days, Thursday, 5 pounds, 5'5",
James Brown, Richard Graham Baltimore MD 5/21/1772, 35 C
    24 days, Monday, 8 dollars, 5'6-7",
John Brown, James Paul Heath Cecil MD 7/26/1739, 21
    16 days, Tuesday, 2 pistoles, tall,
John Brown, Daniel McPherson Lancaster PA 5/26/1768, 23
    19 days, Saturday, 3 pounds, 5'9",
John Brown, Jedediah Allen Salem NJ 3/10/1773, 37
    7 days, Thursday, 4 dollars, 5'5-6",
John Brown, Charles Robinson New Castle DE 3/23/1774, German 20
    10 days, Monday, 5 pounds,
John Brown, Buckler Bond Harford MD 1/10/1771, English 26 C
    8 days, Wednesday, 3.5 pounds, 5'7",
John Brown, Abraham Jarrett Baltimore MD 8/22/1771, English miller C
    18 days, Sunday, 1.5 pounds, middle,
John Brown, Casper Roads Philadelphia PA 12/3/1788, 18 weaver A
    6 days, Thursday, 0.03 pounds, 5'5-6",
John Brown, Buckler Bond Harford MD 5/3/1775, English 30 (2nd escape) C
    39 days, Sunday, 3 pounds, 5'8",
John Brown, Peter Dillon Philadelphia City PA ship captain 8/20/1783, American 39 L
    3 days, Sunday, 5'8",
Margaret Brown, John Leadlie Bucks PA 1/21/1746, Irish 33
    5 days, Saturday, 1 pound, (has had 4 or 5 children)
Margaret Brown, John Leadlie Bucks PA 6/1/1749, Irish 36 (2nd escape)
    4 days, Sunday, 3 pounds,
Martin Brown, Peter Hallem Lancaster PA 7/26/1770, German 23
    16 dollars, middle,
Mary Brown, John Stinson Philadelphia City PA 9/18/1746, Irish 19
    7 days, Thursday, 1.5 pounds,
Mary Brown, John Galbreath Philadelphia City PA shopkeeper 9/13/1759, Irish
    9 days, Tuesday, 2 pounds, (arrived one year ago)
Noah Brown, Daniel Rees Baltimore MD 5/19/1773, English 45 blacksmith L
    555 days, Sunday, 20 dollars, 5'10",
Patrick Brown, Samuel Atkinson Jr Burlington NJ 9/18/1760, Irish 16
    7 days, Thursday, 2 pounds, 5'9",
Patrick Brown, Dennis Whelen Chester PA 9/3/1767, Irish gardener
    7 days, Thursday, 2 pounds, 5'7-8", (lately arrived)
Phillip Brown, John Parry Chester PA 5/17/1739, English 24
    5 days, Saturday, 2 pounds, tall,
Richard Brown, Robert Milburn Essex NJ 9/27/1753, Irish blacksmith
    7 days, Thursday, 3 pounds, 5'8",
Richard Brown, Andrew Sinnickson Jr Salem NJ 6/22/1774, American 18 L
    9 days, Tuesday, 2 pounds, 5'4-5",

Richard Brown, Andrew Sinnickson Jr Salem NJ 8/24/1774, American 18 (2nd escape) L
  9 days, Tuesday, 3 pounds, 5'4-5",
Thomas Brown, John Metcalfe Baltimore MD 1/16/1753, 50 brickmaker
  6 days, Friday, 4 pounds, 5'6",
Thomas Brown, Darby Durell Burlington NJ 8/12/1762, 25
  1.5 pounds, 5'8",
Thomas Brown, Navel Win Hunterdon NJ 9/29/1768, Irish 26 shoemaker
  16 days, Tuesday, 4 pounds, 5'6", (had run away from the navy)
Thomas Brown, Samuel Nicholson Salem NJ 4/13/1796, 30
  10 days, Sunday, 10 dollars, 5'7",
Thomas Brown, Isaac Conroe Burlington NJ 4/26/1753, American 25 L
  4 days, Sunday, 2 pounds,
Thomas Brown, Mord. Moore Philadelphia PA 2/25/1762, English 45 hired L
  10 days, Monday, 2 pounds, short,
William Brown, Joseph Richardson Philadelphia PA 5/17/1733, 21
  11 days, Sunday, 8 pounds, middle,
William Brown, John Dexter Philadelphia City PA sadler 6/21/1730, 20
  2 days, Tuesday, 1.5 pounds, tall,
William Brown, John Jack Chester PA 6/27/1754, Irish 35 weaver
  10 days, Monday, 3 pounds, 5'5",
William Brown, Robert Erwin Philadelphia City PA 8/4/1748, English
  9 days, Tuesday, 3 pounds, middle,
William Brown, Josiah Wallace Kent DE 9/9/1762, 35 gaol sale L
  12 days, Saturday, 3 pounds, 5'8",
John Browne, John Galloway Kent MD 4/9/1777, gardener
  22 days, Wednesday, 4 pounds, 5'7",
John Brownsword, John Gilleylen Chester PA 1/1/1755, English 25
  1.5 pounds, 5'6",
Robert Bruce, Thomas Lowe 9/30/1772, Scot clockmaker
  3 pounds, 5'7-8", (lately arrived)
Carl Bruderlin, Peter Hassenclever EJ ironworks 6/12/1766, German miner
  14 days, Thursday, 5 pounds, 6', (under a 3 year 4 month contract, imported)
Peter Brumgart, Christian Wackey Lancaster PA 6/7/1764, 17 A
  23 days, Tuesday, 2 pounds,
Richard Brushford, George Sharwood shoemaker 6/18/1752, 20 shoemaker
  11 days, Sunday, 4 pounds, 5'7",
Richard Brushford, John Reardon Philadelphia City PA cordwainer 9/28/1752, 21 shoemaker (2nd esc)
  4 days, Sunday, 5 pounds, 5'9",
Adrian Brust, Richard Wistar Salem NJ glassmaker 4/26/1770, German 27 soldier
  10 dollars, 5'7-8", (arrived last fall)
Elizabeth Bryan, Matthew Giffen New Castle DE 11/15/1770, Irish 35
  1 pound, 5'4",
Elizabeth Bryan, John Tolley Philadelphia PA 10/22/1767, English
  6 days, Friday, 1 pound, short,
John Bryan, Joshua McDowell New Castle DE 8/27/1767, Irish 25 ropemaker
  10 days, Monday, 6 pounds, 5'8", (was a soldier)
John Bryan, George Lenard Lancaster PA 9/6/1770, Irish 16
  11 days, Sunday, 1 pound,
John Bryan, William White Lancaster PA 10/26/1774, Irish 20 (2nd escape)
  24 days, Monday, 5 pounds, 5'7",
John Bryan, John Harkins Chester PA 9/8/1768, Irish 35
  5 pounds, 5'6", (has been in the colonies before)
Joseph Bryan, Peter Bard Philadelphia City PA 1/21/1746, 40 sailor L
  45 days, Monday, 3 pounds, tall,
Mary Bryan, George Littel Kent MD 8/3/1769, Irish
  18 days, Sunday, 1 pound, middle,
Michael Bryan, James Casey Chester PA 10/15/1741, Irish 26 sawyer
  10 days, Monday, 2 pounds, short,
Patrick Bryan, John Young Chester PA 11/10/1773, Irish 19
  11 days, Sunday, 3 pounds,
Honor Bryant, John McCarty New Castle DE 4/7/1757, Irish 20 (female)
  2 pounds, short,
James Bryant, Benjamin Vanleer Gloucester NJ 4/19/1775, English 17
  2.5 pounds,
John Bryant, Thomas Smith Philadelphia City PA ship captain 12/2/1742, 29
  2 pounds, middle, (ran from ship)

Zachariah Bryant, Going Lamphier Fairfax VA 6/20/1765, American L
    20 days, Friday, 1 pound,
Timothy Bryen, Joseph Frazer Philadelphia City PA 6/7/1770, Irish 19 baker
    9 days, Tuesday, 5 pounds, 5'5-6",
John Bryn, George Weaver Lancaster PA 12/13/1770, Irish 16
    13 days, Friday, 1 pound,
John Bryn, George Weaver Lancaster PA 3/5/1772, Irish 18 (2nd escape)
    2 pounds, 5'7",
Martha Byers, Andrew McKee New Castle DE 12/20/1770, 22
    16 days, Tuesday, 0.5 pounds,
John Buchanan, Edward Swaynel Chester PA 4/17/1766, Irish 22 wool comber
    2.5 pounds, 5'10",
John Buckley, Francis Moore Chester PA 2/8/1775, English 25 weaver
    6 dollars, 5'8-9", (has been a soldier)
John Buckley, Christopher Anger Philadelphia City PA wool comber 2/7/1760, 24 A
    2 days, Tuesday, 0.25 pounds, 5'5",
Michael Buckley, Hugh Alexander Cumberland PA 7/20/1774, Irish 21
    21 days, Thursday, 8 dollars, 5'9",
Michael Buckley, Hugh Alexander Cumberland PA 8/24/1774, Irish 21 (2nd escape)
    20 days, Friday, 8 dollars, 5'5", (wears an iron collar)
Nathaniel Buffington, Willis Davis Lancaster PA 5/24/1780, 19
    12 days, Friday, 100 dollars, 5'6",
John Bulgen, Joseph Gavin Philadelphia City PA shoemaker 5/19/1768, English shoemaker
    11 days, Sunday, 2 pounds, 5'2-3", (arrived last fall)
Valentine Bullard, Peter Grubb Lancaster PA ironworks 8/2/1759, Irish 25
    2 pounds, 5'7",
Elisha Bullingham, Matthew Forsyth Burlington NJ 7/13/1749, 16 carpenter A
    6 days, Friday, 2 pounds,
William Burchell, James Keemer Philadelphia PA 7/18/1751, English 30
    5 days, Saturday, 1.5 pounds, tall, (lately arrived)
Mary Burd, Hugh Lownes Chester PA 8/19/1789, 16
    9 days, Monday, 0.03 pounds,
Patrick Burgain, Jacob Wright Chester PA 4/6/1732, Irish 23
    3 days, Monday, 2 pounds, middle,
Patrick Burgain, Jacob Wright Chester PA 6/15/1732, Irish 23 (2nd escape)
    4 days, Sunday, 2 pounds, middle,
Christian Ludwick Burger, John H Centher Philadelphia City PA 8/7/1793, German 28 tailor
    3 days, Sunday, 10 dollars, 5'4",
Michael Burges, Greshom Lee Huntingdon PA 9/29/1773, Irish
    10 days, Monday, 6 dollars, 5'8",
Joshua Burgon, Benjamin Vansant Kent MD 10/23/1766, 20 tailor A
    26 days, Saturday, 2 pounds, 5'2",
Peter Buris, William Kille Gloucester NJ 3/24/1763, German-American 25 hired L
    8 days, Wednesday, 5 pounds, 5'8",
Bridget Burk, John Hanna Chester PA 12/22/1763, 20
    1.5 pounds, short,
Eleanor Burk, Henry Pennington Cecil MD 6/30/1743, Irish 22
    4 days, Sunday, 1 pound,
Elizabeth Burk, Thomas Blair Sussex NJ 6/3/1756, Irish 18
    11 days, Sunday, 2 pounds, short,
Elizabeth Burk, George Keith Chester PA workhouse-keeper 7/1/1756, Irish 18 (2nd escape)
    6 days, Friday, 1 pound,
James Burk, Charles Ridgely Jr Baltimore MD ironworks 11/14/1745, Irish carpenter L
    8 pounds, (arrived 12 years ago)
John Burk, Joseph Ludlan Cape May NJ 9/28/1752, Irish 19
    9 days, Tuesday, 2 pounds, short,
John Burk, John Suber Bucks PA 6/16/1773, Irish 20
    10 days, Monday, 3 pounds, 5'5", (arrived last Dec.)
John Burk, John Suber Bucks PA 10/27/1773, Irish 20 (2nd escape)
    21 days, Thursday, 3 pounds, 5'5", (arrived last Dec.)
John Burk, Joseph Osborn Baltimore MD 10/24/1765, 25 C
    4 days, Sunday, 3.5 pounds, 5'4",
Mary Burk, William Scott Sommerset PA 10/6/1748, Irish 18
    2 days, Tuesday, 2 pounds, short,
Matthew Burk, James Cawley Baltimore MD ship captain 8/9/1750, Irish 24 weaver
    4 pounds, tall, (ran from ship)

Michael Burk, Arthur Latimer Chester PA 10/4/1753, Irish 26 weaver
    3 pounds, 6',
Michael Burk, Henry Schultz York PA 6/24/1762, Irish
    10 days, Monday, 5 pounds, 5'9",
Richard Burk, John Beaumont Bucks PA 6/7/1764, Irish 22
    10 days, Monday, 2 pounds, middle, (arrived 5 weeks ago)
Richard Burk, John Beaumont Bucks PA 7/12/1770, Irish 30 (2nd escape)
    11 days, Sunday, 1.5 pounds, (arrived 6 years ago, has a wife)
Thomas Burk, Edward Hughes Philadelphia PA 4/25/1754, Irish 37
    3 days, Monday, 1 pound, 5'9",
Thomas Burk, David Davies Lancaster PA 5/19/1763, American L
    2 pounds, middle,
William Burk, Thomas Stewart Cecil MD 7/2/1741, Irish 23
    3 days, Monday, 1 pound,
William Burk, William Davis Baltimore MD 9/3/1767, Irish 18
    35 days, Thursday, 1.5 pounds,
William Burk, Gabriel Davis Cumberland NJ 3/12/1783, 20
    44 days, Monday, 0.03 pounds,
Catherine Burkhart, Joseph Richardson Bucks PA 7/31/1760, German 19
    24 days, Monday, 1 pound, middle, (bought in Nov. 1756, mother lives in Philadelphia)
Bryan Burn, John Stokes Bucks PA 6/12/1776, Irish 22
    6 dollars, 5'8-9",
Hugh Burn, Edward Richards Chester PA 7/20/1738, Irish
    8 days, Wednesday, 3 pounds,
John Burn, Henry Mitchell Bucks PA 7/21/1748, Irish 20
    8 days, Wednesday, 3 pounds, short,
Matthew Burn, Francis McConnal Chester PA ironworks 4/9/1741, Irish
    3 days, Monday, 3 pounds, middle,
Patrick Burn, William Walker Stafford VA 7/26/1744, Irish C
    28 days, Thursday, 4 pistoles, short,
Simon Burn, Schooner Bennett Kent MD 8/7/1746, Irish
    3 pounds, 5',
Thomas Burn, William Wilkins Gloucester NJ 6/18/1752, Irish shoemaker
    5 pounds, middle,
James Burnes, Thomas Booth New Castle DE 1/10/1787, Irish 21
    62 days, Thursday, 4 dollars, 5'5", (lately arrived)
John Burnes, Hercules Kamp Baltimore MD 1/10/1771, English C
    12 days, Saturday, 3 pounds, 5'6",
Elizabeth Burnet, William Jones Chester PA 7/5/1759, Irish 19
    6 days, Friday, 1 pound, middle,
Arthur Burns, Capt. Seymour NY ship captain 5/2/1745, Irish 38
    4 pounds, (ran from privateer ship)
Arthur Burns, William Ellis Cecil MD 4/30/1747, Irish C
    10 days, Monday, 1 pound,
Christopher Burns, Aaron Leaming Cape May NJ 5/24/1764, Irish 18
    7 days, Thursday, 1.5 pounds, 5'5", (lately arrived)
Edward Burns, David Edmiston 10/11/1764, 42
    36 days, Wednesday, 1 pound, 5'6",
Edward Burns, Charles Risk Philadelphia City PA 12/6/1764, Irish 37
    89 days, Saturday, 2 pounds, 5'5", (arrived last summer)
James Burns, James Webster Baltimore MD ironworks 10/17/1765, Irish 35
    27 days, Friday, 4 pounds, 6',
Philip Burns, Samuel Allen Lancaster PA 8/3/1774, Irish 18
    7 days, Thursday, 4 pounds, 5'5",
Terence Burns, William Ellis Cecil MD 4/30/1747, Irish C
    10 days, Monday, 1 pound,
Thomas Burns, John Herston Baltimore MD 10/17/1771, 24
    18 days, Sunday, 3 pounds, 4'10", (arrived 4 months ago)
Thomas Burns, Richard Barnett Talbot MD 8/10/1774, Irish 22 shoemaker
    25 days, Sunday, 1.5 pounds, 5',
William Burns, John Cox Monmouth NJ 4/19/1759, Irish 45 shoemaker
    32 days, Sunday, 2 pounds, 5'6", (acquainted with most of America)
Henry Burnside, Christian Steer Philadelphia PA 6/29/1774,
    5 pounds, 5'8-9",
Matthew Burrass, Thomas Brown Lancaster PA brickmaker 3/17/1742, English 30 baker
    4 days, Sunday, 2 pounds, short,

John Burridge, William Dewees Philadelphia PA 10/3/1754,
    1 day, Wednesday, 2 pounds, 5'10",
William Burrman, Lyde Goodwin Baltimore MD 3/13/1750, English butcher
    5 pounds, 5'6",
Joseph Burroh, Michael Furbee Kent DE 5/28/1761, English 21 C
    1.25 pounds, 5'8",
George Burrough, William Merritt Kent DE 9/12/1765, English C
    11 days, Sunday, 2.5 pounds, 5'10",
Isaac Burrough, Joseph Harden Gloucester NJ 2/28/1787, 20 A
    13 days, Thursday, 4 dollars, 5'4",
Michael Burrows, Archibald Stewart Philadelphia City PA ship captain 10/10/1751, Irish 24
    2 days, Tuesday, 2 pounds, 5'10", (ran from ship)
Michael Burrows, John Thomas Chester PA 7/16/1752, Irish 25 (2nd escape)
    13 days, Friday, 2.5 pounds, 5'10",
Ricahrd Burrows, John Suber Bucks PA 1/10/1765, American 26 joiner L
    7 days, Thursday, 2 pounds, 5'6",
William Burrows, James Holmes 8/14/1740, 23
    3 days, Monday, 1.5 pounds,
Martin Bush, John Gilleylen Chester PA 1/29/1756, German 23
    10 days, Monday, 2 pounds, 5'6", (father lives nearby, has 4 years left to serve)
Oliver Bush, John Bennet Talbot MD hatter 2/11/1768, A
    2 pounds,
William Buso, Jacob Lippincot Burlington NJ 4/8/1736, 18
    10 days, Monday, 1.5 pounds, short,
Matthias Busset, Peter January Philadelphia City PA 8/11/1768, 18 shoemaker A
    11 days, Sunday, 2 pounds, 5'2-3",
Samuel Butcher, Edward Rockill 10/10/1751, English
    2 pounds, tall,
Catherine Butler, James Patterson Lancaster PA 7/27/1769, Irish 18
    18 days, Sunday, 1.5 pounds, short,
Catherine Butler, James Patterson Lancaster PA 9/7/1769, Irish 18 (2nd escape)
    16 days, Tuesday, 3 pounds, short,
Catherine Butler, James Patterson Lancaster PA 9/1/1773, Irish 22 (3rd escape)
    16 days, Tuesday, 1.05 pounds, (arrived 4 years ago)
Harry Butler, William Kelso Cumberland PA 5/8/1776, Irish 18
    10 days, Monday, 20 dollars, 5'5", (relatives live nearby)
James Butler, William Fishborn Philadelphia City PA 11/17/1737, English carpenter
    5 days, Saturday, 2 pounds, middle,
John Butler, George Sanderson Lancaster PA 1/29/1756, Irish miller
    13 days, Friday, 3 pistols, 5'4", (use to the sea)
Patrick Butler, Archibald Stewart Philadelphia City PA 9/3/1761, Irish 22
    7 days, Thursday, 7 pounds, 5'8", (ran from ship)
Richard Butler, John Bartholomew Philadelphia City PA 3/2/1785, 14 A
    1 dollars, 4'2",
Sarah Butler, John Cottinger Bucks PA tailor 1/15/1745,
    13 days, Friday, 2 pounds, middle,
Thomas Butler, John Young Chester PA 7/12/1786, Irish 19 weaver
    3 days, Sunday, 8 dollars, 5'7-8", (arrived 10 months ago)
William Butler, Hugh Sidwell Chester PA 2/16/1769, Irish 30
    1.5 pounds, 5',
William Butler, Hugh Sidwell Chester PA 6/1/1769, Irish 30 (2nd escape)
    1.5 pounds, 5'6",
William Butler, William Moody New Castle DE 7/7/1773, Irish tailor
    13 days, Friday, 6 dollars,
William Butler, Richard Graham Dumfies VA 5/3/1759, Irish C
    26 days, Saturday, 5 pounds, 5'9",
William Butler, Thomas Hewett Gloucester NJ 4/30/1772, American tailor L
    10 days, Monday, 8 dollars, 5'9-10",
John Buttersoss, Joshua Ely Jr Bucks PA 10/16/1766, German 17
    4 days, Sunday, 2 pounds,
William Butterworth, Joseph Gibson Gloucester NJ 1/7/1762, American 18 L
    1.5 pounds, 5',
Isaac Butterworth Jr, Job Kimsey Gloucester NJ 6/4/1794, 16 A
    80 days, Sunday, 10 dollars, 5'4-5",
Joseph Byard, Jos Lippincott Burlington NJ 2/2/1764, German 21
    11 days, Sunday, 3 pounds, 5'6",

Elizibeth Byer, Aquilla Jones Gloucester NJ 4/13/1785, German (wife to Phillip)
   3 days, Sunday, 2 dollars,
Phillip Byer, Aquilla Jones Gloucester NJ 4/13/1785, German
   3 days, Sunday, 6 dollars, 5'4",
James Byrn, John Inglis Philadelphia City PA 6/11/1752, Irish 17
   5 days, Saturday, 1.5 pounds, middle,
James Byrn, Daniel Walton Philadelphia PA 4/20/1769, Irish 21
   4 days, Sunday, 3 pounds, 5'7",
Patrick Byrne, William Walker Stafford VA 8/20/1747, Irish
   36 days, Wednesday, 5'5", (committed felon)
Matthew Cacey, William White Chester PA 2/4/1768, 26
   4 days, Sunday, 5 pounds, middle,
John Caddils, Garret & Matthews Chester PA 10/23/1776, 19 scythe-maker
   9 days, Tuesday, 8 dollars, 5'8-9",
Moses Cadugan, Josias William Dallam Baltimore MD 7/25/1771, Irish 25 shoemaker
   12 days, Saturday, 5 pounds, (arrived 6 years ago)
Patrick Caign, John Morton Jr Philadelphia PA 3/29/1775, Irish 15
   14 days, Thursday, 4 dollars, 4'7",
Edward Cain, Samuel Howell Philadelphia City PA 7/9/1747, Irish 35 hatter
   4 days, Sunday, 5 pounds, 5'10",
John Cain, Thomas Martin Chester PA 4/2/1752, Irish 20
   18 days, Sunday, 2 pounds, 5'6",
John Cain, Thomas Martin Chester PA 6/25/1752, Irish 21 (2nd escape)
   2 days, Tuesday, 1.5 pounds, 5'6",
John Cain, Edmund Talbot Baltimore MD 5/9/1765,
   3 pounds, 6',
John Cain, Andrew Wilkins Cumberland PA 10/29/1767, hired L
   3 pounds, 5'8",
Matthew Cain, David Scott Cumberland PA 6/1/1769, Irish 22 coachmaker
   10 days, Monday, 5 pounds, 5'6", (arrived last June, use to the sea)
Catherine Caisey, James Hunter Chester PA 7/17/1776, Irish
   5 days, Saturday, 3 dollars, 5'2",
Thomas Cala, David Denny Chester PA 1/5/1785, Irish 18
   4 days, Saturday, 2 pounds, 5'7",
Cornelius Calaghan, Peter Matson Philadelphia PA 11/1/1744, Irish
   4 days, Sunday, 1.5 pounds,
Charles Calahan, William Biddle Philadelphia City PA 12/2/1731, 22
   4 days, Sunday, 2 pounds, short,
Cornelius Calahan, Abel Rees Chester PA 7/28/1773, Irish
   3 days, Monday, 10 pounds, 5'6",
Patrick Calighan, James Gallion Harford MD 1/25/1775, Irish 25 laborer
   17 days, Monday, 2 pounds, 5'4-5",
James Callahan, Alexander Rutherford Philadelphia City PA shoemaker 12/22/1763, shoemaker
   8 pounds,
William Callahan, Andrew Pearce Cecil MD 8/29/1765, Irish 30 plaisterer C
   8 days, Wednesday, 3 pounds, 5'6", (arrived 12 months ago)
William Callahan, Andrew Pearce Cecil MD 9/4/1766, Irish 31 plaisterer (2nd escape) C
   18 days, Sunday, 5 dollars, 5'6-7",
Charles Callehan, William Biddle Philadelphia City PA 4/1/1731, 20
   1 pound, short,
Ephriam Callender, George Stroud Chester PA 5/18/1738, American 30 L
   10 days, Monday, 1 pound, tall,
Melchoir Calvin, Jacob Ove Sommerset PA 8/9/1750, German 21
   5 pounds, short,
John Cambel, Philip Jacobs Gloucester NJ 3/31/1773, 35 sailor
   6 dollars, 5'6",
John Cambel, John Vanderen 8/21/1776, Irish 19
   38 days, Monday, 1.5 pounds, 5'7-8",
Charles Cambell, Henry Hudleston Bucks PA 5/10/1739, Irish 24
   5 days, Saturday, 3 pounds, tall,
James Cambell, Andrew Mitchell Chester PA 7/21/1773,
   3 days, Monday, 1.5 pounds, 5',
Robert Camburn, Richard Cayford 8/10/1774, 20 A
   13 days, Friday, 0.03 pounds,
Dougal Cameron, Robert Horner Charles MD 5/19/1748, (rebel)
   18 days, Sunday, 2.5 pounds, 5'10",

Alexander Campbell, Matthias Boatman Philadelphia PA tavern-keeper 5/26/1763, 16
    3 days, Monday, 2.5 pounds,
Alexander Campbell, Matthias Boatman Philadelphia PA tavern-keeper 10/11/1764, 17 (2nd escape)
    21 days, Thursday, 2 pounds,
Archibald Campbell, Edward Means Cecil MD 9/8/1748, Irish 28
    12 days, Saturday, 2 pounds, tall,
Barney Campbell, Casper Singer Lancaster PA 9/29/1768, Irish 16
    1.5 pounds, 5',
Charles Campbell, Joseph Morrison Lancaster PA 9/27/1753, Irish
    2 pounds, 5'8",
Charles Campbell, Joseph Morrison Lancaster PA 2/5/1754, Irish (2nd escape)
    8 days, Wednesday, 3 pounds, 5'9",
Charles Campbell, Charles Ridgely Jr Baltimore MD ironworks 5/14/1767, English 20
    16 days, Tuesday, 2 pounds, 5'8", (arrived 6 months ago)
Charles Campbell, Charles Ridgely Jr Baltimore MD ironworks 12/6/1770, English 24 (2nd escape)
    3 pounds, 5'8-9", (wears an iron collar)
Duncan Campbell, Robert Arthur Kent DE 8/4/1748, Scot 16
    8 days, Wednesday, 2.5 pounds, short,
Elizabeth Campbell, Thomas Shewell Bucks PA 6/2/1763, 30
    23 days, Tuesday, 1 pound, middle,
Francis Campbell, Lodowick Singles Philadelphia City PA 10/18/1764, Irish 25 butcher
    3 pounds, 5'6",
Francis Campbell, Daniel McPherson Lancaster PA 7/12/1764, Irish 21
    11 days, Sunday, 2 pounds, 5'8",
George Campbell, Thomas Folwell Gloucester NJ 10/29/1783, Irish 22 weaver
    15 days, Tuesday, 12 dollars, 5'8", (lately arrived)
James Campbell, Isaac Rees Philadelphia PA 10/9/1755, Irish weaver gaol sale L
    8 days, Wednesday, 3 pounds, middle, (arrived 12 years ago)
John Campbell, John Richy Philadelphia City PA ship captain 10/5/1752, Irish
    0 days, Thursday, 1.5 pounds,
John Campbell, Unlisted Name Cecil MD 11/23/1749, Irish
    7 days, Thursday, 3 pounds, (ran from ship Prince Snow)
John Campbell, George McDowell Chester PA 12/1/1768, Scot 21 sailor
    9 days, Tuesday, 4 pounds, 5'7", (use to the sea)
John Campbell, John McCalion Chester PA 12/3/1783, Irish 21 carpenter
    21 days, Wednesday, 3 dollars, 5'8-9", (ran from ship, already served 2 years)
John Campbell, William Holmes Frederick VA 2/7/1771, 37 C
    93 days, Tuesday, 14 dollars, 5'7-8",
Mary Campbell, Edward Green Chester PA 11/8/1759,
    8 days, Wednesday, 1 pound, short,
Matthew Campbell, Samuel Moor Lancaster PA 3/27/1776, Irish 30
    44 days, Tuesday, 1 pound, 5'5",
Nelly Campbell, William Dickey 10/4/1764, Irish 26
    19 days, Saturday, 1 pound,
Patrick Campbell, James Johnston Lancaster PA 7/17/1766, Irish 20 soldier
    7 days, Thursday, 3 pounds, 5'9",
Patrick Campbell, John Patton Berks PA ironworks 1/21/1768, Irish 22 soldier (2nd escape)
    17 days, Monday, 4 pounds, 5'9-10",
Peter Campbell, William Watkins Baltimore MD 8/6/1752, Irish C
    18 days, Sunday, 4 pistoles, 5'4",
Robert Campbell, Charles Allen Chester PA 8/26/1772, Irish tailor
    10 days, Monday, 5 pounds, 5'10",
Sarah Campbell, Robert Bell Philadelphia City PA bookseller 2/4/1784, Irish 18
    2 days, Monday, 6 dollars, (arrived last fall)
Valentine Campbell, Abraham Dehaven Philadelphia PA innholder 6/3/1762, 22
    5 pounds, 5'10", (intends to go privateering)
John Campin, Edward Barret Philadelphia PA 9/14/1774, Irish butcher
    5 pounds, 5'6-7", (arrived 6 weeks)
Daniel Canaan, Henry Pennington Cecil MD 6/30/1743, Irish 20
    4 days, Sunday, 1 pound, short,
John Canada, Joseph Burr Burlington NJ 10/1/1747, Irish 23
    3 days, Monday, 3 pounds,
John Cancannon, Colin Ferguson Kent MD 7/11/1754, 21 tailor
    18 days, Sunday,
Barney Cane, Richard Robinson Philadelphia City PA 3/12/1772, 20
    25 days, Sunday, 4 pounds, short,

John Cane, Johnathan Morgan Gloucester NJ 3/5/1794, 23
    6 dollars, 5'10-11",
Thomas Cane, David Kennedy Jr Chester PA 9/22/1763, Irish
    5 pounds, 5', (arrived last May)
James Cangling, William Andrew Philadelphia City PA 11/26/1747, Irish 26 sailor L
    5 days, Saturday, 2 pounds, 5'6",
William Canise, David Davis Chester PA 10/12/1752, 26
    5 pounds, short,
William Canise, David Davis Chester PA 8/2/1753, 27 (2nd escape)
    27 days, Friday, 4 pounds, short,
Ferdinand Cannady, William Taeago Chester PA 8/3/1769, Scot 18
    20 days, Friday, 1.5 pounds,
James Cannady, John Thompson 5/19/1763, American 20 L
    2 pounds, 5'8",
John Cannan, John Rambo Gloucester NJ 5/6/1762, American 18 L
    9 days, Tuesday, 1.5 pounds,
John Cannan, John Rambo Gloucester NJ 7/15/1762, American 19 (2nd escape) L
    7 days, Thursday, 1 pound, 5'2",
Michael Cannan, John Con New Castle DE 12/24/1767, Irish 17
    1 pound, 5'2-3",
Francis Cannon, Adam McCool Chester PA blacksmith 4/18/1751, Irish A
    2 pounds, middle,
James Cannon, Samuel Ruth New Castle DE 3/20/1766, Irish weaver
    1.5 pounds,
John Cannon, Mordecai Cloud Chester PA 7/14/1763, American 20 L
    7 days, Thursday, 1 pound, 5'5",
John Cannon, Thomas Wilson Chester PA 6/6/1765, American 22 (2nd escape) L
    14 days, Thursday, 1.5 pounds, 5'6",
John Cannon, George David Chester PA 1/2/1766, American 23 (3rd escape) L
    7 days, Thursday, 6 dollars, 5'7",
Michael Cannon, Jeremiah Starr Chester PA 8/22/1765, Irish 45
    early June, 1.5 pounds, 5'8-9",
Cornelius Cannor, Moses Coates Chester PA 1/6/1742, Irish 21
    3 days, Monday, 3 pounds, tall,
Philip Cantlon, Thomas Rambo Gloucester NJ 4/26/1753, Irish 30
    4 days, Sunday, 1.5 pounds, middle,
George Canvin, Joseph Gilbons Jr Chester PA 7/26/1770, English 19
    10 days, Monday, 2 pounds,
Charles Cape, Joseph Taylor Philadelphia PA blacksmith 6/8/1791, 17 A
    9 days, Monday, 3 dollars, 5'5-6",
Bernard Cappeler, Henry Haller Berks PA 8/25/1768, German-American 18 tailor A
    25 days, Sunday, 0.5 pounds, 5'7",
Catherine Car, Francis McCutchen Cecil MD 7/30/1777, 21
    5 days, Saturday, 6 dollars,
Matthew Car, John Cromwell Anne Arundel MD 6/1/1758, Irish 30 weaver C
    12 days, Saturday, 3 pistoles, 5'6",
John Carawan, Samuel Davis Philadelphia PA 8/17/1738, Irish 18
    4 days, Sunday, 1.5 pounds, middle, (lately arrived in Brig Hannah)
Hugh Carberry, John Thompson New Castle DE 12/19/1754, Irish 20
    8 days, Wednesday, 2 pounds, (use to the sea)
Weanever Carbrite, James Torbert Bucks PA 7/31/1766, (female)
    82 days, Thursday, 1.5 pounds, 4',
James Cardan, Conyngham & Nesbitt Philadelphia City PA merchants 7/13/1758, 16
    1 pistole,
David Cardew, John Correy Philadelphia City PA 9/14/1769, Irish 30 breeches-maker
    5 dollars,
Joseph Cardey, Jonathan Harris Cumberland NJ 5/15/1760, 25 bricklayer
    26 days, Saturday, 5 pounds, 5',
John Cardiff, William Bonan 5/24/1744, Irish 40
    5 days, Saturday, 1.5 pounds, (arrived 5 months ago)
Catherine Carle, Thomas Leonard Monmouth NJ 12/13/1753,
    5 days, Saturday, 1.5 pounds,
Philip Carle, John Eigener Berks PA 5/15/1766, German
    5 pounds, 5'10",
Robert Carlisle, Benjamin Howell Chester PA 8/23/1753, Irish ship carpenter
    23 days, Tuesday, 2 pounds, 5'5",

Edward Carlow, John Faries New Castle DE 11/28/1765, shoemaker
    12 days, Saturday, 3 pounds, 5'6",
Nail Carlton, William Cloud Chester PA 9/25/1776, Irish 19
    8 days, Wednesday, 2 pounds, 5'4-5",
Neale Carlton, Richard Jones Chester PA 6/1/1785, Irish 30
    some time ago, 6 dollars, 5'6",
Robert Carmack, Robert Pearson Middlesex NJ 7/21/1768, Irish 25
    14 days, Thursday, 2 pounds, 5'10",
John Carman, Richard Croxall Baltimore MD ironworks 5/15/1760, English 30 weaver C
    18 days, Sunday, 4 pounds,
Macaja Carman, John Read Philadelphia City PA 5/26/1743, 19 A
    254 days, Tuesday, 3 pounds, tall,
Richard Carman, Benjamin Young Baltimore MD ironworks 5/15/1760, English weaver C
    18 days, Sunday, 4 pounds,
Jane Carmichael, Roberty Duncan Philadelphia City PA 2/14/1765, Irish 25
    19 days, Saturday, 2 pounds, (arrived last fall)
William Carmichael, William Macarlson Lancaster PA 8/1/1745, Irish 30
    15 days, Wednesday, 2 pounds, 5'10",
John Carnalt, George Curry Chester PA 2/4/1746, English 23
    2 days, Tuesday, 3 pounds, middle,
Hugh Carnan, Samuel Willson Northampton PA 7/15/1762,
    17 days, Monday, 2 pounds,
James Carnee, Jacob Gills Cecil MD 6/5/1740, Irish 30
    12 days, Saturday, 5 pounds, middle,
John Carnell, George Corey Chester PA 4/10/1746, English 23
    46 days, Sunday, 2.5 pounds, middle,
Ann Carney, Peter Robeson Philadelphia City PA gaoler 8/11/1763, Irish 20
    32 days, Sunday, 1 pound, (arrived 11 months ago)
James Carney, William Bennett Chester PA 10/17/1771, Irish 18
    4 days, Sunday, 3 dollars, 5'7",
Lawrence Carney, Jacob Cupp Berks PA 8/9/1775, Irish
    10 days, Monday, 8 dollars,
Matthew Carney, James Leech Lancaster PA 4/4/1771, Irish tailor
    4 pounds, 5'9",
Thomas Carney, Mark Wilcox Delaware PA 12/30/1795, A
    5 days, Friday, 12 dollars, 5'7",
Joseph Carole, Francis West Cumberland PA 6/11/1772, German
    3 pounds, 5'9", (arrived 5 months ago)
Christian Carpenter, Jacob Carpenter Lancaster PA 9/8/1763, 20 A
    10 days, Monday, 3 pounds,
Henry Carpenter, Benjamin Miffin Philadelphia PA 6/17/1742, carpenter
    2 pounds, tall, (has 13 year old son with him)
John Carpenter, Abraham Holmes Lancaster PA 10/27/1768, 25 sailor
    14 days, Thursday, 2 pounds, 5'3-4", (use to the sea)
Michael Carpenter, James Wilson Lancaster PA 8/22/1771, Irish 40 tailor
    11 days, Sunday, 2 pounds, 5'7-8",
Darby Carr, Nicholas Kern Salem NJ 11/24/1773, Irish 21
    5 days, Saturday, 1 pound, 5'6",
Henry Carr, Robert Marcer Cecil MD 11/10/1763, English C
    12 days, Saturday, 3 pounds, 6',
James Carr, John Robinson Philadelphia PA 8/15/1751, Irish
    2 days, Tuesday, 3 pounds, short,
James Carr, George Lownes Chester PA 7/12/1750, Irish 17
    3 pounds,
John Carr, William Leedom Philadelphia PA 2/21/1776, Irish 28 hair-dresser
    3 days, Monday, 2 dollars, 5'7",
John Carr, James Franklin Baltimore MD ironworks 7/26/1770, English 47 bricklayer C
    9 days, Tuesday, 5 pistoles, 5'10", (arrived 2 weeks ago)
John Carr, James Franklin Baltimore MD ironworks 6/6/1771, English 48 bricklayer (2nd esc) C
    35 days, Thursday, 5 pounds, 5'8-9",
Joseph Carr, James Evins Chester PA ironworks 12/16/1746, 20
    8 days, Wednesday, 3 pounds, 6',
Michael Carr, Richard Fowler Baltimore MD 8/8/1765, C
    22 days, Wednesday, 2 pounds, 5'7-8",
Oliver Carr, William Smith Cumberland PA 10/9/1755, Irish 22
    about 2 months ago, 2 pistoles, 5'4",

Peggy Carr, Abraham Mason Philadelphia City PA 6/19/1766, Irish 26
    38 days, Monday, 3 pounds, (lately arrived)
Robert Carr, Richard Dennis New Castle DE 12/17/1761, 20 A
    57 days, Wednesday, 2.5 pounds, 5'10",
James Carragan, Herman Cook Lancaster PA 7/28/1763, Irish 33 weaver (took wife with him)
    11 days, Sunday, 5 pounds, 5'3",
Patrick Carravan, Jeremiah Sherridan Baltimore MD 3/26/1767, Irish blacksmith
    11 days, Sunday, 2 pounds,
John Carrel, William Williams Chester PA 6/6/1745, Irish 26
    15 days, Wednesday, 2.5 pounds, short,
John Carrel, Seth Duncan York PA 1/1/1767, 28 soldier
    5 pounds, 5'8",
Mary Carrel, William Williams Chester PA 6/6/1745, Irish
    15 days, Wedneday, 2.5 pounds, short, (wife to John Carrel)
Thomas Carrelton, Samuel Cheesman Philadelphia City PA 12/3/1767, Irish 21 shoemaker
    3 days, Monday, 3 pounds, 5'6",
Patrick Carril, Walter Thetford New Castle DE 3/3/1747, Irish
    15 days, Wednesday, 2 pounds, short,
William Carrol, Frederick Busard Chester PA 9/8/1768, Irish
    9 days, Tuesday, 3 pounds, 5'10",
Catherine Carroll, George Taylor Monmouth NJ 5/10/1750, Irish 30
    30 days, Tuesday, 5 pounds, middle,
Cornellius Carroll, Charles Batho Philadelphia City PA 1/10/1760, Irish 22
    9 days, Tuesday, 2 pounds, 6',
James Carroll, John Wilson Philadelphia City PA 9/8/1773, Irish 24 school teacher
    16 days, Tuesday, 6 dollars, 5'6-7", (arrived last July)
John Carroll, Jonathan Woodland New Castle DE 3/16/1747, Irish 40
    8 days, Wednesday, 1.5 pounds, middle,
John Carroll, Robert Fulton Lancaster PA 7/9/1767, Irish 27
    11 days, Sunday, 2.5 pounds, 5'7",
John Carroll, Nathan Sparks Queen Anne's MD 5/10/1775, 19
    66 days, Monday, 5'9",
John Carroll, Henry Ewing Chester PA 5/22/1766, gaol sale L
    11 days, Sunday, 2 pounds,
Patrick Carroll, Nathaniel Pope Prince George MD 1/17/1765, Irish butcher C
    77 days, Thursday, 2 pistoles,
Robert Carroll, George Polley Philadelphia City PA shoemaker 6/8/1749, Irish 23
    3 days, Monday, 5 pounds, 5'8",
William Carroll, Patrick Gordon Philadelphia PA 9/13/1770, Irish
    10 days, Monday, 5 pounds, 5'10",
William Carroll, Job Slacum Dorchester MD 2/24/1773, Irish shoemaker
    5 pounds, 5'2-3", (arrived 8 months ago)
Anne Carrowle, Samuel Williams Philadelphia City PA 4/27/1774, English 16 A
    28 days, Thursday, 1 pound, (arrived in 1769)
Ann Carson, Edward Hanlon Philadelphia City PA 9/7/1774, Irish 25
    79 days, Tuesday, 8 dollars, middle, (arrived last May)
John Carson, John Hanna Philadelphia City PA 7/21/1773, Irish 21
    28 days, Thursday, 3 pounds, (lately arrived)
Charles Carter, Carson & Barclay & Mitchell Philadelphia City PA 8/14/1766, Irish 33
    5 days, Saturday, 1.5 pounds, 5'9", (arrived this summer, but was in colonial army earlier)
James Carter, Walter Sterling Philadelphia City PA ship captain 10/10/1754, English 26 carpenter
    6 days, Friday, 5 pounds, 5'9",
John Carter, John Cooper Chester PA 8/12/1772, Irish 23
    3 pounds,
John Carter, James McCabe Queen Anne's MD 7/7/1784, Irish 20
    13 days, Thursday, 9 pounds, 5'6-8",
Philip Carter, George Douglass Berks PA 5/29/1755, Irish 30
    7 days, Thursday, 4 pounds, 5'10", (has wife and child, has been in the army)
Richard Carter, Caleb Way Chester PA 8/25/1768, English blacksmith
    1 pound, short,
Thomas Carter, John Kelle Gloucester NJ 1/6/1773, Irish 30 currier
    14 days, Thursday, 3 pounds, 5'6",
Lawrence Carthner, Cales Brinton Chester PA 9/22/1763, German 16
    7 days, Thursday, 2 pounds, short, (parents live nearby)
Mary Cartney, Joseph Larkin Chester PA 6/5/1776, Irish 25
    3 days, Monday, 3 dollars,

Abner Cartwright, John Briggs Salem NJ 6/10/1795, 23
   9 days, Monday, 4 dollars, 5'7-8",
Henry Cartwright, George Presstman Baltimore MD 5/18/1769, English 24
   11 days, Sunday, 3 pounds, 5'8",
Henry Carty, Benjamin Field Burlington NJ 7/5/1744, Irish 19
   19 days, Saturday, 1 pound, middle,
Jacob Carvel, Nathan Haines Burlington NJ 8/10/1769, 18
   2 days, Tuesday, 2.5 pounds, 5'5-6",
William Carver, James Cheston Baltimore MD 4/6/1774, Scot 26 groom
   9 days, Tuesday, 5 pounds, 5'8-9",
Richard Carvin, Charles Boyles Bucks PA 7/19/1786, Irish
   6 dollars, 5'7",
James Carway, Richard Flower Chester PA 8/1/1751, Irish 27 L
   4 days, Sunday, 2.5 pounds, 5'4",
Matthew Case, Edward Tonkin Burlington NJ 10/4/1764, American 25 brickmaker L
   24 days, Monday, 5 pistoles, 5'4",
Matthew Case, Edward Tonkin Burlington NJ 6/6/1765, American 26 brickmaker (2nd escape) L
   11 days, Sunday, 5 pistoles, 5'6",
Matthew Case, John Hannum Jr Chester PA 8/20/1767, American 28 brickmaker (3rd escape) L
   35 days, Thursday, 6 pounds, 5'6",
Matthias Case, Peter Kier Gloucester NJ 4/12/1775, Irish 29
   33 days, Saturday, 5 pounds, 5'6-7",
William Casedy, Burbridge Brock WJ 8/19/1762, 22
   18 days, Sunday, 5 pounds, 6',
John Casega, John Mitchell Chester PA 8/11/1757, Irish 21
   14 days, Thursday, 1 pound, 5'5",
Peter Casenbury, Anthony Grove tailor 9/22/1773, 19 A
   1.5 pounds, 5',
James Casey, Christopher Divers Baltimore MD 4/28/1748, 23 C
   11 days, Sunday, 5 MD pounds,
John Casey, Nathaniel Parker Hunterdon NJ 7/30/1752, Irish 40
   4 days, Sunday, 3 pounds, 5'6",
Oliver Casey, Bartrem Galbreath Lancaster PA 9/17/1767, Irish 20
   16 days, Tuesday, 2 pounds, 5'6-7", (arrived July 7th last)
William Casey, John Mackey Cecil MD 6/14/1764, Irish 19
   10 days, Monday, 2 pounds, 5'4", (arrived last Dec. 2nd)
Ferdinand Caspar, Jonathan Thomas Philadelphia PA 8/2/1753, German 15
   13 days, Friday, 1.5 pounds,
John Casperson, Samuel Paul Gloucester NJ 4/5/1775, 19
   3 days, Monday, 1 pound,
John Casperson, Samuel Paul Gloucester NJ 8/23/1775, 20 (2nd escape)
   6 days, Friday, 1 pound,
Thomas Cassell, Leonard Jacoby Philadelphia PA 5/11/1785, 18 A
   6 days, Thursday, 0.03 pounds, 5'6-7",
William Castells, Nicholas Hower Lancaster PA hatter 12/11/1766, Irish 18
   10 days, Monday, 3 pounds,
David Castillow, Samuel Howell Philadelphia City PA 7/9/1747, Irish 22 hatter
   4 days, Sunday, 5 pounds, 5'8",
Michael Castle, Robert Collison Bucks PA 6/2/1768, American 18 L
   13 days, Friday, 1.5 pounds, 5'5",
John Castolo, Samuel Webb Baltimore MD tanner 6/28/1744, 22
   19 days, Saturday, 2 pounds, middle,
Francis Caufield, Joseph Clarke Bucks PA tailor 1/2/1753, 19 tailor
   1 day, Wednesday, 1 pound,
Mary Caufield, Joseph Tatnall New Castle DE 4/24/1776, Irish 24
   7 days, Thursday, 1 pound, short,
James Cavanach, William Bennett Baltimore MD 6/16/1748, Irish C
   24 days, Monday, 3 pounds, middle,
Hester Cavanagh, John Shields Burlington NJ 2/19/1777, Irish 18
   14 days, Thursday, 4 dollars, 5',
Michael Cavanagh, John Righter Philadelphia PA 8/21/1776, Irish 16
   7 days, Thursday, 1 pound,
Michael Cavanagh, John Righter Philadelphia PA 3/12/1777, Irish 17 (2nd escape)
   11 days, Sunday, 4 dollars,
Garret Cavannah, Joshua Baker Lancaster PA 6/29/1738, Irish 26
   16 days, Tuesday, 1.5 pounds, tall,

Anthony Cavenaugh, James McCullough Cecil MD 12/13/1753, Irish
   219 days, Tuesday, 3 pounds,
Hugh Cavenaugh, John Stevenson Philadelphia PA 2/24/1747, Irish 20
   5 days, Saturday, 2.5 pounds, middle,
James Cavenaugh, George Aston Chester PA 7/4/1734, Irish
   7 days, Thursday, 2 pounds, middle,
John Cavenaugh, James Breading Cecil MD 2/12/1756, Irish 24 silk weaver C
   9 days, Tuesday, 2 pistoles, 5'4", (arrived last summer)
John Cavenaugh, James Breading Cecil MD 5/13/1756, Irish 24 silk weaver (2nd escape) C
   4 days, Sunday, 5'4",
Eleanor Cavenough, Abraham Shelly Philadelphia City PA 1/26/1744, Irish 35
   about one month ago, 1 pound, short,
Rebecca Cawood, Jonathan Wells Chester PA 4/12/1770, 14
   16 days, Tuesday, 4 dollars,
Philip Ceave, Jacob Ford Morris NJ 5/16/1754, Irish 20 (ran before)
   39 days, Sunday, 3 pounds, 5'6",
John Cely, David Jones Chester PA 3/28/1751, 30 barber
   16 days, Tuesday, 2 pounds, short,
John Ceupenditch, Isaac Baily Chester PA 10/4/1775, English 24
   10 days, Monday, 4 dollars, 5'6",
James Chadick, Peter Richy Queen Anne's MD 6/7/1753, American 27 blacksmith L
   34 days, Friday,
John Chaffy, Nathan Griffith Baltimore MD 8/15/1771, English C
   24 days, Monday, 3 pounds, 5'6-7",
John Chalaner, Nathan Haines Burlington NJ 12/20/1753, American turner L
   6 days, Friday, 3 pounds, 5'6",
David Chamber, Charles Harah Lancaster PA 11/11/1772, Irish 18
   2 pounds, 5'6",
George Chambers, John Townsend Chester PA 3/10/1752, Scot 20
   11 days, Sunday, 2.5 pounds, 5'10",
Jonathan Chambers, Henry Norwood Philadelphia City PA 8/30/1739, 19
   4 days, Sunday, 1.5 pounds,
Mary Chambers Alexander Baird Kent MD 4/25/1754, Irish C
   11 days, Sunday, 1.5 pounds, middle,
Robert Chambers, William Drewry Philadelphia City PA 1/31/1771, Irish 19 (ran before)
   6 days, Friday, 3 pounds, 5'6", (relatives live nearby)
Robert Chambers, William Shewell Bucks PA ironworks 7/2/1761, 18 soldier A
   11 days, Sunday, 3 pounds, 5'9",
Michael Chapman, Thomas Rickey Bucks PA shoemaker 10/25/1750, 16 A
   4 days, Sunday, 1.5 pounds, tall,
Thomas Chapman, Francis Phillips Baltimore MD ironworks 10/1/1767, 25
   9 days, Tuesday, 2 pounds, 5'3-4",
Joseph Alexander Chapney, Seneca Lukens Montgomery PA 4/13/1791, French A
   14 days, Wednesday, 3 dollars, 5'6",
Martin Chard, William Watson Philadelphia City PA shipwright 10/28/1736, English weaver
   5 days, Saturday, 5 pounds, short,
Barbara Charlton, Morris Mattson Chester PA 11/22/1759,
   11 days, Sunday, 0.75 pounds, short,
William Charlton, James Egburts New Castle DE 7/30/1752,
   28 days, Thursday, 5 pounds,
William Cherry, John Longstreth Bucks PA 6/27/1787, Irish 23 tailor
   12 days, Friday, 6 dollars, 5'8", (arrived 1 year ago)
Robert Chesnut, John Shovalter Lancaster PA 11/10/1773, Irish 27
   5 dollars, 5'6-7", (arrived 7 years ago)
Pearce Chessey, David Evans Chester PA 3/23/1769, 35 carpenter gaol sale L
   10 days, Monday, 3 pounds,
Thomas Chesterfield, Edward Barnes Cecil MD 10/4/1744,
   16 days, Tuesday, 2 pounds, tall,
Jeremiah Chichester, Arnold Francis Philadelphia PA 7/4/1751, Irish 21
   7 days, Thursday, 3 pounds, middle, (arrived last Wednesday)
John Child, James Franklin Baltimore MD ironworks 3/8/1764, English 30 gardener C
   13 days, Friday, 5 pounds, 5'10",
John Childs, John Platt Burlington NJ 6/25/1788, American 18 L
   3 days, Sunday, 5 dollars, 5'7",
William Childs, Buckler Bond Harford MD 5/3/1775, English 21 carver
   39 days, Sunday, 3 pounds, 5'6",

Jacob Chooper, George Sellers Salem NJ 7/27/1796, 20 A
   62 days, Thursday, 0.05 dollars,
Elizabeth Christie, Jacob Baker Philadelphia City PA 7/2/1794, 12
   9 days, Monday, 4 dollars, 4'6",
John Christie, Alexander Miller Philadelphia City PA 11/29/1775, Irish
   10 days, Monday, 10 dollars, 5'8-9",
John Christle, John Reedle Philadelphia City PA 5/16/1771, Scot 25 tailor L
   33 days, Saturday, 2 pounds,
Gibbons Christophers, John Douglas MD ironworks 9/14/1769, 18
   25 days, Sunday, 1.5 pounds, 5'5-6",
John Christy, John Baldwin Chester PA 7/30/1767, Irish 26 gaol sale L
   8 days, Wednesday, 3 pounds, 5'10-11",
James Chrystall, James Wilson Lancaster PA 12/16/1772, Irish 30
   5 days, Saturday, 4 dollars, 5'8-9",
William Cinser, Samuel Garrett Jr Chester PA 11/30,/1796, 17 A
   32 days, Saturday, 0.06 dollars, short,
William Citchen, Thomas May Berks PA ironworks 10/10/1765, English 25 brassfounder
   25 days, Sunday, 3 pounds, 5'6-7",
Michael Citsler, John Baccosfoes Lancaster PA 2/7/1771, 17 A
   May 1769, 1 pound, 5'8-9",
Thomas Claborne, Nehemiah Allen Philadelphia City PA 9/1/1748, 18 A
   5 days, Saturday, 1.5 pounds, short,
John Christopher Claouss, John Welsh Baltimore MD ironworks 3/20/1766, German soldier C
   13 days, Friday,
Joseph Clare, William Dewees Jr Lancaster PA ironworks 9/14/1774, Irish 19
   3 days, Monday, 4 dollars, 5'7",
Derby Clark, James Star Chester PA 6/4/1747, Irish 28 weaver
   4 days, Sunday, 5 pounds, 5'9",
Elizabeth Clark, Edward Hicks Chester PA 7/7/1773, English
   3 days, Monday, 4 dollars,
James Clark, James Harrison Philadelphia City PA 9/29/1763, 25 blacksmith
   13 days, Friday, 3 pounds, 5'4",
James Clark, Samuel Scott Lancaster PA 1/16/1766, carpenter
   2.5 pounds, 5'6", (lately arrived)
James Clark, John Wilkinson York PA 1/26/1764, English
   38 days, Monday, 3 pistoles, 5'5",
John Clark, John Mortemor 6/28/1750, Irish 40
   1.5 pounds,
John Clark, Catherine Kirkpatrick New Castle DE 4/4/1751, 35
   4 days, Sunday, 2 pounds, short,
John Clark, Pul Metzger Lancaster PA stocking-weaver 12/11/1766, Irish 22 stocking-weaver
   10 days, Monday, 3 pounds, 5',
John Clark, Nathan Cook 8/3/1769, Irish 18 skinner
   1.5 pounds,
John Clark, Michael Shwarts Bucks PA 6/9/1773, English
   8 days, Wednesday, 6 dollars, 5'4",
John Clark, Jehu Howell Baltimore MD 2/28/1771, carpenter A
   mid-Aug. 1770, 8 dollars, (relatives live nearby)
John Clark, Josiah Bowen Baltimore MD 8/21/1766, 50 C
   11 days, Sunday, 3 pounds, 5'9",
John Clark, George Middleton Dorchester MD 10/2/1755, English 22 C
   2 pounds, 6',
John Clark, Isaac Harris Anne Arundel MD 11/15/1764, English 27 blacksmith C
   25 days, Sunday, 5 pounds, 5'9",
John Clark, W. Buchanan Baltimore MD 6/20/1754, 38 gardener C
   47 days, Saturday, 4 pistoles, 5'8",
John Clark, Philip Marot Burlington NJ 10/18/1750, American 25 carpenter L
   4 days, Sunday, 2 pounds, middle,
Patience Clark, James Thomas Kent MD 3/26/1761, 40 C
   last Nov., 2 pistoles,
Patrick Clark, Joseph McFarland Cecil MD 7/15/1736, Scot 20
   4 days, Sunday, 3 pounds,
Patrick Clark, Jacob Keyser Philadelphia City PA 9/11/1766, English tailor
   8 dollars, 5'6",
Philip Clark, Samuel Landers Chester PA 2/12/1777, Irish
   3 days, Monday, 8 dollars, 5'7-8",

Richard Clark, John Kaighin Gloucester NJ 4/7/1763, English
  2 days, Tuesday, 1.5 pounds, 4',
Thomas Clark, Henry Chalfant Chester PA 11/2/1752, Irish 18
  3 days, Monday, 2 pounds,
Thomas Clark, James Thomas Kent MD 3/26/1761, 40 weaver C
  last Nov., 2 pistoles, 5'4",
William Clark, Renoldo Monk Baltimore MD 7/11/1765, C
  18 days, Sunday, 2 pounds,
John Clarke, Samuel Pritchard VA sheriff 11/16/1752,
  122 days, Friday, 3 pistoles,
Mary Clarke, James Denny York PA 12/22/1757, L
  92 days, Wednesday, 2 pounds, 5'2",
Michael Clarke, Samuel Atkinson Burlington NJ 11/20/1746, 40
  21 days, Thursday, 1.5 pounds, middle,
Sarah Clarke, Joseph Cauffman Philadelphia City PA 3/29/1775, Irish 27
  4 days, Sunday, 2 pounds, (arrived last fall)
Valentine Clarke, Samuel Hurfoot Philadelphia PA 1/18/1733, Irish 19
  4 days, Sunday, 2 pounds, middle,
Joseph Clay, John Houseman Kent DE 10/26738, English
  22 days, Wednesday, 5 pounds,
Thomas Clay, Daniel Gerard Jr Morris NJ 2/8/1770, 50 cooper
  45 days, Monday, 3 pounds, 5'10",
Francis Clayton, Moses Standley Philadelphia City PA 5/17/1753, English 24
  7 days, Thursday, 2 pounds, 5'5", (imported from Bristol)
Thomas Clear, William Nicholson Philadelphia City PA 3/17/1752, English 18
  2 pounds, (arrived last fall)
Andrew Cleara, David Crawford Lancaster PA 5/16/1751, Irish 30
  2 days, Tuesday, 3 pounds, middle,
Anthony Clearry, John Smith Cecil MD 10/23/1755, Irish 25
  9 days, Tuesday, 2 pounds, 5'11",
Peter Clearwater, Ephraim Oliphant Hunterdon NJ 8/8/1751, American 34 L
  8 days, Wednesday, 3 pounds, 6',
Patrick Cleary, John Atchinson Lancaster PA 4/19/1770, Irish 23
  9 days, Tuesday, 3 pounds, 5'6",
Robert Cleary, David Evans New Castle DE 10/19/1752, Irish 22
  24 days, Monday, 2 pounds, 6',
James Cleft, Nathaniel Giles Lancaster PA ironworks 7/16/1761, American L
  10 days, Monday, 5 pounds, 5'8",
Elizabeth Cleland, Elizabeth Robertson Philadelphia City PA 11/15/1775, Irish 17
  6 dollars, 5',
Paul Clem, James Buchanan Philadelphia PA 3/20/1760, German
  5 days, Saturday, 1 pistole, 5',
Thomas Clemans, David Thomson Philadelphia City PA ship builder 9/12/1771, Irish
  9 days, Tuesday, 1.5 pounds,
Eleanor Clemens, William Newman 5/14/1767, 29
  14 days, Thursday, 1 pound,
Martha Clemens, Joseph Dungan Jr Bucks PA 6/1/1769, 15
  5 days, Saturday, 3 dollars,
John Clemm, Thomas Lawrence Philadelphia City PA 4/20/1769, 16 upholsterer A
  23 days, Tuesday, 2 pounds, 5'3",
James Clemmens, Elijah Weed 8/9/1775, Irish waiter
  18 days, Sunday, 3 pounds, 5'8",
Amburst Clemmisson, Edward Bosman Baltimore MD 8/23/1770, English C
  over a year ago, 10 pound, 5'6",
Hugh Clemmons, Richard Gill Philadelphia City PA 4/24/1746, Irish
  middle,
Edward Clemons, James Hinchman Gloucester NJ 8/30/1770, English 23 (ran twice before)
  14 days, Thursday, 4 dollars, 4'4",
John Clerk, John McClellen Burlington NJ 2/25/1795, 16 A
  9 days, Monday, 0.005 dollars,
Valentine Clerk, Lawrence Reynolds Philadelphia City PA currier 7/15/1736, Irish 24
  2 days, Tuesday, 3 pounds, tall,
Anthony Clery, John Smith Cecil MD 7/5/1753, Irish 24
  2 pounds, 5'9",
James Clift, Nathaniel Giles Lancaster PA ironworks 10/16/1760, American 30 L
  93 days, Tuesday, 2 pistoles, 5'8",

James Clift, John Robinson Lancaster PA ironworks 9/2/1762, American 32 (2nd escape) L
    10 days, Monday, 2 pounds,
William Clifton, William McCrea Philadelphia City PA joiner 10/5/1752, 17 A
    12 days, Saturday, 4 pounds, 5'5",
Robert Clinton, James Greenfield Chester PA 11/26/1747, Irish 20 weaver
    4 days, Sunday, 5 pounds, middle,
Thomas Clinton, Jonathan Vaughn Talbot MD ironworks 9/29/1763, Irish
    23 days, Tuesday, 1.5 pounds, middle,
Carberry Cloath, Alexander Watson Philadelphia City PA 6/20/1748, Irish 27
    1 days, Wednesday, 1 pound, middle,
William Clyde, William Moore Philadelphia City PA 10/27/1773, Irish 20 blacksmith
    6 dollars, 5'6", (arrived last June)
Nicholas Coady, Robert McCrea Cumberland PA 9/15/1768, Irish 20
    11 days, Sunday, 2 pounds, 6',
William Coady, Angus McDonald MA 5/26/1773, Irish 27 butcher
    50 days, Wednesday, 20 dollars, 5'5",
John Coale, Richard Jones Chester PA 8/20/1794, Irish 20
    9 days, Monday, 8 dollars, 5'5-6", (lately arrived)
Henry Coarse, Thomas Moore Northampton PA 7/14/1773, German 21
    8 days, Wednesday, 8 dollars, 5'9-10",
Josiah Coather, George Aston Chester PA 7/4/1734, American hired L
    7 days, Thursday, 2 pounds, tall,
James Cobagen, Robert Coleman Philadelphia PA ironworks 7/24/1776, Irish 20 forgeman
    4 days, Sunday, 3 pounds, 5'6-7",
Bleny Cochran, John Shafer Berks PA 8/11/1779, Irish 15
    79 days, Monday, 30 dollars, short,
George Cochran, Hugh Niven Chester PA 10/10/1765, Irish
    2 pounds, 5'8-9",
Moses Cochran, John Chambers New Castle DE 5/30/1771, American 19 L
    9 days, Tuesday, 3 pounds, 5'10",
William Cochran, John Ross Chester PA 12/28/1769, American 17 (ran 4 times before) L
    16 days, Tuesday, 1.5 pounds,
John Cocklin, John Hamilton Chester PA 10/26/1752, English 30
    57 days, Wednesday, 1 pound, 5'9",
Richard Coe, James Braddock Talbot MD 11/23/1774, English C
    21 days, Thursday, 6 dollars, (arrived Feb. 1774)
Anthony Coes, Casper Ulrich Philadelphia City PA baker 8/12/1742, German 16
    11 days, Sunday, 3 pounds,
Patrick Coffe, Robert Steuart Berkeley VA 5/17/1775, Irish 30
    10 days, Monday, 8 dollars, 5'6",
John Coffee, Thomas Griffith Chester PA 5/7/1747, Irish 17
    3 days, Monday, 1.5 pounds, short,
John Coffee, Andrew Moore Lancaster PA miller 8/26/1772, 16
    9 days, Tuesday, 6 dollars, 5',
Edward Coffery, James Hinchman Gloucester NJ 5/7/1752, Irish 20
    5 days, Saturday, 2 pounds, middle,
Daniel Coffey, John Dunwody Chester PA 4/23/1752, Irish 16
    4 days, Sunday, 2 pounds,
Joseph Coffey, William Evans Chester PA 8/4/1773, American 18 L
    45 days, Monday, 3 pounds, 5'7-8",
Mary Coffey, William Sail Chester PA 4/19/1761, Irish 28
    9 days, Tuesday, 1.5 pounds,
Michael Coffey, Michael Kinsor Lancaster PA 10/14/1772, Irish 20
    1 pound, 5'5",
Nicholas Coffey, Richard Richison Chester PA 2/20/1766, Irish 25
    4 days, Sunday, 2 pounds, (been in the army and navy)
William Coffey, William Hudson Chester PA 9/20/1753, Irish 23
    3 days, Monday, 1.5 pounds, short,
Richard Cogan, Robert Fulton Lancaster PA 7/9/1767, Irish 24
    11 days, Sunday, 2.5 pounds, short,
Thomas Cogan, James McSparren Lancaster PA 8/24/1769, Irish 20
    14 days, Thursday, 2 pounds, 5'6-7",
Sidney Cogdal, James Rippeth Lancaster PA 5/1/1776, 13
    44 days, Tuesday, 4 dollars, (relatives live nearby)
John Cogdill, John Michener Philadelphia PA 8/18/1743, Irish 17 teamster
    1 day, Wednesday, 1.5 pounds, short,

John Cogdill, Samuel Morris Philadelphia PA 1/7/1746, Irish 20 teamster (2nd escape)
    10 days, Monday, 2 pounds, short,
Nicholas Coging, George Marpole Bucks PA 4/5/1744, Irish 18
    12 days, Saturday, 2 pounds,
Ephriam Colam, Richard Chow WJ 12/2/1742, American 35 L
    22 days, Wednesday, 2 pounds, tall,
Curtis Cole, Benjamin Vansant Kent MD 10/23/1766, 20 tailor A
    26 days, Saturday, 2 pounds, 5'8",
Henry Cole, John Wright Lancaster PA 4/4/1754, English 22
    5 days, Saturday, 5 pounds, middle,
Henry Cole, John Wright Lancaster PA 6/12/1755, English 23 (2nd escape)
    10 days, Monday, 4 pistoles, (use to the sea)
Henry Cole, Robert Emley Hunterdon NJ 9/15/1763, 18
    24 days, Monday, 3 pounds, 5'10",
William Cole, Richard Wright 4/27/1732, 24
    10 days, Monday, 2 pounds, short,
William Cole, Elizabeth Jeffries Chester PA 7/31/1746, 20
    4 days, Sunday, 2 pounds, middle,
Robert Colebrook, Thomas Maybury Philadelphia PA 7/26/1775, English 28 miller
    8 days, Wednesday, 5 pounds, 5'6", (arrived last fall)
Edward Coleman, Dennis McGlaughland Northumberland PA 10/19/1774, Irish breeches-maker
    16 dollars, 5'7",
Henry Coleman, John Young Lancaster PA 10/19/1752, Irish 20
    30 days, Tuesday, 2 pounds, middle,
Henry Coleman, John Young Lancaster PA 8/2/1753, Irish 21 (2nd escape)
    41 days, Friday, 3 pounds, 5'4",
John Coleman, Israel Lawrence Salem NJ 11/22/1764, 18
    9 days, Tuesday, 2 pounds, 5'6",
Matthew Coleman, John Norman 7/19/1775, Irish gentleman's servant
    31 days, Monday, 6 pounds, 5'6-7",
William Coleman, John McCalion Chester PA 12/3/1783, 18
    20 days, Thursday, 3 dollars, 5'7-8",
Philip Colen, William Prigg Baltimore MD 5/15/1755, C
    17 days, Monday, 1 pistole, 5'5",
Isaac Coley, Richard Martin Philadelphia City PA 7/28/1773, 20 tanner A
    18 days, Sunday, 0.11 dollars, 5'10",
John Colgan, Samuel Dick Salem NJ 11/28/1771, Irish 29
    153 days, Friday, 4 pounds, 5'6-7",
Bernard Colgon, John Simpson Chester PA 10/10/1754, Irish
    7 days, Thursday, 1.5 pounds, middle,
Jane Colgon, John Simpson Chester PA 10/10/1754, Irish
    7 days, Thursday, 1.5 pounds, short,
John Coll, James Hutchings Kent DE 8/26/1772,
    24 days, Monday, 5 pistoles, 5'7",
Margaret Collands, William Chamberland Lancaster PA 2/14/1776, 30
    12 days, Saturday, 4 dollars, 5',
Thomas Collard, Samuel Ramsey Chester PA 8/16/1750, Irish
    4 days, Sunday, 3 pounds,
Thomas Collard, Jonas Rees Salem NJ 2/28/1771, English 21
    27 days, Friday, 4 dollars, 5'7",
William Collemore, Abraham Carlistle Philadelphia City PA 7/12/1744,
    4 days, Sunday, 3 pounds,
Robert Collens, James Franklin Baltimore MD ironworks 3/15/1775, English 25 C
    5 pounds, 5'7-8",
Thomas Collerd, William Jones Queen Anne's MD 7/26/1770, C
    16 days, Tuesday, 2 pounds, 5'7-8",
John Collet, Alexander Crukshank Philadelphia City PA shoemaker 9/18/1740, 19 shoemaker A
    1.5 pounds,
John Collier, Charles Worthington Anne Arundel MD 7/7/1773, English C
    16 days, Tuesday, 20 dollars, 5'6",
Joseph Collier, Daniel Lucken Philadelphia PA 7/23/1761, 18 sadler A
    2 pounds, 5'4",
Michael Collings, Jacob Scott Morris NJ 7/8/1742, Irish 24 weaver
    2 pounds, middle,
Cornelius Collins, Abel Harris Salem NJ 1/9/1753, Irish 22
    43 days, Wednesday, 2 pounds, short,

Daniel Collins, James Crawford Lancaster PA 10/12/1769, Irish 20
   2 pounds, 5'8",
Daniel Collins, James Clark Chester PA 5/9/1771, Irish 22 (2nd escape)
   7 days, Thursday, 3 dollars, 5'7",
Daniel Collins, Peter Covert Philadelphia City PA tobacconist 4/21/1784, Irish
   7 days, Wednesday, 4 dollars, 5'4-5",
Darby Collins, Thomas Donnelin Cumberland PA 6/5/1766, Irish 18
   10 days, Monday, 2 pounds, 5'6",
David Collins, Matthias Meuris Philadelphia PA 10/2/1746, American A
   1.5 pounds, 5'10",
Edmund Collins, John Howard Baltimore MD ironworks 8/22/1765, 25 shoemaker C
   17 days, Monday, 3 pounds, 5'8",
James Blight Collins, Robert Shields New Castle DE 10/4/1775, English 23 ropemaker
   10 days, Monday, 6 dollars, 5'6",
John Collins, Archibald Stewart Sussex NJ ironworks 9/13/1770, English 19
   9 days, Tuesday, 3 pounds, 5'5-6",
John Collins, James Clark Chester PA 5/9/1771, Irish 25
   7 days, Thursday, 3 dollars, 5'9",
John Collins, W. Twaddell Chester PA ironworks 3/22/1775, Irish 25
   10 days, Monday, 6 dollars, 5'5",
John Collins, Hugh Steel New Castle DE 12/1/1773, Irish 17
   6 days, Friday, 1.5 pounds, 5'5-6",
John Collins, Caleb Dorsey Anne Arundel MD ironworks 8/21/1760, English 23 C
   4 pistoles, 5'7",
John Collins, Nathaniel Giles Lancaster PA ironworks 10/16/1760, English 23 (2nd escape) C
   10 days, Monday, 2 pistoles, 5'5",
John Collins, Nathaniel Giles Lancaster PA ironworks 4/16/1761, English 23 (3rd escape) C
   about 15 days, 10 pounds, 5'3",
John Collins, Josiah Slade Baltimore MD ironworks 7/21/1763, English 26 (4th escape) C
   19 days, Saturday, 5 pistoles, 5'8",
John Collins, Josiah Slade Baltimore MD ironworks 9/1/1763, English 26 (5th escape) C
   18 days, Sunday, 5 pounds, 5'6",
John Collins, Dennis Whelen Chester PA 11/20/1793, American 20 forgeman L
   9 days, Monday, 12 dollars, 5'7", (has 7 months left to serve)
Joseph Collins, John Morgan Philadelphia PA 7/19/1780, 14 A
   7 days, Wednesday, 400 dollars,
Margaret Collins, John Douglas Lancaster PA 9/4/1776, 30
   3 pounds,
Maurice Collins, Abraham Holmes Lancaster PA 11/24/1773, Irish 20
   10 dollars, 5'10", (ran because he had been stealing)
Michael Collins, John Scot Morris NJ 3/24/1743, Irish 25
   6 days, Friday, 2 pounds, middle,
Michael Collins, John Grant Sommerset PA 10/20/1748, Irish 22
   3 pounds, short,
Nathan Collins, William Downs Gloucester NJ 6/9/1768, 34
   8 pounds, 5'10",
Edward Colson, Henry Smith Philadelphia PA 6/23/1743,
   10 days, Monday, 5 pounds,
James Coltis, Samuel Savage Chester PA ironworks 9/13/1739, 27 carpenter
   5 days, Saturday, 5 pounds, short,
William Colwell, John Bosman Talbot MD 4/26/1764, 30 school teacher C
   36 days, Wednesday, 4 pistoles, 5'10",
John Combs, John Taylor Chester PA 4/26/1775, Irish 21 weaver
   10 days, Monday, 5 pounds, 5'10", (lately arrived)
Owen Comens, James Clemson Lancaster PA 7/10/1766, Irish
   13 days, Friday, 1 pound, 5'5-6",
Elizabeth Comon, George Rein Lancaster PA 12/22/1763, Scot 31
   16 days, Tuesday, 1.5 pounds, short,
Cornelius Conaway, James Brown Philadelphia City PA cordwainer 1/29/1761, 18 A
   2 pounds, 5'6", (relatives live nearby)
William Conaway, David Allison York PA 3/28/1771, 18
   3 pounds, 5'8",
Garret Condon, William Rush Philadelphia City PA blacksmith 12/2/1742, Irish 23
   10 days, Monday, 3 pounds,
Garret Condon, John Dobbin Philadelphia City PA blacksmith 4/5/1748, Irish 28 (2nd escape)
   2 days, Tuesday, 2 pounds, 5'10",

James Condon, Jonathan Park Chester PA 8/12/1731, Irish 25 weaver
    4 days, Sunday, 2 pounds, middle,
James Condon, James Patterson Lancaster PA 10/4/1764, Irish 27
    13 days, Friday, 1.5 pounds, 5'6",
John Condon, Thomas Boal Lancaster PA 6/1/1774, Irish 19
    31 days, Monday, 2 pounds, 5'6",
Briant Conely, John Reed New Castle DE 12/17/1745, Irish 17
    3 days, Monday, 1 pound,
Henry Conland, Walter Bell Lancaster PA 3/30/1774, tailor L
    17 days, Monday, 10 dollars, 5'5",
James Connaly, James Hart Bucks PA 5/30/1751, Irish 21
    2 pounds,
Michael Connel, Abraham Lewis Chester PA 6/30/1773, Irish 20
    3 days, Monday, 2.5 pounds, 5'5", (relative live nearby)
Micheal Connel, James Buchanan Cecil MD 10/18/1764, Irish 27 tailor
    11 days, Sunday, 5 pounds, middle,
Morris Connel, David Jenkins Lancaster PA 1/5/1774, Irish 19 (female)
    24 days, Monday, 4 pounds, 5'3-4",
Dennis Connell, Caleb Jackson Lancaster PA 8/15/1754, Irish 23
    4 days, Sunday, 2 pounds, 5'6",
John Connell, James Hunter Philadelphia City PA 7/8/1795, Irish 19 cork-maker
    19 days, Friday, 10 dollars, 5'5-6", (lately arrived)
Thomas Connely, William Bronson Jr New Castle DE 7/6/1774, Irish barber gaol sale (ran before) L
    9 days, Tuesday, 10 dollars, 5'5-6",
Barnabas Conner, James Hutton Berks PA 6/26/1766, Irish 19
    2 pounds, 5'3-4",
Bryan Conner, William Oakford Philadelphia PA 7/31/1746, 35
    2 pounds, 6',
Christopher Conner, Benjamin Swett Jr 9/29/1763, Irish 18
    9 days, Tuesday, 3 pounds, 5'4",
James Conner, William McCasland Lancaster PA 5/22/1766,
    15 days, Wednesday, 2 pounds, short,
John Conner, John Buckingham Philadelphia City PA 7/26/1764, Irish coach-driver
    7 days, Thursday, 3 pounds, 5'3",
John Conner, John Chirington Philadelphia City PA 4/27/1769, Irish leather breeches-maker
    2 pounds, 5'5",
John Conner, George Taylor Chester PA 4/25/1771, Irish 28
    11 days, Sunday, 2 pounds, 5'3-4",
John Conner, Elijah Wickersham Lancaster PA 4/6/1774, 21 bricklayer
    10 days, Monday, 3 pounds, 5'7-8",
Mary Conner, Michael Clark Philadelphia City PA 1/12/1769, Irish 23
    9 days, Tuesday, 1 pound, (lately arrived)
Sarah Conner, Samuel Peden York PA 12/10/1767, Irish 23
    1.5 pounds, short, (arrived 9 months ago)
Timothy Conner, George Browning Kent MD 4/12/1770, Irish
    12 days, Saturday, 2 pounds, 5'8-9",
Timothy Conner, George Browning Kent MD 8/22/1771, Irish (2nd escape)
    30 days, Tuesday, 2 pounds, 5'8-9",
Timothy Conner, George Browning Kent MD 9/12/1771, Irish (3rd escape)
    9 days, Tuesday, 4 dollars, 5'8-9",
James Connet, William Glen Berkeley VA 6/19/1776, Irish 24
    3 pounds, 5'7-8",
Pattrick Connolin, George Bratten New Castle DE 7/25/1751, Irish 17
    10 days, Monday, 2 pounds, 5'5",
Mary Connoly, David Wilkin New Castle DE 5/17/1750, Irish 23
    13 days, Friday, 5 pounds, 5'4",
Peter Connoly, Samuel Evans Chester PA 6/11/1747, Irish 29
    7 days, Thursday, 1 pound, middle,
Thomas Connoly, Thomas Miller Cecil MD 9/12/1751, Irish 24
    15 days, Wednesday, 1.5 pounds,
Charles Connor, John Henderson New Castle DE 1/22/1751, Irish 20
    11 days, Sunday, 3 pounds, 5',
Charles Connor, John Henderson New Castle DE 8/8/1751, Irish 20 (2nd escape)
    4 days, Sunday, 3 pounds, 5',
Eleanor Connor, Timothy Scarth Philadelphia PA tanner 8/2/1753, Irish 27
    17 days, Monday, 1.5 pounds,

John Connor, David Caldwell Lancaster PA ironworker 9/20/1753, Irish 22 tailor
   5 days, Saturday, 4 pistoles, 5'4",
John Connor, Thomas Ogle New Castle DE 6/21/1753, 25
   1.5 pounds, middle,
John Connor, Jacob Barge Chester PA 2/28/1765, Irish 19
   3 days, Monday, 1 pound, 5',
Michael Connor, Joseph Ruth New Castle DE 5/2/1771, barber
   6 days, Friday, 2 pounds,
Mille Connor, Abraham Holmes Lancaster PA 10/27/1768, 13 (male)
   4 weeks ago, 2 pounds, 4'6-7",
Patrick Connor, William Pywell Philadelphia City PA tanner 11/27/1731, 27 currier
   9 days, Tuesday, 3 pounds, middle,
Patrick Connor, Samuel Worthington Jr Bucks PA 1/26/1769, Irish
   2 pounds, 5'8", (arrived 1 year ago, claims to have arrived as a freeman)
Phillip Connor, Arthur Alexander Cecil MD 8/15/1754,
   10 days, Monday, 2 pounds, 5'10",
Roger Connor, John Davis Chester PA 10/12/1752, Irish 18
   18 days, Sunday, 1.5 pounds, short,
Thomas Connor, Alexander McIntoch Kent MD 5/13/1762, Irish 50 shoemaker L
   2 pistoles, (was a soldier)
William Connor, Andrew Cochran Cecil MD 5/26/1784, 23 shoemaker
   8 days, Tuesday, 4 dollars, 5'7-8",
James Connoway, David Crawford Lancaster PA 9/15/1773, Irish
   10 days, Monday, 4 dollars, 5'6-7",
Mary Conolly, Alexander Alexander Philadelphia City PA 11/3/1757,
   39 days, Sunday, 2 pounds,
Mary Conolly, Alexander Alexander Philadelphia City PA 2/28/1760, (2nd escape)
   22 days, Wednesday, 2 pounds,
Thomas Conolly, Alexander Alexander Philadelphia City PA 11/3/1757, English blacksmith
   39 days, Sunday, 2 pounds, middle,
Thomas Conolly, Alexander Alexander Philadelphia City PA 2/28/1760, English blacksmith (2nd esc)
   22 days, Wednesday, 2 pounds, 5'6",
Peter Conoly, Samuel Evans Chester PA 12/9/1746, Irish 20
   2 days, Tuesday, 2 pounds,
Peter Conoway, Daniel Shaw Lancaster PA 8/18/1768, Irish
   11 days, Sunday, 2 pounds, 5'6-7",
William Conrad, Peter Young Bucks PA 2/18/1755, German 18
   16 days, Tuesday, 3 pounds, middle,
Margaret Conslatine, Joshua Brown Lancaster PA 4/6/1769,
   55 days, Friday, 2 pounds,
John Const, John Room Gloucester NJ 5/14/1772, English 25
   39 days, Sunday, 5 pounds, 5'4-5",
Redman Conten, Leonard Middlecaff York PA 8/23/1775, Irish 19
   21 days, Thursday, 3 pounds, 5'6-7",
William Conyngham, Matthew Hand Philadelphia City PA 12/28/1774, 16 A
   4 days, Sunday, 4 dollars, 5'6",
Ann Cook, William Griffith York PA 3/29/1775, Irish
   19 days, Saturday, 5 pounds,
George Cook, Peter Lowry Philadelphia City PA butcher 1/12/1774, German 19
   7 days, Thursday, 1 pound, 5'5",
John Cook, Henry Trimble Chester PA 7/3/1760, Irish
   5 days, Saturday, 2 pounds, 6", (was in the army)
John Cook, William Griffith York PA 3/29/1775, Irish
   19 days, Saturday, 5 pounds, 5'7-8",
John Cook, Thomas Reed Chester PA 3/14/1765, English 26 A
   9 days, Tuesday, 2 pounds, 5',
Miles Cook, Captain Crymer Baltimore MD ship captain 8/18/1763, English 30 C
   10 days, Monday, 1 pistole, 5'10",
Samuel Cook, Joseph Gilbert Philadelphia PA 2/19/1745, American 18 L
   4 days, Sunday, 2 pounds,
Samuel Cook, Joseph Gilbert Philadelphia PA 3/15/1746, American 19 (2nd escape) L
   7 days, Thursday, 2 pounds,
William Cook, Thomas Armstrong Chester PA 5/1/1760, 22 brickmaker
   4 days, Sunday, 2 pounds, 5'10",
Richard Cooke, Charles Ridgely Jr Baltimore MD ironworks 8/13/1747, English 30 L
   24 days, Monday, 4 pounds, 5'6",

Richard Cooke, Charles Ridgely Jr Baltimore MD ironworks 4/5/1748, English 31 (2nd escape) L
    155 days, Sunday, 4 pounds, 5'6",
Charles Cookson, Jacob Mattson Chester PA 8/27/1777, 17 weaver
    4 dollars,
James Cooley, Amos Garrett Lancaster PA ironworks 9/20/1753, Irish 29 dyer
    5 days, Saturday, 4 pistoles, 5'6",
John Cooley, Buckler Bond Harford MD 5/3/1775, English 22 plaisterer
    39 days, Sunday, 3 pounds, 5'8",
William Coombs, Patrick Doaren Anne Arundel MD 4/25/1751, English 19 bricklayer
    2.5 pistoles,
Christopher Cooney, Nathan Watson Burlington NJ 1/29/1751, Irish 26 hostler L
    9 days, Tuesday, 2 pounds, short,
Charles Cooper, William Robinson Philadelphia City PA 9/20/1764, 18 A
    48 days, Friday, 1.5 pounds, 5'6",
Samuel Cooper, Robert Milburn Essex NJ 9/27/1753, Irish blacksmith
    7 days, Thursday, 2 pounds, 5'7",
Samuel Cooper, James Gihon Philadelphia City PA 4/17/1776, 18 cordwainer A
    7 days, Thursday, 8 dollars,
Thomas Cooper, Caleb Dorsey Anne Arundel MD ironworks 8/21/1760, English 26 C
    4 pistoles, 5'3",
William Cooper, Stephen Burrows Hunterdon NJ 5/26/1743, English collier
    10 days, Monday, 2 pounds, short,
William Cooper, Matthias Williamson 4/15/1762, English 28 harnessmaker
    6 pounds, 5'8",
Christian Coots, Thomas Grubb Lancaster PA 9/6/1753, Scot
    2 pounds, short,
Jacob Coozar, George Cowin Cumberland PA 10/17/1751, German 24
    17 days, Monday, 5 pounds, short,
John Cope, Edward Kemble Burlington NJ 6/7/1729,
    1.5 pounds, short,
Thomas Copland, David Patten Chester PA 9/8/1768, Irish 20 weaver
    11 days, Sunday, 1 pound, 5'9",
Richard Copple, Daniel Evans Chester PA 4/27/1774, English 18 sawyer
    5 dollars, 5'5",
Richard Corbet, Joseph Smith Baltimore MD ironworks 1/15/1756, Irish
    21 days, Thursdays, 2 pistoles, 5'5",
John Corbett, James McDill Lancaster PA 4/4/1771, Irish tailor
    4 pounds, 5'8",
William Corble, John Dabbin Philadelphia City PA blacksmith 1/27/1743, English 24 blacksmith
    4 days, Sunday, 3 pounds, 5'8",
William Corby, John Dabbin Philadelphia City PA blacksmith 7/7/1743, English
    5 days, Saturday, 3 pounds, 5',
Thomas Coreshill, William Digges MD 1/19/1769, stone mason
    3 pounds, 5'8",
Timothy Corker, Jeremiah Ducker Frederick MD 2/15/1775, Irish tailor
    24 days, Monday, 10 pounds, 5'4",
John Frederick Corn, Stephen Carpenter Philadelphia PA 1/28/1755, German 40
    3 pounds,
Thomas Corner, Jacob Windrode Frederick MD 11/14/1771, Irish 17
    48 days, Friday, 5 pounds, 5',
Martin Cornett, Amos Strettell Philadelphia City PA 7/10/1755, English 16
    4 days, Sunday, 1 pound, (arrived last summer)
James Cornish, Nicholas Castle Philadelphia City PA 2/28/1738, Welsh 21
    1 pound, middle,
Francis Correy, William West Chester PA 9/6/1775, Scot 20 farmer
    18 days, Sunday, 5 pounds, 5'7", (was a soldier)
John Corry, John McCoulough Lancaster PA 3/3/1752, Irish 25
    1 pound, 5'8",
John Frederick Francis Cortine, James Stockhouse Philadelphia City PA 4/4/1754, German 17
    3 days, Monday, 2 pounds, 5'6",
Mary Cortney, Joseph Lapkin Chester PA 11/15/1775, Irish 25
    3 days, Monday, 4 dollars, short,
Mary Cosby, Timothy Brannin Cecil MD 6/7/1750, Irish 20 C
    7 days, Thursday, 1 pound, short,
Robert Cosgraves, Richard Hall Chester PA 1/20/1763,
    16 days, Tuesday, 2 pounds, 5'4",

Charles Cosgrove, Noble Biddle Cecil MD 4/16/1767, Irish 20
   13 days, Friday, 2 pounds, 5'6", (wears an iron collar)
John Cossel, Thomas Griffith Chester PA 7/30/1747, Irish 17
   6 days, Friday, 2 pounds, middle,
John Costeloe, Obadiah Bonfall Chester PA 11/3/1748, Irish 23 shoemaker
   3 pounds, middle,
James Cosway, William Berry Kent DE 8/21/1740, 20
   14 days, Thursday, 1 pound, short,
James Cotter, Mark Elliot New Castle DE 6/14/1764, Irish 20 weaver
   10 days, Monday, 2.5 pounds, 5'10", (arrived last fall)
James Cotter, Henry Weaver Lancaster PA 5/5/1773, American L
   6 dollars, 5'5-6",
Joseph Couch, Joshua Thompson Salem NJ 4/29/1795, 18 A
   30 days, Monday, 8 dollars, 5'3-4",
William Cough, Samuel Butt Bucks PA 5/11/1738, Irish
   14 days, Thursday, 2 pounds, short,
John Coughlan, John Lewis Chester PA 3/14/1771, Irish 22
   9 days, Tuesday, 6 dollars, 5'6",
John Coughlen, James Welsh Baltimore MD 10/5/1774, Irish
   17 days, Monday, 5 pounds, 5'6-8",
Mary Councun, James Brown Philadelphia City PA tavern-keeper 9/15/1773, Irish 20
   14 days, Thursday, 5 pounds,
John Coupleditch, Robert Lamborn Chester PA 11/16/1774, English 24
   18 days, Sunday, 3 dollars, 5'9-10",
James Courbet, Thomas Emory Queen Anne's MD 3/6/1760, English 19 C
   7 days, Thursday, 1 pound,
Jacob Covell, William Thompson Baltimore MD 11/16/1743, 17 tailor
   10 pounds,
William Covert, John Reedle Philadelphia City PA 11/27/1782, 18 A
   2 days, Monday, 0.03 pounds, 5'6",
Nicholas Cowalt, Alexander Murray Hunterdon NJ ironworks 6/8/1749, German 25
   18 days, Sunday, 3 pounds,
Henry Cowan, Matthew Cannon New Castle DE 5/22/1766, Irish 24
   4 days, Sunday, 5 pounds, 5',
John Cowan, Peter Dicks Chester PA 5/9/1751, American 23 L
   7 days, Thursday, 3 pounds, short,
Samuel Cowan, Samuel Owings Baltimore MD 6/16/1773, American 25 joiner L
   162 days, Wednesday, 15 pounds, 5'10",
Susannah Cowden, William Randall Baltimore MD 6/11/1767, 20 C
   30 days, Tuesday, 3 pounds,
Francis Cowell, John Walker Queen Anne's MD 5/23/1771, 40 C
   1.5 pounds, 5'4-5",
Elizabeth Cowen, John Spencer Philadelphia City PA shipwright 12/12/1747, German 25
   14 days, Thursday, 3 pounds,
Jane Cowerder, Isaac Yarnail Chester PA 11/8/1759,
   8 days, Wednesday, 1 pound,
David Cowings, John Chapple Queen Anne's MD 4/26/1775, Irish 40
   28 days, Thursday, 2 pounds,
William Cowling, Richard Croxall Baltimore MD ironworks 8/28/1755, English C
   11 days, Sunday, 4 pistoles, 5'8", (arrived 14 months ago)
Absalom Cox, Samuel Lewis York PA 7/11/1765, 17 A
   10 days, Monday, 1 pound, 5'8-9",
Daniel Cox, Samuel Hough Burlington NJ 10/3/1792, American L
   7 days, Wednesday, 6 dollars, 5'7",
Francis Cox, Daniel Fitzpatrick Chester PA 5/18/1796, 16 A
   10 days, Sunday, 6 dollars,
Moses Cox, Henry Scheet Montgomery PA 8/19/1789, American 21 L
   3 days, Sunday, 4 dollars, 5'7-8",
Richard Cox, William Modesley Queen Anne's MD 5/9/1765, 40 C
   30 days, Tuesday, 5 pounds, 5'5",
Robert Cox, Charles Carroll Baltimore MD ironworks 9/12/1754, English 25 farmer
   43 days, Wednesday, 3 pounds, tall, (arrived this summer, has steel collar around neck)
Samuel Cox, Hugh Coulter Philadelphia City PA 4/28/1748, sailor L
   8 days, Wednesday, 5 pistoles, middle,
William Cox, Thomas Holms Anne Arundel MD 9/11/1746, English 30 butcher
   18 days, Sunday, 5 pounds, tall,

Owen Coyl, William Webb Baltimore MD 6/16/1773, Irish 20 jockey C
   14 days, Thursday, 3 pounds, 5'7-8", (arrived 3 weeks ago)
Charles Coyle, David Jones Berks PA 1/8/1754, Irish 40 cordwainer
   last May, 1 pound,
John Crabb, Joseph Musgrave Chester PA 1/3/1776, English
   3 days, Monday, 2 pounds,
Joseph Cradok, Isaac Mayer Lancaster PA 4/12/1764, Irish 25
   97 days, Thursday, 3 pounds, 5'8",
John Crafford, Thomas Williams Philadelphia PA joiner 2/10/1763, 19 A
   0.06 pounds, 5'9",
Anne Craig, Stephen Anderson Chester PA 4/17/1776, Irish 40
   11 days, Sunday, 1 pound,
Sarah Craig, Andrew Wentz Philadelphia PA 9/18/1776, English
   24 days, Monday, 8 dollars, 5',
William Craige, Colin Ferguson Kent MD 8/27/1747, 19 A
   5 days, Saturday, 2 pounds, middle,
Daniel Craley Jr, James Burd Lancaster PA 2/22/1775,
   3 pounds, 5'10", (relatives live nearby)
Henry Cramer, Mark Bird Berks PA ironworks 6/8/1769, German 27 wheelwright
   25 days, Sunday, 5 pounds, 5'7-8", (arrived last fall)
William Crammer, Barillai Furman Burlington NJ 12/7/1791, 16 weaver A
   16 days, Monday, 1 dollar, short,
William Cramston, John Durborow Philadelphia City PA 8/13/1794, 17 sailmaker A
   12 days, Friday, 8 dollars, 5'7",
John Crarat, Aaron Holman Middlesex NJ 1/12/1774, American 18 L
   8 days, Wednesday, 4 dollars, 5'7",
Richard Cravatt, John Bates Philadelphia City PA 7/17/1766, American shoemaker A
   4 days, Sunday, 5 pounds, 5'7",
Andrew Crawford, Benjamin Moses Clave 7/24/1776, 17 A
   10 days, Monday, 0.03 pounds, 5',
John Crawford, William Wilson Burlington NJ 6/2/1773, Irish 21
   10 days, Monday, 2.5 pounds, 5'6-8",
John Crawford, John Rodman Bucks PA 12/12/1765, Irish 16 hired L
   8 days, Wednesday, 5 pounds, short,
Richard Crawford, Charles Foreman Kent MD 5/24/1750, Irish
   2 pounds, tall,
Rose Crawford, Joseph Kinney Philadelphia City PA mariner 10/25/1759, Irish 40
   7 days, Thursday, 1 pound,
William Crawford, Benjamin Cooper Sussex NJ ironworks 3/19/1761, 30
   21 days, Thursday, 5 pistoles, 6',
William Crawneen, Joshua Way Chester PA 2/6/1772, Irish 18
   5 days, Saturday, 1.5 pounds, 5'8-9",
Francis Crawson, Matthias Boatman Philadelphia PA tavern-keeper 11/22/1759, 18 A
   9 days, Tuesday, 1 pistole, 5',
James Craytan, James Wood Baltimore MD 8/21/1766, English 27 C
   11 days, Sunday, 3 pounds, 5'8-9",
Daniel Creamer, William Flaningan Gloucester NJ 6/29/1774, Irish 20
   10 days, Monday, 6 dollars, 5'8-9",
Daniel Creeley, Stephen Twining Bucks PA 4/22/1795, 16 A
   29 days, Tuesday, 4 dollars, 5'5",
Elizabeth Creely, Hugh Jones Philadelphia PA 1/4/1775,
   11 days, Sunday, 1 pound, middle,
John Creighton, Benjamin Paschall Philadelphia City PA cutler 7/7/1737, English 25 knifemaker
   4 days, Sunday, 2 pounds,
Frederick Creiner, Henry Lisle Philadelphia City PA 7/6/1774, German 18
   3 days, Monday, 2.5 pounds,
Hanse Creiner, Henry Lisle Philadelphia City PA 7/6/1774, German 18
   3 days, Monday, 2.5 pounds,
John Cresswel, Rice Prichard Chester PA 10/2/1729,
   7 days, Thursday, 3 pounds, middle,
Benjamin Creuse, John Wood Hunterdon NJ 1/2/1772, French watchmaker
   10 days, Monday, 1 pound, 5'7-8",
Elizabeth Crileley, James Crawford Lancaster PA 10/12/1769, 20 ,
   2 pounds,
Hanse Martin Crimer, Charles West 10/19/1774, German 18
   3 days, Monday, 2.5 pounds,

Cornelius Crimmen, Richard Jacobs Lancaster PA 8/3/1774, Irish 16
    3 days, Monday, 4 dollars, short, (arrived last fall)
Jacob Crips, Marmaduke Cooper Gloucester NJ 7/12/1775, German 27 butcher
    28 days, Thursday, 10 pounds, 5'8",
Jacob Crips, Marmaduke Cooper Gloucester NJ 9/20/1775, German 27 butcher (2nd escape)
    6 days, Friday, 5 pounds, 5'8",
Joseph Crispin, Nehemiah Allen Philadelphia City PA 1/27/1747, 19 cooper A
    10 days, Monday, 3 pounds, 5'8",
John Croan, Martin Pendergast Philadelphia City PA 6/21/1764, Irish 22 blacksmith
    3 days, Monday, 4 pounds, 5'10", (lately arrived)
Robert Crocket, John Jackson Philadelphia City PA shoemaker 11/28/1751, Scot shoemaker
    4 days, Sunday, 5 pounds,
Robert Crocket, John Jackson Philadelphia City PA shoemaker 4/16/1752, Scot shoemaker (2nd esc)
    8 days, Wednesday, 3 pounds,
Samuel Crockett, Abraham Inskeep Gloucester NJ 7/17/1782, 17 A
    20 days, Thursday, 3 pounds, 5'7",
John Crockland, William Towson Baltimore MD 9/8/1743, English 24
    7 days, Thursday, 5 pounds, middle,
John Crockland, William Towson Baltimore MD 10/11/1744, English 25 (2nd escape)
    3 pounds, middle,
Christopher Crom, Jacob Fox Hunterdon NJ 10/5/1769, German-American 18 A
    7 days, Thursday, 1 pound,
Mary Cromel, Anthony Whitly New Castle DE 8/5/1756, Irish
    44 days, Tuesday, 1 pound, middle,
William Crompton, Captain Hinton Philadelphia City PA ship captain 11/21/1751, English hatter
    1 pound, (ran from ship)
William Croneen, Thomas Meters Chester PA 12/16/1772, Irish 20
    3 days, Monday, 10 dollars, 5'9",
Michael Crook, Joseph Wallen Sussex NJ 8/29/1765, German
    7 days, Thursday, 5 dollars, 5'6",
John Croom, Robert Anderson Lancaster PA 12/15/1773, English 18
    10 days, Monday, 3 dollars,
William Crosberry, James Mackey Philadelphia City PA 12/18/1735, Irish 22 tailor
    6 days, Friday, 1 pound,
Patrick Crosby, Robert Callender Cumberland PA 7/26/1775, Irish 19
    30 days, Tuesday, 3 pounds, 5'9-10",
Edward Cross, Captain Hinton Philadelphia City PA ship captain 11/21/1751, English gardener
    1 pound, (ran from ship)
Thomas Cross, Josiah Hitchcock Baltimore MD 8/26/1772, 25
    12 days, Saturday, 2 pounds, 5'7-8",
James Croswell, Jacob Johnson Burlington NJ 10/26/1732, 30 shoemaker
    2 pounds, tall,
Ann Crotey, William Forrest Philadelphia City PA 10/17/1754, Irish 16
    2 days, Tuesday, 0.75 pounds, middle,
Charles Crouch, W. Dunlap Philadelphia City PA 3/8/1759, American 25 printer L
    3 pounds, 5'10",
Henry Crouch, John Gilks Baltimore MD 10/9/1755, English carver
    4 pistoles, 5'6",
Catherine Crout, Duncan Beard 6/4/1783, A
    68 days, Friday, short,
Ephraim Crow, Jeremiah Holden Philadelphia PA 9/7/1785, American 18 L
    3 dollars,
Joseph Crow, Thomas Evans Philadelphia PA 2/13/1766, American 18 L
    14 days, Thursday, 1.5 pounds, 5'7-8",
George Crowder, Robert Clark Salem NJ 4/12/1775, English 19 (ran before)
    7 days, Thursday, 3 pounds, 5'6",
Dennis Crowley, Joel Bailey Chester PA 7/25/1745, Irish 16
    184 days, Thursday, 4 pounds, short,
Cornelius Crowly, Samuel Thompson Cecil MD 5/24/1770, Irish butcher
    4 dollars, 5'9",
John Crowly, Samuel Miller Cecil MD 1/3/1771, Irish 33 weaver
    16 days, Tuesday, 2 pounds, 5'3-4",
Wilhelm Cruger, Christoph Kugher Philadelphia PA 10/19/1774, German 22
    24 days, Monday, 16 dollars, 5'7-8",
Edmund Cryers, George Lee Westmoreland VA 10/26/1749, English shoemaker (ran before)
    66 days, Monday, 2 pistoles, 5'8", (arrived 4 years ago)

John Cudwell, John Mecaulle New Castle DE 3/11/1755,
    13 days, Friday, 3 pistoles, middle,
Patrick Cuff, Samuel Purviance Salem NJ 11/24/1773, Irish 25
    11 days, Sunday, 2 pounds, 5'9",
John Cuffey, Michael Branin Burlington NJ 8/21/1740, English 35
    10 days, Monday, 1.5 pounds, short,
Edward Cuisick, Thomas Paxton Lancaster PA 9/10/1747, Irish 20
    4 days, Sunday, 3 pounds, 5'6",
Andrew Culbertson, Abner Evans Chester PA 4/23/1752, 23
    11 days, Sunday, 3 pounds, middle,
James Culbertson, Henry Hall Augusta VA 11/16/1774, Irish 30 C
    130 days, Sunday, 5'10", (arrived Oct. 1773)
Patrick Culford, Samuel Nutts Chester PA ironworks 6/5/1740, carpenter
    45 days, Monday, 1 pistole,
Mary Cullen, Alexander Lockart Hunterdon NJ 10/1/1741, 30
    1 pound,
William Cullimoore, John Winterton Kent MD gaoler 12/12/1765, English ditcher C
    61 days, Saturday, 7 dollars, 5'4",
Samuel Cumings, James Adams New Castle DE 6/30/1779, 20 printer A
    100 dollars, 5'8-9",
Thomas Cummings, George Rock Cecil MD 5/24/1750, English 35 blacksmith gaol sale L
    28 days, Thursday, 3 pounds, short,
William Cummings, John Thompson Chester PA 6/16/1768, Irish 35
    11 days, Sunday, 1 pound, 5'9",
Joseph Cummins, Isaac Walker Chester PA 4/23/1730, Irish 22
    4 days, Sunday, 1.5 pounds, middle,
William Cummins, John Gronow Chester PA 11/23/1774, Irish workhouse sale L
    7 days, Thursday, 4 dollars, 5'5-6",
James Cundun, Richard Whitten Philadelphia PA 11/29/1728, Irish 22
    1 pound, short,
Ally Cunningham, Deborah Conard Philadelphia City PA 12/18/1793, Irish 17 (female)
    73 days, Sunday, 4 dollars, short, (has 2 years 4-5 months left to serve)
Dennis Cunningham, James Fulton Lancaster PA 6/11/1767, Irish tailor
    3 dollars, 5'9-10",
Elizabeth Cunningham, Thomas White Lancaster PA 1/28/1768, Irish 23 (pregnant)
    10 days, Monday, 1 pound,
John Cunningham, George Thomas Chester PA 4/24/1776, 24
    10 days, Monday, 12 dollars, 5'7-8",
Patrick Cunningham, Thomas Anderson Philadelphia PA 7/5/1744, 30
    1 pound,
Samuel Cunningham, Thomas Duffield Philadelphia PA 8/2/1753, 16
    11 days, Sunday, 2 pounds, (has relatives nearby)
Thomas Cunningham, George O'Kill Philadelphia City PA 10/2/1746, 18
    3 pounds, tall, (ran from ship)
John Cuppledick, Francis Lamborn Chester PA 5/11/1769, English
    6 days, Friday, 2 pounds, 5'10",
Bridget Curly, Mary Williams Frederick MD 6/12/1776, Irish 20
    355 days, Friday, 5 pounds, (lately arrived)
Nicholas Curran, Joseph Frazer Lancaster PA 6/21/1750, Irish 20
    5 pounds, 5'10",
Thomas Currel, Joseph Yeates Philadelphia City PA 2/9/1769, English 16
    14 days, Thursday, 1.5 pounds, short,
George Curren, David Davies Chester PA 11/10/1729, Irish 21
    7 days, Thursday, 1 pound, middle,
John Currey, James Pennall Chester PA 11/13/1776, American 18 L
    7 days, Thursday, 6 dollars, 5'2",
Edward Curry, Abraham Bryan Burlington NJ 6/14/1739, Irish 26 L
    5 days, Saturday, 1 pound, short,
William Curry, George Trenchard Salem NJ 8/26/1762, Irish 35 barber
    9 days, Tuesday, 3 pounds, 5'2",
Joseph Curse, Peter January Philadelphia City PA shoemaker 11/3/1763, Irish 23 shoemaker
    11 days, Sunday, 5 pounds, 5'4",
John Curtin, John Rankin Chester PA 5/30/1771, Irish 23 L
    10 days, Monday, 2 pounds, 5'8",
John Curtis, Peter Browne Philadelphia City PA 10/3/1745, 17
    2 days, Tuesday, 2 pounds, 5',

Polly Curtiss, James Whitehead Philadelphia City PA workhouse-keeper 10/11/1759, Irish 19
    2 months ago, 1 pistole, middle,
Edward Cutter, Morris Hayes Philadelphia City PA 11/3/1763, 18
    5 pounds, 5'6",
Jane Dagnon, John Mackey Cecil MD 8/11/1757, Irish
    11 days, Sunday, 1 pound, middle, (arrived last June)
Michael Dailey, Joseph Hugg Gloucester NJ 2/13/1766, Irish 17
    11 days, Sunday, 2 pounds, 5'2-3",
Thomas Dailey, Joseph Neide Chester PA 5/3/1775, Irish
    9 days, Tuesday, 4 dollars, short,
Andrew Daily, Joshua Brick Salem NJ 5/14/1741, Irish
    10 days, Monday, 2.5 pounds, tall,
Dennis Daily, William Bird Philadelphia PA 6/21/1744, Irish 22
    1.5 pounds,
Dennis Daily, William Bird Philadelphia PA 4/18/1745, Irish 23 (2nd escape)
    2 pounds,
John Daily, Alexander Lowery Lancaster PA 1/17/1765, Irish 19
    30 days, Tuesday, 2 pounds, 5'8",
John Daily, Joseph Anderson Philadelphia City PA 5/4/1769, Irish 25 miller (2nd escape)
    3 pounds, 5'9-10", (arrived some time ago)
George Dale, Charles Carroll Baltimore MD ironworks 9/12/1754, English 22
    20 days, Friday, 3 pound, short, (arrived this summer)
Dennis Daley, Samuel Sloss Kent MD 8/22/1754, Irish 24
    8 days, Wednesday, 1.5 pounds,
Dennis Daley, Mary Kneesberry Cecil MD 11/14/1754, Irish 24 (2nd escape)
    10 days, Monday, 2 pounds, 5'8",
Dennis Daley, John Connor Cecil MD 9/18/1755, Irish 25 (3rd escape)
    6 days, Friday, 1.5 pounds, 5'8",
Honour Daley, Timothy Pickering 9/27/1786, Irish 28
    16 days, Monday, 4 dollars, 5', (arrived 14 months ago)
James Daley, Hugh Coupland Baltimore MD 6/9/1748, Irish 40 weaver C
    18 days, Sunday, 2 pounds, (arrived 20 months ago)
John Daley, Robert Bigham York PA 5/26/1768, soldier L
    14 days, Thursday, 3 pounds, 5'7",
Owen Daley, William Hamilton Philadelphia City PA 5/10/1750, Irish 25
    8 days, Wednesday, 3 pounds, short,
Peggy Daley, Timothy Pickering 9/27/1786, Irish 18
    16 days, Monday, 4 dollars, 5', (arrived 14 months ago)
Joseph Dalloway, John Lloyd Philadelphia City PA 9/10/1730, 35 blacksmith
    1.5 pounds, middle,
Richard Dalton, Peter Sigfreidusalrichs New Castle DE 5/17/1753, Irish 23
    7 days, Thursday, 1.5 pounds, 5'4",
William Dalton, Samuel Mendenhall Chester PA 8/24/1769, Irish 21
    3 days, Monday, 8 dollars, 5'8-9",
Roger Damagan, Rynar Tyson Philadelphia PA 11/8/1764, Irish 40
    3 days, Monday, 2 pounds, 5'5", (has served some time in the colonies)
Margaret Dampsey, William Hall Philadelphia City PA 5/7/1741, Irish 18
    19 days, Saturday, 3 pounds, short,
Henry Damsel, William Nichols Chester PA 7/8/1731,
    4 days, Sunday, 3.5 pounds, short,
Thomas Dance, Sweatnam Burn Queen Anne's MD 9/18/1766, English
    28 days, Thursday, 1 pound, 5'4-5",
Howell Dandy, Curtis Trenchard Salem NJ 11/28/1771, 26
    14 days, Thursday, 4 pounds, 5'9",
William Dane, Simon Wicks Kent MD 8/2/1764, English 40 blacksmith C
    60 days, Sunday, 20 dollars,
Sarah Danelley, George Leadbetter Philadelphia City PA 6/21/1764, 16
    23 days, Tuesday, 0.75 pounds,
Samuel Dangerfield, William Lyon Baltimore MD 9/15/1773, English 30 whitesmith
    20 dollars, 5'7", (arrived 2 years ago)
Daniel Daniel, Arthur Park Chester PA 6/21/1764, 16 tanner A
    10 days, Monday, 5 pounds, 5'8",
Richard Daniel, Humphrey Wall Burlington NJ 6/21/1764, Irish
    10 days, Monday, 2 pounds, 4'11",
Richard Daniels, Joseph Beaks Philadelphia City PA drayman 6/20/1745, English
    7 days, Thursday, 3 pounds, short,

George Dannefelder, Peter Hoffenclever 7/4/1765, Danish butcher
   5 pounds, 5'6",
William Darbey, Thomas Talman Burlington NJ 6/6/1754, American 19 L
   10 days, Monday, 3 pounds, 5'8",
William Darbey, Thomas Talman Burlington NJ 8/1/1754, American 19 (2nd escape) L
   2 days, Tuesday, 1 pound, 5'8",
Thomas Darby, John Bringhurst Philadelphia PA 11/9/1769, English 24 soldier
   10 days, Monday, 4 dollars, 5'7-8",
Cornelius Darbyson, Samuel Webster Philadelphia City PA tailor 8/1/1754, Irish 25 tailor
   4 days, Sunday, 1.5 pounds, 5'7",
George Darley, Joseph Height Burlington NJ 5/29/1766, English 30
   4 days, Sunday, 2 pounds, 5'6-7",
William Darlinton, William Beeks New Castle DE 7/15/1736, English 30 L
   1.5 pounds, middle,
Joseph Daton, Henry Shriner Cumberland NJ 7/2/1794, 17 tailor A
   122 days, Sunday, 4 dollars, 4'9",
Francis Davenport, Benjamin Vernor Lancaster PA 3/31/1768, Irish 16
   8 days, Wednesday, 2 pounds, 5'3",
Francis Davenport, Benjamin Vernor Lancaster PA 8/24/1769, Irish 17 (2nd escape)
   9 days, Tuesday, 2 pounds, 5'8",
James Davenport, James Boyd Chester PA 3/16/1769, English 30 school teacher
   120 days, Wednesday, 6 dollars, 5'8-9", (11 years in army, 2.5 years teaching in Chester)
Amos David, John Rowland Chester PA 11/13/1746, Welsh 20
   11 days, Sunday, 2 pounds,
John David, Thomas Weir Philadelphia City PA 5/24/1775, English 22 hair-dresser
   16 days, Tuesday, 1 pound, 5'6",
Joseph David, Thomas Mayhew Salem NJ 5/5/1763, German 30
   2445 days, Monday, 8 dollars, 5'3", (enlisted in army but is now discharged)
William David, Henry Housholder Baltimore MD 10/25/1770, Irish 21
   11 days, Sunday, 2.5 pounds, 5'4",
Catherine Davidson, George Buchannan Baltimore MD 2/13/1750, C
   9 days, Tuesday, 5 pounds, (lately arrived)
James Davie, Dell Pennell Chester PA 7/21/1784, English 24
   3 days, Sunday, 6 dollars, 5'4",
William Davies, Benjamin Smith Hunterdon NJ 10/6/1737, English 25
   11 days, Sunday, 1.5 pounds, short,
Abraham Davis, Charles Black Chester PA 6/13/1765, 16
   6 days, Friday, 4 dollars, 4'8",
Edward Davis, James Franklin Baltimore MD ironworks 6/6/1771, English 30
   17 days, Monday, 5 pounds, 5'2",
Edward Davis, Joseph Earle Cecil MD 2/6/1766, English 30 perukemaker C
   7 days, Thursday, 4 pounds, 5'4",
Edward Davis, John Calvert Baltimore MD 6/28/1764, English sailor C
   3 pounds, 5'9", (use to the sea)
Eleanor Davis, James Buller Queen Anne's MD 9/27/1775, English L
   17 days, Monday, 2 pounds, 5'3-4",
Evan Davis, David Rees Philadelphia City PA shoemaker 6/3/1756, Welsh shoemaker
   4 days, Sunday, 1.5 pounds, 5'5",
Evan Davis, Samuel Blunt Queen Anne's MD 4/27/1769, Welsh 30 C
   30 days, Tuesday, 2.5 pounds, 5'9-10", (arrived Nov. 1768)
Henry Davis, John Glen Cumberland PA 7/19/1770, Irish 29 (ran before)
   8 dollars,
Henry Davis, John Glen Cumberland PA 6/13/1771, Irish 30 (2nd escape)
   4 dollars, 5'10",
Hugh Davis, John Hamilton Lancaster PA 6/18/1752, Irish 22
   3 pounds, middle,
James Davis, Samuel Richey Philadelphia City PA weaver 8/1/1745, Irish 30 weaver
   12 days, Saturday, 2 pounds, tall,
John Davis, Daniel Cooper Philadelphia City PA 5/30/1745, 18
   1 day, Wednesday, 3 pounds,
John Davis, Thomas Sligh Baltimore MD 6/10/1742, English 40
   11 days, Sunday, 5 pounds,
John Davis, Thomas James Lancaster PA 7/19/1750, clockmaker
   3 pounds, 5'4",
John Davis, James Galbreath Lancaster PA 1/24/1749, Welsh 25
   35 days, Thursday, 3 pounds,

John Davis, Aaron Fithian Cumberland NJ 10/27/1768, sadler
    4 dollars, 5'4",
John Davis, Thomas Clayton Chester PA 10/16/1776, Irish weaver
    16 days, Tuesday, 7.5 dollars, 5'8",
Joseph Davis, Pennel Evans Berks PA 4/25/1754, Welsh 18
    24 days, Monday, 3 pounds, 5'6",
Joseph Davis, John Nemo Kent DE 7/26/1753, English
    4 days, Sunday, 5 pounds, middle, (has sailed out of Philadelphia)
Joshua Davis, John Byars Lancaster PA shoemaker 9/27/1750, Welsh-American 18 A
    3 pounds, 5'6",
Mary Davis, Evan Morgan Philadelphia City PA shopkeeper 7/1/1731,
    short,
Michael Davis, Joseph Anderson Philadelphia City PA 7/27/1769, Irish 40
    2 pounds, 5'6-7",
Sarah Davis, William Plaskett Hunterdon NJ 9/17/1747, Welsh 27
    6 days, Friday, 1 pound, middle,
Sarah Davis, William Plaskett Hunterdon NJ 11/26/1747, Welsh 27 (2nd escape)
    6 days, Friday, 2 pounds, middle,
Thomas Davis, John Wilson Queen Anne's MD 5/8/1760, English 25 C
    6',
Thomas Davis, John Trapnall Chester PA 7/7/1768, Welsh 35 L
    4 days, Sunday, 2 pistoles, 5'7-8",
William Davis, Jacob Lightfoot Chester PA 8/8/1734, Welsh 35 miner
    5 pounds, middle,
William Davis, John Roe Queen Anne's MD 3/5/1751, Irish 30
    37 days, Tuesday, 1 pound,
William Davis, Joseph Frazier Gloucester NJ 6/11/1752, Irish 21
    4 days, Sunday, 1.5 pounds, short,
William Davis, Thomas Cobourn Chester PA 5/15/1766,
    14 days, Thursday, 3 pounds, 5'4-5",
William Davis, Joseph Starr Chester PA 2/26/1777, English 21
    59 days, Monday, 8 dollars, 5'8",
John Davison, Philip Clampher 1/11/1775, Irish 19 barber
    4 dollars, 5'3-4",
William Davy, John Smith Philadelphia PA 2/19/1761, English 24
    4 days, Sunday, 5 pounds, 5'6", (arrived last spring, was in the colonies before)
Ann Dawson, Hugh Stewart Chester PA 3/14/1765, Irish 18
    2 pounds,
Betty Dawson, Joshua McDowell Chester PA 7/14/1768, 22 gaol sale L
    6 days, Friday, 2 pounds,
John Dawson, Robert Ritchie Chester PA 11/3/1763, Scot 22 sailor
    1 pound, 5'9", (lately arrived)
John Dawson, Robert Clench Lancaster PA 5/21/1767, Scot 22 soldier
    11 days, Sunday, 1.5 pounds, 5'5-6", (arrived 2 years ago)
John Dawson, Hugh Bryarly Baltimore MD 9/1/1773, English 36 C
    22 days, Wednesday, 4 pounds, 5'5",
Thomas Dawson, Peter Businton Chester PA 3/27/1750, German 20 A
    5 pounds, short,
William Dawson, Henry Callister Talbot MD 1/29/1756, English 30 laborer C
    last July, 5 pounds, short,
Bryan Day, Charles Ridgely Jr Baltimore MD ironworks 2/8/1744, English
    about 18 months ago, 6 pounds, middle,
James Day, Robert Mendenhall Chester PA 6/22/1774, American 24 L
    10 dollars, 5'6-7",
Susannah Day, John Stuart Frederick VA 9/21/1758, 30 C
    82 days, Saturday, 2 pistoles,
Thomas Day, Samuel Rhoads Philadelphia City PA 7/25/1771, English 15 miller
    11 days, Sunday, 1 pound,
Thomas Day, Jonathan Booth 4/27/1774, English 18 miller (2nd escape)
    6 days, Friday, 6 dollars, 5'2-3",
Thomas Day, Benjamin Thackrey Gloucester NJ 12/27/1775, English 20 miller (3rd escape)
    3 days, Monday, 2 pounds, 5'4-5",
Catherine Dayerman, Alexander Scott Lancaster PA 8/18/1748, Irish
    46 days, Sunday, 2 pounds, short, (is married)
Michael Deace, John Bartholomew Chester PA 6/7/1786, Irish 17
    4 days, Saturday, 8 dollars, 5'6-7",

Thomas Deal, Peter Jones Gloucester NJ 4/4/1754, 36
    10 days, Monday, 5 pounds, 5'6",
Samuel Deale, Mark Alexander Baltimore MD 3/14/1771, English 24
    87 days, Monday, 6 pounds, 5'6-7",
Samuel Deale, Mark Alexander Baltimore MD 8/8/1771, English 24 (2nd escape)
    18 days, Sunday, 7 pounds, 5'6-7",
William Dealy, John Stevenson Baltimore MD 3/15/1764, Irish C
    about 42 days, 10 pounds, 5'8",
Edward Dean, Jonathan Crathorn Philadelphia City PA ship captain 10/17/1751, 17
    4 days, Sunday, 1 pound, (ran from ship)
John Dean, Joseph Clark Chester PA sadler 5/15/1760, American 17 A
    2 pounds,
Thomas Dean, Michael Cario Philadelphia City PA jeweller 12/18/1744, 21
    4 days, Sunday, 1 pound, short,
Joseph Dearah, Andreas Stahl Philadelphia PA 5/19/1757, German 14 shoemaker A
    4 days, Sunday, 2 pounds,
Franciscp Deberara, Jonathan Johnson Chester PA 7/12/1775, Spanish
    4 days, Sunday, 4 dollars, 5'7",
Anne Debolly, Robert Davis Philadelphia City PA 7/19/1753, German 13
    6 days, Friday,
Henry Decker, John Gresler Lancaster PA 6/30/1773, 21 weaver A
    31 days, Monday, 3 pounds, 5'9",
Henry Michael Deemer, John Righter Philadelphia PA 7/25/1771, German 26
    4 days, Sunday, 2 pounds, 5'4-5",
James Deering, James Chambers Charles MD 11/6/1760, barber L
    5'8",
Margaret Deermod, William Hannum Chester PA 12/7/1774, Irish 18
    1 pound,
Daniel Degan, Elisha Price Chester PA 12/13/1780, German 21 soldier
    13 days, Thursday, 5'9-10",
Daniel Degan, Elisha Price Chester PA 5/16/1781, German 21 soldier (2nd escape)
    19 days, Friday, 5'10", (relatives live nearby)
Abraham Dehaven, John Sharer Philadelphia PA 4/28/1768, 19 L
    9 days, Tuesday, 2 pounds, 5'6-7",
Francisco De Herarra, Jonathan Johnson Chester PA 5/8/1776, Spanish 31
    April, 2 pounds, 5'7-8",
Daniel Delaney, William Mills Lancaster PA 8/11/1773, 22 A
    10 days, Monday, 2 pounds, 5'7",
James Delaney, John Miller Berkeley VA 6/19/1776, Irish 22
    3 pounds, 5'8-9",
Mary Delany, John Cooper Cecil MD 9/24/1767, Irish 24
    1 pound, 5'6",
Nelly Delany, Thomas Kittera Lancaster PA 4/25/1765, Irish 20
    1 pound,
Richard Delany, Marquis Stephenson Berkeley VA 7/17/1776, 25 gilder C
    6 dollars, 5'7",
William Delany, David Barclay Baltimore MD 5/21/1772, Irish 45 C
    19 days, Saturday, 7 pounds,
George Delap, Widow Rinedoller Philadelphia City PA 4/5/1775, A
    8 days, Wednesday, 5'2-3",
John Deley, Thomas Ewings Chester PA 7/10/1755, Irish 22
    16 days, Tuesday, 1 pistole, 5'9",
Thomas Deley, Daniel McMichael Chester PA 7/10/1755, Irish 25
    16 days, Tuesday, 1 pistole,
Waliburg Demen, Hugh Roberts 6/10/1756, German 22
    6 days, Friday, 1.5 pounds,
Peter Dempsey, Robert Campbell Chester PA 5/27/1762, Irish 27
    2 pounds, 5'7",
Edward Demsy, Thomas Chittami 7/11/1754, Irish 26 barber C
    2 pistoles, 5'3",
Simon Denck, Peter Hassenclever EJ ironworks 6/12/1766, German 25 miner
    14 days, Thursday, 5 pounds, (under a 3 year 4 month contract, imported)
Thomas Dene, George Fling Philadelphia City PA 5/4/1749, Irish 30 hired L
    2 days, Tuesday, 2 pistoles, short,
William Denim, Joseph Reed Hunterdon NJ merchant 7/17/1732, tailor
    16 days, Tuesday, 3 pounds,

John Denison, James Pryor Chester PA 7/16/1747, Irish
    5 pounds, short,
Timothy Denison, William Attwood Philadelphia City PA ship captain 10/23/1740, Irish 15
    4 days, Sunday, 1.5 pounds, tall,
Edmund Denney, George Smedly Chester PA 4/13/1769, Irish 20 weaver
    8 days, Wednesday, 3 pounds, 5'5",
William Denning, Thomas Walker Philadelphia City PA butcher 8/29/1754, English 22
    11 days, Sunday, 3 pounds, short,
Hugh Dennis, John Rowan Salem NJ 6/8/1785, Irish 20
    16 days, Monday, 3 pounds, short,
John Dennis, Edward Evans 10/23/1740, 18 A
    4 days, Sunday, 1 pound, middle,
Joseph Dennis, John Nemo Kent MD 7/11/1754, English 25
    19 days, Saturday, 2 pounds, 5', (has been in the colonies before)
Barnabas Dennison, Robert Penrose Bucks PA 9/18/1760, Irish 40
    11 days, Sunday, 2 pounds,
Hannah Dennison, Daniel Campbell Frederick VA 5/24/1753,
    last Feb., 3 pounds, middle,
John Dennison, Daniel Campbell Frederick VA 5/24/1753, 32 shoemaker
    last Feb., 3 pounds, 5'6",
John Dennison, Navel Win Hunterdon NJ 9/29/1768, Irish 30 laborer
    16 days, Tuesday, 4 pounds,
Patrick Dennison, John Bleakley Philadelphia City PA 12/21/1742, Irish 35
    8 days, Wednesday, 2 pounds, tall, (ran from ship)
Anthony Densely, John Cooper Cecil MD 9/21/1758, English 40 C
    2 pistoles, tall,
Joseph Dent, William Fitzhugh Calvert MD 7/24/1766, French gardener
    2.5 pounds, 5'8",
Carolina De Pool, Joseph Kaighin Gloucester NJ 2/10/1773, German 23
    14 days, Thursday, 1.5 pounds, (arrived last fall)
Carolina De Pool, John Bispham Burlington NJ 4/16/1777, German 27 (2nd escape)
    110 days, Friday, 4 dollars,
Christopher Derrick, Jonathan Wood Salem NJ 6/21/1775, German-American 24 L
    11 days, Sunday, 4 dollars, 5'5-6",
Henry Desell, Samuel Forwood Baltimore MD 8/15/1754, English 18
    8 days, Wednesday, 3 pounds, 5'7",
James Deslin, Joseph Ennalls Dorchester MD 6/19/1760, Irish 35 tailor
    31 days, Monday, 5 pounds, (has relatives in the colonies)
Lewis Detreval, Charles Brown Queen Anne's MD 5/13/1742, French 24
    37 days, Tuesday, 2.5 pounds, 6', (lately arrived)
Isaac De Vase, Joshua Moore 8/11/1768, 18 joiner A
    11 days, Sunday, 2 pounds, 5',
No Name Deveny, Jeremy Miller Lancaster PA 3/29/1775, Irish 22 shoemaker
    18 days, Sunday, 5 pounds, (arrived last summer)
James Devine, Caleb Emlen 10/25/1775, Irish 18
    9 days, Tuesday, 5 dollars, 5'6-7",
Richard Devine, Wallace & Bryan Philadelphia City PA 4/11/1754, Irish
    7 days, Thursday, 2.5 pounds, middle,
Anthony Devir, Josiah Lockhart Lancaster PA 8/26/1772, Irish
    10 dollars, 5'4-5",
John Devonshire, James Day Chester PA 5/10/1753, Irish 20
    6 days, Friday, 1.5 pounds, 5'7",
Cornelius Dewees, Thomas May Berks PA ironworks 3/8/1764, collier
    52 days, Monday, 5 pounds,
James Dey, John Cromwell Anne Arundel MD 6/1/1758, English 35 laborer C
    12 days, Saturday, 3 pistoles,
Margery Diamond, Henry Braken New Castle DE 7/16/1772, 25
    25 days, Sunday, 4 dollars,
James Diar, Joshua Gist Frederick MD 4/6/1774, Irish 27
    15 pounds, 5'4-5", (wears an iron collar, has been in the colonies before)
James Dick, Thomas Carney Jr Salem NJ 6/23/1773, Scot 30 (ran 7 times before)
    8 days, Wednesday, 4 dollars, 5'8-9", (wears an iron collar)
James Dick, Thomas Carney Jr Salem NJ 9/8/1773, Scot 30 (2nd escape)
    12 days, Saturday, 3 dollars, 5'8", (wears an iron collar)
James Dick, Thomas Carney Sr Salem NJ 6/28/1775, Scot 32 (3rd escape)
    12 days, Saturday, 4 dollars, 5'8-9",

James Dick, Thomas Carney Jr Salem NJ 8/14/1776, Scot 33 (4th escape)
  2 days, Tuesday, 4 dollars, 5'9-10",
John Dick, Robert Hall Talbot MD 6/16/1768, Scot tailor
  40 days, Saturday, 4 pounds, 5'8",
John Dick, John Jarvis Hunterdon NJ 11/2/1774, English
  6 dollars, 5'9", (lately arrived)
John Dick, James Cumming 3/30/1785, Scot 22 tailor
  5 days, Friday, 8 dollars, 5'10-11", (arrived last fall)
Carson Dickerson, Obadiah Dingee New Castle DE 9/4/1782, 15 A
  15 days, Tuesday, 10 dollars, 5',
Joseph Dickinson, James Adams Chester PA 5/20/1762, 19 tailor A
  9 days, Tuesday, 1.5 pounds, 5'5",
Samuel Dickson, Robert Robinson New Castle DE 1/29/1756, Irish 18
  9 days, Tuesday, 2 pistoles, 5'6",
Francis Didger, Frederick Holstein Philadelphia City PA 10/26/1752, German 36 wigmaker
  last week, 4 pounds, 5'5",
Hance Dieder, Barnet Vanhorne Bucks PA 4/25/1754, German 35
  4 days, Sunday, 2 pounds, 5'6",
Catherine Diel, Daniel Robinson 10/23/1755, Irish (with 6 month old male child)
  95 days, Sunday, 1 pound,
John Diermond, Archibald Thompson Philadelphia PA 7/23/1767, Irish 22
  21 days, Thursday, 4 dollars, 5'8-9",
Simon Dietz, Michael Haberstich Lancaster PA 7/16/1767, German
  16 days, Tuesday, 5 pounds, 5'6-8",
Robert Diffey, William Bowers Chester PA 6/16/1773, English 40 joiner
  16 days, Tuesday, 5 pounds, 5'8",
John Daniel Digg, John Taylor Lancaster PA 8/30/1753, German 21 cooper
  5 pounds, 5'9",
Mary Diggens, Ann Parke Philadelphia City PA 3/10/1768, English
  January, 5 pounds, (served some time in MD)
Frederick Dighmeyer, Martin Rittenhouse Philadelphia PA 1/10/1776, German
  16 days, Tuesday, 3 dollars, 5'5",
Bryan Dignan, Randal Marshall Chester PA ironworks 5/28/1747, Irish 20
  4 days, Sunday, 2 pounds, short,
Lorenzo Dihm, George Weiler Lancaster PA 6/29/1774, German 35
  10 days, Monday, 2 pounds, 5'6",
Philip Henderick Dill, Wallace & Donaldson Philadelphia City PA 11/17/1784, German
  2.5 pounds, 5'6", (ran from ship)
James Dilland, William Ellis Cecil MD 10/2/1746, Irish C
  12 days, Saturday, 1.5 pounds, (lately arrived)
John Dillis, Robert Lamborn Chester PA 11/16/1774, American 20 L
  18 days, Sunday, 3 dollars, 5'8-9",
John Dillis, William Kerlin Chester PA 7/10/1776, American 22 (2nd escape) L
  38 days, Monday, 2 pounds, 5'10-11",
John Dillywy, David Cuming Philadelphia City PA 7/27/1769, Irish
  4 days, Sunday, 1.5 pounds, (lately arrived)
Joseph Dinnehay, Johan Miller Berkeley VA 6/19/1776, Irish 19
  3 pounds, 5'7-8",
Jeremiah Disman, Abel Rees Chester PA 5/12/1784, Irish
  10 days, Sunday, 3 pounds, 5'6",
Neal Dispen, Richard Erwin Chester PA 10/9/1766, Irish 25 weaver
  2 pounds, 5'8", (arrived 2 weeks ago)
William Ditchett, Thomas Croasdale Burlington NJ 3/15/1739, English 24
  2 days, Tuesday, 2 pounds, short,
George Ditterline, Conrad Sheetz Philadelphia City PA 1/26/1791, 19 hatter A
  8 days, Tuesday, 12 dollars,
George Ditterline, Conrad Sheetz Philadelphia City PA 2/22/1792, 20 hatter (2nd escape) A
  9 days, Monday, 0.03 pounds,
Henry Dixon, Abraham Chattin Jr Gloucester NJ 5/24/1750, English 19
  4 days, Sunday, 2 pounds, short,
John Dixon, James Craick 9/4/1755, Scot 20
  4 pistoles, 5'6",
William Dobbins, Enoch Fenton 9/12/1754, Irish 20
  11 days, Sunday, 2 pounds,
William Dobin, Thomas James Philadelphia PA 5/9/1751, Irish 18
  4 days, Sunday, 1 pound,

James Doby, Charles Greenbury Griffith Frederick MD 5/26/1768, 40 C
   16 days, Tuesday, 5 pounds, 5'8-9",
Thomas Docart, Thomas Mawhorter Northampton PA 10/6/1790, 19 A
   17 days, Sunday, 20 dollars, 5'7",
John Dockerty, John Black Chester PA 11/9/1774, Irish 18
   1 pound, 5'5",
Thomas Dodd, John Righter Philadelphia PA 10/14/1772, Irish 26
   13 days, Friday, 5'4",
Thomas Dodd, John Righter Philadelphia PA 10/27/1773, Irish 27 (2nd escape)
   26 days, Saturday, 2 pounds, 5'4", (married)
Thomas Dodd, Samuel Morris Chester PA 10/12/1774, Irish 28 (3rd escape)
   115 days, Monday, 3 pounds, 5'4-5",
Zachariah Dodds, Richard Strode Chester PA 4/14/1773, 19 blacksmith A
   10 dollars, 5'6-7",
Mark Dogan, Joseph Bell Philadelphia City PA 5/6/1756, Irish 19 cook
   1 day, Wednesday, 1.5 pounds,
Edward Doherty, Robert Law Chester PA 11/3/1773, Irish 20
   16 days, Tuesday, 5 dollars, 5'2",
John Doherty, John Peden Lancaster PA 6/28/1775, Irish 20
   6 dollars, 5'7-8",
John Doherty, James Pennell Chester PA 8/19/1772, Irish 22
   6 dollars, 5'8-9", (arrived 6 years ago)
Michael Doherty, James Jackson New Castle DE 4/20/1774, Irish 16
   3 pounds, 5'4",
Michael Doherty, James Jackson New Castle DE 10/4/1775, Irish 17 (2nd escape)
   11 days, Sunday, 2 pounds,
Thomas Doil, Samuel Allen Lancaster PA 8/18/1768, Irish
   11 days, Sunday, 2 pounds, 5'4-5",
James Dolan, John Tells Chester PA 6/19/1776, Irish 22
   6 days, Friday, 8 dollars, 5'4-5",
John Dolin, William Tateham Gloucester NJ 6/14/1739, Irish 18
   1 days, Wednesday, 2 pounds, short,
John Dolin, James Bonsall Philadelphia PA 7/25/1754, Irish 31 (2nd escape)
   11 days, Sunday, 1.5 pounds, 5'6",
John Dolin, James Bonsall Philadelphia PA 7/26/1753, Irish 30
   7 days, Thursday, 2 pounds, (knows country well)
William Dollaha, Mary Lownes Philadelphia PA 3/12/1745, Welsh 30
   6 days, Friday, 1.5 pounds, middle,
Patrick Dollar, Rodger Conner Lancaster PA 11/24/1743, Irish 30 hatter
   9 days, Tuesday, 3 pounds,
Richard Dolton, James McKachern Chester PA 4/11/1771, Irish 18
   14 days, Thursday, 2 pounds, 5'3-4",
William Dolton, William Bassrt Salem NJ 4/9/1767, Irish 20
   3 days, Monday, 1.5 pounds, 5'5",
William Dome, Robert Roberts Kent MD 4/26/1764, English C
   15 days, Wednesday, 8 dollars,
Peter Dominick, Jacob Duffield Philadelphia PA 3/17/1779, French
   1 dollars, 5'6",
Daniel Donahew, John Yoder Philadelphia PA 7/9/1747, Irish 40 miller
   4 days, Sunday, 3 pistoles, middle,
Michael Donahue, Archibald McElroy Philadelphia City PA 6/28/1764, Irish 15 barber
   7 days, Thursday, 3 pounds, (arrived 2 days ago)
Joseph Donaldson, William Woodside Philadelphia City PA ship captain 4/26/1750, 50
   7 days, Thursday, 6 pounds, 5'10", (ran from ship)
Thomas Donaldson, Uriah Blue New Castle DE 3/28/1751, Irish 35 soldier
   9 days, Tuesday, 1.5 pounds, 6',
James Donbar, Richard Wescot Cape May NJ 4/12/1764, Spanish-Indian-American L
   17 days, Monday, 5 pounds, 5'4",
John Donefan, Robert Simonton Lancaster PA 10/19/1749, Irish 24
   3 pounds, tall,
Patrick Donehey, Adam Orth Lancaster PA 8/8/1771, Irish 20
   15 days, Wednesday, 4 dollars, 5'8",
John Donelan, Enoch Anderson Philadelphia City PA innkeeper 9/25/1740, Irish tavern-keeper
   10 days, Monday, 3 pounds, middle,
No Name Donelly, Simon Tribet Philadelphia City PA 7/6/1785, Irish mason
   8 dollars, 5'9",

Arthur Donely, Abraham Holmes Lancaster PA 5/23/1771, Irish 21 driver
    11 days, Sunday, 4 dollars, 5'4-5",
Patrick Donnachy, James Foster Lancaster PA 8/24/1769, 16
    24 days, Monday, 2 pounds,
John Donnally, James Black Chester PA 2/2/1785, 26 weaver
    25 days, Saturday, 8 dollars, 5'7-8",
John Donnaly, David Bell Augusta VA 4/9/1772, Irish 20
    18 days, Sunday, 3 pounds, 5'6-7",
William Donnavan, Conyngham & Nesbitt Philadelphia City PA merchants 6/14/1764, 28
    4 days, Sunday, 5'6", (ran from ship)
Cornelius Donnevan, Thomas Yorks Philadelphia PA 4/22/1742, Irish 20
    10 days, Monday, 1 pound, short,
John Donnohon, Robert Siminton Lancaster PA 11/30/1749, Irish 24
    46 days, Sunday, 5 pounds,
John Donnohon, Theophilus Siminton Lancaster PA 3/13/1750, Irish 24 (2nd escape)
    9 days, Tuesday, 2.5 pounds,
John Donnohon, Robert Siminton Lancaster PA 5/31/1750, Irish 24 (3rd escape)
    17 days, Monday, 2 pounds,
Eleanor Donoboge, Elisha Mitchell 9/20/1759, Irish
    45 days, Monday, 2 pounds,
Philip Donohow, Jacob Mayer Philadelphia City PA 7/4/1771, Irish 16
    6 days, Friday, 6 dollars, 5'3",
James Donoson, Captain Crymer Baltimore MD ship captain 8/18/1763, English 26 C
    10 days, Monday, 1 pistole, 5'5",
Charles Doogwood, James Anderson Jr Lancaster PA 12/7/1769, Irish
    10 days, Monday, 2 pounds, 5'4-5",
John Doon, Hugh Kirkpatrick Baltimore MD 4/6/1774, Irish 27
    11 days, Sunday, 8 dollars,
Daniel Door, James McCraken Philadelphia City PA 10/29/1767, Irish 22
    13 days, Friday, 3 pounds, short,
Brian Doran, Isaac Janney Cecil MD 11/10/1763, Irish 20
    12 days, Saturday, 2 pounds, 5'6",
Patrick Doran, Anthony Pritchard Chester PA 12/27/1753, Irish 20
    2 days, Tuesday, 2 pounds, 5'4", (use to the sea)
Bryan Doron, Batholomew Tims Chester PA 3/13/1750, Irish 35 weaver
    5 pounds, 5'6",
Richard Dorrel, Isaac Gibbs Cecil MD 12/12/1754,
    2 pounds,
Dennis Dorrough, George Kennedy Chester PA 4/5/1775, Irish 40
    9 days, Tuesday, 4 dollars, 5'6-7",
Daniel Dorthety, Thomas Ogle Jr New Castle DE 11/10/1763, Irish blacksmith
    19 days, Saturday, 3 pounds, 5'5",
Edward Doud, John Merick Bucks PA 9/29/1784, Irish hostler
    10 days, Sunday, 6 dollars, 5'6",
Richard Doud, Samuel Blair Hunterdon NJ 9/16/1742, Irish 20
    3 days, Monday, 5 pounds, 5',
George Doude, Ralph Whitsitt Lancaster PA 8/17/1749, 20
    3 pounds, short,
Archibald Dougherty, John Brown Baltimore MD 12/26/1771, 13 A
    24 days, Monday, 0.13 pounds, 4'9-10",
Hugh Dougherty, Robert Jack New Castle DE 5/31/1770, Irish 35 weaver gaol sale L
    11 days, Sunday, 5'4-5",
John Dougherty, Henry Lawrence Chester PA 7/25/1751, weaver
    2 days, Tuesday, 1.5 pounds, middle,
George Douglas, Simon Sherlock Philadelphia City PA 7/14/1763, Scot 40 gardener C
    6 days, Friday, 6 pounds, 5'7", (a rebel)
Francis Douglass, Simon Tribet Philadelphia City PA 7/6/1785, English
    8 dollars, 5'8",
Joseph Dovey, Thomas Harrison Anne Arundel MD ironworks 5/15/1760, English C
    12 days, Saturday, 5 pounds, short, (arrived June 1758)
Henry Dow, John Footman Baltimore MD 10/18/1770, English 30 C
    101 days, Monday, 1 pound, 5'6",
James Dowdall, Adam Hope Cumberland PA 11/23/1752, (2nd escape)
    14 days, Thursday, 2 pounds, 5'4",
James Dowdall, Hugh Wright Philadelphia City PA ship captain 9/21/1752, laborer
    3 days, Monday, 2 pounds, 5'4", (ran from ship, has been in the colonies before)

James Dowdel, Silas Jones Philadelphia PA 9/9/1772, Irish
   10 days, Monday, 8 dollars, 5'7-8",
James Dowelin, Valentine Bower Lancaster PA 9/29/1773, English 19
   24 days, Monday, 5 pounds, 5'7",
Phillip Dowen, Thomas Wills Chester PA 10/19/1738, Irish 20
   4 days, Sunday, 2 pounds, middle,
Martin Dowland, Corbin Lee Baltimore MD ironworks 8/18/1768, Irish
   15 days, Wednesday, 50 dollars, 6',
Pat Dowling, Sharp Delaney 7/14/1784, Irish 25
   3 days, Sunday, 10 dollars, 5'6",
Samuel Dowling, Joseph Fox Philadelphia City PA 12/1/1773, English blacksmith
   7 days, Thursday, 5 pounds, (arrived last Sept.)
Jacob Down, Pzrsifor Frazer Chester PA 8/2/1775, English 19
   4 dollars, 5'10", (lately arrived)
Jane Down, Peter Pechin Chester PA 3/17/1768, Irish 19
   10 days, Monday, 2 pounds, middle,
John Down, Zacharia Hood Philadelphia City PA 3/10/1757, American 32 blockmaker L
   21 days, Thursday, 3 pounds, 5'8",
William Downes, Unlisted Name Chester PA 6/20/1751, 33 weaver L
   16 days, Tuesday, 5 pistoles, short,
James Downey, Zebulon Cook Monmouth NJ 5/17/1744, Irish 35
   7 days, Thursady, 3 pounds, middle,
Terrence Downey, Samuel Levis Chester PA 10/16/1766, Irish
   5 days, Saturday, 2 pounds, 5'10",
Timothy Downey, David Perry 10/1/1767, Irish 27 tailor A
   3 pounds, 5'4",
Anstis Downing, John Clark Bucks PA 3/13/1730, Irish 22 (female)
   5 days, Saturday, 1 pound, middle,
James Downing, John Read New Castle DE 4/6/1738, Irish
   9 days, Tuesday, 1 pound, short, (second trip as an indentured emigrant)
Robert Downing, William Carlin Fairfax VA 3/31/1768, English breeches-maker
   26 days, Saturday, 8 dollars, 5'5-6",
Samuel Downing, William Clark Cecil MD miller 6/27/1765, English
   2 pounds, 5'8",
Daniel Downs, William Quillen Kent MD 6/28/1770, Irish 30
   11 days, Sunday, 1 pound,
Mary Downs, Joseph Miles Chester PA 4/19/1764,
   1 pound,
Patrick Downs, Richard Porter Talbot MD 8/7/1740, Irish 25 tailor
   6 days, Friday, 3 pounds, middle,
William Downy, John Bayley Lancaster PA 5/1/1766, Irish 30
   13 days, Friday, 2 pounds, 5'8',
John Dowsman, Cornelius Vanstavoren Kent MD 11/13/1766, German 20 baker
   2 pounds, 5'8-9", (arrived 2 years ago)
Thomas Doyl, Curtis Grubb Lancaster PA ironworks 4/25/1771, Irish 16
   14 days, Thursday, 8 dollars, 5',
David Doyle, Thomas Sligh Baltimore MD 12/15/1743, Irish 30 cooper
   10 pounds, 6',
George Doyle, John Anderson Lancaster PA 12/5/1771, 15 A
   62 days, Friday, 4 dollars, 5'2",
Lawrence Doyle, William Andrew Philadelphia City PA 11/26/1747, Irish 26 sailor L
   5 days, Saturday, 2 pounds, 5'6",
Michael Doyle, William Wiley Chester PA 4/11/1754, Irish 22
   4 days, Sunday, 5 pounds, 5'10",
Michael Doyle, William Berry Kent DE 9/20/1744, Irish blacksmith C
   8 days, Wednesday, 0.5 pounds,
Patrick Doyle, Messer Brown Chester PA 7/24/1766, Irish 30
   10 days, Monday, 3 pounds, 5'8-9",
Patrick Doyle, Messer Brown Chester PA 10/23/1766, Irish 30 (2nd escape)
   10 days, Monday, 6 pounds, 5'8",
Thomas Doyle, Benjamin Asbleman Lancaster PA 9/10/1747, Irish 24
   4 days, Sunday, 3 pounds, middle,
Thomas Doyle, Alexander Carlyle Philadelphia City PA 5/11/1774, Irish 45 tanner
   9 days, Tuesday, 4 dollars, 5'6-7", (arrived last July)
William Doyle, Anthony Wayne Chester PA 10/4/1775, 23
   2 days, Tuesday, 8 dollars, 5'9-10",

John Doyles, William Dieley Philadelphia City PA 7/21/1773, Irish
    10 days, Monday, 8 dollars, 4'5", (lately arrived)
John Doyling, William Tateham Gloucester NJ 2/28/1738, Irish 17
    4 days, Sunday, 2 pounds, middle,
Stephen Draper, Anthony Bright Philadelphia City PA silversmith 9/20/1739, 27
    4 days, Sunday, 3 pounds, middle,
Valentine Draper, William Hooper Queen Anne's MD 5/20/1742, English 40
    11 days, Sunday, 2 Maryland pounds, 5'8",
Peter Drew, Alexander Campbell Dumfries VA 11/18/1772, Irish 25 sawyer
    11 days, Sunday, 7 pounds, 5'8", (arrived 3 weeks ago)
William Drisdall, James Gallt Cecil MD 5/26/1779, American 18 L
    16 days, Monday, 30 dollars,
John Driseall, Martin Pendergast Philadelphia City PA 7/19/1764, Irish 22 blacksmith
    18 days, Sunday, 6 pounds, 5'10", (lately arrived)
Hopkins Driver, Joseph Holdstock Philadelphia City PA 8/4/1768, English 34 blacksmith
    2 pounds, 5',
Hopkins Driver, Joseph Holdstock Philadelphia City PA 6/1/1769, English 35 blacksmith (2nd esc)
    2 pounds, 5', (has runaway 20 times before)
Hopkins Driver, Joseph Holdstock Philadelphia City PA 8/31/1769, English 35 blacksmith (3rd esc)
    (23rd time to runaway)
Hopkins Driver, Joseph Holdstock Philadelphia City PA 2/1/1770, English 35 blacksmith (4th esc)
    (24th time to runaway)
Hopkins Driver, Joseph Holdstock Philadelphia City PA 7/16/1772, English 38 blacksmith (5th esc)
    10 days, Monday, 1 pound, 5',
Michael Drury, Joseph James Chester PA 9/4/1766, Irish 35
    18 days, Sunday, 3 pounds, 5'6",
William Dryskyl, Ralph Lees Philadelphia City PA tailor 1/23/1734, Irish 17 tailor
    1.5 pounds,
Garret Dubise, Joel Miller Jr Cumberland NJ 5/20/1789, 19 A
    18 days, Saturday, 2 dollars, 5'6-7",
Robert Duddleston, Samuel McCormick Cumberland PA 8/24/1785, Irish 30
    66 days, Sunday, 8 dollars, 5'8-9",
John Dudgen, James Moore Harford MD 10/26/1774, Irish 24 shoemaker C
    27 days, Friday, 10 dollars, 5'4",
Joseph Dudgen, James Fisher Harford MD 10/26/1774, Irish shoemaker C
    27 days, Friday, 10 dollars,
William Duey, Jacob Lemmon Harford MD 5/31/1775, Irish 24 breeches-maker
    10 days, Monday, 4 pounds, 5'5-6",
John Duff, John Kugler Bucks PA 10/2/1766, Irish 18
    12 days, Saturday, 1.5 pounds, 5',
Neal Duffey, Francis Alison Chester PA 6/18/1767, Irish
    11 days, Sunday, 3 pounds, 5'8",
Peter Duffey, William Ellis Cecil MD 10/2/1746, Irish C
    12 days, Saturday, 1.5 pounds, (lately arrived)
Francis Duffy, John Glenn Chester PA 7/6/1749, Irish 18
    11 days, Sunday, 2 pounds,
James Duffy, George Shieve Montgomery PA 11/18/1789, Irish 22
    18 days, Saturday, 4 pounds, 5'4-5",
Robert Dugall, Henry Baker Cecil MD 6/14/1750, Scot 35 carpenter
    3 pounds,
Robert Dugall, Henry Baker Cecil MD 5/21/1752, Scot 37 carpenter (2nd escape)
    2 pounds,
James Dugan, Daniel Stuart Philadelphia PA 8/6/1747, Irish
    5 days, Saturday, 2.5 pounds, 5'10",
Charles Dugray, John Hughs WJ ironworks 10/7/1762, Irish 30 C
    11 days, Sunday, 10 pounds,
Martha Dulin, Felix Donnally Lancaster PA gaolkeeper 8/11/1763, English C
    1 pounds, 5'6", (has 2.25 years to serve)
Edward Dumphy, Phebe Morton 10/26/1774, Irish 19
    9 days, Tuesday, 3 pounds, 5'6-7",
James Dun, Jones Scoggin Salem NJ 6/14/1753, Irish 35
    11 days, Sunday, 3 pounds, 5'10", (has a wife)
Patrick Dun, William Hamilton Philadelphia City PA ship captain 4/25/1754,
    2 days, Tuesday, 0.5 pounds,
George Michael Dunabour, Joshua Littler New Castle DE 4/24/1755, German 19
    10 days, Monday, 2 pounds,

Johanna Dunagon, Thomas Wire Burlington NJ doctor 3/13/1766, Irish 20
    4 days, Sunday, 5 pounds, middle,
James Dunbar, Jonathan Doan Burlington NJ 6/24/1795, 18 A
    56 days, Wednesday, 10 dollars, 5'7-8",
John Dunbar, George O'Kill Philadelphia City PA 10/2/1746, Irish 18
    3 pounds, (ran from ship)
John Dunbar, Calvin Cooper Lancaster PA 5/10/1750, Irish 22 (2nd escape)
    32 days, Sunday, 1.5 pounds, 5'9",
Weldon Dunbar, Josias William Dallam Baltimore MD 7/25/1771, Irish 16 barber (ran twice before)
    12 days, Saturday, 5 pounds,
Weldon Dunbar, Josias William Dallam Baltimore MD 11/11/1772, Irish 17 barber (2nd escape)
    9 days, Tuesday, 5 pounds, 5'5-6",
William Dunbar, William Whitehill Lancaster PA 1/26/1785, Irish 20 weaver
    32 days, Saturday, 10 dollars, 5'6",
William Dunbar, William Whitehill Lancaster PA 12/7/1785, Irish 21 weaver (2nd escape)
    20 days, Thursday, 0.25 pounds, 5'8",
David Dunblass, Adam Stephens Frederick VA doctor 10/25/1750, Scot
    5 pistoles,
Daniel Duncan, William Adair Cumberland PA 1/3/1776, Irish 18
    3 pounds, 5'5",
John Duncan, Job Bacon Philadelphia City PA 8/11/1763, hatter A
    18 days, Sunday, 2 pounds, 5'4",
David Dundas, Jonathan Hugh Burlington NJ 6/16/1748, Scot 35
    19 days, Saturday, 3 pounds,
James Dundass, William Brogden Queen Anne's MD 12/5/1749, Scot 24
    4 pounds, short,
Samuel Dundee, Michael Moses Philadelphia City PA 2/16/1769, 14 A
    113 days, Sunday, 1 dollar,
Charles Dunevan, James Kiemer Chester PA 6/21/1744, Irish
    5 days, Saturday, 2 pounds, short,
Patrick Dunfee, Jacob Leany Chester PA 12/10/1767, Irish 30 tailor
    9 days, Tuesday, 3 pounds, 5'7-8",
Lawrence Duning, John Robert Philadelphia PA miller 3/16/1774, 40
    3 days, Monday, 1 pound, middle,
Isaac Dunlap, Isaac Roberts Philadelphia PA wheelwright 11/17/1763, 18 A
    9 days, Tuesday, 2 pounds, 5'8",
Martha Dunlap, Cal Phipps Chester PA 10/12/1769, 21
    4 dollars, short,
William Dunmead, Francis Kay Gloucester NJ 5/31/1775, English
    4 days, Sunday, 3 pounds, 5'4",
Andrew Dunn, William Walker Burlington NJ 12/26/1752, Irish
    (no other information)
Catherine Dunn, Amos Garrett Baltimore MD 5/14/1747, Irish 20
    10 days, Monday, 1.5 pounds, middle,
Daniel Dunn, David Ogden 8/7/1740, Irish 30
    11 days, Sunday, 1.5 pounds,
Daniel Dunn, John Forwood Baltimore MD 10/18/1770, English 35 C
    8 days, Wednesday, 3 pounds, 5'7",
Elizabeth Dunn, John Bennett Chester PA 6/12/1766, Scot 19
    11 days, Sunday, 1 pound,
John Dunn, John Town Salem NJ 5/24/1775, carpenter
    22 days, Wednesday, 3 pounds, 5'9-10",
John Dunn, Adam Vandebeer Cecil MD 10/11/1750, Irish C
    11 days, Sunday, 3.5 pounds, middle,
John Dunn, Jonathan Youngs Cumberland NJ 10/13/1784, 17 A
    10 days, Sunday, 0.5 pounds,
Michael Dunn, William Darragh Philadelphia City PA 9/13/1764, Irish 17
    11 days, Sunday, 2 pounds, 5'3",
Murtha Dunn, Joseph England New Castle DE 4/5/1753, Irish
    8 days, Wednesday, 3 pounds, 5'7",
Patrick Dunn, John Michener Philadelphia PA 4/16/1752, Irish 30
    4 days, Sunday, 5 pounds, middle,
Thomas Dunn, Abraham Bonsall Chester PA 4/9/1752, 23
    4 days, Sunday, 2 pounds, middle,
Thomas Dunn, Orr Glenholme Philadelphia City PA merchant 6/19/1766, Irish 30 nailer
    12 days, Saturday, 1.5 pounds, 5'6", (ran from ship)

Thomas Dunn, David Cowpland Jr Chester PA 2/17/1773, Irish 40 soldier L
    9 days, Tuesday, 4 dollars, 5'6-7",
Dennis Dunnavon, Captain Morrison Baltimore MD 9/29/1763, Irish tailor
    11 days, Sunday, 1.5 pounds, middle,
Francis Dunne, William Sutton Philadelphia PA 4/10/1793, German 25 tallowchandler
    24 days, Sunday, 16 dollars, 5'4", (arrived Sept. 9, 1792)
Lawrence Dunning, John Roberts Jr Philadelphia PA 7/30/1767, Irish 26
    4 days, Sunday, 2 pounds, middle,
Lawrence Dunning, John Roberts Jr Philadelphia PA 6/8/1769, Irish 27 (2nd escape)
    4 days, Sunday, 1 pound, middle,
John Dunnivin, Henry Counsill Queen Anne's MD 12/5/1751, Irish 19
    71 days, Wednesday, 5 MD pounds, middle,
Joseph Dunstore, Thomas Lennon New Castle DE 1/12/1764, French
    16 days, Tuesday, 2 pounds,
John Durbin, Benjamin Chandlee Chester PA 7/12/1764, 20 A
    15 days, Wednesday, 2 pounds, 6',
John Durck, Peter Hassenclever EJ ironworks 6/12/1766, German miner
    14 days, Thursday, 5 pounds, (under a 3 year 4 month contract, imported)
Bartholomew Durham, Ann Burn Philadelphia City PA 11/21/1745, Irish 20
    4 days, Sunday, 5 pounds, middle,
Bartholomew Durham, Thomas Anderson Philadelphia PA 7/23/1747, Irish 22 (2nd escape)
    4 days, Sunday, 2 pounds, 5'6",
James Durham, Nathaniel Grubb Chester PA 4/23/1752, 18
    4 days, Sunday, 2 pounds,
Daniel Durrah, William Carson New Castle DE 12/1/1773, Irish
    3 pounds, 5'3-4",
Mary Durrason, Henry Martin Bucks PA 1/19/1764, Irish
    last may, 1.5 pounds,
Thomas Dyer, Robert Hinson Kent MD 4/4/1771, English 21 C
    13 days, Friday, 2 pounds, 5'6", (arrived Aug. 1770)
Michael Eades, Joshua Cowpland Chester PA 8/13/1730, 24 shoemaker
    6 days, Friday, 2 pounds, short,
John Eagen, Timothy Scarth Philadelphia PA tanner 6/15/1738, Irish 20 hatter
    11 days, Sunday, 2 pounds,
Matthias Eames, Israel Robeson Berks PA 9/22/1763, German
    19 days, Saturday, 3 pounds, 5'6",
Robert Early, Curtis Grubb Lancaster PA ironworks 6/8/1785, Irish 23 schoolmaster
    10 days, Sunday, 8 dollars, 5'9-10",
Conrad Hendrick Earns, John Leadlie Philadelphia PA 6/13/1754, German 45 doctor
    12 days, Saturday, 2 pounds,
John Easerly, Thomas Johnson Worcester MD 7/16/1788, German 18
    65 days, Monday, 3 pounds, 5'5",
Charles East, Isaac Nicolls Dorchester MD 1/25/1770, English schoolmaster
    24 days, Monday, 4 pounds, 5'5",
Charles East, Isaac Nicolls Dorchester MD 10/3/1771, English schoolmaster (2nd escape)
    20 dollars,
Thomas Easton, John Randall Anne Arundel MD 7/27/1774, Scot joiner
    47 days, Saturday, 5 pounds, 5'6-7", (arrived last Feb.)
Habbakkuk Eastwood, Robert Maghee Middlesex NJ 5/24/1770, L
    12 dollars,
William Eaton, Thomas Kennard 8/2/1764, English 21
    16 days, Tuesday, 4 dollars, 5'4",
David Ecklin, Thomas Ogle New Castle DE 8/14/1755, Irish
    4 days, Sunday, 1.5 pounds,
Ebenezer Eddy, Thomas Croasdale Burlington NJ 8/7/1735, American ship carpenter L
    4 days, Sunday, 3 pounds,
Elizabeth Edgworth, Edward Henderson Hunterdon NJ 11/10/1773,
    14 days, Thursday, 4 dollars, tall,
Anne Edmund, John Reedle Philadelphia City PA 5/16/1771, Welsh 19
    33 days, Saturday, 1.25 pounds, (arrived 1 year ago)
Patrick Edonovan, James Baxter New Castle DE 12/29/1743, 21 tailor
    3 days, Monday, 1.5 pounds, 6',
Edward Edwards, Robert Warburton Chester PA 1/8/1751, English 30 fuller (ran before)
    6 days, Friday, 1.5 pounds,
Edward Edwards, James Bennet Chester PA 8/30/1750, Irish 26
    3 pounds, middle

Edward Edwards, Nathan Hoopes Chester PA 9/6/1753, English
    3 days, Monday, 2 pounds, 5'10",
Henry Edwards, John Riley Chester PA 4/27/1732, English wool comber
    7 days, Thursday, 2 pounds, tall,
John Edwards, James Boyd Chester PA 3/21/1734,
    16 days, Tuesday, 1 pound, short,
John Edwards, William Davies 10/14/1731, bookbinder
    4 days, Sunday, 1 pound, middle,
John Edwards, Nathan Boys Jr Gloucester NJ 7/3/1766, Welsh 35
    11 days, Sunday, 3 pounds, 5'6",
John Edwards, Joshua Ely Bucks PA 10/16/1766, American L
    17 days, Monday, 2 pounds,
Joseph Edwards, Henry Ward Pearce Cecil MD 3/15/1770, English 20 wool comber
    5 pounds,
Joseph Edwards, James Gallion Harford MD 1/25/1775, English 25 wool comber (2nd escape)
    17 days, Monday, 2 pounds, 5'5-6",
Richard Edwards, John Williams Bucks PA ferryman 10/26/1752, Welsh 18
    9 days, Tuesday, 3 pounds, 5'6", (arrived last fall)
William Edwards, Nathaniel Grubb Chester PA 11/18/1736, Welsh 35 miller
    11 days, Sunday, 3 pounds,
Francis Edwin, Robert Teves Baltimore MD 11/6/1766, (2nd escape) C
    10 dollars, 5'5",
Francis Edwin, Robert Teves Baltimore MD 9/12/1765, C
    11 days, Sunday, 1 pound, 5'5",
James Egberton, Abner Hetfield EJ 6/27/1765, blacksmith
    5 pounds, 5'5",
Hans Wulf Eifman, Christian Grafsholt Philadelphia PA 11/16/1733, German 22 tailor
    4 days, Sunday, 1 pound,
James Elington, John Leacock ironworks 5/30/1734, English 14
    4 days, Sunday, 2 pounds,
John Casper Eliot, William Ridgway Burlington NJ 8/13/1788, German shoemaker
    4 days, Saturday, 3 pounds, 5'10",
John Elisha, Alexander Campbell Dumfries VA 11/18/1772, English 35 bricklayer
    11 days, Sunday, 7 pounds, 6', (arrived 3 weeks ago)
Charles Ellick, Charles Engle Philadelphia PA 1/27/1790, tanner A
    11 days, Saturday, 2 dollars, 5'8",
Charles Elliot, John Baker Philadelphia PA carpenter 5/16/1751, Irish 25
    4 days, Sunday, 2 pounds, middle,
James Elliot, Nicholas Diehl Philadelphia City PA 8/10/1769, Irish 16
    10 days, Monday, 4 dollars, 4'8-9",
James Elliot, John Cooper Burlington NJ 3/29/1786, Irish 20 baker
    15 days, Tuesday, 8 dollars, 5'6-7",
James Elliot, John Cooper Burlington NJ 4/9/1788, Irish 22 baker (2nd escape)
    11 days, Saturday, 1 pound,
William Elliot, Samuel Ogden Gloucester NJ 12/9/1795, A
    76 days, Thursday, 0.06 dollars, 5'10",
Thomas Ellis, Charles Christie Philadelphia City PA 5/2/1754, Welsh sailor
    2 days, Tuesday, 2 pistoles, 5'7",
Thomas Elmore, John Evans Lancaster PA 9/4/1760, Irish
    3 pounds, 5'8",
Thomas Elton, Thomas Rutland Anne Arundel MD 6/1/1769, 25 butcher (ran before) C
    28 days, Thursday, 4 dollars, short,
Jacob Emlin, Phineas Caril Cumberland NJ 1/20/1790, 15
    7 days, Wednesday, 3 pounds,
John Emmerton, Stephen Stewart 9/24/1761, English tanner
    36 days, Wednesday, 3 pistoles, 5'6",
Elizabeth Ems, James Cox Bucks PA 1/18/1786, American 19 L
    26 days, Friday, 3 dollars,
John Endless, William Hey New Castle DE 11/30/1758, English 40
    11 days, Sunday, 3 pounds, 5'8", (was discharged from the army last April)
Adam Enger, Abraham Williams Philadelphia PA 2/5/1756, German 25
    10 days, Monday, 2 pounds, middle,
John Engle, Peter Ten Eick NJ 8/8/1754, German miller hired L
    11 days, Sunday, 3 pounds, middle,
Nelly English, Edward Breston Baltimore MD 11/10/1768, 40 C
    11 days, Sunday, 2 pounds,

Margaret Ereson, Christian Groves Philadelphia PA 12/1/1763, 25
    1 pound, middle,
John Ermus, John Ladd Gloucester NJ 1/22/1754, German-American 28 L
    4 days, Sunday, 2 pounds, middle,
Jared Ervin, George Eberly Lancaster PA gaolkeeper 12/28/1774, 30 gaol sale L
    10 days, Monday, 8 dollars, 5'9-10",
Andrew Erwin, Arthur Taggart Lancaster PA 1/26/1769, Irish 21 weaver
    17 days, Monday, 2 pounds, 5'6",
Dick Erwin, Robert Allison Chester PA 2/11/1784, Irish 21
    7 days, Wednesday, 3 pounds,
Francis Erwin, George Plater St Mary's MD 3/15/1759, Irish blacksmith C
    25 days, Sunday, 8 pistoles, 6',
James Erwin, Samuel Fisher Chester PA 5/10/1750, English 14
    2 pounds,
Thomas Erwin, Robert Givanes Cecil MD 12/15/1743, Irish 16 brickmaker
    12 days, Saturday, 1 pound,
Thomas Erwin, Lawrence Potter Philadelphia PA 7/23/1747, Irish 19 brickmaker (2nd escape)
    5 days, Saturday, 2 pounds, tall,
Thomas Erwin, Morial Allen Chester PA 6/20/1754, Irish 26 brickmaker (3rd escape)
    9 days, Tuesday, 2 pounds, 5'8",
Paul Eslinger, Jacob Swope Baltimore MD 5/7/1777, German 18
    12 days, Saturday, 16 dollars, 5'6",
James Ethrington, Andrew Mitchell Chester PA 7/21/1773,
    3 days, Monday, 1.5 pounds, 5'8",
Daniel Etter, George Fitler Philadelphia City PA 7/31/1776, 19 shoemaker A
    1 pound, 5'5",
John Eugene, Robert Young Chester PA 6/28/1750, 30
    7 days, Thursday, 3 pounds, middle,
Belle Evans, Hugh De Haven 10/18/1786, Irish 26
    4 days, Saturday, 1 pound, 5'2-3",
Daniel Evans, Thomas Yarnall Chester PA 4/5/1753, Welsh 22 blacksmith
    6 days, Friday, 2 pounds, 5'8",
David Evans, James Gibbons Chester PA 9/12/1771, Welsh 19
    17 days, Monday, 3 pounds, 5'6-7",
Ezekiel Evans, Arthur Campbell Philadelphia PA 5/31/1780, 16 A
    28 days, Wednesday, 20 dollars, 5'6-7",
George Evans, James Riggs Anne Arundel MD 4/25/1765, Irish
    16 days, Tuesday, 2 pounds, 5'10",
Griffith Evans, Mary Mitchel Prince George MD 4/19/1753, Welsh 48 hired L
    9 days, Tuesday, 3 pistoles, tall,
John Evans, George Monro New Castle DE 6/27/1745, 25
    19 days, Saturday, 3 pounds, 5'8",
John Evans, Robert Teves Baltimore MD 11/6/1766, 21 shoemaker C
    10 dollars, 5'8-9",
John Evans, James Graham VA 11/23/1752, Welsh sailor L
    21 days, Thursday, 1 pistole,
Lewis Evans, Thomas Leedom 8/17/1796, 18
    9 days, Monday, 5 dollars, 5'8",
Morgan Evans, Lawrence Debow Philadelphia PA 8/2/1753, Welsh
    8 days, Wednesday, 2 pounds, 5'8",
Morris Evans, Nathaniel Scott Queen Anne's MD 4/5/1753, 36 C
    10 days, Monday, 3 pounds, 5'7",
Thomas Evans, Benjamin Thaw 7/28/1784, 13 A
    19 days, Friday, 0.03 pounds,
William Evans, Edward Man Sherwood Talbot MD 8/14/1735, Welsh 28 carpenter
    2 pounds, tall,
William Evans, Robert Evans Cecil MD 8/3/1769, English 20
    16 days, Tuesday, 1.5 pounds, 5'9",
William Evans, Edward French Burlington NJ 11/9/1785, 20 A
    24 days, Sunday, 2 dollars, tall,
William Evans, Isaac Dusnane New Castle DE 5/19/1763, Irish tailor gaol sale L
    3 pounds,
William Evens, George Benner Philadelphia PA 10/22/1794, 17 A
    15 days, Tuesday, 2 dollars,
John Everest, Charles Brown Queen Anne's MD 5/13/1742, English 22
    37 days, Tuesday, 2.5 pounds, short,

John Everit, John Denton Hunterdon NJ 7/25/1771, 19 A
 108 days, Monday, 16 dollars,
Jonathan Everston, Joseph Lusby Baltimore MD 5/23/1751, Irish
 38 days, Monday, 3 pistoles, 5'2",
John Ewing, Samuel Huggans Salem NJ 8/20/1794, 42 tailor (ran before)
 16 days, Monday, 10 pounds, 5'8-9", (ran off with master's wife)
John Ewing, Andrew Miller Cumberland PA 9/26/1771, 25 L
 18 days, Sunday, 6 dollars, 5'10",
George Ewings, William Goldsborough Talbot MD 8/15/1745, Irish schoolmaster
 10 days, Monday, 5 pounds, middle,
Joseph Eyers, Curtis Grubb Lancaster PA ironworks 9/1/1773, English 20
 22 days, Wednesday, 7 dollars, 5'6-7", (lately arrived)
William Eyres, John Hopkins 9/16/1756, Irish C
 1 pound,
Thomas Ezaar, James Jack Cumberland PA 7/2/1767, Irish
 16 days, Tuesday, 3 pounds, 5'6",
Patrick Fachy, Charles Ridgely Jr Baltimore MD ironworks 5/14/1767, Irish
 16 days, Tuesday, 2 pounds, 5'6", (arrived 6 months ago)
Jeremiah Fagan, William Haines Cecil MD 9/28/1796, American 18 L
 98 days, Wednesday, 10 dollars, 5'8-9",
Francis Fagen, George Hooke York PA 6/27/1751, Irish
 9 days, Tuesday, 2 pounds, short,
Judith Fagen, Thomas Morgan Bucks PA 7/23/1772, Irish 15
 10 days, Monday, 1 pound,
Judith Fagen, Thomas Morgan Bucks PA 6/16/1773, Irish 16 (2nd escape)
 13 days, Friday, 3 dollars,
Mary Fagen, George Hooke York PA 6/27/1751, Irish
 9 days, Tuesday, 2 pounds, short,
William Fagen, Edward Scanlon Chester PA 8/26/1772, Irish tailor
 10 days, Monday, 5 pounds, 5'8-9",
Garret Fagon, Thomas Darrach Kent DE 9/12/1765, Irish 30 C
 11 days, Sunday, 2.5 pounds, 6',
Samuel Fail, Joseph Dixon Chester PA 4/12/1750, 25 miller L
 11 days, Sunday, 3 pounds, short,
John Fair, Daniel Lucken Philadelphia PA 5/28/1772, Irish 19
 4 days, Sunday, 12 dollars, 5'6-7",
William Fair, William Anderson Philadelphia City PA 11/12/1788, 11 A
 8 days, Tuesday, 0.03 pounds,
Thomas Fairbrother, John Philips Philadelphia City PA carpenter 7/24/1746, English 27 carpenter
 1 pound, 5',
William Fanton, Rynier Probasco Monmouth NJ 1/31/1771, 21
 11 days, Sunday, 1.5 pounds, 5'6-7",
William Far, Benjamin Vanleer Gloucester NJ 4/19/1775, English 22
 2.5 pounds, 6',
James Faran, Robert Wilson Salem NJ 5/25/1774, Irish 30 gaol sale L
 9 days, Tuesday, 4 dollars, 5'9-10",
Robert Faries, William Smith New Castle DE 12/5/1754, 20
 11 days, Sunday, 1.5 pounds,
Edward Farl, Daniel Larew Jr Bucks PA 5/9/1771, Irish 24
 13 days, Friday, 6 dollars, 5'8-10",
Roger Farrall, Isaac Whitelock Lancaster PA 12/6/1745, Irish 45
 41 day, Friday, 1 pound, 5'6",
Charles Farran, Henry Hollingsworth Cecil MD 6/13/1765, Irish 20
 5 pounds, 5'6",
Charles Farran, Henry Hollingsworth Cecil MD 8/7/1766, Irish 21 (2nd escape)
 15 days, Wednesday, 4 pounds, 5'6",
Francis Farrel, John Hammond Baltimore MD 9/6/1750, Irish
 46 days, Sunday, 8 pounds,
Michael Farrel, Andrew Richman Gloucester NJ 7/7/1773, Irish gaol sale L
 5 days, Saturday, 8 dollars, 5'9-10",
Michael Farrell, Patrick Motley Philadelphia City PA baker 10/9/1766, Irish 16
 2 pounds,
William Farrell, Joseph Jackson Chester PA 8/16/1750, Irish
 4 days, Sunday, 3 pounds, middle,
Felix Farrill, Henry William Stiegal Lancaster PA glassmaker 11/21/1771, 23
 20 days, Friday, 10 pistoles, 5'6",

Lawrence Farroll, Richard Croxall Baltimore MD ironworks 4/3/1760, Irish 23 C
    10 days, Monday, 5 pounds, 5'10",
Grace Faulkner, James Smith Lancaster PA 12/7/1774, 16
    6 days, Friday, 3 dollars, short,
Richard Faulkner, John Singleton New Castle DE 8/21/1755, painter
    4 days, Sunday, 2 pounds, short,
William Faulkner, William Lux Baltimore MD 4/18/1754, English 24 C
    3 pounds,
John Favrite, Unlisted Name Philadelphia PA 2/18/1768, French (with his 2 children and wife)
    8 days, Wednesday, 1.5 pounds, middle
Peggy Favrite, Unlisted Name Philadelphia PA 2/18/1768, French
    8 days, Wednesday, (wife to John Favrite)
Thomas Fea, Thomas Segrmes Queen Anne's MD 5/24/1764, Irish 25
    11 days, Sunday, 5 pounds, 5'5",
Henry Featherstone, George Goddard Philadelphia PA blacksmith 3/15/1786, 25
    0.12 pounds, 5'7",
Agnes Fee, Boax Boyce New Castle DE 1/29/1754, Irish
    44 days, Tuesday, 1.5 pounds, short,
Edward Feely, Matthew Potter Philadelphia PA 12/25/1755, Irish
    10 days, Monday, 1.5 pounds, 6',
Francis Feghan, David Watson York PA 6/14/1750, 27
    3 pounds, middle,
Bryan Feilia, Ephraim Moore Lancaster PA 7/28/1768, Irish
    18 days, Sunday, 2 pounds, 5'5-6",
Hannah Felirs, John Grosch 1/16/1772, 25
    53 days, Sunday, 1 pound, short,
William Fell, James Dimmitt Baltimore MD 8/2/1750, English wig-dresser C
    24 days, Monday, 3 pounds, middle,
Michael Feltmire, Joseph Whollen Philadelphia PA 6/28/1753, German 17
    3 days, Monday, 2 pounds, short,
No Name Female, William Williams Baltimore MD ironworks 5/29/1746, German
    (no other information)
James Fennell, James Willcox Chester PA 8/14/1766, Irish 20
    5 pounds, 5'10", (arrived last fall)
Thomas Fenton, Frederick Hagenes Monmouth NJ 8/23/1764, American 18 tailor A
    4 days, Sunday, 2 pounds, middle,
James Ferguson, Jonathan Walton Bucks PA 2/7/1765, Irish 30
    3 pounds, 5'8", (lately arrived)
John Ferguson, Alexander Russel Chester PA 4/29/1795, 19 A
    36 days, Tuesday, 4 dollars,
Margaret Ferguson, William Starr New Castle DE 4/24/1776, Irish 40
    7 days, Thursday, 1 pound, tall,
William Ferguson, Joseph Pennock Chester PA 10/26/1769, Irish 20
    4 days, Sunday, 2 pounds, middle,
Andrew Ferncorn, George Philip Bucks PA 9/28/1774, German 23 weaver
    6 days, Friday, 6 pounds, short,
Michael Ferol, Robert Mendenhall Chester PA 6/8/1774, 21
    8 days, Wednesday, 3 pounds, 5'10",
Michael Ferral, John McKemey Augusta VA 6/23/1768, 28 C
    53 days, Sunday, 4 pounds, 5'9-10",
Hugh Ferran, James Moore Lancaster PA 5/21/1772, hired L
    9 days, Tuesday, 2 pounds, 5'6",
Catherine Ferrell, Samuel Anderson Cumberland PA 9/23/1762, Irish 24 L
    87 days, Monday, 3 pounds, short,
Eleanor Ferrell, Thomas Talman Burlington NJ 7/23/1761, Irish 27 L
    6 days, Friday, 2 pounds, short,
Eleanor Ferrell, Henry Jamison Bucks PA innkeeper 5/27/1762, Irish 28 (2nd escape) L
    3 pounds,
Eleanor Ferrell, Abraham Emmit Chester PA 9/8/1763, Irish 29 (3rd escape) L
    23 days, Tuesday, short,
Garret Ferrell, James Hunter York PA 11/30/1769, Irish 30 tailor
    20 days, Friday, 1.5 pounds, 5'8",
Nicholas Ferrell, John Culbreton Chester PA 12/5/1765, 20 butcher
    4 days, Sunday, 1 pound, 5'4-5",
Patrick Ferrell, James Partridge New Castle DE 8/22/1771, Irish 18
    10 days, Monday, 1 pound, 5'2-3",

Elizabeth Ferringhan, John Chevalier Philadelphia City PA 9/8/1763, German 16
   17 days, Monday, 1 pound, short,
George Ferver, William Hall Philadelphia City PA 5/15/1776, German 16
   3 days, Monday, 4 dollars, short,
Anne Fetchman, Samuel Hart Baltimore MD 8/14/1746, English C
   11 days, Sunday, 3 pounds,
William Fetherson, William Bennet Queen Anne's MD 4/28/1768, 36 schoolmaster
   2 pounds, 5'10",
Johannes Fetterly, John Naglee Philadelphia PA butcher 12/23/1729, German 34 soldier
   23 days, Tuesday, 3 pounds, middle,
Benjamin Feurt, Benjamin Marrot Philadelphia City PA 11/19/1794, 18 tailor A
   6 days, Thursday, 40 dollars, 5'3",
Frederick Fie, James McConnaughy Chester PA 10/23/1776, German 17
   4 days, Sunday, 6 dollars, 5'6-7",
James Field, John Jones New Castle DE 5/25/1769, Irish 20
   30 days, Tuesday, 3 pounds, 5'4-5",
Thomas Field, John Thomson Chester PA 8/24/1774, Irish 21
   8 days, Wednesday, 4 dollars, 5'10-11",
James Fieldgate, Alexander Scott Lancaster PA 8/3/1774, English 24
   23 days, Tuesday, 4 dollars, 5'3-4",
James Fields, William Selman Anne Arundel MD 12/9/1772, 22 C
   30 days, Tuesday, 2 pounds, 5'8-9",
William Fields, Joshua Owings Jr 8/18/1768, Irish 24 weaver
   23 days, Tuesday, 3 pounds, 5'7-8",
Thomas Filer, Thomas Andrews Burlington NJ 4/18/1754, English 33
   9 days, Tuesday, 6 pounds, 5'6", (has 3.5 years yet to serve)
William Filston, Archibald Graham Chester PA 5/12/1773,
   5 days, Saturday, 8 dollars, 5'6", (was in the navy)
Caspar Fince, Joseph Pemberton Jr Philadelphia City PA glazier 8/31/1774, German 18
   6 dollars, 5'6",
Eleanor Find, Charles Mense Philadelphia PA mustard-maker 2/16/1774, Irish 18
   9 days, Tuesday, 5 dollars,
Alexander Finlab, John Rankin Chester PA 2/20/1772, Irish 28 L
   4 pounds, 5'8",
Anthony Finley, Levy Marks Philadelphia City PA tailor 8/5/1762, Irish tailor
   96 days, Saturday, 5 pounds,
John Finley, Mary Stockdale Burlington NJ 4/5/1729, 20 farmer
   2 pounds,
William Finley, James Brinton Chester PA 11/22/1764, Irish 25
   4 days, Sunday, 5 pounds, 5'8",
David Finly, John Shankland Sussex NJ 12/1/1737, Irish blacksmith
   19 days, Saturday, 3 pounds, middle,
Catherine Finnety, William Brackin New Castle DE 4/17/1776, Irish 22
   118 days, Thursday, 4 dollars, middle,
Joseph Finnety, William Brackin New Castle DE 4/17/1776, Irish cooper
   15 days, Wednesday, 4 dollars, 5'5",
John Finsley, John Kerr Lancaster PA 8/15/1771, Irish 19
   17 days, Monday, 1.5 pounds, 5'4",
John Firmstone, Volantine Standley 5/17/1764, English
   24 days, Monday, 2 pounds, 5'8",
Moses Firrill, John Van Fessen Bucks PA 4/28/1773, A
   25 days, Sunday, 3 goats, 5'7-8",
Frederick Fisher, Joseph Sears Philadelphia PA 11/9/1752, German 18
   4 days, Sunday, 2 pounds, 4'4",
George Fisher, Hazeal Thomas Chester PA 1/25/1775, Irish 30 laborer
   10 days, Monday, 4 dollars, 5'6",
Joseph Fisher, John Welsh Queen Anne's MD 9/6/1759, 40 C
   95 days, Sunday, 2 pounds, 5'8",
Christian Fistmire, Samuel Flowers Chester PA ironworks 4/10/1755, German 22
   64 days, Wednesday, 2 pounds,
William Fitch, John Metcalfe Baltimore MD 5/10/1753, C
   6 pounds,
Abraham Fitched, John Van Etten Northampton PA 4/28/1773, English-American 34 soldier L
   16 days, Tuesday, 10 dollars, 5'8",
Abraham Fitched, John Van Etten Northampton PA 11/3/1773, English-American 34 soldier (2nd esc) L
   10 days, Monday, 6 dollars, 5'6",

Abraham Fitched, John Van Etten Northampton PA 10/12/1774, English-American 35 soldier (3rd esc) L
    10 dollars, 5'6",
James Fitzgerald, Jonathan Fister Philadelphia City PA glover 10/8/1730, 18 glover
    3 days, Monday, 1 pound,
James Fitzgerald, Isaac Corin Philadelphia City PA 9/23/1731, 19 glover (2nd escape)
    4 days, Sunday, 1.5 pounds,
James Fitzgerald, John Cross Sommerset PA 12/6/1743, Irish
    91 days, Tuesday, 1.5 pounds, short,
James Fitzgerald, Captain Hinton Philadelphia City PA ship captain 11/21/1751, Irish 19 sawyer
    1 pound, (ran from ship)
James Fitzgerald, Daniel Surrell Queen Anne's MD 7/16/1752, Irish 20 sawyer (2nd escape)
    11 days, Sunday, 2 pistoles, 5'6",
John Fitzgerald, Samuel Patterson Lancaster PA 7/23/1741, 24
    5 days, Saturday, 1 pound, tall,
John Fitzgerald, Daniel Howell New Castle DE 5/4/1749, Irish 20
    4 days, Sunday, 5 pounds,
John Fitzgerald, Samuel Patterson Lancaster PA 9/20/1764, Irish 22 tailor
    2 pounds, 5'7", (lately arrived, was in the navy)
John Fitzgerald, Samuel McMichan Chester PA 1/21/1768, Irish 26 tailor (2nd escape)
    39 days, Sunday, 8 dollars, 5'9",
John Fitzgerald, William Turner Lancaster PA 1/25/1770, Irish 18 A
    17 days, Monday, 2 pounds, 5'6",
John Fitzgerald, William Turner Lancaster PA 1/31/1771, Irish 19 (2nd escape) A
    25 days, Sunday, 3 pounds, 5'6-7",
Margaret Fitzgerald, Thomas Mease Chester PA 6/22/1774, Irish 25 (pregnant)
    12 days, Saturday, 0.1 pounds, 5'2",
Morris Fitzgerald, Michael Wills Philadelphia PA 4/13/1774, Irish 18
    3 days, Monday, 8 dollars, 5'5-6",
Morris Fitzgerald, Michael Wills Philadelphia PA 8/17/1774, Irish 18 (2nd escape)
    3 days, Monday, 8 dollars, 5'5-6",
Nicholas Fitzgerald, Samuel Henry Philadelphia City PA 8/24/1769, Irish 24
    11 days, Sunday, 20 dollars, 6',
Thomas Fitzgerald, William Cochran Winchester VA 6/26/1760, Irish 40 spinning-wheel-maker
    31 days, Monday, 10 pounds, 6',
William Fitzgerald, Timothy Dargen Prince William VA 9/11/1735, Irish 25 sailor
    168 days, Thursday, 2.5 pounds,
David Fitzgerrald, William Murray Boston MA perukemaker 4/12/1753, Irish 26
    25 days, Sunday, 5 dollars,
Gilbert Fitzgibbon, Unlisted Name Philadelphia City PA 3/29/1775, 33 horseman
    8 days, Wednesday, 1 pound, 5'8-9",
Richard Fitzmorris, Roger Magrah Philadelphia City PA tailor 8/2/1753, Irish 23 tailor
    17 days, Monday, 3 pounds, short, (arrived 7 weeks ago)
Dennis Fitzpatrick, William Hitchman Cecil MD 9/20/1750, Irish 35
    10 days, Monday, middle,
John Fitzpatrick, John Allison Cumberland PA 9/15/1768, Irish 20
    11 days, Sunday, 2 pounds, 5'6",
Miles Fitzpatrick, George Brinton Chester PA 1/12/1758, Irish 21
    6 days, Friday, 1 pistole, 5'7",
Patrick FitzPatrick, George Fudge Philadelphia City PA bricklayer 9/3/1747, Irish 22
    5 days, Saturday, 5 pounds, 6', (lately arrived)
Philip Fitzpatrick, Thomas Canby New Castle DE 8/15/1754, Irish cooper
    4 days, Sunday, 1.5 pounds,
Philip Fitzpatrick, Thomas Canby New Castle DE 1/14/1755, Irish cooper (2nd escape)
    25 days, Sunday, 1.5 pounds, short,
Philip Fitzpatrick, Thomas Canby New Castle DE 3/18/1755, Irish cooper (3rd escape)
    6 days, Friday, 1.5 pounds, middle,
Philip Fitzpatrick, Thomas Canby New Castle DE 5/1/1755, Irish cooper (4th escape)
    24 days, Monday, 1.5 pounds, short,
Richard Fitzpatrick, Joseph Smith Chester PA 6/6/1751, Irish 19
    13 days, Friday, 1.5 pounds, 5'4",
James Fitzsimmons, John Gregory Chester PA 9/3/1761,
    7 days, Thursday, 3 pounds, short,
Richard Fitzsimmons, Samuel Bettle Chester PA 8/28/1746, Irish 22 baker
    2 pounds,
Joseph Fitzwater, Jacob Hite Frederick VA 10/25/1750, English 20 C
    5 pistoles, short,

Thomas Flagherty, Thomas Halliday Lancaster PA 9/11/1766, Irish 17
   11 days, Sunday, 4 dollars, 5',
Catherina Flakes, Richard Thatcher Chester PA 7/7/1757, German 35 gaol sale (pregnant) L
   13 days, Friday, 1 pound, short,
Terence Flanagan, Benjamin Tasker Baltimore MD ironworks 5/29/1746, Irish 24 C
   10 days, Monday, 4 pounds, middle,
Roger Flanagen, Samuel Swift Philadelphia PA 12/12/1749, Irish
   9 days, Tuesday, 1.5 pounds,
Grace Flannegan, John Stricker Philadelphia PA 6/9/1757, Irish 19
   11 days, Sunday, 1 pound, short,
James Flannigan, Joseph Hugg Gloucester NJ 1/28/1768, Irish
   7 days, Thursday, 6 dollars, 5'11",
Paultus Flatt, Joseph Mickle Gloucester NJ 12/9/1756, German 19
   7 days, Thursday, 1.5 pounds, 5'5",
John Flaugh, Michael Withers Lancaster PA 9/7/1796, German 27 mason
   1 day, Tuesday, 20 dollars, short,
Thomas Fleaming, Abraham Warner 8/25/1768, 19 mason A
   25 days, Sunday, 3 pounds, 5'8-9",
Charles Fleming, Robert Smith Bucks PA 1/7/1768, Irish
   12 days, Saturday, 1.5 pounds, 5'7",
John Fleming, Nathan Hayes Chester PA 8/9/1770, Irish 21
   11 days, Sunday, 1.5 pounds, short,
Patrick Fleming, William Griffitts Philadelphia City PA 11/15/1753, Irish 21
   10 days, Monday, 1 pound, 5'6",
Richard Fleming, Joshua Way Chester PA 12/16/1772, Irish 25 tailor
   3 days, Monday, 10 dollars, 5'3",
Thomas Flemming, Nathaniel Grubb Chester PA 4/18/1754, Irish 22
   7 days, Thursday, 3 pounds,
John Flenn, Robert Slater Lancaster PA 9/16/1762, 22 A
   11 days, Sunday, 3 pounds, 5'5", (has 5 years to serve)
Richard Fletcher, George Phipps Chester PA 5/3/1770, C
   34 days, Friday, 2 pounds, 5'4-5",
Frederick Fletman, Adam Guier Philadelphia City PA 3/31/1768, German 30 butcher
   5 days, Saturday, 2 pounds, (arrived last fall)
Michael Flewharty, George Perkin Kent MD 9/8/1763, 18 A
   1 pound,
James Flin, James Williams Chester PA 4/18/1754, Irish 30 cooper
   3 days, Monday, 1.5 pounds, 5'6",
Cornelius Fling, Thomas Walker Philadelphia City PA butcher 6/28/1739, 40 butcher
   51 days, Tuesday,
Edward Fling, Thomas Green Charles MD 7/8/1742, Irish 18
   67 days, Sunday, 3 Maryland pounds, short,
Edward Fling, Humphrey Johnson Chester PA 2/26/1751, Irish 30
   9 days, Tuesday, 3 pounds, short, (arrived last summer as a return immigrant)
Rebecca Fling, John Hamilton Lancaster PA tanner 9/29/1743, English 25
   6 days, Friday, 1 pound, short,
Peter Floyd, James Davis Cumberland PA 5/18/1774, 22 L
   254 days, Tuesday, 4 pounds, 5'8",
John Flud, Jacob Wright Chester PA 6/15/1732, Irish 20 weaver
   4 days, Sunday, 2 pounds, short,
James Flynn, Robert Casey Baltimore MD 9/12/1781, Irish 30 tanner
   10 days, Sunday, 30 dollars, 5'8",
George Foell, Peter Care Philadelphia PA 11/28/1771, German 25
   31 days, Monday, 6 pounds, 5'3",
John Fogarthy, Thomas Price Anne Arundel MD 4/20/1774, Irish 22 bricklayer
   14 days, Thursday, 5 pounds, 5'10", (a free-willer)
Andrew Fogle, Michael Withir Lancaster PA 8/20/1777, 14 gunsmith A
   6 dollars,
James Foran, Peter Kline Lancaster PA 4/23/1767, Irish 21 blacksmith
   11 days, Sunday, 3 pounds, 5'9-10", (arrived 10 months ago)
John Foran, Isaac Hewes New Castle DE 9/14/1769, Irish 30
   30 days, Tuesday, 3 pounds, 5',
Jane Forbes, Richard Wells Philadelphia City PA 4/3/1776, Scot 20
   44 days, Tuesday, 2 pounds,
William Forbush, Micajah How Burlington NJ 5/19/1737, 20 shoemaker
   3 days, Monday, 2 pounds,

Samuel Force, David Fenton Philadelphia City PA 11/4/1789, 19 shoemaker A
 23 days, Monday, 8 dollars, 5'5",
John Ford, Matthew Hughes Bucks PA 6/4/1730, 17
 15 days, Wednesday, 2 pounds, short,
John Ford, George Cunningham Cumberland PA 8/17/1774, Irish 18
 17 days, Monday, 3 pounds, 5'7-8",
Robert Ford, James Graham VA 11/23/1752, sailor L
 21 days, Thursday, 1 pistole,
John Forder, Brian Wilkinson Philadelphia City PA carver 5/3/1750, English 17
 17 days, Monday, 1.5 pounds,
John Foren, Evan Evans Chester PA 8/6/1767, Irish 25
 4 days, Sunday, 2.5 pounds,
Fendey Forlindey, Richard Stanley Philadelphia City PA potter 6/17/1731, Irish 30 weaver
 4 days, Sunday, 3 pounds,
Thomas Forrest, Jonathan Fister Philadelphia City PA glover 7/30/1730, 30 skinner
 8 days, Wednesday, 5 pounds, middle,
Robert Forset, Adam Weaver Philadelphia City PA 9/17/1767, tailor A
 4 days, Sunday, 4 dollars,
Samuel Forster, John Murray Baltimore MD 10/6/1768, 30
 10 days, Monday, 2 pounds, 5'10",
Ann Fortey, John Fortey Baltimore MD 3/29/1748,
 4 days, Sunday, 5 pounds, short,
Simeon Fortner, Israel Hallowell 7/20/1774, 20 carpenter A
 2 pounds, 5'10",
Renard Fosser, Margaret Pocklenton 3/28/1749, English caulker A
 11 days, Sunday, 6 pounds, 5', (has 3.75 years to serve)
Jonathan Fossit, Joseph Shinn Salem NJ 12/27/1764, 19 joiner A
 4 pounds, 5'6",
David Foster, Andrew Moynihan PhiladelphiaCity PA breechesmaker 8/19/1772, Irish 21 breechesmaker
 17 days, Monday, 3 dollars, 5'6-7",
Edward Foster, John Lovering Cecil MD 7/5/1750, 30
 12 days, Saturday, 2 pistoles, middle,
Jacob Foster, Joe Ridgway Burlington NJ 12/24/1767, 18
 5 days, Saturday, 1 pound, middle,
John Foster, Matthew Brooks Philadelphia PA 10/23/1776, English 19
 3 days, Monday, 8 dollars, 5'6",
Christiana Fothergale, Robert Armor Lancaster PA 8/12/1756, German 23 (& female child age 2)
 23 days, Tuesday, 1.5 pounds,
David Fothergale, Robert Armor Lancaster PA 8/12/1756, German 26
 23 days, Tuesday, 1.5 pounds, 5'10",
Conrad Founder, Frederick Houssman York PA butcher 9/29/1773, 18 butcher
 17 days, Monday, 3 pounds, 4'10",
John Fowler, James Bennett Chester PA 5/20/1742, Irish 21 tailor
 1 day, Wednesday, 1.25 pounds, short,
John Fowler, George Scott Anne Arundel MD 12/7/1769, Irish 30 tanner C
 5 pounds, 5'10",
Peter Fowler, William Hartley Chester PA 2/24/1743, Irish 20
 6 days, Friday, 2.5 pounds, short,
Peter Fowler, William Hartley Chester PA 6/27/1745, Irish 22 (2nd escape)
 10 days, Monday, 3 pounds, (arrived 4 years ago, but has 4 years yet to serve)
Peter Fowler, William Hartley Chester PA 3/3/1747, Irish 25 (3rd escape)
 8 days, Wednesday, 5 pounds, (arrived serval years ago)
Thomas Fowler, George Ross Lancaster PA 11/19/1761, Irish soldier L
 11 days, Sunday, 3 pounds, 5'2",
Andrew Fox, Frederick Rapp hatter 7/18/1781, A
 20 days, Thursday, 8 dollars, 5'10",
John Fox, John Coope Lancaster PA 6/10/1762, American 27 L
 8 days, Wednesday, 1.5 pounds, 5'6",
Patrick Fox, Robert Clark Lancaster PA 4/19/1770, Irish 18
 4 days, Sunday, 3 pounds, 5'4",
Patrick Fox, Robert Clark Lancaster PA 10/17/1771, Irish 20 (2nd escape)
 10 days, Monday, 2 pounds, 5'6",
Charles Foy, Abraham Holmes Lancaster PA 11/1/1775, Irish 18
 23 days, Tuesday, 8 dollars, 5'4",
John Foy, Thomas Euthorp Cecil MD 4/23/1752, Irish
 4 days, Sunday, 4 pounds, middle,

John Foy, John Town Salem NJ 5/24/1775, carpenter
  22 days, Wednesday, 3 pounds, 5'5-6",
Robert Fraim, John Mackey New Castle DE 6/20/1771, Irish
  15 days, Wednesday, 5 pounds, 5'7-8", (arrived 4 years ago)
James Francis, James Ringgold, Kent MD 3/25/1755, English 26
  14 days, Thursday, 4 pistoles, middle,
James Francis, Stephen Bordley Jr Kent MD 8/1/1771,
  5 pounds,
Thomas Francis, Isaac Coran Philadelphia City PA 8/24/1749, English 22 skinner
  2 pounds, 5'5",
Henry Frankferden, Benjamin Morgan Philadelphia City PA 3/29/1775, German 15
  7 days, Thursday, 6 dollars, (arrived 2 years ago)
James Frasher, Alexander Ware Salem NJ 5/26/1768, Scot 23 shoemaker
  12 days, Saturday, 3 pounds, 5'10",
John Frasier, Isaac Piles Chester PA 8/12/1762, English
  2 pounds, (has on a steel collar)
George Paul Frazer, John Pearson Chester PA 4/30/1772, German 21
  4 days, Sunday, 3 pounds, 5'10-11",
Henry Frazer, Adin Pancoast Frederick MD 7/14/1773, English 26 C
  18 days, Sunday, 10 pounds, 5'8-9",
William Frazier, Samuel Henry Hunterdon NJ 9/22/1763, Scot 25 gaol sale L
  17 days, Monday, 5 pounds, 5'7",
Johannes Jacob Frederickson, Daniel Trimble Chester PA 9/3/1788, German 18
  6 days, Thursday, 2 dollars, 5',
Isaac Freeborn, Matthew Atkinson Lancaster PA 9/27/1750, 19 A
  2 pounds, 5',
Daniel Freeman, Peter Footman Somerset MD 10/10/1765, Irish tailor
  28 days, Thursday, 4 pounds, 5'4",
Jacob Freeman, Jacob Vagdes Chester PA 2/1/1770, German A
  31 days, Monday, 0.05 pounds, 5'8",
Samuel Freeman, Daniel Bacon Burlington NJ 1/18/1732, 23
  3 days, Monday, 5 pounds, short,
Thomas Freeman, Samuel Flower Chester PA ironworks 7/4/1754, English 23 soldier (ran before)
  3 pounds, 5'8", (arrived 4 years ago)
Thomas Freeman, Samuel Shivers Gloucester NJ 5/13/1756, English 25 (2nd escape)
  4 days, Sunday, 1.5 pounds, middle,
Joseph Freemiller, Samuel Burrows Gloucester NJ 3/6/1750, German 18
  2 pounds, short,
John Milcus Freits, Thomas Lee NY 12/14/1758, German
  566 days, Friday, 3 pounds, 5'8",
Michael French, John Hall Baltimore MD 10/25/1753, Irish 20
  11 days, Sunday, 5 pounds, (arrived 7 years ago)
William French, James Walker Winchester VA 4/14/1790, 20 hatter A
  46 days, Saturday, 8 dollars, 5'8",
Johannes Fretzel, Robert Meade Philadelphia City PA 11/27/1746, German
  about 10 months ago, 5 pistoles,
Mrs. Fretzel, Robert Meade Philadelphia City PA 11/27/1746, German
  about 10 months ago, 5 pistoles, (wife to Johannes Fretzel)
Conrad Freyberger, Isaac Moore Montgomery PA 5/25/1796, German 23 baker
  3 days, Sunday, 20 dollars, 5'6",
Nazareth Frieland, Stephen Phipps Philadelphia City PA 8/1/1771, American 20 tailor A
  6 dollars, 5'7-8",
Christian Frits, John Coryell Hunterdon NJ 4/7/1754, German 20
  4 days, Sunday, 1.5 pounds, 5'4",
Harmon Frivall, Robert Meade Philadelphia City PA 1/22/1745, German 24
  10 days, Monday, 3 pistoles, middle,
Mrs. Frivall, Robert Meade Philadelphia City PA 1/22/1745, German
  10 days, Monday, 1 pistole, middle, (wife to Harman Frivall)
George Frizell, James Hunter Philadelphia City PA 12/2/1762, Irish 19
  18 days, Sunday, 2 pounds, (went privateering)
Henry Frocher, Jacob Lighty Philadelphia PA 8/31/1774, German 16
  16 days, Tuesday, 5 pounds, 5'3", (arrived 1 year ago)
Henry Froeherden, Thomas Underhill Cecil MD 5/17/1753, English 28
  7 days, Thursday, 5 pounds,
John Frost, Evan Morgan Philadelphia City PA shopkeeper 5/7/1730, 30 tailor
  32 days, Sunday, 4 pounds,

John Frounds, Henry Ewald Philadelphia PA 9/16/1772, Irish stocking-weaver gaol sale L
    3 pounds, 5'3-4",
Henry Fry, James Cloyd Chester PA 1/1/1755, German
    3 days, Monday, 1 pound, 5'5",
Thomas Fry, Martin Freiley Northampton PA 8/2/1770, English 16
    7 days, Thursday, 2 pounds, 5',
William Fry, Brain Philpot Baltimore MD 6/7/1764, English
    15 days, Wednesday, 3 pounds, 5'8",
John Fryer, Abraham Gudding New Castle DE 1/5/1731, gaol sale L
    2 pounds, middle,
John Fryer, Francis Phillips Baltimore MD ironworks 1/8/1767, 30 wheelwright C
    11 days, Sunday, 10 pounds, 5'7",
Gottlieb Fuhrman, Leonard Jenawein York PA 4/27/1774, German
    5 pounds, 5'7-8",
Peter Fulham, William Craddock Philadelphia City PA 11/3/1743, Irish tailor
    0.5 pounds, short,
John Fulk, John Hide Philadelphia City PA 1/22/1783, German-American 16 L
    6 days, Thursday, 3 pounds,
Alexander Fullerton, Orr Glenholme Philadelphia City PA merchant 9/1/1768, 19 A
    22 days, Wednesday, 3 pounds, 5'7",
Charles Fullerton, James Hamilton Chester PA 11/23/1755, Scot
    4 days, Sunday, 2 pounds, 5'8",
William Fulton, Edward Turner Philadelphia PA 4/12/1753, Irish 24
    7 days, Thursday, 2 pounds, 5'9",
John Furio, Frances Sholey Chester PA 11/12/1747, Irish 30
    8 days, Wednesday, 3 pounds, short,
Christopher Furman, George Miller Salem NJ 9/30/1772, German 35 linen-weaver
    11 days, Sunday, 16 dollars, 5'7-8",
Simon Fury, Martin Waltz Berks PA 5/24/1770, Irish shoemaker
    38 days, Monday, 3 pounds, 5'6",
Michael Futrill, Ephraim Blaine Cumberland PA 6/13/1765, Irish 26 soldier L
    3 pounds, 5'8",
Solomon Gabriel, Thomas Jones Baltimore MD 7/12/1764, English painter C
    11 days, Sunday, 5 pounds, 5'3",
Timothy Gafny, James Willcox Chester PA 11/12/1767, Irish 19
    3 pounds, middle,
Michael Galacher, Hugh McCleland Lancaster PA 3/3/1747, Irish 14
    40 days, Saturday, 1.5 pounds,
Robert Galbraith, John Cochran Chester PA 11/13/1766, Irish 20 shoemaker
    4 days, Sunday, 2 pounds, 5'10",
Michael Gallaber, Archibald Henderson Lancaster PA 5/3/1770, Irish 23
    13 days, Friday, 4 dollars, 5'7",
Bridget Gallacher, Robert Williams Cecil MD 9/14/1749, 30
    12 days, Saturday, 2 pounds,
Thomas Gallacher, William Foster Lancaster PA 3/15/1744, Irish
    2 pounds, short,
Margaret Gallagher, Conyngham & Nesbitt Philadelphia City PA merchants 7/13/1758, 17
    1 pistoles,
Robert Gallagher, Joseph Wiley York PA 10/4/1775, Irish
    38 days, Monday, 5 pounds, 5'10",
Timothy Gallaham, Jehu Maris Chester PA 4/17/1776, Irish 18
    10 days, Monday, 1 pound, 5'6-7",
Richard Gallaher, James Patterson Lancaster PA 1/17/1771, Irish 23
    11 days, Sunday, 3 pounds, 5'7-8",
Richard Gallaher, James Patterson Lancaster PA 3/21/1771, Irish 23 (2nd escape)
    4 dollars,
Hugh Gallaspy, Robert Grace Philadelphia PA ironworks 4/5/1748, Irish
    10 days, Monday, 3 pounds, middle,
Arthur Gallaway, Robert Ritchie Chester PA 8/9/1764, Irish 16
    6 days, Friday, 1 pound,
James Gallegher, George Speir 1/5/1769, 19
    14 days, Thursday, 1.5 pounds, 5'7",
Hannah Galley, William Kurtz Berks PA 10/20/1763, Irish 30 (has 9 year old son)
    30 days, Tuesday, 3 pounds, 5'6", (arrived last summer)
Michael Galloher, Joseph Philips Chester PA 4/18/1771, Irish 21 weaver
    6 dollars, 5'7-8",

Matthew Gallop, Alexander Stuart Cecil MD 9/18/1755, English 30 C
    10 days, Monday, 2 pistoles, 5'8", (arrived 6 weeks ago)
John Galloway, Cornealius Tobit Salem NJ 4/29/1736, English 22
    14 days, Thursday, 3 pounds, tall,
John Galloway, Hinson Wright Queen Anne's MD 6/27/1745, 25 shoemaker
    9 days, Tuesday, 9 pounds, middle,
James Galohown, Richard Willmot Baltimore MD 9/19/1754, Irish 24
    45 days, Monday, 7 pounds, 5'7",
Philip Galser, George Nyce Philadelphia PA tanner 7/28/1757, 18 horse doctor
    11 days, Sunday, 1 pound, middle,
Richard Gamble, Thomas Hanaway, Lancaster PA 1/8/1745, English 26 farrier L
    14 days, Thursday, 2 pounds, middle, (arrived 10 years ago)
Robert Garnell, Balster Spangler York PA 3/24/1768, 19
    6 dollars, 5'4",
John Gammel, John Murphy Cecil MD 4/9/1772, A
    16 days, Tuesday, 1 pound,
James Ganthony, Peter Bard Philadelphia City PA 1/21/1746, 35 sailor L
    45 days, Monday, 3 pounds, tall,
Peter Garagan, George Middleton Burlington NJ 2/6/1750, Irish 20
    3 days, Monday, 3 pounds, short,
Peter Garagan, George Middleton Burlington NJ 4/5/1750, Irish 20 (2nd escape)
    1 days, Wednesday, 1.5 pounds, short,
Peter Garagan, Bennet Bard Burlington NJ 7/26/1750, Irish 21 (3rd escape)
    4 days, Sunday, 2 pounds, short,
George Gardener, William Bond MD 9/11/1740, English 28 husbandman
    18 days, Sunday, 3 pounds,
George Gardiner, Abraham Merriott Burlington NJ 3/10/1742, 40
    9 days, Tuesday, 1.5 pounds, middle,
John Gardiner, David Barr New Castle DE 9/1/1768, English 22
    14 days, Thursday, 2 pounds, 5'8-9"
Nichols Gardiner, Stephen Onion Baltimore MD ironworks 7/4/1754, German 35
    32 days, Sunday, 3 pounds, short,
Benjamin Gardner, Amos Cooper Gloucester NJ 10/14/1789, 17 A
    2 days, Monday, 4 dollars, 5'4",
Jacob Gardner, Samuel Erwin Philadelphia PA 2/9/1769, German 17
    6 days, Friday, 1.5 pounds, 5'4-5",
James Gardner, John Howell Philadelphia City PA tanner 11/21/1745, 30 tanner
    4 days, Sunday, 5 pounds, middle,
John Gardner, James Nicholls Philadelphia City PA ship captain 11/23/1752, Irish 18
    2 pounds, (ran from ship)
John Gardner, William Bright Cumberland NJ 1/11/1775, American L
    8 days, Wednesday, 4 dollars, 5'10",
Joseph Garison, Cornelius Austin Salem NJ 2/5/1777, 20 A
    last March, 0.01 pounds,
James Garland, Matthew Brogan Lancaster PA 6/13/1765, Irish
    11 days, Sunday, 5 pounds, 5'8",
Nicholas Garland, Archibald Getteys New Castle DE 12/30/1762, 24 tailor
    3 pounds, 6',
William Garland, Thomas Blair Bucks PA ironworks 2/22/1739, Irish
    502 days, Sunday, 4 pounds, middle,
James Garlen, Hugh Russell Lancaster PA 9/15/1763, Irish 25
    5 pounds, 5'6",
Joseph Garley, James Davis Chester PA 10/18/1759, Irish 25 schoolmaster L
    16 days, Tuesday, 4 pounds, 5'7",
George Garner, Benjamin Lodge Gloucester NJ 5/9/1771, American 21 L
    2 pounds, 5'7",
Henry Garner, Charles Brown Queen Anne's MD 5/13/1742, 18
    37 days, Tuesday, 2.5 pounds, short,
John Garner, Nathan Chapman Stafford VA ironworks 4/16/1748, Scot 21
    6 days, Friday, 2 pistoles, middle,
John Garnish, Isaac Wayne Chester PA 8/16/1770, English tanner
    4 days, Sunday, 2 pounds, 5'5",
Malachi Garvi, Samuel Worthington Philadelphia PA 2/1/1733, Irish 34 L
    8 days, Wednesday, 3 pounds,
Mary Gathen, Joseph Cannon Chester PA 12/18/1740, 11
    28 days, Thursday, 0.5 pounds,

Jane Gau, Thomas Laycock Philadelphia PA 11/6/1776, Irish
  6 days, Friday, 2 pounds, short,
William Gawlin, Isaac Foster Frederick MD 7/19/1775, Irish perukemaker
  33 days, Saturday, 5 pounds, 5'11",
John Peter Geable, William Maclay Northampton PA 8/11/1773, German 25 carpenter
  10 days, Monday, 16 dollars, 5'8-9",
Thomas Gearran, William McClure New Castle DE 9/19/1771, Irish 21
  1.5 pounds, 5'6-7",
Charles Geifinger, Martin Halter Salem NJ 7/9/1767, German 27 soldier
  4 days, Sunday, 16 dollars, 5'4", (arrived last fall)
Johann George Geissel, William Stiles PhiladelphiaCity PA stonecutter 11/15/1786, German 20 mason
  3 days, Sunday, 4 dollars, (lately arrived)
George Leonard Geist, Adam Leberger Salem NJ 6/1/1758, German 20
  17 days, Monday, 2 pounds, middle,
Con Gellaher, Samuel Hughes Frederick MD 8/3/1774, Irish 25
  14 days, Thursday, 3 pounds, 5'6", (arrived 1 month ago)
William Gemeinbower, Baltiss Fleisher Philadelphia City PA 10/9/1782, 15 A
  2 dollars,
John Frederick Gentnen, Jonathan Lewis Philadelphia City PA 8/9/1753, German 15
  16 days, Tuesday, 2 pounds,
James Gerald, Alexander Hill Salem NJ 4/27/1774, Irish 30
  2 days, Tuesday, 5 pounds, 5'9-10",
George Thomas Gerhard, Matthias Folk Philadelphia City PA skinner 12/14/1769, German 20 A
  27 days, Friday, 3 pounds, 5'7",
Edward German, Colin Ferguson Kent DE 7/26/1753, English carpenter
  4 days, Sunday, 5 pounds, short,
Hugh German, Hugh Fraser Baltimore MD 8/16/1770, 28 tailor
  8 days, Wednesday, 5 pounds, 5',
William German, Garret Barry Chester PA 9/8/1757, 18
  22 days, Wednesday, 1 pound, (has been privateering)
John Germon, John Querns Baltimore MD 11/30/1769, Irish 24
  5 pounds, middle,
Elizabeth Gest, Benjamin Jones Chester PA 4/2/1783, American 22 L
  5 days, Friday, 2 pounds,
Christian Getz, Robert Miller Chester PA 9/13/1753, German 20
  15 days, Wednesday, 2 pounds, short,
Charles Gheiseler, Joseph Wharton Jr Philadelphia City PA 12/16/1772, German 19
  6 days, Friday, 1.5 pounds, 5'9", (arrived 1 week ago)
Charles Gheiseler, Joseph Wharton Jr Philadelphia City PA 1/27/1773, German 19 (2nd escape)
  6 days, Friday, 1.5 pounds, (arrived 2 months ago)
John Gibbons, James Reynolds Philadelphia City PA gilder 8/23/1770, gilder
  0.05 pounds, 6',
Hugh Gibson, William Foott New Castle DE 2/23/1774, Irish 24
  13 days, Friday, 6 dollars, 5'7",
Joseph Gibson, John Allen Frederick VA 4/4/1765, English 20 C
  2 pounds, 5'5",
William Gibson, Alexander Scott Lancaster PA 10/3/1771, Irish 18
  10 days, Monday, 3 pounds, 5'10",
John Christopher Giel, William Von Phul 2/1/1792, German 26 cooper
  3 days, Sunday, 3 pounds, 6',
Tobit Gilder, Robert Story Philadelphia PA 12/15/1737,
  10 days, Monday, 2.5 pounds,
Richard Gilding, John McIntire 12/15/1768, English 25 breeches-maker
  4 days, Sunday, 2 pounds, 5'4-5",
Patrick Gile, Nicholas Wilson New Castle DE 3/18/1755, Irish bricklayer
  6 days, Friday, 1.5 pounds, middle,
John Gilespy, Robert Nivin New Castle DE 5/18/1749, Irish 21 drummer
  2 days, Tuesday, 3 pounds,
Mary Gilgin, Robert Drybrugh 8/10/1758, 17
  3 days, Monday, 2 pounds, short,
John Gilgrew, George Hinkel Lancaster PA 8/30/1775, Irish 25
  18 days, Sunday, 4 dollars, 5'4-5",
Charles Gill, Barbara Hook Cumberland PA 5/6/1762, English 28
  15 days, Wednesday, 3 pounds,
Charles Gill, Edward Teal Baltimore MD 10/22/1761, English 30 jockey C
  15 days, Wednesday, 4 pistoles, 5'6",

Patrick Gill, Nicholas Wilson New Castle DE 3/13/1753, Irish bricklayer
   1 day, Wednesday, 1.5 pounds, middle,
James Gillalen, James Adams Lancaster PA 3/29/1764, 19
   9 days, Tuesday, 2 pounds, 5'6",
James Gillcreace, Richard Borden Hunterdon NJ 12/3/1767, Irish shoemaker
   13 days, Friday, 4 dollars, 5'4",
Patrick Gillespie, David Davis New Castle DE 3/21/1765, Irish 26
   1.5 pounds, 5'10",
Patrick Gillespie, Patrick McColgan New Castle DE 8/29/1765, Irish 26 (2nd escape)
   9 days, Tuesday, 8 dollars, 5'9-10",
David Gillmore, John Moodey Philadelphia City PA 2/20/1772, Irish 20
   26 days, Saturday, 4 dollars, 5'9-10", (arrived last fall)
Joseph Gillpatrick, Josiah Sherrald Philadelphia City PA 9/15/1768, English 28 turner
   18 days, Sunday, 30 dollars, 5'5",
John Baptist Gilman, James Plunket 5/21/1772, French 21
   2 pounds, 5'5",
Valentine Gilman, Daniel Lucken Philadelphia PA 2/22/1770, German 19
   6 days, Friday, 6 dollars, 5'4-5", (relatives live nearby)
Thomas Gilpin, William Havelton Philadelphia City PA 8/11/1768, 18 A
   149 days, Tuesday, 1 pound,
Isaac Gingle, John Metcalfe Baltimore MD 10/5/1752, English farmer C
   79 days, Tuesday, 5 pounds,
John Ginnens, Bryan Murphy Lancaster PA 9/5/1751, American 19 A
   209 days, Sunday, 5'6",
William Gipson, William Zane Gloucester NJ 6/12/1776, English 16
   14 days, Thursday, 3 dollars,
No Name Girl, Gerhard Brenner Lancaster PA 11/4/1762, German 15
   2 pounds, middle,
No Name Girl, James Cummins New Castle DE 1/10/1760, Irish 26
   8 days, Wednesday, 1.5 pounds, middle,
No Name Girl, William Kerlin Chester PA 10/23/1776, German 25
   12 days, Saturday, 4 dollars,
John Gittens, John McDermott Chester PA 10/11/1753, English 40
   29 days, Wednesday, 1.5 pounds, middle,
John Glanding, Henry Wrench Queen Anne's MD 1/29/1767, 25 shoemaker
   23 days, Tuesday, 2 pounds, 5'7-8",
Johannas Glann, William Quillen Kent MD 6/28/1770, Irish (male)
   11 days, Sunday, 1 pound, 5'9",
Hugh Glasgow, Joseph Chick Cecil MD 6/28/1750, 35
   21 days, Thursday, 2 pounds, 5'10",
Ludwick Glass, William Lawrence Gloucester NJ 4/16/1788, German
   6 days, Thursday, 4 dollars, 5'5-6",
John Glassham, David Morgan Lancaster PA 8/29/1771, Irish 20
   2 pounds, 5'6-7", (lately arrived)
John Glassham, John Evans Lancaster PA 8/19/1772, Irish 21 (2nd escape)
   5 pounds, 5'5",
William Glen, Isaac Janney Cecil MD 3/27/1753, Irish 15
   8 days, Wednesday, 3 pounds, short,
William Glen, Isaac Janney Cecil MD 6/26/1755, Irish 18
   11 days, Sunday, 2 pounds,
Hugh Glenn, Mark Wilcox Delaware PA 12/30/1795, 19 A
   5 days, Friday, 12 dollars, 5'10",
Samuel Glenn, Thomas Clark New Castle DE 1/23/1772, 19 A
   17 day, Monday, 4 dollars, 5'9-10",
Cannon Gleson, James McNair Bucks PA 8/16/1764, Irish
   6 days, Friday, 2 pounds, 5'6",
Matthew Gloster, William Drewry Philadelphia City PA 3/26/1772, Irish 18
   5 days, Saturday, 2 pounds, 5'4", (arrived 3.5 years ago)
William Goddin, William Gray Philadelphia City PA baker 4/12/1744,
   10 days, Monday, 2 pounds, short,
Edward Godfrey, Azarian Thomas Chester PA 5/9/1771, Irish 19
   15 days, Wednesday, 3 pounds, 5'4-5", (arrived 3 years ago)
Edward Godfrey, Azarian Thomas Chester PA 3/5/1772, Irish 20 (2nd escape)
   7 days, Thursday, 2 pounds, 5'1-2",
Edward Godfrey, William Clever Philadelphia PA 9/21/1774, Irish 22 gaol sale (ran before) L
   12 days, Saturday, 4 dollars, short,

Jacob Godwin, Josiah Jones Philadelphia PA 7/26/1764, American 19 A
   3 pounds, 5'6",
Casper Goedenberg, Isaac Merrit Burlington NJ 12/13/1764, German 33 clockmaker
   4 days, Sunday, 3 pounds, 5'3",
Frederica Goettle, Hilary Baker 9/15/1790, German 14
   39 days, Saturday, 2 dollars,
Charles Goff, Thomas Norris Salem NJ 3/31/1773, waterman
   10 dollars, 5'2-3",
Edward Goff, Thomas Penrose Philadelphia City PA 12/15/1763, American 20 A
   2 days, Tuesday, 20 dollars, 5'8",
Joseph Gold, Thomas Atkinson, Bucks PA 3/12/1788, 14
   2 days, Monday, 2 dollars, 5'7-8",
Andrew Golden, Benjamin Bartholemew Chester PA ironworks 4/10/1755, German 20
   64 days, Wednesday, 2 pounds, short,
Richard Golden, Martha Humphries Talbot MD 3/14/1771, English
   16 days, Tuesday, 2 pounds, 5'10", (already served 4 years in New York)
Elizabeth Gollin, Alexander Crukshank Philadelphia City PA shoemaker 6/14/1753, German 14
   14 days, Thursday, 1 pound,
Stephen Gom, David Dewar Philadelphia City PA ship captain 12/26/1752, English gardener
   1 pound, 5'6", (ran from ship)
Thomas Good, Charles Greenbury Griffith Frederick MD 5/26/1768, English 35 miller C
   16 days, Tuesday, 5 pounds, 5'7-8",
William Gooden, John Summers Huntingdon PA 6/19/1793, 18 A
   16 days, Monday, 8 dollars, 5'7-8",
John Goodenough, Thomas Mullan Philadelphia City PA 5/28/1741, English
   4 days, Sunday, 1.5 pounds, short,
William Goodfellow, James Claxton Philadelphia PA 8/14/1746, 15 (ran 7 times before)
   15 days, Wednesday, 1.5 pounds,
John Goodman, William Scott Philadelphia City PA 3/20/1760, 16 tailor A
   15 days, Wednesday, 2 pounds,
Matthew Goodman, John Taylor Lancaster PA 6/13/1754, English 18
   4 days, Sunday, 2 pounds, 5'8",
William Goodman, Richard Lloyd Chester PA 5/9/1745, Irish 30
   11 days, Sunday, 1.5 pounds, short,
Gilbert Goodridge, Edmund Ball Baltimore MD 11/28/1754, English C
   18 days, Sunday, 1.33 pounds, (arrived April 1753)
Andrew Goodson, Timothy Matlack Gloucester NJ 7/12/1744, English
   4 days, Sunday, 3 pounds,
John Goodwin, William Snow Anne Arundel MD ship captain 2/15/1770,
   1 pound, 5'7", (ran from ship)
Thomas Goodwin, John Jackson Cecil MD 9/6/1744, Irish 45 C
   1 pound, middle,
John Gorden, Patrick Hayes Lancaster PA 12/2/1772, Scot 26
   17 days, Monday, 4 dollars, 5'10",
Adam Gordon, Robert Graham 4/16/1777, Scot 21
   10 days, Monday, 10 dollars, 5'9-10",
George Gordon, Mr Jones Philadelphia City PA joiner 7/15/1756, English 17 A
   12 days, Saturday, 2 pistoles, 5',
James Samuel Gordon, Edmund Milne Philadelphia City PA goldsmith 8/3/1769, English 24 jeweller
   18 days, Sunday, 2 pounds, 5'1",
James Samuel Gordon, Edmund Milne Philadelphia City PA goldsmith 4/4/1771, English 26 jeweller
   11 days, Sunday, 8 dollars, 5'1", (2nd escape)
John Gordon, Andrew Gibson Cecil MD 7/5/1753, Scot 30
   4 days, Sunday, 3 pistoles, middle,
John Gordon, Samuel Sharp Cecil MD 8/14/1766, Scot 18
   4 days, Sunday, 3 pounds, 5'6",
Robert Gordon, Daniel Offley Philadelphia City PA 10/17/1754, Irish 19 blacksmith
   5 days, Saturday, 3 pounds, 5',
Robert Gordon, Daniel Offley Philadelphia City PA 6/20/1755, Irish 20 blacksmith (2nd escape)
   5 days, Saturday, 3 pounds, 5'4",
William Gordon, Samuel Smith New Castle DE 10/3/1765, Scot 23
   16 days, Tuesday, 3 pounds, 5'8-9",
William Gordon, Casper Johnson Philadelphia City PA 1/15/1783, 19
   19 days, Friday, 0.02 pounds, 5'6",
William Gordon, Jacob Wismer Philadelphia PA 11/5/1783, 20 (2nd escape)
   6 dollars,

William Gordon, Jacob Wismer Philadelphia PA 12/10/1783, 20 (3rd escape)
    8 days, Tuesday, 10 dollars, 5'5-6",
Daniel Gordy, Jacob Hagie Philadelphia PA papermaker 4/11/1751, 17 A
    1 pound,
Patrick Gore, Isaac Starr New Castle DE 11/3/1773, Irish 21
    13 days, Friday, 5 pounds, 5'8-9", (arrived 2 years ago)
Thomas Gore, Nathan Bolden New Castle DE 7/23/1772, Irish 16
    13 days, Friday, 4 dollars,
John Gorman, John Smith Chester PA 10/8/1767, Irish 24
    7 days, Thursday, 3 pounds, 5'6",
Michael Gorman, Abraham Levan Berks PA 11/15/1775, Irish 18
    10 days, Monday, 3 pounds, 5'3-4",
Michael Gorman, Abraham Levan Berks PA 3/13/1776, Irish 18 (2nd escape)
    12 days, Saturday, 3 pounds, 5'3-4",
Thomas Gormand, Robert Newell Cumberland PA 12/25/1755, American 22 carpenter L
    24 days, Monday, 3 pounds,
Herman Gosser, Michael Dotterer Philadelphia PA 8/16/1770, German
    4 days, Sunday, 1 pound, 5',
Mary Gossit, Robert Patterson Cecil MD 5/14/1761, American 20 L
    51 days, Tuesday, 1.5 pounds, short,
George Gothley, Patrick Creagh MD 12/30/1742, 30
    4 months ago, 3 pounds, middle,
William Gould, Samuel Hill Chester PA 1/18/1743, Irish 20
    7 days, Thursday, 2 pounds, middle,
Michael Gouldsboury, George Browning Kent MD 8/22/1771, Irish
    30 days, Tuesday, 2 pounds, 5'6-7",
Aaron Gover, Thomas Middleton Philadelphia City PA 8/7/1776, English 20 baker
    7 days, Thursday, 1 pound,
Henry Gowmiller, Henry Wolff Berks PA 3/12/1754, German 37
    7 days, Thursday, 5 pounds, 5'5",
John Clark Grace, Edward Rummey Anne Arundel MD 8/16/1744, American 30 L
    39 days, Sunday, 3 pounds, middle,
John Clark Grace, John Pennill Chester PA 1/31/1749, American 34 (2nd escape) L
    8 days, Wednesday, 2 pounds, 5'9",
William Grace, William Davis Stafford VA 5/31/1750, 24 C
    5 pounds, 5',
Luke Grady, John Edwards New Castle DE 10/16/1766, Irish 29
    4 days, Sunday, 4 pounds, 5'9",
George Graff, Henry William Stiegal Lancaster PA ironworks 8/24/1766, German 29 sadler
    5 days, Saturday, 10 pistoles, 5'4",
David Graham, Robert Ritchie Chester PA 11/3/1763, Scot 28 pewterer
    1 pound, 5'6", (lately arrived)
Edward Graham, Henry Rice 4/6/1785, Irish 19
    9 days, Monday, 8 dollars, 5'6",
John Graham, Boaz Boyce New Castle DE 6/6/1751, Irish 25 weaver
    4 pounds, 5'5",
John Graham, Joseph Mitchell Philadelphia City PA merchant 11/20/1755, Irish
    2.5 pounds, 5'9",
John Graham, James Ewing York PA 9/13/1775, Irish 18
    1.5 pounds, 5'4-5", (arrived in 1773)
Samuel Graham, Joseph Thomas Bucks PA 7/26/1770, Irish 16
    44 days, Tuesday, 6 dollars, 5'1-2",
William Graham, James Christie Jr Baltimore MD 1/29/1767, C
    7 days, Thursday, 5 pounds, 5'6-7",
William Graham, John Montgomery New Castle DE 11/24/1763, Irish 30 soldier L
    1 pound, middle,
Francis Grahams, Isabella Nevins New Castle DE 8/13/1747, Irish 22
    3 days, Monday, 1 pound,
Lucina Granger, Nicholas Pyle Chester PA 4/17/1755, Irish
    14 days, Thursday, 1.5 pounds, short, (arrived last fall)
Alexander Grant, Adam Shank Philadelphia PA 4/14/1790, 12 A
    0.03 pounds,
Daniel Grant, Thomas Adams New Castle DE 11/22/1753, Irish 19
    8 days, Wednesday, 2 pounds, 5'8",
James Grant, John Coward Monmouth NJ 8/14/1740, Irish 21
    3 days, Monday, 1.5 pounds,

Edward Gray, William Kerlin Chester PA 7/10/1776, English 26 miller gaol sale L
   11 days, Sunday, 5 pounds, 5'6",
John Gray, John Bentley Chester PA 3/1/1729, English
   2.5 pounds, short,
John Gray, Jacob Forwood New Castle DE 8/29/1765, English 21
   4 days, Sunday, 2 pounds, 5'8-9",
Martha Gray, Barney Cain Philadelphia PA 10/28/1772,
   14 days, Thursday, 3 dollars, 4'10",
William Gray, Stephen Webb Chester PA 2/28/1776, English 21 wool comber L
   3 pounds, 5'5",
Hugh Grayly, Richard Brown York PA 1/22/1767, Irish 20 tailor
   2 pounds, 5'8", (arrived last Nov. 25th at Baltimore)
Edward Greagin, James Portell Chester PA 2/9/1731, Irish 20
   5 pounds,
James Greeing, Robert Adair Chester PA 9/7/1758, English shoemaker
   11 days, Sunday, 2 pounds, 6',
Anne Green, Thomas Cresap Frederick MD 6/1/1749, English 45
   30 days, Tuesday, 7 pounds, short,
Catherine Green, Adam Poet Philadelphia City PA 9/14/1774, German
   2 pounds, 5',
Edward Green, Samuel Wright Burlington NJ 1/13/1729, Irish
   about 323 days, 3 pounds, middle,
James Green, Samuel Bunting Jr Burlington NJ 6/14/1775, Irish 23
   10 days, Monday, 5 dollars, 5'9", (arrived 2 years ago)
John Green, Robert Christie Philadelphia City PA 8/20/1741, Irish 24 barber
   10 days, Monday, 2 pounds, middle,
John Green, John Gill Gloucester NJ 10/14/1742, Irish 25 barber (2nd escape)
   52 days, Monday, 3 pounds, middle,
John Green, George Ward Gloucester NJ 5/26/1743, Irish 25 barber (3rd escape)
   7 days, Thursday, 2 pounds, middle,
John Green, Charles Elliot Salem NJ 3/19/1772, 20 A
   10 days, Monday, 4 dollars, 5'3",
John Green, William Kelso Cumberland NJ 9/9/1772, Irish 21 sailor (ran before) L
   124 days, Friday, 5 pounds, 5'8-9",
Joseph Green, Samuel Swerigen 12/10/1761, 21 C
   11 days, Sunday, 2.5 pounds, 5',
Matthew Green, David Dewar Philadelphia City PA ship captain 12/26/1752, English 20 printer
   1 pound, (ran from ship)
Peter Green, Samuel Read Frederick MD 4/12/1753, English 42 C
   3 pounds, 5'4",
William Green, John Comely Philadelphia PA 5/13/1731, 20
   3 days, Monday, 1.25 pounds, middle,
Stephen Greenleaf, Jonathan Ingham Bucks PA 5/25/1749, 23 sailor
   8 days, Wednesday, 1.5 pounds, middle,
Giles Greenwich, Moses White Chester PA 7/8/1731,
   4 days, Sunday, 3.5 pounds, short,
James Greenwood, James Vahan Monmouth NJ 6/9/1748, English
   2 pounds, middle,
Jane Greenwood, Benjamin Randolph Philadelphia City PA cabinetmaker 1/5/1769, English
   3 days, Monday, (has 4 years 7 months to serve)
Henry Greeses, Thomas Chrisholm Baltimore MD 8/31/1769, Welsh 40 C
   10 days, Monday, 2 pounds, 5'6-7",
John Greevy, James Dougherty Chester PA 4/4/1745, Irish 35
   18 days, Sunday, 5 pounds, 5',
James Gregg, James Blair Westmoreland VA 5/31/1750, Scot 11
   75 days, Saturday, 2 pistoles, short,
Richard Gregory, Nathan Rigbie MD 2/22/1744, 30 joiner
   43 days, Wednesday, 5 pounds, middle,
Thomas Gregory, Frederick Mouse Philadelphia City PA 11/20/1776, English 16 A
   17 days, Monday, 4 dollars,
John Grenan, Robert Alison Chester PA 9/11/1766, Irish
   32 days, Sunday, 3 pounds, 5'8",
James Grier, John Kidd Berks PA 6/23/1773, 18 tinker A
   7 days, Thursday, 8 dollars, 5'9-10",
Edward Griffin, Edward Rummey Anne Arundel MD 8/16/1744, 45 C
   39 days, Sunday, 3 pounds sterling, short

Joannah Griffin, Thomas Faulkner Bucks PA 11/15/1750, Irish 28
   45 days, Monday, middle,
John Griffin, James Childs 8/8/1751, Irish blockmaker
   7 days, Thursday, 2.5 pounds, (lately arrived)
William Griffin, William Hamilton Chester PA 5/25/1738, Welsh
   3 pounds, middle,
Philip Griffis, Andrew Hickman Kent MD 5/9/1771, Welsh
   10 days, Monday, 2 pounds, 5'7-8",
Edward Griffith, James McCan Chester PA 12/6/1764, 18 weaver A
   5 days, Saturday, 1 pound, 5'6",
George Griffith, Cromwell McVity Lancaster PA 9/28/1769, Irish 20
   16 days, Tuesday, 5 pounds, 5'6-7",
George Griffith, Edward Wells Philadelphia City PA 6/30/1779, 18 A
   17 days, Monday, 8 dollars, 5'5-6",
John Griffiths, Edward Wyatt Philadelphia City PA tailor 8/30/1739, 20
   4 days, Sunday, 1.5 pounds, middle,
Nelly Griffiths, William Smith Philadelphia PA 11/17/1757, American 20 L
   6 days, Friday, 3 pounds,
Thomas Griffiths, Baldwin Wake Burlington NJ 2/9/1774, English 35 tavern-keeper
   5 pounds,
Mary Griffitts, Peter Row Lancaster PA 6/26/1766, English 20 C
   20 days, Friday, 3 pounds, (arrived in 1763)
Phillip Griffitts, Richard Ashton Lancaster PA 7/19/1739, English 30
   2 pounds, tall,
George Grift, John Taylor Chester PA shoemaker 9/18/1755, 19 A
   about 62 days, 1.5 pounds, 5'7",
Thomas Grigg, Thomas Hart Philadelphia City PA bricklayer 9/17/1730, 18 mason
   3 days, Monday, 2 pounds,
Francis Grimes, Hugh Rendels New Castle DE 2/14/1749, Irish 22
   8 days, Wednesday, 2.5 pounds, 5'6",
John Grimes, Robert McCeay Cumberland PA 5/12/1763, Irish 19
   14 days, Thursday, 2 pounds, 5'4",
Mary Grimes, Henry Cooper Burlington NJ 6/25/1747, Irish
   4 days, Sunday, 2.5 pounds, short,
Samuel Grimes, John Craig Bucks PA 7/2/1772, Irish 19
   16 days, Tuesday, 4 dollars, 5'4-5",
Edmund Grimshaw, Charles Ridgely Jr Baltimore MD ironworks 8/13/1767, English 21 weaver C
   11 days, Sunday, 2 pounds, 5'9",
John Grimshaw, John Jones Baltimore MD 4/5/1764, 40 C
   about 16 days, 2.5 pounds, 5'2",
Anna Catherina Grobin, James Moore Chester PA storekeeper 8/15/1754, German 26
   8 days, Wednesday, 1.5 pounds,
John Grocott, John Newton Westmoreland VA 9/2/1762, English 40 bricklayer
   32 days, Sunday, 8 pounds, 5'9",
Sophia Groton, Joseph Cauffman Philadelphia City PA 3/8/1786, German 25
   19 days, Friday, 8 dollars, 4'10",
James Groves, Thomas Foster Anne Arundel MD 8/16/1764, English 40 C
   46 days, Sunday, 5 pounds, (arrived Aug. 1763)
Henry Gruber, Charles Gemberling Philadelphia City PA 7/17/1766, German 19 shoemaker L
   17 days, Monday, 5 pounds,
Honos Yerack Grumble, William Albertson Gloucester NJ 2/6/1750, German 29
   2 pounds, middle,
John Gubby, Edward Collings Philadelphia PA mason 4/19/1739, English 35
   7 days, Thursday, 2 pounds, short,
Andrew Guffen, William Henderson Philadelphia City PA 8/26/1772, Irish 16
   4 days, Sunday, 5 pounds,
Edward Guin, Joseph Clark Chester PA 11/8/1770, Irish 18
   19 days, Saturday, 4 dollars, 5'6", (arrived Oct. 16th last, relatives live nearby)
Felix Gunahan, Conyngham & Nesbitt New Castle DE merchants 9/1/1784, Irish shoemaker
   8 days, Tuesday, 3 pounds, 5'10", (ran from ship)
Johannes Gunen, Water Leeve Chester PA 5/25/1796, German 32
   3 days, Sunday, 20 dollars, 5'6-7", (was a soldier)
Jonathan Guy, Joseph Pratt Philadelphia City PA 10/13/1763, American 19 joiner A
   11 days, Sunday, 5 pounds, 5'4",
Richard Guy, Alexander Henderson Philadelphia PA 6/11/1777, 15 A
   0.03 pounds,

Johannes Haas, Daniel Lefever Lancaster PA 5/3/1753, German 18
    15 days, Wednesday, 2 pounds, 5'2",
Hans Yerrick Haase, Thomas Jones Bucks PA 3/6/1750, German 24 shoemaker
    3 pounds, short,
Jacob Hackaliver, Abraham Smith Chester PA 7/17/1755, German 22
    9 days, Tuesday, 2 pounds, 5'3",
Jacob Hackaliver, Abraham Smith Chester PA 7/8/1756, German 23 (2nd escape)
    15 days, Wednesday, 1 pound, 5'4",
Magdalene Hackaliver, Abraham Smith Chester PA 7/17/1755, German 29
    9 days, Tuesday, 2 pounds, (wife to Jacob Hackaliver)
Magdalen Hackaliver, Abraham Smith Chester PA 7/8/1756, German 30 (2nd escape)
    15 days, Wednesday, 1 pound, (wife to Jacob Hackiler, has a 5 month child)
John Hackertee, David Miller Philadelphia City PA 10/27/1790, A
    1 dollars, 5',
Edmund Hacket, Patrick O'Hanlon Burlington NJ 8/7/1755, Irish 24 shoemaker
    3 days, Monday, 2 pounds,
John Hackett, Benjamin Thompson Cumberland NJ 8/18/1743, American 28 L
    15 days, Wednesday, 2 pounds, short,
George Hadams, Samuel Lefever Lancaster PA 2/15/1770, English 45 schoolmaster L
    18 days, Sunday,
Andrew Haddock, John Lewis Jr Albermarle VA 5/8/1766, Irish school teacher
    10 pounds, 5'10",
Mary Hadley, James Reynolds Philadelphia City PA gilder 5/30/1771, English
    5 days, Saturday, 6 dollars, 5'4", (arrived 2 days ago)
Benjamin Haethbourn, Robert Parrish Philadelphia City PA carpenter 11/28/1751, Scot 21
    4 days, Sunday, 2.5 pounds, middle,
James Hagan, Benjamin Engle Philadelphia PA 8/18/1748, Irish
    26 days, Saturday, 3 pounds, short,
John Hagan, Robert McKee Chester PA 1/22/1751, Irish
    24 days, Monday, 3 pounds, 5'8",
James Hagen, Peter Rose Burlington NJ 11/24/1737, Irish 35
    10 days, Monday, 2 pounds, tall,
John Hagen, Phillip Alexander Stafford VA 4/22/1742, Irish 25 shoemaker C
    18 days, Sunday, 2 pistoles, tall,
John Hagenbook, Andrew Hertzog Philadelphia City PA 8/24/1785, German 21 tailor
    3 days, Sunday, 12 dollars, 5'5",
John Hager, Frederick Dietz Philadelphia City PA tailor 8/12/1772, 21
    7 days, Thursday, 10 dollars, 5'4",
Michael Hagerty, Henry Miller Cecil MD 5/21/1767, Irish mill-tender
    9 days, Tuesday, 3 pounds, 5'10",
Thomas Haggarty, David Caldwell Lancaster PA ironworks 10/30/1760, Irish 25
    11 days, Sunday, 2 pistoles, 5'6", (lately arrived)
Thomas Haggarty, James Old Lancaster PA ironworks 5/6/1762, Irish 27 (2nd escape)
    17 days, Monday, 3 pounds, middle,
Thomas Haggarty, George Maxton 12/3/1767, Irish 32 (3rd escape)
    8 days, Wednesday, 0.5 pounds,
Catherina Hagges, Robert Harris Anson NC 8/29/1754, German
    118 days, Friday, 2 pistoles, (wife to Herman Hagges)
Herman Hagges, Robert Harris Anson NC 8/29/1754, German 30
    118 days, Friday, 2 pistoles, short,
Thomas Hagins, William Logan Chester PA 2/24/1773, Irish 34
    5 days, Saturday, 2 pounds, 5'10",
Roger Hagon, James Porter Chester PA 8/27/1767, 16
    25 days, Sunday, 4 dollars, 5', (lately arrived)
George Hails, Tobias Rudisley Baltimore MD 8/7/1766, 22 brickmaker C
    18 days, Sunday, 20 dollars, 5'8-9", (lately arrived)
Thomas Haily, William Lynn Fredericksburg VA 10/9/1746, Irish 21
    67 days, Sunday, 2 pistoles, 5'8",
John Hain, Isaac Perkins Kent MD 6/28/1775, English 32 malster
    14 days, Thursday, 2 pounds, 5'11",
Anthony Haines, Jonathan Ellis Gloucester NJ 5/26/1748, A
    2 days, Tuesday, 3 pounds, short,
John Haines, Joseph Ellis Gloucester NJ 4/20/1749, English 30
    7 days, Thursday, 5 pounds, short,
Robert Haines, Michael Byrne Kent MD 11/9/1769, English 22 C
    15 days, Wednesday, 2 pounds, 5'7-8",

Thomas Haines, Josiah Foster Burlington NJ 11/15/1770, 22
    3 days, Monday, 10 dollars, 5'7-8",
Thomas Haines, Adam Poate Philadelphia City PA 1/4/1775, Irish 34
    2 pounds, 5', (arrived last Sept.)
William Hains, Martin Ryerson Hunterdon NJ 5/7/1741,
    2 pounds,
Jeremiah Hairliky, George McDowell Chester PA 11/24/1768, Irish
    21 days, Thursday, 8 dollars, 5'7", (lately arrived)
Daniel Haley, William Maugridge Berks PA 12/2/1762, Irish 18
    41 days, Friday, 3 pounds, 5'7",
Daniel Haley, Michael Christ Berks PA 9/13/1764, Irish 20 (2nd escape)
    11 days, Sunday, 5 pounds, short,
John Haley, William Niven Anne Arundel MD 7/3/1766, English 24 baker
    14 days, Thursday, 5 pounds, 5'4-5",
Patrick Halfpenny, William Pennell Chester PA 5/26/1773, American L
    3 days, Monday, 5 dollars, 5'10",
Archibald Hall, Richard Gill Philadelphia City PA 4/24/1746, Irish
    middle,
George Hall, John Grant Kent MD 4/26/1770, 18 C
    10 days, Monday, 2 pounds, 5'3",
Hugh Hall, John Catheringa tailor 6/14/1750, 18 A
    4 days, Sunday, tall,
Jesse Hall, William Dewees Jr Lancaster PA ironworks 9/14/1774, American 17 L
    12 dollars,
John Hall, John Ingram bricklayer 6/3/1736, English 19
    4 days, Sunday, 1 pound, middle,
John Hall, Caleb Way Jr Chester PA 8/3/1774, 15
    1.5 pounds,
John Hall, Caleb Way Jr Chester PA 9/20/1775, 16 (2nd escape)
    5 days, Saturday, 1.5 pounds, 5'5",
John Hall, Caleb Way Jr Chester PA 6/12/1776, 17 (3rd escape)
    9 days, Tuesday, 1.5 pounds, 5'6-7",
John Hall, Isaac Forsyth Philadelphia City PA 7/19/1780, A
    50 dollars, (apprenticed to a ship)
John Hall, John Hall Baltimore MD 8/16/1764, Irish C
    38 days, Monday, 5 pounds,
Lawrence Hall, James Scott Chester PA 7/30/1752, German 16
    14 days, Thursday, 2.5 pounds, 4'8",
Richard Hall, James Armitage New Castle DE 11/19/1730, Irish 22
    2 pounds, Tuesday, 2.5 pounds, tall,
Thomas Hall, Swan Justis Philadelphia PA 3/19/1754, English 21
    3 days, Monday, 3 pounds, 5'8",
Thomas Hall, Thomas Grubb Lancaster PA 8/8/1754, English 21 (2nd escape)
    3 pounds, 5'8",
William Hall, William Bell Philadelphia City PA 4/16/1752, English
    8 days, Wednesday, middle,
William Hall, Charles Postley Chester PA 11/5/1767, Irish 21 weaver
    6 days, Friday, 5 dollars, 5'5",
William Hall, Cockey Owings Baltimore MD 8/2/1775, English 25 shoemaker
    40 dollars, 5'10",
William Hall, John Alexander Philadelphia City PA shoemaker 7/29/1772, English 24
    7 days, Thursday, 1.5 pounds,
Mary Halls, John Kent MD ironworks 4/22/1762, 25 C
    30 days, Tuesday, 5 pounds, 5',
David Hamar, John Platt Burlington NJ 6/25/1788, American 18 L
    3 days, Sunday, 5 dollars, 5'10",
Charles Hamble, John Smith Chester PA 1/28/1755, Irish 20 weaver
    8 days, Wednesday, 2 pounds, 5'6",
Robert Hambleton, Joseph Burleigh Bucks PA 8/7/1735, 21
    4 days, Sunday, 3 pounds,
William Hamblin, Thomas Lovering Cecil MD 9/21/1758, English 25 C
    2 pistoles, tall,
Gilbert Hamell, Thomas Woods Lancaster PA 7/19/1775, Irish 30
    6 days, Friday, 2 pounds, 5'5",
George Leonard Hamels, Clement Hall Salem NJ 9/18/1755, German
    2.5 pounds, 6',

Alexander Hamilton, Job Haines Chester PA 10/25/1764, Scot 17
    11 days, Sunday, 2 pounds, 5'4",
Alexander Hamilton, James McMullen York PA 11/6/1766, Irish 35 soldier
    14 days, Thursday, 3 pounds, (arrived last Sept., has been in the colonies before)
Catherine Hamilton, Richard Gay Cecil MD 9/23/1762, Irish (with 7 month old child)
    40 days, Saturday, 4 dollars,
Francis Hamilton, Charles Williams Bucks PA 7/7/1748, 19 A
    1.5 pounds, 6',
George Hamilton, George May Gloucester NJ 8/29/1754, Scot
    5 days, Saturday, 6 pounds, middle,
James Hamilton, Rachael Graydon 1/17/1765, Irish 18
    3 days, Monday, 2 dollars, 5'6", (lately arrived)
James Hamilton, John Hill Bucks PA 1/1/1761, Irish 27
    4 days, Sunday, 3 pounds, 5'7",
John Hamilton, Joseph Kaighin Gloucester NJ 5/31/1744, Irish 15
    5 days, Saturday, 2 pounds,
John Hamilton, Peter Kleinott Cecil MD 6/4/1761, 26
    25 days, Sunday, 3 pounds, 5'6",
John Hamilton, Stephen Anderson Chester PA 6/26/1766, Irish 34
    11 days, Sunday, 3 pounds, 5'9",
John Hamilton, Henry Caldwell Chester PA 3/10/1752, Irish 22 L
    1.5 pounds, middle,
Patrick Hamilton, Samuel Hawthorn Lancaster PA 6/2/1768, Irish 27
    25 days, Sunday, 1 pound, 5'3",
Patrick Hamilton, Samuel Kennedy Chester PA doctor 7/9/1772, Irish 17
    33 days, Saturday, 4 dollars, 5'6", (arrived June 13th last)
Robert Hamilton, David Wiley Chester PA 4/8/1742, Irish 24
    4 days, Sunday, 2 pounds, middle,
Robert Hamilton, Joseph Mitchell Philadelphia City PA merchant 3/20/1766, Scot 30 shoemaker
    end of Oct., 6 dollars, short,
William Hamilton, John Brandon Lancaster PA 1/29/1745, Irish 20
    7 days, Thursday, 1 pound, short,
William Hamilton, Charles Porter Cecil MD 11/25/1772, Irish 26
    10 days, Monday, 5 pounds, 5'8-9", (arrived June, 1771)
John Hammel, Samuel Woods Lancaster PA 4/21/1773, Scot 20 (2nd escape)
    13 days, Friday, 5 pounds, 5'9-10",
John Hammel, Samuel Woods Lancaster PA 12/2/1772, Scot 20
    19 days, Saturday, 3 pounds, 5'9-10",
David Hammer, John James Salem NJ 9/23/1789, 19 A
    4 dollars, 5'8-9",
John Hammer, John Gill Gloucester NJ 12/30/1772, English 20
    4 days, Sunday, 2 pounds, 5'7-8",
Henry Hamrick, Peter Wilterberger Philadelphia City PA shoemaker 1/13/1763, German 18 A
    128 days, Tuesday, 5 pounds, 5', (was advertised in Oct. in German newspapers)
George Han, John Rup Philadelphia City PA 4/6/1774, German shoemaker
    4 days, Sunday, 5 pounds, 5'2",
James Hand, John Ware Cumberland NJ 3/23/1796, 16
    8 dollars,
Silas Hand, James Young Salem NJ 8/26/1762,
    2 pounds, 5'9",
Thomas Handfield, John Howard Anne Arundel MD 10/28/1742, 19 C
    32 days, Sunday, 3 pounds,
John Handley, George MacKrill Lancaster PA 8/30/1753, Irish 19 (ran 4 times before)
    5 days, Saturday, 2 pounds, 5'6",
John Handley, George MacKrill Lancaster PA 12/20/1753, Irish 20 (2nd escape)
    7 days, Thursday, 2 pounds,
Richard Handley, John Roberts Salem NJ 7/7/1768, Irish 19
    6 days, Friday, 3 pounds, short,
Richard Handley, John Roberts Salem NJ 6/6/1771, Irish 22 (2nd escape)
    10 days, Monday, 3 pounds, 5'4",
Thomas Handley, Nicholas Dillon Bucks PA 2/23/1764, Irish 25
    14 days, Thursday, 5 pounds, 5'5", (arrived 6 weeks ago)
William Handley, John Fitz Dorchester MD 11/15/1750, English cooper
    43 days, Wednesday, middle,
Valentine Handlin, Richard McCarthy Philadelphia City PA ship captain 12/4/1740, Irish 30
    2 days, Tuesday, 1 pound, (ran from ship)

Patrick Hanes, Lawrence Howard Chester PA 9/5/1754, Irish
  2 days, Tuesday, 2 pounds, 5'6",
Polly Hanes, John McCalla Philadelphia City PA 10/30/1766, Irish 19
  1.5 pounds, short,
Thomas Haney, Joseph Durborow shipwright 4/28/1737, Irish 18
  2 days, Tuesday, 1.5 pounds, middle,
John Hanglin, Patrick Porter Burlington NJ 10/11/1753, Irish 26 L
  11 days, Sunday, 3 pounds, middle, (arrived 8 years ago)
William Hanker, Thomas Sligh Baltimore MD 6/10/1742, English 30
  11 days, Sunday, 5 pounds,
Elizabeth Hanlen, John Tobert 10/23/1766, English
  1.5 pounds, (has 4 years to serve)
Dudley Hanley, James Moore New Castle DE 9/19/1751, Irish 20
  3 days, Monday, 2 pounds,
Dudley Hanley, Thomas Hastings Lancaster PA 7/30/1752, Irish 21 (2nd escape)
  21 days, Thursday, middle,
James Hannah, Robert Young Philadelphia City PA ship captain 7/30/1747, Irish
  5 days, Saturday, 2 pounds, 5'8",
James Hannah, Joseph Hutchinson Lancaster PA 5/15/1776, 18
  10 days, Monday, 8 dollars, 5'7-8",
William Hannah, Hugh Glasford Cecil MD 12/13/1764, Irish 39
  15 days, Wednesday, 3 pounds, 5'8",
William Hannah, John McCool Lancaster PA 6/19/1766, Irish 44 (2nd escape)
  278 days, Saturday, 3 pounds, 5'8-9",
Richard Hannaly, Richard Hacket Salem NJ 6/4/1767, Irish 20
  3 days, Monday, 2 pounds, short,
Daniel Hannan, Samuel Allen Chester PA 8/23/1750, Irish
  9 days, Tuesday, 2 pounds, 5'10", (lately arrived)
Christopher Hanns, William Top Philadelphia City PA 8/24/1769, English 26 painter
  9 days, Tuesday, 2.5 pounds, 5',
Thomas Hanraty, James Maxwell Chester PA 8/28/1746, Irish 19
  22 days, Wednesday, 2 pounds, short,
Matthias Hanson, Alexander Perry Philadelphia City PA 10/22/1783, 21 soapboiler A
  0.32 dollars,
Thomas Hanson, Peter Hall 5/12/1743, American 24 blacksmith L
  17 days, Monday, 1.5 pounds, short,
Thomas Hanway, William Parrish Baltimore MD 10/25/1770, Irish 30 C
  11 days, Sunday, 2.5 pounds, 5'5",
Adrian Haplitzel, Nicholas Hower Cecil MD 11/30/1769, Swiss 21 hatter
  4 pounds, 5',
Edward Harah, William McPherson Lancaster PA 8/16/1770, Irish 15
  11 days, Sunday, 2 pounds, (arrived this year)
Robert Hardey, Charles Ridgely Jr Baltimore MD ironworks 8/10/1774, English C
  56 days, Thursday, 50 dollars, 5'9",
John Harding, Widow Wragg Philadelphia City PA 8/5/1731, 30 butcher
  8 days, Wednesday, 1 pound, short,
John Harding, Jonathan Gilbert Chester PA 6/2/1763, English 40 L
  2 pounds, 5'4",
Simon Harding, Joseph Helm Frederick MD 7/1/1756, American 15 L
  15 days, Wednesday, 4 pounds,
William Harding, Richard Jones Baltimore MD 1/13/1763, English 30 C
  32 days, Sunday, 2 pounds, 5'9",
Coles Hardwick, Alexander Parker Philadelphia City PA 8/24/1749, English 23
  4 days, Sunday, 3 pounds, middle,
John Hardy, Charles Ridgely Jr Baltimore MD ironworks 8/13/1767, English 38 C
  11 days, Sunday, 2 pounds, 5'9",
John Harford, Thomas Harrison Philadelphia City PA 11/28/1765, Irish tailor
  25 days, Sunday, 8 dollars, 5'7",
John Harken, James Henderson Chester PA 11/16/1774, Irish
  4 days, Sunday, 2 pounds, 5'6",
Jonathan Harker, Benjamin Bickerton Philadelphia City PA 5/30/1781, 14 shoemaker A
  4 days, Saturday, 0.2 pounds, 4'8-9",
Dennis Harkin, John Byars Lancaster PA shoemaker 4/17/1755, 19
  4 days, Sunday, 3 pounds, 5'9",
James Harley, John Herthorn Lancaster PA 9/13/1770, Irish 22
  59 days, Monday, 3 pounds, 5'6",

William Harley, George Dowllenger Lancaster PA 10/2/1746, Irish 19
    21 days, Thursday, 2 pounds, 5'9",
William Harley, William Bell Philadelphia City PA 1/28/1752, English coachmaker
    last Dec., 7 pounds,
Manus Harly, John Edwards New Castle DE 2/26/1751, Irish 25
    17 days, Monday, 3 pounds, short,
Jacob Harman, John Tiller Lancaster PA 4/20/1774, German 30
    11 days, Sunday, 2.5 pounds,
Thomas Harnet, Charles Ridgely Jr Baltimore MD ironworks 11/23/1774, Irish 25 L
    10 dollars, 5'5-6",
Jacob Harper, Christopher Binks Philadelphia City PA 8/7/1776, German-American 18 A
    2 dollars, 5'6",
William Harper, James Smith Chester PA 5/8/1776, Irish 20
    16 days, Tuesday, 4 dollars, 5'7",
William Harper, Charles Morgan Kent MD 4/4/1771, English 21 C
    13 days, Friday, 2 pounds, 5'4", (arrived 9 months ago)
Conrad Harr, Luke Nethermark Philadelphia PA 4/17/1755, German
    11 days, Sunday, 3 pounds, 6',
Samuel Ponsonby Harrington, Samuel Lafever Lancaster PA 8/22/1771, Irish 40 wool comber
    2 pounds, 5'4-5",
Barney Couzens Harris, Richard Dennis New Castle DE 12/17/1761, 17 A
    57 days, Wednesday, 2.5 pounds,
George Harris, Jonathan Peasley Philadelphia City PA chocolate-grinder 3/26/1741, English 26
    1 days, Wednesday, 2 pounds, short,
Jesse Harris, Jeremiah Reese Cumberland PA 6/9/1768, Irish 30
    21 days, Thursday, 3 pounds, 5'6",
John Harris, Humphrey Brooke King William VA 9/21/1738, Welsh
    68 days, Saturday,
John Harris, John England Chester PA 7/5/1775, Irish 20 shoemaker
    9 days, Tuesday, 4 dollars, 5'3-4",
John Harris, John Moore Kent MD 9/6/1770, English (ran before) L
    5 pounds,
Joseph Harris, Jacob Shinn Burlington NJ 7/31/1776, English 16
    33 days, Saturday, 4 dollars, 5',
Robert Harris, Peter Bard Philadelphia City PA 1/21/1746, 40 sailor L
    45 days, Monday, 3 pounds, tall,
Samuel Harris, John Beaumont Jr Bucks PA 6/21/1780, 18
    15 days, Tuesday, 200 dollars,
Samuel Harris, John Richy Philadelphia City PA ship captain 6/21/1759, 16 A
    3 pounds,
Thomas Harris, Robert Valentine Chester PA 9/9/1772, English 20
    9 days, Tuesday, 2 pounds, 5'5",
James Harrison, Andrew Philler Philadelphia City PA 12/20/1775, Irish 19 shoemaker A
    2 pounds, 5'6-7", (arrived 2 years ago)
John Harrison, Henry Miller Bucks PA 6/28/1786, 18 A
    2 dollars, short,
Philip Harrison, William Kendall Philadelphia PA 8/16/1750, Irish 23
    9 days, Tuesday, 3 pounds, 5'5",
Philip Harrison, George Monro New Castle DE 2/5/1756, Irish 28 (2nd escape)
    6 days, Firday, 1.5 pounds,
William Harrison, David Logan Frederick VA 6/6/1751, Irish 28 C
    15 days, Wednesday, 2 pistoles,
George Hart, Paul Livezy Philadelphia PA 5/28/1788, 20
    9 days, Monday, 16 continental paper dollars,
Patrick Hart, Thomas Tobin New Castle DE 4/2/1772, 30
    32 days, Sunday, 8 dollars, 5'6-7",
William Hart, William Dames Kent MD 8/14/1746, Irish 26 C
    10 days, Monday, 2 pounds, middle,
Patrick Hartin, Joseph Newlin New Castle DE 9/16/1762, Irish 16
    1.5 pounds, 5',
Agnes Hartman, John Moor Philadelphia PA 3/6/1776, German 25
    25 days, Sunday, 2 dollars, 5'2-3",
John Hartman, Matthias Sheifele Montgomery PA ironworks 7/27/1785, German 20 stockingweaver
    10 days, Sunday, 8 dollars, 5'6",
Edward Harvey, Michael Branin Burlington NJ 4/29/1756, English
    3 days, Monday, 2 pounds, 5'4",

John Harvey, John De Nyce Philadelphia City PA 2/4/1752, English
    4 days, Sunday, 2 pounds, short, (use to the sea)
Patrick Harvey, Francis Morris Chester PA 1/15/1756, Irish 20 blacksmith
    25 days, Sunday, 5 pounds, short,
Thomas Harvey, Alexander Hill Salem NJ 4/27/1774, Irish 20
    2 days, Tuesday, 5 pounds,
Thomas Harvey, William Bowers Chester PA 6/16/1773, English 28 joiner
    16 days, Tuesday, 5 pounds, 5'6",
William Haselton, Benjamin Howell Chester PA 12/13/1759, collier
    26 days, Saturday, 1 pound, 5'5",
George Haslop, William Ferguson Chester PA 4/28/1757, Irish 25
    12 days, 1 pound, 5'5",
John Jacob Hass, John Taylor Lancaster PA 6/12/1755, German 22
    11 days, Sunday, 2 pounds, 5',
Michael Hatchet, James Webb Lancaster PA 6/26/1776, Irish 18
    7 days, Thursday, 2 pounds, 5'5",
William Hatton, William Baxter Cecil MD 9/20/1764, English 25 stocking-weaver C
    16 days, Tuesday, 5 pounds, 5'6", (arrived June 1764)
William Hatton, Francis Phillips Baltimore MD ironworks 10/1/1767, English 28 weaver (2nd esc) C
    9 days, Tuesday, 2 pounds, 5'6-7",
William Hatton, Francis Phillips Baltimore MD ironworks 9/15/1768, English 29 weaver (3rd esc) C
    16 days, Tuesday, 3 pounds, 5'6-7",
William Hatton, Francis Phillips Baltimore MD ironworks 7/6/1769, English 30 weaver (4th esc) C
    51 days, Tuesday, 3 pounds, 5'6-7",
Christopher Hauffe, James Comings Bucks PA 10/12/1749, German 22
    5 days, Saturday, 2.5 pounds,
Regina Hauffe, James Comings Bucks PA 10/12/1749, German
    5 days, Saturday, 2.5 pounds,
Charles Haughans, James Paul Jr Bucks PA 6/16/1773, Irish 20
    10 days, Monday, 3 dollars, 5'3-4",
Michael Haun, Benjamin Levering Philadelphia PA 8/23/1753, German 19 tailor
    1 pound,
John Haverbach, Francis Smith Burlington NJ 6/20/1734, German 40 soldier
    2 days, Tuesday, 2 pounds, middle,
William Hawk, John Shipley Anne Arundel MD 12/9/1772, C
    30 days, Tuesday, 2 pounds, 5'7-8",
John Hawkerday, Michael Earle Cecil MD 4/17/1766, English 40 (ran before) C
    8 days, Wednesday, 5 pounds,
James Hawkins, Edward Costolow Kent MD 3/28/1765, English butcher C
    2 pistoles, 5'10", (arrived Jan. 1765)
John Hawkins, Amos Garrett Baltimore MD 5/14/1747, Irish 28 (ran before)
    10 days, Monday, 5 pounds, short, (arrived some time ago)
John Hawkins, William Sellers 2/18/1768, 19 printer A
    11 days, Sunday, 3 pounds, 5',
Stephen Hawkins, Joseph Watkins Anne Arundel MD ironworks 7/22/1762, English 27 C
    7 days, Thursday, 4 pounds, 6', (arrived January 1762)
Stephen Hawkins, Joseph Watkins Anne Arundel MD ironworks 9/23/1762, English 27 (2nd esc) C
    4 pounds, 6', (arrived Feb. 1762)
John Hawsford, John Dodd New Castle DE 10/13/1743, Irish 25
    47 days, Saturday, 3 pounds, short,
William Hawthorn, Edmund Kean Cumberland PA 8/28/1776, Irish 25 shoemaker
    10 days, Monday, 8 dollars, 6', (was a soldier)
James Hay, Goerge Mifflin 9/25/1776, Scot 17
    early Aug., 8 dollars, 5'3",
James Hayes, William Williams Bucks PA 11/30/1749, Irish 20
    7 days, Thursday, 3 pounds, middle,
John Hayes, William Dallam Baltimore MD 5/21/1741, Irish 26
    18 days, Sunday, 8 Maryland pounds, middle,
John Haygen, Isaac Baker Lancaster PA 7/14/1743, Irish
    31 days, Monday, 2 pounds, short,
Michael Hayne, R. Grisham Kent MD 7/6/1769, German 32 tailor C
    10 days, Monday, 10 dollars, 5'7",
George Haynes, William Harris Philadelphia City PA ship captain 12/6/1733, English 28 cooper
    2 pounds, (ran from ship Vigor from Bristol)
Eleanor Hays, Joseph Hobb Sr Anne Arundel MD 8/30/1775, Irish 18
    43 days, Wednesday, 10 dollars, 5'3-4",

John Hays, Joseph Hobb Sr Anne Arundel MD 8/30/1775, Irish 25 shoemaker
    43 days, Wednesday, 10 dollars, 5'10",
John Hazely, Peter Bard Philadelphia City PA 1/21/1746, 30 sailor L
    45 days, Monday, 3 pounds, tall,
Robert Hazlit, William Bywater Philadelphia City PA joiner 9/13/1759, 18 A
    46 days, Sunday, 2 pounds,
Andrew Head, Benjamin Morgan Gloucester NJ 1/28/1752, German 22
    3 pounds, tall,
Thomas Head, Charles Reilles Chester PA 3/15/1748, Irish 22
    19 days, Saturday, 5 pounds,
John Headley, Hugh Mearns Bucks PA 9/27/1753, 17
    8 days, Wednesday, 2 pounds, short,
Daniel Headon, John Cox Burlington NJ 9/26/1751, Irish 29 blacksmith
    11 days, Sunday, 2 pounds, 5'7",
Cornelius Healy, George Evans New Castle DE 7/23/1761, Irish soldier
    2 pounds, 5'8",
Sarah Heames, William Bannister Baltimore MD 9/29/1768, English 22
    22 days, Wednesday, 3 pounds, 5'4", (enticed away by sailors)
Mary Heany, James Whitall Gloucester NJ 11/25/1762, Irish
    1.5 pounds, short,
Samuel Heap, Stephen Onion Baltimore MD ironworks 3/17/1752, 25 carpenter
    3 pounds, middle,
Richard Heaslip, Abraham Taylor Chester PA 8/8/1771, Irish 21
    2 days, Tuesday, 2 pounds, 5'8",
Richard Heaslip, John Taylor Chester PA 12/23/1772, Irish 22 (2nd escape)
    5 days, Saturday, 2 pounds, 5'8",
William Heaton, John Hutchinson Bucks PA 9/21/1749, 20 A
    4 days, Sunday, 5 pounds, 5'5", (has 18 months to serve)
Daniel Heavey, Larkin Randall Baltimore MD 11/8/1770, Irish 26 whitesmith
    21 days, Thursday, 10 dollars, 5'8-9",
John Hedford, White & Taylor 5/14/1730,
    2 pounds, middle,
Conrad Heidi, Frederick Bicking Montgomery PA papermaker 12/17/1794, German 22
    6 dollars, 5'5-6",
Christian Heidiach, William Curlis Jr Burlington NJ 11/17/1773, German
    3 days, Monday, 6 dollars, (lately arrived)
Jacob Heighford, George Sellers Salem NJ 7/9/1794, 18 blacksmith A
    21 days, Wednesday, 0.03 pounds, 5'6-7",
Christianus Heisterberg, William Nicholson NY ship chandler 8/16/1753, German 30 limer
    11 days, Sunday, 5 pounds, 5'6",
Francis Henderson, John Potts Philadelphia PA 5/28/1747, Irish 24
    9 days, Tuesday, 3 pounds, tall,
James Henderson, John Craig Bucks PA 6/8/1769, Irish 26 school teacher
    2 pounds, 5'5",
John Henderson, James Steward Chester PA 8/17/1774, 18 wheelwright A
    3 days, Monday, 2.5 pounds,
John Henderson, Samuel Simpson Philadelphia City PA 4/24/1760, American 18 cordwainer A
    11 days, Sunday, 2 pounds, 5'4",
Samuel Henderson, James Bennet Chester PA 4/14/1737, Irish 20 tailor
    14 days, Thursday, 2 pounds, short,
William Henderson, Nathaniel Waller Somerset MD 3/27/1740, American gaol sale L
    45 days, Monday, 5 pounds,
Edward Hendrick, Benjamin Heritage Burlington NJ 8/4/1748, Irish 25
    2 days, Tuesday, 1.5 pounds, 5'9",
Thomas Hendrick, Joseph Burrough Gloucester NJ 1/17/1776, Irish 20
    36 days, Wednesday, 1 dollars, 5'9-10",
Darby Hendry, James Wilson Chester PA 8/30/1750, Irish
    3 days, Monday, 1.5 pounds, 5'10",
John Hendry, George House Philadelphia City PA 11/20/1735, Irish 22 shoemaker
    4 days, Sunday, 5 pounds, middle,
Margaret Henley, Nathan Lewis Chester PA 11/22/1750, Irish 30
    8 days, Wednesday, 1.5 pounds, (lately arrived)
John Hennen, Henry Troth New Castle DE 8/15/1754, Irish spinning-wheel-maker
    4 days, Sunday, 1.5 pounds, middle,
Jacob Henney, Rynear Halloway Philadelphia PA 3/10/1779, German 18
    6 days, Thursday, 8 dollars in silver, 5'8",

Johan Henry Henning, Samuel Weatherill Jr Philadelphia PA 7/4/1787, German 45 tallow-chandler
  8 dollars, (arrived last fall)
Darby Henry, James Wilson Chester PA 11/9/1749, Irish 26
  3 days, Monday, 3 pounds, 5'9",
Darby Henry, James Wilson Chester PA 4/26/1750, Irish 26 (2nd escape)
  5 days, Saturday, 3 pounds, 5'10",
George Henry, Richard McWilliam New Castle DE 9/2/1772, Irish 20 weaver
  mid-June, 4 dollars, 5'3",
George Henry, Richard McWilliam New Castle DE 6/2/1773, Irish 21 weaver (2nd escape)
  4 dollars, 5'2-3",
George Henry, Richard McWilliam New Castle DE 9/1/1773, Irish 21 weaver (3rd escape)
  8 days, Wednesday, 4 dollars, 5'5", (arrived 3 years ago)
James Henry, William Ramsey Bucks PA 5/11/1785, Irish 20
  4 days, Saturday, 3 pounds, 5'7-8",
John Henry, John Purdon Philadelphia City PA 11/1/1764, Irish
  11 days, Sunday, 8 dollars, (lately arrived, but has been in the colonies before)
John Henry, Cromwell McVity Lancaster PA 6/8/1774, Irish 30
  10 days, Monday, 2 pounds, 5'6-7",
Thomas Henry, Heslop & Blair Fredericksburg VA 1/30/1772, English schoolmaster C
  76 days, Friday, 15 dollars,
William Hensley, Jacob Binder Philadelphia City PA 1/15/1783, 18 comb-maker A
  14 days, Wednesday, 4 dollars, middle-tall,
Benjamin Hensly, Henry Callister Talbot MD 1/29/1756, English barber C
  87 days, Monday, 5 pounds,
Conrad Hents, Stephen Onion Baltimore MD ironworks 7/4/1754, German 23
  32 days, Sunday, 3 pounds, middle,
George Hepburn, John Houlton Chester PA 6/10/1756, Irish 20
  11 days, Sunday, 2 pounds, middle,
John Heran, Conrad Smith Baltimore MD 6/12/1766, bricklayer gaol sale L
  2 pounds, 5'9",
Christopher Hergesheimer, Matthew Potter Jr Philadelphia PA 7/19/1759, German 19 blacksmith A
  6 days, Friday, 2 pounds, middle,
Daniel Herkins, Jacob Wheeler Baltimore MD 8/16/1770, Irish 25 ship carpenter
  11 days, Sunday, 2.5 pounds, 5'8-9",
John George Herman, Philip Moses 3/19/1767,
  11 days, Sunday, 8 dollars,
Samuel Hermon, Philip Broudrike Lancaster PA 4/2/1767, German 27 shoemaker
  3 pounds, 5'6",
Daniel Hern, John Aubrey Lancaster PA 4/8/1742, Irish C
  2 pounds, middle,
Richard Hern, John Johnston Lancaster PA 6/14/1753, English 19
  2 pounds, 5'8",
Lawrence Herne, Nicholas Skull Philadelphia City PA innholder 12/23/1729, 22
  18 days, Sunday, 2 pounds, short,
John Adam Herner, David Davis Chester PA 5/9/1754, German 20
  1.5 pounds, 5',
John Heron, Conrad Smith Baltimore MD 3/13/1766, Irish 26 mason
  17 days, Monday, 2.5 pounds, 5'9",
William Herrogan, Benjamin Debow Salem NJ 1/23/1772, Irish 25
  10 days, Monday, 8 dollars, 5'7-8", (arrived in 1769)
Jacob Heselgaser, Joseph Inslee Bucks PA 10/31/1751, German 21
  10 days, Monday, 3 pounds, middle,
David Hesschin, Henry Miller Augusta VA 3/30/1791, Irish 22 teacher
  191 days, Monday, 40 dollars, 5'5-6", (arrived Nov. 1786)
Paul Hetchelbery, John Simpers Cecil MD 4/29/1762, German
  3 pounds,
Joseph Hewes, Christopher Hansman Philadelphia City PA 7/31/1766, English-American 20 tailor L
  3 pounds, 5'6",
William Hewes, Henry Wall New Castle DE 2/19/1767, American 21 L
  40 days, Saturday, 1.5 pounds, 5'4",
Benajab Hewit, Aaron Learning Cape May NJ 3/15/1775, 19 A
  35 days, Thursday, 1.5 pounds,
Thomas Hewitt, Robert Willmott Baltimore MD ironworks 7/19/1770, English 27 bookbinder
  10 days, Monday, 10 pounds, 5'6",
Edward Hewke, James Smith Frederick MD 10/25/1775, 45 butcher
  14 days, Thursday, 2 pounds, 5'10",

Sarah Hews, Eleanor Gray Cumberland PA 10/14/1762, Irish
    55 days, Friday, 3 pounds,
William Heyward, John Ensor Jr Baltimore MD 4/25/1765, English 25 shoemaker C
    10 pounds, 5'8",
John Hickay, David Rees Chester PA 6/25/1741, blacksmith
    1.5 pounds, (middle-aged)
Francis Hickey, Peter Bard Philadelphia City PA 1/21/1746, 24 sailor L
    45 days, Monday, 3 pounds, short,
Richard Hickham, Thomas Shaw Philadelphia PA 4/7/1784, 16
    3 days, Sunday, 6 dollars,
John Hickins, Ephraim Howard Anne Arundel MD 7/28/1773, C
    9 days, Tuesday, 6 pounds, 5'8", (arrived 6 years ago)
Katherine Hickleson, Joseph Brown Chester PA 10/30/1760, German 30
    47 days, Saturday, 1.5 pounds, middle, (has 2 years and 8 months to serve)
James Hickman, Alexander Wells Baltimore MD 7/7/1773, English 22 C
    17 days, Monday, 5 pounds, 5'7-8",
Benjamin Hicks, Henry Smith Philadelphia PA 4/2/1741, English 26
    about 2.5 months ago, 3 pistoles,
Edward Hicks, Thomas Baker Gloucester NJ 11/9/1758, American L
    17 days, Monday, 3 pounds, 5',
Elias Hicks, John Jones Baltimore MD 4/5/1764, 25 shoemaker C
    about 16 days, 2.5 pounds,
John Higginbothom, Thomas Reed Charles VA 12/4/1740, 60 cooper
    5 pounds,
Barnaby Higgins, Thomas Brook St Mary's MD 7/13/1738, Irish 25 joiner
    112 days, Saturday, 5 Maryland pounds, short,
Edward Higgins, James McClasky Chester PA 6/24/1762, English 17
    5 days, Saturday, 2 pounds, 5',
Edward Higgins, Abraham Stout Bucks PA 8/19/1772, English 27 (2nd escape)
    11 days, Sunday, 2 pounds, 5'9",
John Higgins, Michael McGuire Chester PA 6/8/1732, worstedcomber
    54 days, Saturday, 3 pounds, middle,
William Higgins, Edward Wright Queen Anne's MD 6/16/1757, English 36 miller C
    15 days, Wednesday, 1.5 pounds, 5'6",
Anthony Hill, Alexander Hickinbottom Philadelphia City PA bricklayer 11/18/1742,
    1 pound, middle,
Edward Hill, Leonard Vandegrift Bucks PA 1/23/1750, hired L
    2 pounds,
James Hill, Joseph Claypoole Philadelphia City PA hatter 9/12/1771, English 20 shoemaker
    10 days, Monday, 10 dollars, 5'6",
John Hill, Thomas Cookson Lancaster PA 9/6/1750, English 30 dyer
    3 pounds, middle, (arrived 2 months ago)
John Hill, Matthew Ridley Baltimore MD 8/30/1770, 26 glassmaker C
    9 days, Tuesday, 4 pounds, 5'4", (lately arrived)
John Hilyear, Edward Norwood Baltimore MD 11/21/1771, 30 C
    67 days, Sunday, 3 pounds, 5'6-7",
Benjamin Himes, John McCracken Chester PA 1/25/1792, 18 A
    6 dollars, 5'8-9", (relatives live nearby)
Thomas Hinds, John Love Baltimore MD 11/28/1754, English 23 C
    18 days, Sunday, 1.33 pounds, 5'7", (arrived in 1752)
James Hines, Daniel Ryan Philadelphia PA 10/6/1768, Irish 25
    4 days, Sunday, 4 dollars, middle,
John Hines, John Wilson Bucks PA 11/15/1750, Irish 18 plaisterer
    9 days, Tuesday, 2 pistoles, middle,
Nathaniel Hines, John Barratt Queen Anne's MD 6/3/1762, American carpenter L
    2 pounds, 6',
Patrick Hines, Lawrence Howard Chester PA 4/8/1756, Irish 20
    10 days, Monday, 2 pistoles, 5'7",
Thomas Hines, Samuel Purviance Philadelphia City PA 3/2/1774, English 15
    3 days, Monday, 4 dollars,
Richard Hinkings, Samuel Jones Lancaster PA 5/1/1766, English
    18 days, Sunday, 5 pounds, 5'9",
John Hinson, Stephen Talman Monmouth NJ doctor 9/11/1755, American 30 L
    10 days, Monday, 3 pounds, 5'11",
William Hipit, Daniel Reese Baltimore MD 7/11/1771, English 40 collier L
    37 days, Tuesday, 6 pounds, 5'10-11",

John Hiron, Hugh Parke Kent DE hatter 1/14/1768, 20 A
  2 pounds,
Eberhard Hirshman, John Odenheimer Philadelphia City PA 11/19/1767, German 22
  23 days, Tuesday, 10 pounds,
William Hockly, James Shirley Philadelphia City PA ship captain 6/13/1754, 35 sawyer
  3 days, Monday, 0.75 pounds, 5'6",
Thomas Hodgson, William Sadler 7/28/1784, English 25
  3 days, Sunday, 12 dollars, 5'7", (lately arrived)
George Hoffman, George Mayer Philadelphia City PA 3/24/1790, German 28 baker
  3 days, Sunday, 4 dollars, 5',
James Hoffman, John Lloyd Salem NJ 12/27/1764, American 17 shoemaker A
  4 pounds, 5'7",
Margaret Hoffman, John Sibbald Philadelphia City PA 9/11/1766, German 16
  10 days, Monday, 1.5 pounds, 5',
Dominick Hogan, Benjamin Tasker Baltimore MD ironworks 7/11/1745, Irish C
  16 days, Tuesday, 2 pounds, short, (wears an iron collar)
John Hogan, William Foster Lancaster PA 4/16/1752, Irish 18 clerk
  3 pounds, 5'3",
John Hogan, James Anderson Lancaster PA 7/5/1753, Irish 19 clerk (2nd escape)
  11 days, Sunday, 3 pounds, short,
John Hogan, John Anderson Lancaster PA 4/18/1754, Irish 20 clerk (3rd escape)
  2 pounds, 5'7",
William Hogan, Alexander Alexander Philadelphia City PA 7/5/1750, Irish blacksmith
  2 pounds, 5'10",
George Hogg, Joseph Armit 10/30/1740, 19 A
  11 days, Sunday, 2 pounds, middle,
Richard Holand, Zachariah Robins Monmouth NJ 8/8/1745, English 20 shoemaker
  9 days, Tuesday, 10 pounds,
William Holand, Thomas Maule Philadelphia City PA joiner 4/17/1746, 16 A
  5 days, Saturday, 1 pound,
Thomas Holburn, David Beaty Chester PA 6/8/1769, Irish 25
  4 days, Sunday, 2 pounds, 5'8-9",
Edward Holder, John Footman Baltimore MD 10/18/1770, English 40 (been transported before) C
  101 days, Monday, 1 pound, 6',
John Holder, Thomas Stedham Caroline MD 11/30/1774, 16
  2 pounds, 5',
John Holeger, Augustine Boyer Jr Kent MD 4/10/1760, American soldier hired L
  12 days, Saturday, 5 pounds, 6',
John Hollace, John Garret Chester PA 7/4/1765, 18 A
  10 days, Monday, 1 pound, 5'6",
John Hollahon, John Penington Bucks PA 6/1/1769, Irish
  18 days, Sunday, 4 dollars, 5'2",
Arthur Holland, Richard Nolan Hunterdon NJ 10/6/1737, Irish 30
  11 days, Sunday, 1.5 pounds, tall,
John Holland, Joseph Brubacher Lancaster PA 10/10/1765, German
  16 days, Tuesday, 3 pounds, 5'5",
Joseph Holland, Richard Croxall Baltimore MD ironworks 10/23/1760, English C
  19 days, Saturday, 5 pounds,
Richard Holland, Benjamin Kendall Philadelphia City PA 1/31/1749, English 23 shoemaker
  1 days, Wednesday, 5 pounds, 5'4",
Timothy Holland, John Brown Philadelphia City PA 12/20/1775, Irish 25
  11 days, Sunday, 5'6", (ran from ship)
Jacob Holler, Edward Tonkin Burlington NJ 6/6/1765, German
  11 days, Sunday, 5 pistoles, 5'7",
Charles Hollingsworth, William Drake Salem NJ 9/18/1776, 15
  17 days, Monday, 6 dollars, short,
Hannah Hollington, John Douglas MD ironworks 10/3/1745, Irish 16
  5 days, Saturday, 1 pound, (lately arrived)
Joseph Holmes, Abechnegs Botfield Talbot MD 6/13/1754, English 31 C
  24 days, Monday, 3 pounds, middle, (arrived in 1753)
Samuel Holmes, William Taite Northumberland VA 5/30/1765, English tailor C
  29 days, Wednesday, 3 pounds, 6',
Samuel Holmes, William Taite Northumberland VA 5/15/1766, English tailor (2nd escape) C
  5 pounds, 5'5",
Samuel Holmes, William Taite Northumberland VA 7/17/1766, English tailor (3rd escape) C
  5 pounds,

Stephen Holmes, John Byars Lancaster PA shoemaker 3/2/1769, Irish carpenter
  17 days, Monday, 2 pounds, 5'6",
Henry Holms, John Brown Philadelphia City PA 6/11/1772, Irish 19
  1 pound, 5'7-8",
Thomas Holse, John Patton Berks PA ironworks 7/25/1765, German 28
  17 days, Monday, 3 pounds, 5'9",
John Holt, John Thomas Chester PA 11/22/1739, 23
  2 pounds, middle,
Thomas Holt, Stephen Armit Philadelphia City PA joiner 1/11/1733, Irish 21 joiner
  17 days, Monday, 1 pound,
Thomas Holt, James Baldwin Philadelphia PA 4/23/1741, Irish 29 joiner (2nd escape)
  3 days, Monday, 1 pound, middle,
Stephen Holtstyn, Andrew Campbell Orange VA 6/17/1742, 33
  tall,
John Homer, Thomas Willis Chester PA 3/7/1732, shoemaker
  6 days, Friday, 1 pound, short,
John Hooper, John Jones Philadelphia PA 10/20/1737, English 21
  9 days, Tuesday, 2 pounds, middle,
Daniel Hooseman, John Potts 6/17/1756, German
  8 days, Wednesday, 1.5 pounds,
Hopkins Hopkin, William Lux Baltimore MD 4/13/1774, 25 shoemaker C
  7.5 pounds,
John Hopkins, George Fleming Philadelphia City PA 11/1/1733, English cook
  2 pounds, (ran from ship)
John Hopkins, John Guest Philadelphia City PA 6/18/1767, English 24 shoemaker
  10 days, Monday, 2 pounds, 5'7",
John Hopkins, Jesse Holingsworth Anne Arundel MD ironworks 2/6/1766, English gaol sale L
  2 pounds, 5'9",
Patrick Hopkins, Andrew McClement Kent MD 3/22/1748, Irish 30 L
  59 days, Monday, 2 pounds, short,
William Hopkins, Charles Read Burlington NJ ironworks 7/4/1771, 20
  12 days, Saturday, 5 pounds, 5'6-7",
William Hopper, Leonard Kroesen Bucks PA 1/16/1788, 21
  26 days, Friday, 0.02 pounds, 5'8",
John Horan, Abigail Wheatly New Castle DE 3/26/1761, Irish 35 miner gaol sale L
  11 days, Sunday, 1 pound, short,
Patrick Horan, George Ewing Cecil MD 2/9/1769, Irish 25 C
  9 days, Tuesday, 4 dollars, 5'5-6",
Thomas Horbin, John Lester Bucks PA 10/23/1776, English 18
  9 days, Tuesday, 5 dollars,
Richard Horn, John Knight Queen Anne's MD 5/24/1764, English 60 C
  4 dollars, 5'10",
William Horn, David Jones Chester PA 7/18/1754, American 21 L
  38 days, Monday, 1 pound, 6',
William Horn, Abraham Hayter Bucks PA 9/18/1755, American 22 (2nd escape) L
  50 days, Wednesday, 2 pounds, 6',
Poolino Horne, Alexander Henderson MD 11/16/1774, English 24 C
  19 days, Saturday, 5 pounds, 5'8-9", (arrived Sept. 1774)
John Horner, Joseph Lloyd Chester PA 10/18/1775, Irish 20
  3 days, Monday, 8 dollars, 5'9-10",
Joseph Horsley, John Wallace Chester PA blacksmith 2/2/1731, 25
  3 days, Monday, 5 pounds,
Jacob Hose, John Taylor Lancaster PA 6/13/1754, 23
  4 days, Sunday, 2 pounds,
William Hose, Sampson Darrell Fairfax VA 7/25/1751, 45
  24 days, Monday, 2 pistoles, (has been 3 years in VA)
Mary Hosk, Mary Phipps Chester PA 10/9/1766, 16
  12 days, Saturday, 1 pound,
Ludwick Hosman, Griffith Minshall New Castle DE 11/21/1754, German 20
  5 days, Saturday, 3 pounds, middle,
Jacob Houber, Isaac Myars Lancaster PA 10/24/1754, German 25
  25 days, Sunday, 3 pounds, 5',
Frederick Houck, William Trotter Philadelphia PA 3/2/1785, 18 A
  12 days, Friday, 0.04 pounds,
Thomas Houghy, William Galbreath York PA 8/31/1769, Irish 20
  6 dollars, 5'6",

John Houre, Nathan Lewis Chester PA 6/29/1738, English 20
 1 day, Wednesday, 1 pound, short,
Thomas House, James Gregory Burlington NJ ironworks 5/26/1773, 22 A
 9 days, Tuesday, 6 dollars, 5'10",
Michael Houseal, Henry Denuss Lancaster PA 10/12/1774, sadler A
 10 days, Monday, 1 dollar, 5'8-9",
William Houston, Jacob Rapine Philadelphia PA 12/4/1793, 17 weaver A
 8 days, Tuesday, 3 dollars, 4'10-11",
Edward Houton, Jacob Giles Cecil MD 3/6/1750, English 35 sawyer (ran before) C
 26 days, Saturday, 3 pistoles, (arrived June 12, 1743)
Gilbert How, Thomas Nevell Philadelphia City PA 5/8/1766, 18 A
 8 days, Wednesday, 1.5 pounds, 5'2",
James How, Andrew Campbell Orange VA 2/18/1746, English C
 84 days, Tuesday, 2 pounds sterling, 5'9",
Benjamin Howard, Isaac Haines Burlington NJ 6/19/1793, 18 A
 5 days, Friday, 8 dollars, 5'9",
Essingham Howard, William Pennell Chester PA 7/17/1776, English 24
 68 days, Saturday, 2.5 pounds, 5'8",
James Howard, William Smith Salem NJ 6/20/1771, English 22
 9 days, Tuesday, 2 pounds, 5'7",
Matthew Howard, John Sheerwood Talbot MD 1/22/1751, English 35 farrier C
 36 days, Wednesday, 3 pounds, short,
Nancy Howard, Thomas Duncan Cumberland PA 3/23/1769, 13
 1.5 pounds, 5'3",
John Howell, Samuel Burrows Gloucester NJ 5/1/1760, Irish 28 C
 20 days, Friday, 2 pounds,
John Howell, John Hughs WJ ironworks 10/7/1762, Irish 30 (2nd escape) C
 11 days, Sunday, 10 pounds,
Loranz Howsar, John Jerret Philadelphia PA 8/20/1747, German 20
 11 days, Sunday, 2 pounds,
Thomas Hoxson, Gawes Burrows Philadelphia City PA ship captain 8/21/1755, A
 11 days, Sunday, 1.5 pounds, 5'5",
Thomas Hoyd, Thomas Montgomery New Castle DE 8/1/1754,
 3 days, Monday, 2 pounds, middle, (has been in the colonies before)
Henry Hrubb, William Carnagie Sommerset PA 10/25/1753, German 35 weaver
 76 days, Friday, 3 pounds, 5'6",
John Hubbard, James Hood Anne Arundel MD 12/6/1764, English 25 sailor C
 3 pounds, 5'8",
John Christian Hubner, Nathaniel Lewis Philadelphia PA 8/29/1787, German 21 baker
 8 days, Tuesday, 10 dollars, 5'6-7",
William Huckster, Robert Barns Lancaster PA 12/3/1783, English 33 soldier L
 9 days, Monday, 20 dollars, 5'9",
Margaret Hudson, John Price Berks PA 6/20/1765, English 18
 11 days, Sunday, 1 pound,
Patrick Huffey, John Roberts Salem NJ 6/4/1767, Irish 21
 3 days, Monday, 2 pounds, 5'10",
John Huffman, William Walmsley Salem NJ 9/10/1783, 18 joiner A
 25 days, Saturday, 2 dollars, 5'7-8",
David Hughes, Peter Wagener Prince William VA 6/9/1748, Welsh 40 blacksmith C
 5 pistoles,
Ferdinando Hughes, Nathaniel Bowser Philadelphia City PA tailor 1/30/1750, Irish 23 tailor
 7 days, Thursday, 4 pounds, middle,
Ferdinando Hughes, Robert Savage Monmouth NJ 10/24/1751, Irish 25 tailor (2nd escape)
 151 days, Saturday, 3 pounds, short,
James Hughes, Andrew Caldwell Philadelphia City PA 11/10/1773, A
 3 pounds, 5'6-7", (ran from ship Jupiter)
John Hughes, William Moses Philadelphia City PA blacksmith 10/15/1747, Irish 20
 3 days, Monday, 2.5 pounds, 5'5",
John Hughes, Thomas Collins Philadelphia PA 11/2/1749, Irish 22 (2nd escape)
 5 pounds, short,
John Hughes, Samuel Butcher Philadelphia PA 8/1/1745, 15
 13 days, Friday, 1.5 pounds, short,
John Hughes, Joseph Jeanes Philadelphia PA 1/6/1747, 17 (2nd escape)
 7 days, Thursday, 1.5 pounds,
John Hughes, John Mackey Chester PA 11/10/1743, Irish 18
 3 days, Monday, 1 pound, middle,

John Hughes, William Grant Kent MD 11/3/1768, Irish 20 smith
    2 pounds, 5',
Joseph Hughes, Joseph Hugg Gloucester NJ 7/21/1763,
    6 days, Friday, 3 pounds, 5'4",
Joseph Hughes, Frederick Hagenes Monmouth NJ 8/23/1764, American 17 tailor A
    4 days, Sunday, 2 pounds,
Levi Hughes, Joseph Day New Castle DE 8/1/1787, A
    16 days, Monday, 4 dollars, 5'8",
Nicholas Forster Hughes, James Loughrey Bucks PA 5/28/1767, Irish 28 school teacher
    13 days, Friday, 3 pounds, short,
Nicholas Foster Hughes, James Old Lancaster PA ironworks 6/15/1769, Irish 30 teacher (2nd esc)
    3 pounds, 5'5-6",
Peter Hughes, Andrew Frazer Cecil MD 10/18/1770, Irish weaver
    1.5 pounds, (lately arrived)
Peter Hughes, Andrew Frazer Cecil MD 1/17/1771, Irish weaver (2nd escape)
    7 days, Thursday, 8 dollars, 5'6-7", (arrived last Sept.)
Samuel Hughes, John Wallace Chester PA 4/30/1730, English 30
    1 pound, short,
Thomas Hughes, Calen Dorsey Anne Arundel MD ironworks 1/19/1769, 30 carpenter (ran before) C
    12 days, Saturday, 10 pounds, 5'5",
Henry Hulbeas, John Stricker Philadelphia PA 10/22/1761, German 20
    19 days, Saturday, 2 pounds, 5',
John Hull, Joshua Anderson Bucks PA 4/27/1774, Irish 45
    11 days, Sunday, 2 pounds, 5'7-8",
William Humber, William Ridgely Anne Arundel MD 10/10/1771, English 20 C
    32 days, Sunday, 8 dollars, 5'7-8",
John Humble, Joseph Warner New Castle DE 8/9/1775, English 22
    7 days, Thursday, 6 dollars, 5'7", (arrived 3 months ago)
Eve Humel, Jacob Humen Chester PA 4/16/1777, German 15
    32 days, Sunday, 0.15 pounds,
George Humphrey, John Heard St Mary's MD 7/13/1738, English 19
    112 days, Saturday, 5 Maryland pounds,
Edward Humphreys, James Baker Baltimore MD 8/18/1773, English C
    16 dollars,
Elizabeth Humphreys, Samuel Moore Philadelphia City PA 7/5/1753, Welsh 25 mantuamaker
    25 days, Sunday, 1.5 pounds, short,
Matthew Humphreys, William Wrench Queen Anne's MD 4/12/1764, English 33 C
    18 days, Sunday, 3 pounds, short,
Thomas Humphreys, Stephen Bordley Kent MD 5/15/1760, 42 blacksmith C
    21 days, Thursday, 3 PA pounds, tall,
Peter Humphries, John Fruin baker 12/2/1731, 26
    4 days, Sunday, 2 pounds, middle,
Thomas Humphries, John Cook Kent DE 10/9/1760, English 41 blacksmith
    46 days, Sunday, 3 pounds, 6',
Charles Hunt, Alexander Parker Salem NJ 3/13/1750, 25
    13 days, Friday, 1 pound, short,
John Hunt, James Johnson Frederick MD 5/22/1766, English 20 wheelwright
    16 days, Tuesday, 1 pound, 5'8-9",
John Hunt, Unlisted Name Philadelphia City PA 3/15/1770, English 13
    2 days, Tuesday, 0.75 pounds,
John Hunt, Thomas Stewart Chester PA 8/26/1772, English 15 (2nd escape)
    18 days, Sunday, 1.5 pounds, (not a new arrival)
Michael Hunt, William Vogan Lancaster PA weaver 1/14/1752, Irish 25 L
    10 days, Monday, 2 pounds, 5'3",
Richard Hunt, Robert Lewis Philadelphia PA 4/5/1764, English 30
    4 days, Sunday, 5 pounds, 5'9", (arrived last Oct., was in the navy)
Thomas Hunt, Adam Funk Philadelphia City PA blacksmith 8/18/1790, 16 A
    2 days, Monday, 0.03 pounds,
William Hunt, William Robinson Philadelphia City PA 9/20/1764, 15 A
    48 days, Friday, 1.5 pounds, 5',
Archibald Hunter, John Caldwell Philadelphia PA 10/18/1775, 20 weaver
    1 day, Wednesday, 5 pounds, 5'7-8",
Hungerford Hunter, William McAtee Charles MD 7/8/1742, 26 C
    67 days, Sunday, 3 MD pounds, tall,
Jacob Hunter, Jacob Messmer Philadelphia PA 7/16/1772, 18 weaver A
    4 days, Sunday, 4 pounds, 5'4",

Peter Hunter, William Fox Burlington NJ 2/11/1762, American 22 L
    3 days, Monday, 2 pounds,
Dennis Hurly, Jacob Pollard 5/14/1767, Irish 26 bricklayer
    165 days, Sunday, 0.5 pounds, 5'8",
Margaret Hurly, Isaac Cadwallader Philadelphia PA 2/27/1766, 20
    9 days, Tuesday, 1.5 pounds,
Richard Husband, Joseph Luckens Philadelphia City PA innholder 2/20/1772, Irish
    3 pounds, 5'10-11",
Thomas Husbands, Peter Bard Philadelphia City PA 1/21/1746, 23 sailor L
    45 days, Monday, 3 pounds, middle,
William Hustler, William Ward Cecil MD 8/13/1752, American hired L
    46 days, Sunday, 2.5 pounds, 5'6", (has a wife)
Elizabeth Huston, Edward Connor Chester PA 12/2/1756, German 21
    9 days, Tuesday, 4 pounds, short,
Robert Huston, Edward Wier Cecil MD 6/28/1775,
    12 days, Saturday, 2 pounds, 5'7",
Thomas Huston, Isaac Richardson Lancaster PA 10/3/1765, English
    11 days, Sunday, 1 pound, 5'8-9",
John Hutchenson, Thomas Clark New Castle DE 11/12/1741, Irish 20
    9 days, Tuesday, 1.5 pounds, short,
George Hutchinson, George Hepler Philadelphia PA 8/2/1770, shoemaker A
    9 days, Tuesday, 1 pound, 5'4",
Jairus Hutchinson, Joseph Harden Gloucester NJ 2/28/1787, 18 A
    13 days, Thursday, 8 dollars, 5'6",
John Hutchinson, William Nelson New Castle DE 9/15/1773, Irish 18 A
    26 days, Saturday, 1 pound, 5'6-9",
John Hutchison, John Buckingham New Castle DE 7/3/1746,
    5 days, Saturday, 1.5 pounds, short,
Peter Hutschar, Peter Hassenclever EJ ironworks 6/12/1766, German miner
    14 days, Thursday, 5 pounds, 5'6", (under a 3 year 4 month contract, imported)
James Hutton, George Stevenson Cumberland PA 8/28/1776, Irish 20
    10 days, Monday, 8 dollars, 5'7-8", (arrived 2 years ago)
John Huxely, Jacob Paullin Salem NJ 4/23/1772, American L
    9 days, Tuesday, 4 dollars, 6',
David Huxly, Joseph Wharton Philadelphia PA ironworks 6/28/1739, Welsh 40
    4 pounds, middle,
Samuel Hyatt, Thomas Coomes New Castle DE 8/7/1782, A
    37 days, Monday, 16 dollars, 5'6",
Cefar Hyde, Daniel Palmer Bucks PA 7/11/1729, 28
    1.5 pounds, short,
Charles Hysley, Richard Graves Kent MD 1/23/1766, 25
    2 pounds, 5'6",
John Iden, John Hallowell Philadelphia City PA shoemaker 10/26/1749, 19
    10 days, Monday, 1 pound,
James Ilegins, Thomas Folwell Bucks PA 10/11/1764,
    3 days, Monday, 1.5 pounds, 5'8",
John Impy, Henry Smith Lancaster PA 11/24/1737, 22
    6 days, Friday, 3 pounds,
William Ingle, Andrew Sinnickson Jr Salem NJ 6/22/1774, English 18
    9 days, Tuesday, 2 pounds, 5'5-6",
Michael Inglehart, Jacob Asleman Lancaster PA 12/13/1748, German 19
    2 days, Tuesday, 2 pounds, middle,
John Ingles, John Malcolm Philadelphia City PA sailmaker 5/6/1762, Scot 45 gardener
    14 days, Thursday, 20 dollars, 5'8", (was a soldier)
Thomas Ingram, William Garwood ropemaker 4/10/1760, English 23 ropemaker A
    4 days, Sunday, 2 pounds, 5'4",
John Inman, Michael Bateman Queen Anne's MD 4/28/1773, C
    17 days, Monday, 3 pounds, 5'3",
James Ireland, John Thompson Chester PA 6/16/1768, Irish 17
    11 days, Sunday, 1 pound, 5'3",
Francis Irwin, Thomas West Loudoun VA 11/3/1773, Irish blacksmith C
    23 days, Tuesday, 20 dollars,
Peter Jabil, Israel Wright Burlington NJ 2/7/1771, German 40
    7 days, Thursday, 15 dollars, 5'7",
Anthony Jackson, John Hood Anne Arundel MD 9/20/1770, English 20 C
    18 days, Sunday, 10 pounds, 5'8", (arrived July 1770)

Daniel Jackson, Thomas Bivens Kent MD 7/16/1772, 16 A
    34 days, Friday, 4 dollars, 5'4-5",
James Jackson, James Moore Lancaster PA 11/9/1752, Scot 21
    3 days, Monday, 3 pounds, 5'6",
James Jackson, Benjamin Thompson Gloucester NJ 10/31/1771, English 19
    13 days, Friday, 1.5 pounds, 5'6",
Jane Jackson, Jacob Jones Philadelphia City PA 4/5/1775, Irish 23
    3 pounds, 5'2", (arrived July 27th last)
John Jackson, William Clayton Queen Anne's MD 6/15/1758, C
    45 days, Monday, 1.5 pounds, 5'8",
John W Jackson, James Colvin EJ 10/21/1795, 17 weaver A
    6 dollars, (relatives live nearby)
Mary Jackson, William Clayton Queen Anne's MD 6/15/1758, C
    45 days, Monday, 1.5 pounds, 5'8",
Samuel Jackson, William Bennett Lancaster PA ironworks 9/25/1760, English 25 gaol sale L
    3 pounds, 5'6",
Susannah Jackson, John Miller Lancaster PA 11/6/1760, Irish (with daughter age 2)
    4 days, Sunday, 1 pound,
Adam Jacobs, David Watson Lancaster PA 9/27/1770,
    106 days, Wednesday, 2 pounds, 5'4",
James Jacobs, Isaac Taylor Philadelphia City PA 5/8/1746, 19 carpenter A
    5 days, Saturday, 3 pounds, tall,
Michael Jacobs, Captain Hinton Philadelphia City PA ship captain 11/21/1751, Danish caulker
    1 pound, (ran from ship)
John James, John Hoopes Chester PA 1/17/1738, English 20 L
    12 days, Saturday, 1.5 pounds, short, (arrived 9 years ago)
Martha James, John Jones Philadelphia PA 10/25/1753, 28
    1.5 pounds, middle,
Morgan James, John Fogwell Kent MD 8/1/1754, Welsh 32
    1 pound,
Peter James, John Knight Queen Anne's MD 5/24/1764, English 45 C
    4 dollars,
Thomas James, Ely Dorsey Anne Arundel MD 7/2/1761, American L
    15 days, Wednesday, 10 pistoles, 6',
Thomas James, Patrick Reynolds Burlington NJ 5/3/1753, American 19 L
    44 days, Tuesday, 2 pounds,
John Jarvis, Peter Butler Baltimore MD 7/19/1770, English 25 C
    8 days, Wednesday, 1.5 pounds, 5'7", (lately arrived)
John Jarvis, Peter Butler Baltimore MD 8/23/1770, English 25 (2nd escape) C
    8 days, Wednesday, 1 pound, 5'6",
John Jebb, John Grines Howard Baltimore MD 8/6/1752, English 30 shoemaker C
    18 days, Sunday, 4 pistoles, tall,
Lewis Jeck, Conrad Abel Philadelphia City PA 7/4/1787, German 25
    8 dollars, 5'1-2", (arrived last fall)
Margaret Jefferies, John Blyth Cumberland PA 10/20/1773, Scot 24
    24 days, Monday, 4 dollars, (wife to Michael Jefferies)
Michael Jefferies, John Blyth Cumberland PA 10/20/1773, Irish 30
    24 days, Monday, 4 dollars, 5'5-6",
William Jefferis, Jacob Carter Queen Anne's MD 7/1/1756, 30 shoemaker C
    4 pistoles, 5'6",
Thomas Jeffers, William Bradford Philadelphia City PA 7/10/1755, English 17
    4 days, Sunday, 1 pound, (arrived last summer)
William Jeffreys, Job Haines Chester PA 4/12/1775, Irish 25
    9 days, Tuesday, 2.5 pounds, 5'9-10",
John Jeffris, Isham Randolph Philadelphia City PA ship captain 4/16/1748, sailor L
    2 pounds, 5'5",
David Jenkins, Thomas Sharp Chester PA 9/17/1767, 28 soldier
    8 days, Wednesday, 3 pounds, 5'5", (arrived 1 year ago, has been in the colonies before)
Israel Jenkins, Joseph Hart Bucks PA 10/16/1776, American 16 L
    17 days, Monday, 2 pounds, short,
John Jenkins, Isaac Hains Burlington NJ 1/26/1769, Welsh 26
    3 days, Monday, 3 pounds, 5'4",
Thomas Jenkins, Moses Harris Cumberland NJ 5/30/1787, 19 cooper A
    6 dollars, 5'8-9",
William Jenkison, Samuel Lamb Cumberland PA 11/7/1751, English 14
    112 days, Thursday, 3 pounds, (has an uncle in Philadelphia)

Charles Jennings, Samuel Wheeler Philadelphia City PA 7/11/1771, English cutler
  6 days, Friday, 5 dollars, 5',
John Jennings, Benjamin Kirby Queen Anne's MD 5/25/1769, English shoemaker C
  16 days, Tuesday, 6 pounds, 5'9-10",
Thomas Jennings, William Bird Philadelphia PA 4/18/1745, English
  1 pound,
Edward Jerman, John Nemo Kent MD 7/11/1754, English 25 ship carpenter
  19 days, Saturday, 2 pounds,
William Jewel, Samuel Dorsey Jr Baltimore MD ironworks 9/20/1775, 23 C
  32 days, Sunday, 3.75 pounds, 5'6",
Thomas Jobson, Robert Farthing Philadelphia City PA ship captain 8/10/1758, 17 tall,
William Jochain, Augustine Musk Caroline VA 4/16/1747, English 19 dance teacher
  39 days, Sunday, 2 pistoles, 5'8",
David John, Daniel Howell New Castle DE 5/4/1749, 23
  4 days, Sunday, 5 pounds,
David John, Sarah Miles Bucks PA 9/6/1775, Welsh 29 hired L
  22 days, Wednesday, 5'2",
Dolly John, Jacob Fouts Lancaster PA 9/27/1764, Irish 24
  8 days, Wednesday, 2 pounds,
Reuban John, Richard Brown Monmouth NJ 2/10/1790, 18 A
  15 days, Tuesday, 4 dollars, 5'7-8",
Jeremiah Johns, Thomas Johnson Queen Anne's MD 1/12/1764, 40 shoemaker C
  2 pistoles,
Jacob Johnson, James Graham Chester PA 4/20/1749, English 24
  7 pounds, 6', (travelled all over and been privateering)
Jacob Johnson, James Cherry Chester PA 11/28/1765, 20 tailor A
  5 days, Saturday, 1.5 pounds, 5'3",
James Johnson, John Welsh Chester PA 6/8/1774, Irish
  15 days, Wednesday, 3 pounds, 5'9", (arrived 3 weeks ago)
James Johnson, Samuel Lippencott Burlington NJ 8/26/1772, English
  2 pounds, 5'6",
John Johnson, William Crosthwaite Philadelphia City PA perukemaker 3/6/1740, English 30 barber
  3 days, Monday, short, (2nd escape)
John Johnson, William Crosthwaite Philadelphia City PA perukemaker 9/20/1739, English 25 barber
  1 days, Wednesday, 1 pound, short,
John Johnson, Robert Thornburgh Cumberland PA ironworks 6/6/1765, Irish 26
  5 pounds, 5'8",
John Johnson, Joseph Richardson Philadelphia PA 9/29/1768, 30
  4 days, Sunday, 3 pounds, 5'7", (relatives live nearby)
John Johnson, Roger Hartley Bucks PA 5/14/1767, English 23 (2nd escape)
  14 days, Thursday, 3 pounds, middle,
John Johnson, James Boyles Bucks PA 11/20/1766, English 22
  11 days, Sunday, 8 dollars, 5'8",
John Johnson, John Herston Baltimore MD 10/17/1771, 24
  18 days, Sunday, 3 pounds, (arrived 4 months ago, use to the sea, was in the navy)
John Johnson, Andrew Stalcop New Castle DE 5/28/1767, American 22 L
  5 days, Saturday, 2 pounds, 5'8",
Jonathan Johnson, Laurance Allwine Philadelphia City PA windsor-chair-maker 11/23/1791, 20 A
  52 days, Sunday, 8 dollars, 5'5-6",
Simon Johnson, James Jeck York PA 5/9/1771, English 35
  20 days, Friday, 2 pounds, 5'3-4", (use to the sea)
Thomas Johnson, Alexander Lawson Baltimore MD ironworks 4/20/1749, English 30 C
  1.5 pounds, tall,
Daniel Johnston, George Rock Cecil MD 7/5/1753, Scot 25
  4 days, Sunday, 3 pistoles, short, (was a drummer in the army)
Elizabeth Johnston, James Frier Chester PA 3/20/1766, Irish 30
  11 days, Sunday, 1.5 pounds,
Jacob Johnston, Walter Fullam 8/26/1772, American tailor L
  3 pounds, 5'6-7",
James Johnston, Moore & Chestnut Philadelphia City PA 7/27/1769, Irish 26
  8 days, Wednesday, 4 dollars, 5'10",
James Johnston, John Harry Philadelphia PA 11/7/1771, Irish 23 L
  24 days, Monday, 2 pounds, 5'5",
John Johnston, Nathaniel Chew Chester PA ship captain 6/20/1751, 25 gardener
  16 days, Tuesday, 5 pistoles, short, (ran from ship)

John Johnston, William McCord Lancaster PA ironworks 7/24/1766, 24
  16 days, Tuesday, 6 pounds, 5'7-8",
John Johnston, John Menough Jr Chester PA 8/26/1795, Irish 17
  16 days, Monday, 7 dollars, 5'4-5", (relatives live nearby)
John Johnston, Charles Baker Baltimore MD 1/10/1771, English C
  12 days, Saturday, 3 pounds, 5'5",
No Name Johnston, Collin Ferguson Kent MD 4/3/1766, C
  2.5 pounds,
Richard Johnston, Samuel Hazard 6/12/1755, English 30
  4 days, Sunday, 1 pound, 6',
Robert Johnston, John Grady Bucks PA 8/18/1784, 17
  14 days, Wednesday, 4 dollars, 5'6",
Thomas Johnston, Thomas Ogle New Castle DE 6/21/1753, 30
  1.5 pounds, middle,
William Johnston, John Grattan Augusta VA 11/19/1767, 30
  5 pounds, 5'7", (arrived 2 weeks ago)
Patrick Joice, Isaac Wayne Chester PA 1/6/1773, Irish 26
  5 days, Saturday, 2.05 pounds, 5'7", (lately arrived)
Patrick Joice, Isaac Wayne Chester PA 8/18/1773, Irish 26 (2nd escape)
  3 days, Monday, 2 pounds, 5'7",
Thomas Jolley, John Wigmore Philadelphia City ship-rigger 7/2/1783, ship-rigger A
  2 days, Monday, 4 dollars,
Matthew Jolly, Benjamin Tasker Baltimore MD ironworks 7/11/1745, Irish 22 C
  16 days, Tuesday, 2 pounds, short,
Matthew Jolly, Benjamin Tasker Baltimore MD ironworks 5/29/1746, Irish 23 (2nd escape) C
  10 days, Monday, 4 pounds, short,
Richard Jolly, James Dobbins Philadelphia City PA 5/5/1748, sailor L
  21 days, Thursday, 4 pistoles,
Anne Jones, William Jenkins Baltimore MD 10/10/1754, Irish C
  7 days, Thursday, 1 pistole,
Catherine Jones, Thomas Davis Chester PA 9/15/1768, Irish
  11 days, Sunday, 3 pounds,
Charles Jones, James Day Chester PA 6/17/1762, 16 A
  7 days, Thursday, 2 pounds, 5',
David Jones, John Mickel Gloucester NJ 9/12/1734, Welsh
  1 day, Wednesday, 2 pounds, middle,
David Jones, Nathan Yarnall Chester PA 5/17/1744, Welsh 21
  3 days, Monday, 1.5 pounds, middle,
David Jones, Joshua Humphreys Chester PA 9/26/1751, Welsh 34
  2 pounds, middle,
David Jones, Joshua Humphreys Chester PA 6/18/1752, Welsh 35 (2nd escape)
  7 days, Thursday, 3 pounds, short,
Edward Jones, Nathaniel Chew Chester PA ship captain 6/20/1751, shoemaker
  16 days, Tuesday, 5 pistoles, middle, (ran from ship)
Edward Jones, Francis Harris Philadelphia City PA 8/13/1767, English 35
  3 days, Monday, "fame",
Ellis Jones, Nathan Evans Chester PA 2/1/1775, Welsh 23 glover
  6 dollars, 5'11", (arrived last summer)
Henry Jones, William Rigden Philadelphia City PA painter 7/29/1762, English 24 painter
  6 days, Friday, 3 pounds, 5',
Henry Jones, Abraham Ferree Lancaster PA 5/30/1765, 28 C
  11 days, Sunday, 1.5 pounds, 5'5",
Henry Jones, Isham Randolph Philadelphia City PA ship captain 4/16/1748, sailor L
  2 pounds, 5'8",
Hugh Jones, George Randell Baltimore MD ironworks 9/22/1768, Irish 30 miller C
  15 dollars, 5'5",
Isaac Jones, James Starr Philadelphia City PA 4/12/1764, American 21 cordwainer A
  2 pounds, (has 1 year to serve)
James Jones, Benjamin Bradford Cecil MD doctor 5/17/1750, Irish 16
  1 day, Wednesday, 1 pound,
James Jones, Otho Othoson Cecil MD 3/27/1753, Irish 19 (2nd escape)
  10 days, Monday, 1 pound, short,
James Jones, Patrick Flynn New Castle DE 10/2/1755, Irish 21 (3rd escape)
  2 pounds, 5'5",
James Jones, William Carson Philadelphia City PA perukemaker 9/15/1763, English 20
  2 days, Tuesday, 2 pounds, 5'10",

James Jones, Samuel Wheeler Philadelphia City PA 8/16/1775, blacksmith
    73 days, Monday, 2 pounds, 5'9-10",
James Jones, William Hayman Chester PA 2/27/1788, 20
    10 days, Sunday, 4 dollars, 5'7-8",
John Jones, Jacob Scuten Philadelphia PA 6/8/1732, 22
    4 days, Sunday, 2 pounds, middle,
John Jones, Edward Wells Philadelphia City PA 5/7/1747, English 25
    6 days, Friday, 1 pound, 5'6",
John Jones, Lewis Lewis Bucks PA 8/10/1738, English 21
    about 1.5 months ago, 2 pounds, short, (lately arrived but has been in America before)
John Jones, Joseph Moore Burlington NJ 11/22/1750, English
    1.5 pounds,
John Jones, Thomas Timms Talbot MD 1/27/1757, Irish 29 schoolmaster
    23 days, Tuesday, 5'4",
John Jones, Cales Perkins New Castle DE 1/28/1762, English 50
    3 pounds,
John Jones, Joseph Anderson Philadelphia City PA 5/4/1769, 40
    1 pound, 5'8",
John Jones, William Higbee Burlington NJ 5/25/1774, English 17
    6 days, Friday, 2 pounds, 5'6",
John Jones, Samuel Dennis Cumberland PA 9/27/1764, 22 tanner A
    36 days, Wednesday, 2 pounds,
John Jones, Timothy Kirk Jr Chester PA 1/27/1773, weaver A
    18 days, Sunday, 0.5 pounds, 5'6",
John Jones, John Jones Frederick MD ironworks 7/24/1776, Welsh 40 forgeman
    24 days, Monday, 10 pounds, 5'6",
John Jones, James Davis Philadelphia City PA 7/12/1744, A
    4 days, Sunday, 3 pounds,
John Jones, Robert Bryerly Baltimore MD 5/15/1755, C
    17 days, Monday, 1 pistole, 5'7",
John Jones, William Jenkins Baltimore MD 10/10/1754, Irish C
    7 days, Thursday, 1 pistole, 5'10", (been in the colonies before)
Joseph Jones, Burroughs Abit Gloucester NJ 8/28/1766, 17 A
    13 days, Friday, 2 pounds, 5'6-7",
Margaret Jones, Abraham Pennel Chester PA 6/14/1786, Irish 18
    3 days, Sunday, 6 dollars, short,
Morgan Jones, George Emlen Philadelphia City PA 7/12/1744, Welsh 20
    4 days, Sunday, 3 pounds, short,
Moses Jones, William Baxter ironworks 11/17/1757, English 25 collier C
    105 days, Thursday, 3 pounds, 5'7",
Nelly Jones, Hugh Jones Philadelphia PA 5/11/1769, Irish 24
    15 days, Wednesday, 1 pound,
Owen Jones, Edward Thomas New Castle DE 4/8/1731, Welsh 25
    13 days, Friday, 1 pound,
Reuben Jones, John French Burlington NJ 4/18/1751, America L
    14 days, Thursday, 2.5 pounds, 6',
Robert Jones, Hugh Meredith Chester PA 3/5/1751, Welsh 22 tailor
    8 days, Wednesday, 3 pounds, 5'10",
Robert Jones, John Morris Chester PA tavern-keeper 12/13/1753, Welsh 24 tailor (2nd escape)
    2 days, Tuesday, 1.5 pounds, 5'10",
Robert Jones, John Smith Lancaster PA 6/20/1765, Irish
    11 days, Sunday, 3 pounds, 5'3-4",
Robert Jones, William Fray Kent MD 1/8/1756, 19
    21 days, Thursday, 1 pound, 5'2",
Robert Jones, Allen Gillespie New Castle DE 9/7/1769, Irish
    8 days, Wednesday, 5 pounds, 5'8-9",
Robert Jones, Thomas Robinson New Castle DE 12/21/1791, 18
    11 days, Saturday, 4 dollars, 5'6",
Samuel Jones, William Rush Philadelphia City PA blacksmith 6/5/1760, English nailer
    2 pounds, 5'6",
Samuel Jones, Curtis Grubb Lancaster PA ironworks 9/1/1773, English 18
    22 days, Wednesday, 7 dollars, short, (lately arrived)
Thomas Jones, William Dewees Philadelphia PA 10/3/1754,
    1 day, Wednesday, 2 pounds, 5'10",
Thomas Jones, John Read York PA 4/2/1752, English 19
    2.5 pounds,

Thomas Jones, Edmund Beakes EJ 3/31/1763, shoemaker
   12 days, Saturday, 3 pounds, middle,
Thomas Jones, Joseph Morrison York PA 7/4/1765, Welsh 25 tanner
   3 pounds,
Thomas Jones, James Whitehead Philadelphia City PA workhouse-keeper 2/19/1761, Welsh 22
   5 days, Saturday, 3 pounds, middle,
Thomas Jones, Joseph Glasentine Philadelphia PA 7/24/1760, Welsh 22
   5 days, Saturday, 3 pounds, 5'2",
Thomas Jones, Joseph Anderson Philadelphia City PA 7/27/1769, Irish 40
   1.5 pounds, 5'6",
Thomas Jones, John Righter Philadelphia PA 6/13/1771, English 25
   4 days, Sunday, 1.5 pounds, 5',
Thomas Jones, Elijah Weed 10/31/1771, 30
   4 days, Sunday, 6 dollars, 5'2",
Thomas Jones, William Webb Harford MD 8/7/1776, Welsh 25 C
   72 days, Tuesday, 16.5 dollars, 5'8",
Thomas Jones, Samuel Cary Bucks PA 4/24/1755, American 18 L
   4 days, Sunday, 4 pounds, middle,
William Jones, John Roe Queen Anne's MD 10/28/1742, 30 weaver
   18 days, Sunday, short,
William Jones, Charles Carroll Baltimore MD ironworks 6/9/1743, Welsh 25
   40 days, Saturday, 5 Pennsylvania pounds, (has 3 years left to serve, ran from ship)
William Jones, Robert Hartshorf Monmouth NJ 10/4/1750, Irish
   4 days, Sunday, 3 pounds, short,
William Jones, Samuel Vallacot 8/8/1751, Welsh plaisterer
   7 days, Thursday, 2 pounds, middle, (arrived last year)
William Jones, William Taylor Monmouth NJ 2/14/1765,
   18 days, Sunday, 6 pounds, middle,
William Jones, Robert Holland Philadelphia City PA 2/19/1767, Welsh 25 tanner
   11 days, Sunday, 2 pounds, 5'9", (arrived last fall, was in colonies before as a soldier)
William Jones, Joseph Reynolds Frederick MD 4/14/1768, Welsh C
   16 days, Tuesday, 5 pounds, 5'8-9",
Hugh Jopp, Stephen Steward Anne Arundel MD 7/6/1774, Scot tailor
   19 days, Saturday, 4 pounds, 5'9",
Rachel Jordan, Thomas Scholfield 1/2/1772, workhouse sale L
   42 days, Thursday, 1 pound, middle,
William Jordan, Benjamin Ingram Baltimore MD ironworks 8/22/1765, 32 C
   17 days, Monday, 3 pounds, 5'5",
John Jorden, George Lamb Kent MD 8/30/1775, Irish 19 weaver
   4 dollars, 5'6-7",
Richard Jordon, Alexander Scott Lancaster PA 10/12/1769, Irish 19
   9 days, Wednesday, 1.5 pounds, 5'8",
Catherine Jortanin, Joseph Caufman Philadelphia City PA 4/14/1757, German
   24 days, Monday, 1.5 pounds, short,
John Jose, Gideon Gilpin Chester PA 1/26/1774, German 19
   30 days, Tuesday, 10 dollars,
Richard Jose, William Webb Chester PA 9/18/1755, Irish 20
   3 days, Monday, 2 pounds, 5'6",
Richard Jose, Daniel Webb Chester PA 9/25/1755, Irish 20 (2nd escape)
   4 days, Sunday, 1.5 pounds, 5'6",
Abraham Josep, James Hunt Philadelphia PA 9/10/1741, English 24 shoemaker
   20 days, Friday, 3 pounds, middle,
Joseph Joslyne, Henry Feddeman Queen Anne's MD 11/30/1752, English plaisterer
   279 days, Wednesday, 3 pounds, 5'9",
Patrick Joyce, John Grant Philadelphia City PA 11/8/1764, Irish 40 tailor
   10 days, Monday, 3 pounds, 5'3", (was in the army)
Philip Jung, Philip Hahn Philadelphia PA 10/30/1776, German
   3 days, Monday, 8 dollars,
Ann Justice, George Emlen Philadelphia City PA 5/26/1763, Irish 24
   5 days, Saturday, 1 pound, short, (arrived last summer)
Hans William Kabe, George Miller Hunterdon NJ 5/30/1751, 16
   13 days, Friday, 5 pounds,
Frederick Kablemacher, Michael Miller Philadelphia City PA 6/20/1792, German 26 joiner
   3 days, Sunday, 20 dollars, 5'4-5",
Fergus Kagan, Willing & Morris Philadelphia City PA merchants 5/2/1765, Irish 26 coachman
   4 days, Sunday, 8 dollars, 5'8", (lately arrived, ran from ship)

John Kahar, Evan Ellis Chester PA 3/22/1739, Irish 24
    about 1 month ago, 1.5 pounds, short,
John Kaighn, John McDowell Chester PA 4/26/1775, Irish
    4 dollars, 5'7-8",
Henry Kain, John Taylor Chester PA 7/27/1785, Irish 22
    8 days, Tuesday, 20 dollars, 5'7",
James Kain, Arney Lippincott Burlington NJ 7/14/1784, Irish 17
    3 days, Sunday, 8 dollars, 5'2-3", (arrived last fall)
William Kaine, Thomas Slipper Kent MD 7/22/1762, English 48 C
    18 days, Sunday, 4 pounds, short,
Francis Kane, James Starr Berks PA 5/17/1775, Irish 21
    8 days, Wednesday, 1.5 pounds, 5'8-9",
Margaret Kane, Joseph Reed Hunterdon NJ merchant 5/12/1748, Irish
    1 day, Wednesday, 1 pound, middle,
Francis Kanton, John Harper Philadelphia PA 8/1/1745, 22
    5 days, Saturday, 1.5 pounds, middle,
James Karman, James Duncan Philadelphia City PA 9/21/1785, Irish 16
    3 days, Sunday, 8 spanish dollars, 5'2-3",
Thomas Karr, Edward Castelloe Kent MD 3/5/1761, Irish 21
    20 days, Friday, 2 pistoles, short,
William Karragan, Andrew McCallem Salem NJ 8/9/1770, Irish 21 smith
    11 days, Sunday, 8 dollars, 5'5-6",
Jacob Katts, Martin Bish Philadelphia City PA 4/30/1783, 20 A
    30 dollars, 5'8-9",
Ludowick Katts, Christian Warner Philadelphia PA blacksmith 5/17/1744, 19
    3 days, Monday, 1 pound,
Hans Peter Kaul, Thomas Lawrence Philadelphia City PA 7/19/1753, German tailor
    4 days, Sunday, 1.5 pounds, short,
James Kay, William Webb Harford MD 8/7/1776, Irish 23 C
    72 days, Tuesday, 16.5 dollars, 5'7",
Barney Kean, John Mitchell Lancaster PA 7/7/1773, Irish 25
    9 days, Tuesday, 2 pounds, 5'8",
John Kean, Francis Fisher Chester PA 4/26/1753, Irish 20
    3 days, Monday, 1.5 pounds, middle,
Thomas Kean, John Graham Chester PA 8/31/1785, Irish 25 shoemaker
    10 days, Sunday, 2.5 pounds, 5'8-9",
Charles Keanon, Richard Ford Cecil MD 12/8/1784, Irish 20
    10 days, Sunday, 3 pounds, 5'2",
John Kearns, Isaac Hersay New Castle DE 1/30/1753, 23 cooper
    8 days, Wednesday, 3 pounds, 5'8",
Lawrence Keas, James McDowell Chester PA 7/5/1770, Irish 21
    4 days, Sunday, 2 pounds, 5'8",
Ignatius Keating, Joshua Evans Berks PA 7/14/1773, Irish
    12 days, Saturday, 6 dollars, 5'7-8",
Catherine Keeler, Robert Tomkins 1/25/1775, 17
    0.03 pounds,
James Keen, Nathaniel Giles Lancaster PA ironworks 7/16/1761, American 21 L
    10 days, Monday, 5 pounds,
Henry Keer, John Keer Lancaster PA 11/20/1776, 15 tailor A
    67 days, Sunday, 0.05 pounds, 5'5",
John Hendrick Keese, Christian Van Phull NY baker 7/5/1775, German baker
    13 days, Saturday, 10 dollars, 5',
James Keevan, James Read Lancaster PA 6/5/1766, Irish 20
    2 pounds, 5'5",
David Keighn, Thomas Antram Burlington NJ 12/18/1755, Irish 20
    12 days, Saturday, 1.5 pounds, short,
Maria Kelcon, John Hopkins Lancaster PA tavern-keeper 10/31/1754, German 40
    5 days, Saturday, 2 pounds, middle, (arrived 2 weeks ago)
Archibald Kelley, John Pierse 2/28/1765, Irish 16
    4 days, Sunday, 2 pounds, 5'6",
Augustin Kelley, Silas Jones Philadelphia PA 11/24/1784, 16
    8 dollars,
Dennis Kelley, Daniel Jones Philadelphia PA 12/21/1738, Irish 22
    5 days, Saturday, 1.5 pounds, short,
John Kelley, Joseph Williams Chester PA 6/20/1754, Irish
    4 days, Sunday, 1.5 pounds, middle,

John Kelley, John Jenkin Jr Lancaster PA 7/14/1773, Irish 17
    10 days, Monday, 2.5 pounds, 5'4",
Peter Kelley, Thomas Duffell Philadelphia PA 4/30/1730, Irish
    5 days, Saturday, 2.5 pounds, middle,
William Kelley, George Eberly Lancaster PA gaolkeeper 6/4/1772, 18
    10 days, Monday, 1 pound,
Alexander Hamilton Kelly, John Boyle Bucks PA 3/2/1785, 22 carpenter L
    14 days, Wednesday, 12 dollars, short, (arrived 1.5 years ago)
Arthur Kelly, William Blair Philadelphia City PA 9/4/1760, Irish 35
    8 days, Wednesday, 2 pounds, 5'8",
Barnabus Kelly, Edward Roberts Philadelphia PA 5/5/1773, Irish 21
    10 days, Monday, 10 dollars, 5'6",
Bartholomew Kelly, Thomas Pain Chester PA 7/19/1753, Irish 45 turner
    7 days, Thursday, 3 pounds, short,
Cornelius Kelly, Nathan Dix Chester PA 2/9/1731, Irish 20
    5 pounds, tall,
Corneilus Kelly, Mahlon Stacy Burlington NJ ironworks 8/24/1738, Irish 27 (2nd escape)
    19 days, Saturday, 2 pounds, tall,
Daniel Kelly, Robert Towers 10/2/1766, Irish 19 breeches-maker
    7 days, Thursday, 1.5 pounds, 5'6",
David Kelly, Matthew Robertson Chester PA 9/14/1769, Irish 17
    2 pounds, 5'6",
Edward Kelly, John Stirling Lancaster PA 9/11/1766, Irish 45
    20 days, Friday, 2 pounds, 5'8",
Honor Kelly, William Moore New York NY ship captain 10/27/1763, Irish 19
    2 pounds, (ran from ship)
Hugh Kelly, Samuel Hodge NY perukemaker 10/20/1748, Irish 19
    3 pounds, short, (ran from privateer ship in Bermuda)
Hugh Kelly, George Monro New Castle DE 6/28/1750, Irish 21 (2nd escape)
    8 days, Wednesday, 2 pounds,
James Kelly, Thomas Underhill Cecil MD 8/20/1752, Irish 18
    4 days, Sunday, 5 pounds, 5'5",
James Kelly, Thomas Underhill Cecil MD 5/17/1753, Irish 19 (2nd escape)
    7 days, Thursday, 5 pounds,
James Kelly, Alexander Lewis Chester PA 11/16/1774, Irish 19
    5 days, Saturday, 1 pound, 5'6", (arrived 2 months ago)
John Kelly, Thomas Forman Burlington NJ 9/23/1762, 18
    15 days, Wednesday, 3 pounds, 5'4",
John Kelly, Robert English New Castle DE 5/22/1755, Irish 19
    1.5 pounds,
John Kelly, Joseph Williams Chester PA 1/29/1756, Irish 20 (2nd escape)
    10 days, Monday, 2 pounds, 5'9",
John Kelly, John Jenkins Lancaster PA 12/1/1773, Irish
    8 days, Wednesday, 4 dollars, 5'3-4",
John Kelly, John Ferree Lancaster PA 9/28/1785, Irish 20
    15 days, Tuesday, 16 dollars, 5'7-8",
Margaret Kelly, Samuel Hodge NY perukemaker 8/11/1748, Irish 18
    11 days, Sunday, 3 pounds, tall,
Margaret Kelly, John Porter Philadelphia PA 8/31/1774, Irish 22
    40 days, Saturday, 3 dollars, middle,
Margaret Kelly, John Boyer 11/6/1776, Irish 24 (2nd escape)
    16 days, Tuesday, 4 dollars, 5'2-3",
Martin Kelly, Jonathan Vaughn Talbot MD ironworks 9/29/1763, Irish
    23 days, Tuesday, 1.5 pounds, middle,
Mary Kelly, Samuel Boggs Gloucester NJ 6/11/1752, Irish
    4 days, Sunday, 1.5 pounds, short,
Michael Kelly, James McCabe Queen Anne's MD 7/7/1784, Irish 32
    13 days, Thursday, 9 pounds, 5'6-8",
Michael Kelly, James Hutchinson Baltimore MD 9/14/1769, Irish 24 C
    11 days, Sunday, 5 pounds, 5'8", (arrived 1 month ago)
Nicholas Kelly, Nathan Giles Baltimore MD 3/26/1767, Irish
    11 days, Sunday, 2 pounds, middle,
Owen Kelly, Joel Bailey Chester PA 4/17/1766, Irish breeches-maker
    2.5 pounds, 5'7",
Patrick Kelly, David Wheeler Morris NJ 3/24/1743, Irish 26
    6 days, Friday, 2 pounds, middle,

Patrick Kelly, Benjamin Benson Cecil MD 7/20/1749, Irish silk-weaver
    50 days, Wednesday, 0.5 pounds, middle,
Patrick Kelly, William Kelso Cumberland PA 5/1/1776, Irish 13
    55 days, Friday, 4 dollars,
Redmond Kelly, William Daily Kent MD 2/15/1775, Irish 20
    4 dollars, 5'6-7", (arrived last July)
Richard Kelly, William McClelan Chester PA 4/24/1755, Irish 19
    5 days, Saturday, 3 pounds, 5'5",
Thomas Kelly, Robert Evans Cecil MD 7/5/1753, Irish 23
    2 pounds, 5'6",
Thomas Kelly, Robert Evans Cecil MD 8/23/1753, Irish 24 (2nd escape)
    1 pound, 5'6", (has an iron collar on neck)
Thomas Kelly, Samuel Scott Lancaster PA 3/12/1751, Irish
    10 days, Monday, 3 pounds, 6',
Thomas Kelly, Samuel Howey Philadelphia PA 8/6/1767, 19 soldier
    8 days, Wednesday, 6 dollars, 5'5",
Thomas Kelly, Thomas Harrison Philadelphia City PA 9/2/1772, Irish 17 tailor
    10 days, Monday, 15 dollars, 5'7-8",
William Kelly, George Ross York PA ironworks 7/23/1777, Irish 20
    10 days, Monday, 20 dollars, 5'7-8",
John Keloe, William Carlile Chester PA 7/5/1770, Irish
    4 days, Sunday, 2 pounds, 5'8",
Stephen Kelso, Micajah James Baltimore MD 3/8/1775, American 35 caulker L
    29 days, Wednesday, 5 pounds, 5'8-9",
Hezekiah Kemble, Benjamin Olden Philadelphia City PA 8/13/1777, 18 shoemaker A
    3 days, Monday, 20 dollars, 5'3-4", (relatives live nearby)
William Kemp, Samuel Hill Chester PA 10/29/1741, English 27 wool comber
    7 days, Thursday, 2 pounds, middle,
William Kemp, John Glenn Cecil MD 7/5/1753, Scot 24
    4 days, Sunday, 3 pistoles, 5'3",
John Kench, John Shellenberg Philadelphia PA 7/21/1773, American butcher L
    15 days, Wednesday, 3 pounds, 5'6",
Wilhem Kenig, Peter Hassenclever EJ ironworks 6/12/1766, German miner
    14 days, Thursday, 5 pounds, (under a 3 year 4 month contract, imported)
William Kenly, William Dunlap Lancaster PA 5/1/1755, 15 A
    10 days, Monday, 2 pounds,
Catherine Kennedy, James Smith Lancaster PA 12/7/1774, Irish 22
    6 days, Friday, 3 dollars,
Catherine Kennedy, James Smith Lancaster PA 9/20/1775, Irish 23 (pregnant) (2nd escape)
    43 days, Wednesday, 0.25 pounds,
Edward Kennedy, William Coale Baltimore MD 4/19/1764, Irish C
    5 pounds, 5'2",
Ferdinand Kennedy, Richard Jacobs Lancaster PA 12/13/1770, Scot 19
    6 days, Friday, 3 pounds, 5'6",
James Kennedy, David Lewis Chester PA 5/10/1786, English shoemaker
    10 days, Sunday, 8 dollars, 5'10",
John Kennedy, Henry Weatherby Gloucester NJ 9/26/1765, 22
    3 pounds, 5'7",
John Kennedy, Robert Adair Chester PA 12/25/1766, Irish 20
    19 days, Saturday, 2 pounds, 5'9",
John Kennedy, Abraham Kendick Lancaster PA 8/25/1773, Irish 18
    24 days, Monday, 5 pounds, 5'4",
John Kennedy, William Rogers Chester PA 2/28/1776, Irish 16
    9 days, Tuesday, 5 dollars, 5'4",
John Kennedy, Susannah Terry Philadelphia City PA widow 6/13/1754, American 16 blockmaker A
    6 days, Friday, 1 pound,
Mary Kennedy, Thomas Waters Chester PA 7/7/1768, Irish maid
    10 days, Monday, 1.5 pounds,
Samuel Kennedy, Richard Richison Chester PA 8/4/1748, Irish 23 soldier
    1 day, Wednesday, 3 pounds, 5'8",
Susanna Kennedy, John Bing Chester PA 10/28/1772, Irish
    3 pounds, 5',
Thomas Kennedy, Mark Bird Berks PA ironworks 5/2/1765, Irish
    5 pounds, 5'5",
Thomas Kennedy, William McCalla Bucks PA 8/24/1785, Irish 20
    3 days, Sunday, 6 dollars, 5'4-5",

William Kennedy, William Nicholson Philadelphia City PA 3/17/1752, English 25 surgeon
    1.5 pounds, 5'10", (arrived last fall)
Daniel Kenney, George Ross Lancaster PA 7/26/1764, Irish 23
    5 pounds, 5'8", (arrived last fall)
Samuel Kenning, Ezekiel Hunter Queen Anne's MD 8/3/1769, 18 shoemaker
    43 days, Wednesday, 2.5 pounds,
William Kenny, John Harvey Burlington NJ 4/30/1741, Irish 23 tanner
    4 days, Sunday, 2.5 pounds,
John Kensey, Richard Naylor Philadelphia City PA 11/28/1745, Scot 19
    8 days, Wednesday, 1 pound, middle,
John Kent, Benjamin Coates Chester PA 5/21/1767, Irish 22 wool comber
    4 days, Sunday, 5 pounds, 5'9",
Richard Kent, James Dobbins Philadelphia City PA 5/5/1748, sailor L
    21 days, Thursday, 4 pistoles,
Bryan Keran, Daniel McDermot Kent MD wheelwright 11/10/1773, A
    2 pounds, 5'4-5",
John Kerby, Robert Clinch Lancaster PA 10/18/1764, English 30 soldier L
    2 pounds, 5'5",
Michael Kerevan, William Huse Baltimore MD 9/21/1752, 18
    48 days, Friday, 1 pistole,
Abraham Kerflake, Stephen Onion Baltimore MD ironworks 9/27/1739, English 30
    10 Maryland pounds, short,
Neal Kerigan, Paul Connor Philadelphia City PA 1/26/1785, Irish 23 shoemaker
    8 dollars, 5'6-7", (arrived last May)
Patrick Kerlan, Robert Nivin New Castle DE 9/19/1745, Irish 19
    2.5 pounds,
John Kerlin, George Hinckel Lancaster PA 1/16/1766, Irish 16
    20 days, Friday, 2.5 pounds,
Timothy Kerly, Robert McKey Lancaster PA 12/29/1773, Irish 25
    58 days, Tuesday, 4 dollars, 5'6-7",
Michael Kern, Richard Gresham Kent MD 3/23/1769, German tailor C
    11 days, Sunday, 20 dollars, 5'7",
John Kerner, John Andrew Messerschmids Philadelphia City PA 11/15/1770, 20 tinplate-maker
    4 dollars, 4'9",
Catherine Kerney, James Ham Philadelphia City PA 9/30/1762, 10
    17 days, Monday, 0.5 pounds,
John Kerney, Thomas McCaughery Kent MD 4/25/1765,
    6 dollars,
Thomas Kerney, William Thomas Chester PA 4/13/1785, Irish
    3 days, Sunday, 5 dollars, 5'6",
Lawrence Keron, Rees Pritchard Chester PA 12/12/1734, Irish 22
    31 days, Monday, 2 pounds,
John Kerr, James Morgan Bucks PA ironworks 3/15/1775, Irish 22
    10 days, Monday, 2 pounds, 5'7-8",
John Kerr, James Morgan Bucks PA ironworks 9/27/1775, Irish 22 (2nd escape)
    1.5 pounds, 5'9",
Robert Kerr, James Morgan Bucks PA ironworks 3/15/1775, Irish 24
    10 days, Monday, 2 pounds, 5'6-7",
Robert Kerr, James Morgan Bucks PA ironworks 9/27/1775, Irish 24 (2nd escape)
    1.5 pounds, 5'9",
Manus Kerregan, Richard Hughs Chester PA 8/20/1747, Irish 30
    11 days, Sunday, 5 pounds, 6',
John Peter Kesslar, John Bockias Philadelphia PA 3/8/1764, German 28 tailor
    11 days, Sunday, 5 pounds, 5'4",
Jacob Kessler, Wallace & Donaldson Philadelphia City PA 11/17/1784, German
    2.5 pounds, 5'7", (ran from ship)
William Kettsendorf, Nathan Lewis Chester PA 12/6/1738, German 18
    8 days, Wednesday, 1 pound,
James Key, Conrad Waltecker Philadelphia City PA butcher 9/18/1746, Irish 18
    4 days, Sunday, 3 pounds,
John Key, Caleb Evans Philadelphia City PA blacksmith 4/20/1758, English 35
    5 days, Saturday, 2 pistoles, 5'6",
Simon Key, Richard Collings Gloucester NJ 8/13/1767, American 14 A
    19 days, Saturday, 1 pound,
Mary Keys, John Wharton Philadelphia City PA 7/29/1762, Irish 19
    10 days, Monday, 1.5 pounds, middle,

John Kicks, James Dickey Augusta VA 9/8/1773, 20
    43 days, Wednesday, 3 pounds, 5'8",
Robert Kid, William Rush Philadelphia City PA blacksmith 7/19/1750, English blacksmith
    4 days, Sunday, 5 pounds, small,
Thomas Kiegan, Samuel England Chester PA 10/11/1764, Irish 17
    11 days, Sunday, 2 pounds, short,
Archibald Kier, Mr. Warrell Hunterdon NJ 12/8/1737, Scot 24
    8 days, Wednesday, middle,
Philip Kieve, Hugh McCleland Lancaster PA 12/24/1751, Irish 19
    3 pounds, middle,
Philip Kieve, Hugh McCleland Lancaster PA 5/7/1752, Irish 19 (2nd escape)
    15 days, Wednesday, 1.5 pounds, middle,
Patrick Kilday, Christian Stake Lancaster PA 5/2/1792, Irish 19
    17 days, Sunday, 10 dollars, 5'8-9",
William Killpatrick, William Sittelton Chester PA 3/23/1774, 26
    3 days, Monday, 4 dollars, 5'6",
Caleb Kimble, Frederick Christian Philadelphia City PA 6/24/1789, 19 biscuit baker A
    10 days, Sunday, 4 dollars,
John Valentine Kinberger, Davis Bevan Chester PA 6/1/1774, German 18
    3 days, Monday, 4 dollars,
Matthew Kinchlow, Robert Warburton Chester PA 8/30/1750, Irish 19
    3 pounds, (arrived 10 weeks ago)
John Kindel, Richard Wistar Philadelphia City PA 4/19/1770, German 16
    10 dollars, 5'3",
Peter Kindley, William Miller Chester PA 10/19/1738, Irish 30 tailor
    5 days, Saturday, 2 pounds, tall,
Charles King, John Fuller Baltimore MD 6/26/1740, 23
    16 days, Tuesday, 1 pound, middle,
Charles King, Samuel McConaughy York PA 8/22/1771, Irish 20
    60 days, Sunday, 3 pounds, 5'5-6",
Charles King, George Brown Baltimore MD 7/11/1745, English 30 C
    4 pounds, short,
Henry King, Thomas Riche Bucks PA 4/27/1774, English
    10 days, Monday, 3 pounds, 5'8-9",
Hugh King, George McCallay Philadelphia City PA shipbuilder 8/2/1759, Scot 20 ship carpenter A
    5 pounds, 5'8",
James Corlina King, William Crum Frederick MD 5/29/1776, English 23
    3 pounds, 5'6-7",
John King, Ralph Sandiford 9/26/1732, English weaver
    2 pounds, short,
John King, Thomas Hallam Baltimore MD 11/7/1751, English 40 weaver
    3 pounds,
John King, Robert North Baltimore MD 4/3/1746, 25 C
    5 pounds, middle,
Peter King, Frederick Greiner Philadelphia City PA 9/20/1775, Irish 20 tailor
    3 days, Monday, 8 dollars, 5'6-7", (arrived last July)
Thomas King, Joseph Helm Frederick MD 7/1/1756, 25
    15 days, Wednesday, 4 pounds, short,
Thomas King, Richard Sprigg Anne Arundel MD 7/27/1774, English 30 bricklayer
    47 days, Saturday, 5 pounds, (arrived last March)
Thomas King, Amos Jones New Castle DE 10/24/1754, 18 A
    0.25 pounds, short,
Thomas King, Edward Mortimore Baltimore MD 7/25/1745, Irish 36 sawyer L
    8 days, Wednesday, 10 MD pounds, 5'6", (arrived 20 years ago)
William King, John Glen Cumberland PA 6/13/1771, Irish 30
    4 dollars, 6', (arrived 1 year ago)
William King, John Collier Berks PA 4/7/1773, American tailor L
    10 days, Monday, 2 pounds, 5'8.5",
James Kinley, John Maque Kent DE 4/12/1764, 26 L
    26 days, Saturday, 2 pounds, middle,
Richard Kinnersley, Archibald Mickle Gloucester NJ 11/27/1755, English 30
    3 days, Monday, 3 pounds, 5'9",
Eleanor Kinney, John Carmichael Chester PA 5/30/1765, Irish 25
    2 pounds,
Eleanor Kinney, John Carmichael Chester PA 8/20/1767, Irish 27 (2nd escape)
    1 pound, short,

Hezekiah Kinnicut, Thomas Stevenson Hunterdon NJ 1/17/1738, 24 joiner
    11 days, Sunday, 3 pounds, middle,
Michael Kinnin, Benedict Liddick Frederick MD 8/9/1775, Irish 23
    27 days, Friday, 4 pounds, 5'2",
John Kinsey, Isaac Grubb New Castle DE 5/14/1783,
    3 pounds, 5',
John Kinsiner, Michael McGuire Frederick MD 1/6/1773, German 35 tailor
    10 pounds, 5'6", (relatives live nearby)
John Kirby, Henry Miller Philadelphia City PA 11/3/1784, Irish 24 butcher
    3 days, Sunday, 0.03 pounds, 5'5-6", (arrived last May)
Mary Kirby, Matthias Boatman Philadelphia PA tavern-keeper 5/5/1763, 30
    7 days, Thursday, 2.5 pounds,
William Kirgan, Stephen Webb Chester PA 2/28/1776, American 21 L
    3 pounds, 5'10-11",
Henry Kirk, Benjamin Tasker Baltimore MD ironworks 7/11/1745, Irish 22 butcher C
    16 days, Tuesday, 2 pounds, middle,
Henry Kirk, Benjamin Tasker Baltimore MD ironworks 5/29/1746, Irish 23 butcher (2nd escape) C
    10 days, Monday, 4 pounds,
Patrick Kirk, Luke Morris Philadelphia City PA ropemaker 12/5/1749, Irish 21
    9 days, Tuesday, 5 pounds, middle,
Elizabeth Kirkbride, Alexander McDowell Philadelphia City PA 11/3/1773, 16
    11 days, Sunday, 0.25 pounds,
William Kirkpatrick, Peter Heisler 8/13/1788, Irish 18
    11 days, Saturday, 0.03 pounds,
William Kitchen, Alexander Miller Cumberland PA 10/19/1752, English 35
    55 days, Friday, 3 pounds, 5'6",
William Kitchen, Benjamin Boyers Chester PA 5/31/1764, English
    8 days, Wednesday, 3 pounds, 5'8",
Thomas Kitchin, John Coyell Bucks PA 11/3/1763, American 22 L
    19 days, Saturday, 5 pounds, 5'10",
William Kitchingman, Henry Willis Frederick VA 4/12/1739, English linen-printer C
    47 days, Saturday, 2 pistoles,
Edward Kite, Samuel Jaques Essex NJ 6/6/1751, English 30
    9 days, Tuesday, 5 pounds, middle,
John Kittle, Jonathan Vaughn Talbot MD ironworks 9/29/1763, Irish
    23 days, Tuesday, 1.5 pounds, middle,
John Kives, Robert Magill Bucks PA 6/2/1773, 15
    15 days, Wednesday, 2 pounds,
John Kline, William Kune Philadelphia City PA 5/22/1766, A
    14 days, Thursday, 2 pounds, 5'4",
Anthony Henry Knaighler, John Carpenter Lancaster PA 11/15/1775, German 25
    10 days, Monday, 2 pounds, 5'10-11",
William Knellers, Micajah James Baltimore MD 4/6/1774, English 22 forgeman
    19 days, Saturday, 8 dollars, 5'6-7",
Joseph Knight, Thomas Moore New Castle DE 3/22/1733,
    7 days, Thursday, 1.25 pounds, short,
Robert Knight, John Deaver Baltimore MD 5/20/1762, English
    46 days, Sunday, 5 pistoles, 5'3", (has wife with child)
Robert Knight, John Pinchback Philadelphia PA 9/20/1775, English
    9 days, Tuesday, 3 dollars, 5'3-4",
William Knight, John Justice 8/4/1768, English 29
    2 pounds, 5'9",
Frederick Knodle, Richard Flower Chester PA 9/14/1785, German 30
    5 days, Friday, 6 dollars, 5'5",
Maria Knodle, Richard Flower Chester PA 9/14/1785, German 32
    5 days, Friday, 6 dollars, (wife to Frederick Knodle)
Christopher Knoferinck, William Hannum Chester PA 8/30/1775, German 45
    29 days, Wednesday, 4 dollars, 5'9-10",
Patrick Knowler, Arney Lippincott Burlington NJ 7/14/1784, Irish 17
    3 days, Sunday, 8 dollars, (arrived 6 weeks ago)
Holliday Knowles, John Crosby Chester PA 7/16/1772, 20
    4 days, Sunday, 3 pounds, 5'6-7",
James Knox, Thomas Fitzwater Philadelphia PA blacksmith 11/3/1748, Irish blacksmith
    9 days, Tuesday, 2 pounds, 5'6",
Sarah Knox, David Currie Lancaster VA 2/20/1753, English C
    292 days, Monday,

George Koffman, John Eualt Berks PA 12/20/1759, German 16
    1 pound, (drove a team in the army)
Charles Godfrey Kossman, P. Marmie 4/14/1790, German 15
    2 dollars,
Nicholas Peter Koster, Thomas Tilbury Philadelphia City PA 3/16/1774, German 26 silk dyer
    6 days, Friday, 8 dollars, 5',
George Kraft, Nicholas Mayer Berks PA weaver 6/14/1764, German 17 A
    379 days, Tuesday, 5 pounds, middle,
Phillip Kramer, Peter Neff Philadelphia PA 5/30/1792, 19 blacksmith A
    17 days, Sunday, 6 pounds, 5'3-4",
Conrad Kratz, Michael Withers Lancaster PA 9/7/1796, German 24
    1 day, Tuesday, 20 dollars, tall,
Daniel Kreely, John Heston Jr Bucks PA 2/22/1770, 25
    10 days, Monday, 5'9-10",
John Godfrey Kritner, Jacob Vanderveer Somerset NJ 8/4/1763, German 28 sailor
    4 days, Sunday, 4 pounds, middle,
John Godfrey Kritner, Mark Bird Berks PA ironworks 12/29/1763, German 28 miller (2nd escape)
    32 days, Sunday, 3 pounds, 5'10",
Jacob Krotehous, Rachael Hawn Philadelphia City PA 6/22/1769, German-American 19 skin-dresser A
    3 days, Monday, 1.5 pounds, 5'8",
Martin Krytz, William Clifton Philadelphia City PA 5/23/1771, German 26 blacksmith
    4 days, Sunday, 8 dollars, 5'6", (arrived 10 months ago)
Hans Kuhn, Richard Philips Hunterdon NJ 1/29/1754, German 28
    11 days, Sunday, 2 pounds,
John Kuhn, George Keehmle Philadelphia City PA 6/20/1781, 17 barber
    2 days, Monday, 0.5 crowns, 4'6-7",
Maria Kummerfield, John Cuming Hunterdon NJ 4/11/1754, German 26
    41 days, Friday, 1 pounds,
Joseph Kunley, George Myer Cumberland PA 12/22/1773, German 21
    49 days, Thursday, 7 pounds, 5'4",
Philip Kuntzman, George Yeager Berks PA hatter 9/2/1789, 18 hatter A
    17 days, Sunday, 5 pounds, 5'4",
Andreas Kurfis, John Singer Philadelphia PA 4/9/1794, German 24
    17 days, Sunday, 30 dollars, 5'8-9",
John Kyly, Martin Howard RI 7/5/1733, Irish 32
    38 days, Monday, 2.5 pounds, short,
Johann Hendrick Kyser, John West Philadelphia City PA 10/3/1765, German 20
    3 pounds, 5'3-4",
Cornelius Lacey, Peter Robeson Philadelphia City PA gaoler 4/5/1775, 18
    mid-March, 4 dollars,
Thomas Lacey, Philip Lidig Baltimore MD 10/7/1772, English 23 cobler C
    16 days, Tuesday, 5 pounds, 5'6-7",
Patrick Lachay, Willing & Morris Philadelphia City PA merchants 5/2/1765, Irish 25 weaver
    4 days, Sunday, 8 dollars, 5'6", (lately arrived, ran from ship)
John Lad, Marquis Stephenson Berkeley VA 7/17/1776, 30 C
    6 dollars, 5'8",
No Name Lad, Henry Styner Salem NJ 11/11/1795, 18
    4 dollars, 5'9",
John Jacob Laedel, Andrew Boshart 10/5/1785, German 24 shoemaker
    3 days, Sunday, 3 pounds, 5'7",
John Laird, Henry Dills Northampton PA 4/5/1786, Irish 25
    8 days, Tuesday, 8 dollars, 5'6-7",
James Laky, Thomas Swayne Chester PA 8/12/1772, Irish 20
    8 days, Wednesday, 1 pound, 5'6",
William Lamare, Jacob Yearsley Chester PA 7/17/1793, American 19 L
    16 days, Monday, 8 dollars, 5'10-11",
Francis Lamb, George Perkin Kent MD 9/8/1763, 18 A
    1 pound,
John Lamb, John Grattan Augusta VA 11/19/1767, 30 tailor
    5 pounds, middle, (arrived 2 weeks ago)
James Lamberd, Charles Ridgely Jr Baltimore MD ironworks 8/10/1774, English 31 C
    56 days, Thursday, 50 dollars, 5'6",
Patrick Lamenon, Robert Deglish ship captain 1/27/1729, Irish 30 cooper A
    8 days, Wednesday, 1 pound,
Thomas Lamprey, Nathan Farrow Queen Anne's MD 7/16/1767, 28 wool comber C
    19 days, Saturday, 3 pistoles, 5'10",

Henry Lancaster, John Rees Lancaster Pa 8/24/1758, 25
    10 days, Monday, 1 pound,
Thomas Lanciscus, Michael Hillegas Philadelphia City PA potter 6/29/1738, 19 A
    4 days, Sunday, 2 pounds, middle,
James Land, Samuel Ellis Gloucester NJ 8/24/1774, 30 L
    10 pounds, 5'4-5",
Joseph Land, Thomas Stapleford Philadelphia City PA joiner 9/19/1734, 18
    3 days, Monday, 2 pounds, short,
William Land, David Clement Gloucester NJ 5/28/1794, 14 A
    14 days, Wednesday, 0.03 pounds, short,
John Landon, William Inman Anne Arundel MD 9/7/1769, English 22 C
    5 pounds, 5'8-9",
William Landram, Patrick Steward NY tailor 4/15/1742, Scot 28
    59 days, Monday, 1.5 pounds,
John Lane, Stephen Duncan Cumberland PA 4/19/1775, American 25 driver L
    58 days, Tuesday, 3 pounds, 5'9",
Richard Lane, Benjamin Thompson Cumberland NJ 8/18/1743, American 28 L
    15 days, Wednesday, 2 pounds, middle,
Thomas Lane, Daniel Goldsmith Chester PA 6/13/1751, American 35 shoemaker L
    8 days, Wednesday, 2 pounds, short,
Thomas Lane, James Belford Lancaster PA ironworks 5/7/1752, American 36 shoemaker (2nd esc) L
    12 days, Saturday, 2 pounds, 5'2",
Thomas Lane, John Wood Hunterdon NJ 5/22/1755, American 39 shoemaker (3rd escape) L
    44 days, Tuesday, 1.5 pounds, 5',
William Lane, Nathan Dorsey Anne Arundel MD 6/21/1764, 25 C
    5 pounds, 5'9",
John Langley, Nathan Shepherd Cumberland NJ 5/29/1776, 17 A
    20 days, Friday, 4 dollars, 5'6-7",
William Langley, Abraham Patton Baltimore MD 6/27/1771, English 26
    5 pounds, 5'7-8",
Joseph Langwieder, Peter Hassenclever EJ ironworks 6/12/1766, German 36 miner
    14 days, Thursday, 5 pounds, 5'6", (under a 3 year 4 month contract, imported)
Andrew Lanin, Philip Fitzgerald Salem NJ 7/25/1754, Irish 23
    3 days, Monday, 2 pounds, 6',
John Lannen, John Schofield Bucks PA 8/6/1752, Irish 19
    6 days, Friday, 4 pounds, middle,
Johannes Lantzell, Jacob Hagie Philadelphia PA papermaker 10/10/1751, German 17
    2 days, Tuesday, 1.5 pounds,
John Lap, Benjamin Kendall Philadelphia City PA 10/19/1758, German 20 A
    5 days, Saturday, 3 pounds, 5'8",
Cormack Lappen, Rinian Beall Frederick MD 10/24/1771, Irish butcher
    last July, 3 pounds, 5'9",
James Lapsley, Jacob Stern Sussex NJ ironworks 3/4/1762, Irish 28 peddler L
    about 43 days, 5 pounds, 6',
Cornelius Larey, Peter Robinson Philadelphia City PA 8/30/1775, Irish 19
    4 dollars,
Jacob Lasant, Herman Richman Salem NJ 6/7/1739, German 20 butcher
    15 days, Wednesday, 2.5 pounds, middle,
John Lascomb, Joseph Morris Philadelphia City PA 8/15/1771, English 15
    11 days, Sunday, 2 pounds,
Philip Laughen, James Martin Baltimore MD 3/5/1751, Irish 25
    8 days, Wednesday, 2 pounds, 5'6",
James Laughlin, Robert Coleman Philadelphia PA ironworks 5/24/1775, Irish 19 forgeman
    6 pounds, 5'7-8",
Daniel Lauhler, Abraham Musgrave Chester PA 8/8/1771, Irish 19
    5 days, Saturday, 4 dollars, 5'6-7",
Thomas Lavellan, Robert Cummins Cumberland PA 3/28/1765,
    2 pounds, 5'6",
Alexander Laverdy, Thomas Cockran Lancaster PA 6/23/1743, Irish 22
    2 pounds, tall,
Peter Lavote, Peter Soullard Cumberland NJ 3/7/1765, French shoemaker
    2 pounds,
Adam Lavour, William Lawrence Gloucester NJ 8/30/1775, German 17
    6 days, Friday, 8 dollars,
Robert Lawler, Samuel Simpson Philadelphia City PA 9/14/1769, Irish 21 shoemaker
    11 days, Sunday, 2 pounds, 5'6",

John Lawless, John Bowen Chester PA 8/29/1751, Irish 35 soldier
   3 days, Monday, 4 pounds, 6',
Mary Lawless, Joseph Mifflin Philadelphia City PA 2/25/1784, Irish 20
   3 pounds, (arrived last Nov., relatives live nearby)
David Lawrence, Robert Elliot Philadelphia PA 5/19/1784, 19 A
   8 days, Tuesday, 4 dollars, 5'9", (has 2 years left to served)
Henry Lawrence, John Wall Chester PA 3/26/1761, English 24
   4 days, Sunday, 3 pounds,
Johannes Lawser, John Bringhurst Philadelphia PA 10/21/1756, German 16
   18 days, Sunday, 1.5 pounds, 5',
Diana Lawson, Thomas Adams New Castle DE 7/20/1758, English (2nd escape)
   18 days, Sunday, 1 pound,
Diana Lawson, Isaac Richards Chester PA 6/16/1757, English
   16 days, Tuesday, 1 pound, middle,
Abraham Lay, Lewis Howell New Castle DE 4/12/1739, English 26 carpenter
   6 days, Friday, 2 pounds,
Abraham Lay, John Gooding New Castle DE 10/23/1740, English 27 carpenter (2nd escape)
   4 days, Sunday, 5 pounds, middle,
Joseph Layman, John Todd Bucks PA 5/21/1794, 19
   10 days, Sunday, 8 dollars, 5'3-4",
Anthony Lea, John Leacock ironworks 5/30/1734, English
   4 days, Sunday, 2 pounds, tall,
Anthony Lea, John Leacock ironworks 9/12/1734, English (2nd escape)
   tall,
Francis George Leader, William Tod Philadelphia City PA 5/24/1770, English 25
   17 days, Monday, 2 dollars, 5'8-9",
Patrick Leadon, Andrew Smyth Lancaster PA 4/5/1775, Irish 21 horseman
   19 days, Saturday, 3 pounds, 4'10",
Cadry Leary, Richard Lemmon New Castle DE 1/18/1770, Irish
   9 days, Tuesday, 1 pound, 5'5",
Cornelius Leary, James Thomas Chester PA 4/21/1773, Irish 15
   1 pound,
Daniel Leary, John Phipps Chester PA 8/17/1769, Irish 22
   5 days, Saturday, 3 pounds, 5'10",
John Leary, William Fitzhugh Calvert MD 7/24/1766, English caulker
   2.5 pounds, 5'8",
Patrick Ledden, David Allison York PA 3/28/1771, 16
   3 pounds, 5'2",
Charles Lee, Joseph Osborn Baltimore MD 10/24/1765, 30 watchmaker C
   4 days, Sunday, 3.5 pounds, 5'10",
Daniel Lee, John Alison Lancaster PA 9/27/1750, Irish 17 hatter
   10 days, Monday, 1.5 pounds, 5',
Daniel Lee, John Alison Lancaster PA 10/31/1751, Irish 18 hatter (2nd escape)
   4 days, Sunday, 2 pounds, 5'7",
Matthew Lee, John McNair Northampton PA 7/19/1753, Irish 19
   4 days, Sunday, 3 pounds, 5'6",
Purmott Lee, John Jones 4/27/1769, American 25 L
   8 dollars, 6',
Shadrach Lee, William Underwood New Castle DE 2/18/1762, 19 shoemaker A
   11 days, Sunday, 2 pounds, 5'8",
Thomas Lee, John Lewis Gloucester VA 6/15/1738, 50 C
   51 days, Tuesday, 1 pistole, tall, (arrived last March)
William Lee, David Scholefield New Castle DE 1/7/1768, Irish 21 L
   4 days, Sunday, 2 pounds, 5'3",
Benjamin Leech, Benjamin Engle Philadelphia PA 7/9/1761, tanner A
   11 days, Sunday, 3 pounds, 5'6",
Catherine Leech, James Abraham Montgomery PA 11/22/1786, 16
   0.03 pounds, short,
Eleanor Leech, Robert Mendenhall Chester PA 5/15/1760, 20
   44 days, Tuesday, 1.5 pounds,
Nicholas Leech, John Light Chester PA 1/4/1770,
   2 pounds, 5'8",
Jacob Leeman, Samuel Read Philadelphia City PA baker 9/27/1753, German 15
   6 days, Friday, 2 pistoles, (relatives live nearby)
Christian Leer, William Flentham Burlington NJ 5/19/1763, German 19
   10 days, Monday, 2 pounds,

Ann Leeson, John Rankin Lancaster PA fuller 2/16/1769, 35
    6 days, Friday, 5 pounds, tall,
Cornelius Leeson, George Ashbridge Chester PA 8/29/1765, Irish
    4 days, Sunday, 2 pounds, 5'8", (arrived 12 days ago, but was in the colonies before)
Solomon Leetch, John Kayton Baltimore MD 10/17/1771, English 25
    18 days, Sunday, 3 pounds, 5'5", (arrived 4 months ago)
Martin Leib, Abraham Schleiffer Chester PA 3/13/1776, German 20
    10 days, Monday, 5 pounds, 5'4",
Aaron Leidinbury, John Hirst Bucks PA 9/28/1749, English 31 schoolmaster
    9 days, Tuesday, 2 pounds, 5'9",
Solomon Leighthle, John Bailey Bucks PA 3/19/1794, American 19 L
    37 days, Monday, 6 dollars, 5'7-8",
John Leister, William Wilson Lancaster PA 9/7/1774, Irish 32
    3 days, Monday, 2 pounds, 5'4", (has been in the colonies before)
Thomas Leitch, Joshua Bisphan Burlington NJ 7/25/1754, Scot 40 carpenter
    19 days, Saturday, 5 pounds, 5'9",
Patrick Lekey, Thomas Pim Chester PA 8/6/1767, Irish 17
    7 days, Thursday, 2 pounds,
Joseph Lemon, Hugh Hutchin Monmouth NJ 6/8/1769, American 23 L
    10 days, Monday, 5 pounds,
Joseph Lemon, Hugh Hutchin Monmouth NJ 11/1/1770, American 24 (2nd escape) L
    17 days, Monday, 5 pounds, 5'7-8",
Christopher Lennord, Benjamin Galey Lancaster PA 10/31/1751, Irish 18
    4 days, Sunday, 2 pounds, 5'6",
John Conrad Lentersmith, John Lloyd Montgomery PA 8/9/1786, German 35
    3 days, Sunday, 4 dollars, 5'4",
Andrew Leonard, James Evans Chester PA 11/8/1770, Irish cooper
    11 days, Sunday, 2.5 pounds, 5'8-9",
Bryan Leonard, Robert Robeson Philadelphia City PA gaoler 5/22/1755, Irish 23 carpenter
    12 days, Saturday, 5 pounds, 5'4",
John Leonard, John Croker Philadelphia City PA 11/4/1736, Irish tailor
    3 pounds,
John Leonard, William Pancoost Burlington NJ 9/11/1740, English 18 weaver
    2 pounds, short, (arrived 8 weeks ago)
John Leonard, Robert Bishop Burlington NJ 12/6/1770,
    2 days, Tuesday, 8 dollars, 5'8",
Matthew Leonard, William Taite Northumberland VA 5/30/1765, Irish soldier C
    29 days, Wednesday, 3 pounds, 6',
William Leonard, William Allen Lancaster PA 3/8/1775, Irish 24
    10 days, Monday, 3 pounds, 5'9",
John Lesley, Josiah Porterfield Chester PA 9/11/1766, American 18 L
    13 days, Friday, 4 dollars, 5'7-8",
John Lesley, Josiah Porterfield Chester PA 4/7/1768, American 19 (2nd escape) L
    8 days, Wednesday, 2 pounds, 5'8",
Thomas Lesly, George Moore Lancaster PA 5/26/1768, 25 soldier
    13 days, Friday, 3 pounds, 5'5",
Ann Lester, Jonas Peterson New Castle DE 5/18/1774, Irish 30
    8 days, Wednesday, 4 dollars, middle,
John Lester, William Wilson Lancaster PA 3/29/1775, Irish 30
    3 days, Monday, 2 pounds, 5'4-5",
John Letthridge, Joseph Riggs Middlesex NJ 8/4/1773, Irish
    3 pounds, 5'8-9",
Isaac Levan, William Byers Chester PA 12/13/1775, German 20
    31 days, Monday, 2 pounds, 5',
William Leverson, Curtis Grubb Lancaster PA ironworks 5/19/1773, Irish gaol sale L
    15 days, Wednesday, 5 pounds, 5'7",
William Leveston, William McConnel Cumberland PA 10/26/1774, Irish 30
    4 dollars, 5'10",
Charles Levett, Widow Watson New Castle DE 11/19/1730, Irish 18
    2 days, Tuesday, 2.5 pounds, short,
John Levetu, Robert Andrews Lancaster PA 4/10/1755, German
    11 days, Sunday, 2 pounds,
Mary Levetu, Robert Andrews Lancaster PA 4/10/1755, German
    11 days, Sunday, 2 pounds, (wife to John)
Michael Levey, Edward Costolow Kent MD 9/22/1773, Irish
    2 pistoles, 5'6",

Elizabeth Levington, Phebe No Name Montgomery PA 7/1/1795,
   13 days, Thursday, 0.03 pounds,
William Lewed, Skellton Standiford Baltimore MD 9/5/1771, C
   16 days, Tuesday, 3 pounds, 5'7-8",
Thomas Lewellyn, Abel James Philadelphia PA 4/13/1769, Welsh 28 mason
   11 days, Sunday, 3 pounds, 5'10",
John Lewes, John Bennett Queen Anne's MD 5/8/1766, Welsh 20
   21 days, Thursday, 10 pounds, 5'9",
David Lewis, Samuel MacFerran Cumberland PA 8/13/1752, Welsh-American 18 carpenter L
   10 days, Monday, 3 pistoles, 5'10",
Edward Lewis, Benjamin Aritage Jr Philadelphia City PA 11/25/1772, English
   1.5 pounds,
Elizabeth Lewis, John Smith Kent MD 8/2/1764, C
   16 days, Tuesday, 3 pounds,
Isaac Lewis, Marmaduke Cooper Gloucester NJ 2/1/1775, 24 L
   5 pounds, 5'10-11",
Jenkins Lewis, William Hartley Chester PA 2/24/1743, American 23 gaol sale L
   34 days, Friday, 2.5 pounds,
John Lewis, John Wright Cecil MD 4/4/1754, English 22
   5 days, Saturday, 5 pounds, short,
John Lewis, Matthew Hines Philadelphia PA 8/7/1776, Irish 18 soldier
   5 dollars, 5'7",
Silas Lewis, John Hart Philadelphia City PA 7/16/1794, 14
   7 days, Wednesday, 0.01 dollars,
Silas Lewis, John Hart Philadelphia City PA 7/23/1794, 14 (2nd escape)
   5 dollars,
Susannah Lewis, Belchior Preston Philadelphia City PA 7/9/1741, Welsh 20
   3 days, Monday, 1 pound, middle,
Thomas Lewis, William Hugg Gloucester NJ 10/2/1755, 22 (ran before)
   2 days, Tuesday, 2 pounds, 5'3",
William Lewis, Benjamin Marklay Philadelphia PA 9/20/1775, English blacksmith
   10 days, Monday, 6 dollars, 5'8-9",
John Leycer, Thomas Morgan Chester PA 4/17/1746, buttonmaker
   4 days, Sunday, 1 pound, middle,
James Libo, Samuel Henry Hunterdon NJ 6/28/1775, Irish 20
   9 days, Tuesday, 10 dollars,
Joseph Lideard, Pryor & Joy 6/27/1765, English 19
   3 days, Monday, 5'3-4",
Martin Lieberknecht, Philip Dietrict Lancaster PA 5/22/1793, Swiss 40
   22 days, Tuesday, 15 pounds, 5'10",
John Lifter, James Williamson, Calvert MD 8/18/1737,
   5 pounds, middle,
Richard Lightborne, Samuel Massey Queen Anne's MD 7/16/1752, English 40 C
   11 days, Sunday, 2 pistoles, 5'8",
Anne Lightfoot, Thomas Rutherford Frederick VA sheriff 2/5/1745, Irish 37 C
   39 days, Sunday, 5 pounds,
Jane Lightfoot, Francis Maybury Jr Philadelphia PA 3/24/1743, 24
   last month, 1 pound, middle,
John Lightfoot, Thomas Rutherford Frederick VA sheriff 2/5/1745, English 27 mason C
   39 days, Sunday, 5 pounds, middle,
Emanuel Lightin, John Roberts miller 12/16/1762, 20
   2 days, Tuesday, 3 pounds, 5'8",
George Limeburd, Joseph Walker Philadelphia PA 5/1/1755, German 20
   end of Jan., 2 pounds, 5'6",
David Linch, John Cox Philadelphia PA 7/11/1754, Irish 27
   9 days, Tuesday, 3 pounds, 5'5",
Michael Linch, Lawrence Howard Chester PA 9/29/1773, Irish 29
   9 days, Tuesday, 4 dollars, 5'4-5",
Nicholas Linch, Thomas Palmer Philadelphia City PA 7/12/1775, Irish 26 brassfounder
   15 days, Wednesday, 3 pounds, 5'8",
Patrick Linch, George Taylor Chester PA 9/4/1746, Irish 20
   9 days, Tuesday, 2.5 pounds, middle,
Peter Linch, Alexander Mitchell Lancaster PA 9/15/1768, 23 harness-maker
   11 days, Sunday, 1 pound, 5'9",
Thomas Linch, Evan Jones Philadelphia PA 1/11/1770, Irish 19
   10 days, Monday, 2 pounds, 5'8",

Timothy Linch, Thomas Hooton Burlington NJ 8/23/1753, Irish 25
   60 days, Sunday, 2 pounds, 5'6",
Timothy Linch, Thomas Hooton Burlington NJ 12/18/1755, Irish 27 (2nd escape)
   7 days, Thursday, 1.5 pounds, 5'7",
Catherine Lindon, Robert Darlington Cumberland PA 8/21/1776, Irish (pregnant)
   1 pound,
John Lindsay, John Test Philadelphia City PA 8/16/1753, 20 A
   18 days, Sunday, 3 pounds, 5'7",
David Lindsey, Caleb Hewes Philadelphia City PA 9/1/1773, 17 hatter A
   4 days, Sunday, 12 dollars, 5'8-9",
Luke Lindsey, Samuel White Cecil MD 3/18/1731, Irish 17
   4 days, Sunday, 1 pound, short,
Robert Lindsey, John Wilkerson York PA ironworks 10/6/1763, Scot
   3 pounds, 5'8",
Walter Lindy, James Bennet Chester PA 11/26/1767, English 24
   3 days, Monday, 2 pounds, 5'8",
Walter Lindy, John Firth Salem NJ 2/11/1768, English 24 (2nd escape)
   11 days, Sunday, 3 pounds, 5'8-9", (arrived last fall)
Walter Lindy, John Firth Salem NJ 8/9/1770, English 26 (3rd escape)
   7 days, Thursday, 2 pounds, 5'9-10", (10th time to run away)
George Linenger, William Willis York PA 2/27/1766, German 25 weaver
   5 pounds, 5'8-9",
John Linn, Theophilus Davies Chester PA 2/2/1791, American 18 farmer L
   14 days, Wednesday, 3 dollars, 5'6", (relatives live nearby)
Edward Linnard, William Connely Philadelphia PA 4/4/1754, Irish 24
   9 days, Tuesday, 2 pounds, 5'8",
Michael Linsey, Joseph Baker Chester PA 8/2/1744, Irish 25
   1.5 pounds, middle,
Thomas Linsey, Joseph Decow Hunterdon NJ 9/24/1741, Irish
   4 days, Sunday,
Jacob Lippencott, Frederick Engle Chester PA 4/21/1773, 19 A
   15 days, Wednesday, 3 pounds, 5'8", (has 2 years left to serve)
John Lipscomb, John Eastburn Philadelphia PA 8/9/1739, 18
   7 days, Thursday, 1.5 pounds, middle,
Ann Liston, Jonas Peterson New Castle DE 2/17/1773, Irish
   7 days, Thursday, 4 dollars,
George Little, Michael Masser Lancaster PA tanner 11/1/1775, English 17 A
   6 dollars, 5'6-7",
Richard Little, Thomas Renick Lancaster PA 12/21/1769, English 19 weaver
   74 days, Sunday, 2 pounds, short,
Thomas Little, Isaac Bailey Chester PA 3/29/1770, Irish gaol sale L
   13 days, Friday, 3 pounds, 5'8-9",
John Liveston, Samuel McCrory Philadelphia City PA 2/24/1773, 16 A
   22 days, Wednesday, 3 pounds, 5',
Peter Livingston, William Bell Philadelphia City PA 7/23/1783, 16 tailor
   6 days, Thursday, 3 pounds,
Margaret Llewllin, Edward Lewis Philadelphia City PA 1/7/1755, Welsh 30
   late Oct., 2 pounds, middle,
Edward Lloyd, Samuel Wheler Philadelphia PA 1/18/1739, English 22 hired L
   5 days, Saturday, 1 pound, middle,
Luther Lloyd, Robert Lewis Philadelphia City PA 10/20/1768, English 19
   4 days, Sunday, 5 pounds, 5'6-7",
Richard Lloyd, John Cox Monmouth NJ 4/12/1744, Welsh 25 potter
   8 days, Wednesday, 1 pound, short,
Richard Lloyd, Arthur Murphy Bucks PA 8/22/1745, Welsh 26 potter (2nd escape)
   3 days, Monday, 3 pounds, short,
Thomas Lloyd, Philip Thomas Chester PA 6/23/1737, Welsh 22 sailor
   4 days, Sunday, 1.5 pounds, middle,
William Loadsman, Tobias Griscom Queen Anne's MD 6/17/1742, Irish joiner
   18 days, Sunday, 4 pounds, 6',
John Loag, Andrew Caldwell Philadelphia City PA 11/10/1773, A
   3 pounds, 5'8", (ran from ship Jupiter)
John Lobach, Casper Greff Philadelphia City PA 9/26/1765, German 24 tailor
   3 pounds, 6',
Thomas Lockhart, John Almore Baltimore MD 8/17/1769, C
   44 days, Tuesday, 5 pounds, 6',

Mary Lofters, Ann Jones Philadelphia City PA 3/3/1763,
  10 days, Monday, 2 pounds, short,
Bartholomew Logan, William Spear Lancaster PA 6/21/1750, American wampum-maker L 5'8",
Henry Logan, William Starrett Chester PA 6/2/1784, Irish 21
  5 days, Friday, 8 dollars,
James Logan, Edmund Milne Philadelphia City PA goldsmith 8/3/1769, Irish 16 silversmith
  18 days, Sunday, 2 pounds,
John Logan, James Alexander gardener 5/22/1766, shoemaker
  11 days, Sunday, 3 pounds, 5'6",
Samuel Logan, Joseph Rhoads Philadelphia City PA 6/18/1767, Irish 25 carpenter
  3 pounds, 5'8-9",
Joseph Lokey, Samuel Morris 12/18/1760, American L
  35 days, Thursday, 1.5 pounds, 5'6",
Edward Loller, John Climson Lancaster PA 3/10/1747, Irish 17
  21 days, Thursday, 1 pound, middle,
John Lollers, Thomas Harvey 7/24/1755, Irish 40 weaver C
  5 pounds,
Francis Lolley, William Boulton Queen Anne's MD 4/18/1754, English
  18 days, Sunday, 5 pounds, 5'5",
Mark Lolor, Hugh Clark New Castle DE 2/13/1750, Irish
  1 pound, 6',
Mark Lolor, Hugh Clark New Castle DE 8/23/1750, Irish (2nd escape)
  2 pounds, 5'9",
Larke Londergan, James Gorrel Philadelphia City PA 7/16/1741, Irish 18
  3 days, Monday, 1 pound, (ran from ship)
Edward Loney, William Snow Anne Arundel MD ship captain 2/15/1770,
  1 pound, 5'7", (ran from ship)
Abraham Long, Robert Arthur Kent DE 8/4/1748, Irish 18
  8 days, Wednesday, 2.5 pounds, short,
Christian Long, Frederick Shimer Chester PA 6/6/1765, German 23 weaver
  4 days, Sunday, 3 pounds, short, (has 3.5 years left to serve)
Christian Long, Frederick Shimer Chester PA 2/6/1766, German 24 weaver (2nd escape)
  10 pounds, 5',
George Long, James Hutchings Baltimore MD 1/21/1784, Irish shoemaker
  8 days, Tuesday, 5 pounds, 5'6-7", (ran from ship)
Moses Long, Samuel Hart Baltimore MD 8/14/1746, English C
  11 days, Sunday, 3 pounds, tall,
Nathan Long, Jacob Hufty Salem NJ 5/20/1795, 18 A
  18 days, Saturday, 4 dollars,
Thomas Long, Isaac Gibbs Cecil MD 12/12/1754,
  18 days, Sunday, 3 pounds, 5'10",
William Long, John Ellick Philadelphia City PA 9/20/1764, Irish 21 tailor
  4 dollars, 5'5",
William Long, Jacob Falconer Kent MD 3/2/1774, German turner
  4 dollars, 5'6",
William Long, Samuel Shaw Delaware PA 10/15/1794, weaver A
  10 days, Sunday, 1 dollar, 5'8-9",
Thomas Longue, John Lamborn Chester PA 10/14/1772, Irish 18
  3 days, Monday, 2 pounds, 5'9",
Patrick Looby, James Brown Chester PA 6/21/1786, Irish
  9 days, Monday, 10 dollars, 5'11",
Edward Looney, Lleweling Davis Chester PA 10/22/1741, Irish 16
  3 days, Monday, 1.5 pounds,
Aaron Loper, Thomas Proctor Kent DE 8/30/1775, American 30 wheelwright L
  66 days, Monday, 14 dollars, 5'8-9",
Frederick Lorsboach, Michael Boyer Philadelphia City PA 8/27/1761,
  6 days, Friday, 2 pounds, 5',
John Lott, John Ely Bucks PA 7/25/1781, 20
  138 days, Friday, 0.25 pounds, 5'11",
Charles Love, Philip Ludwell Lee Westmoreland VA 9/29/1757, 60 musician
  31 days, Monday, 10 pounds, tall,
James Love, Patrick Miller Chester PA 8/16/1750, Irish 20
  5 pounds, short,
John Lovegrove, Stephen Sturgiss Kent MD 5/3/1750, cooper
  25 days, Sunday, 5 pounds, 5'2", (use to the sea)

Robert Lovegrove, Robert McClellend York PA 10/5/1769, English 20 school teacher
    31 days, Monday, 3 pounds, 5'5",
William Lovejoy, Charles Rass Philadelphia City PA 12/26/1754, 16 A
    12 days, Saturday, 0.5 pounds, middle,
Thomas Lovely, Andrew Meek Baltimore MD 7/2/1772, English C
    12 days, Saturday, 3 pounds, 6',
Joseph Lovett, Joseph Bell Burlington NJ ironworks 7/5/1775, French
    10 days, Monday, 5 dollars, 5'9-10",
John Low, John Tate Cumberland PA 8/31/1774, Scot 20 wheelwright
    5 pounds, 5'6",
Robert Low, Daniel Ruffin Philadelphia City PA ship captain 3/29/1733, 24
    middle,
John Lowe, Robert Stewart Lancaster PA 6/8/1749, 23
    10 days, Monday, 3 pounds, 5'6",
John Lowe, Daniel Smith Philadelphia City PA 12/15/1773, English
    4 days, Sunday, 12 dollars, 5'7", (arrived this fall)
David Lowery, Thomas Burney Cumberland PA 5/6/1762, 40 blacksmith L
    181 days, Friday, 2 pounds, 5'10",
Philip Lowman, Michael Withir Lancaster PA 8/20/1777, 16 gunsmith A
    6 dollars,
Hugh Lowry, Robert Fulton Lancaster PA 11/27/1766, Irish weaver
    16 days, Tuesday, 3 pounds, 5'8",
Nathaniel Lowry, Peter Horning Philadelphia PA 8/28/1766, 19 A
    14 days, Thursday, 0.04 pounds and a nib of punch,
Robert Lowry, Daniel Turner Cecil MD 6/23/1768,
    227 days, Sunday, 5 pounds, 6',
Frederick Loy, Samuel Edward 2/5/1794, German silk-weaver
    23 days, Monday, 100 dollars, short,
Thomas Loyder, William Hamilton Philadelphia City PA ship captain 4/25/1754,
    2 days, Tuesday, 0.5 pounds, tall,
George Lucas, George Lytle Baltimore MD 5/16/1771, English 26 C
    23 days, Tuesday, 2 pounds, 5'6",
Peter Lucas, Charles Elliot Salem NJ 11/1/1764, 30 shoemaker L
    25 days, Sunday, 3 pounds, 5'9",
Frederick Luderiz, Bejamin Levy Philadelphia City PA 12/10/1767, German 21
    2 days, Tuesday, 3 pounds, 6'1-2", (arrived last year)
Englehod Ludwick, Matthias Landenberger Philadelphia City PA 5/26/1773, 16
    10 days, Monday, 3 dollars,
Thomas Lump, Isaac Towers Philadelphia City PA 12/9/1762, English 22
    2 pounds, 5'2",
John Lupton, Alexander Rutherford PhiladelphiaCity PA shoemaker 4/9/1767, American 18 shoemaker A
    6 days, Friday, 2 pounds, 5'3-4",
Christian Luterman, Nathaniel Fitzrandolph Hunterdon NJ 8/14/1755, German
    15 days, Wednesday, 2 pounds, 6',
Philip Lutts, Edward Milner Philadelphia PA 4/11/1771, German 18
    4 days, Sunday, 5 pounds, 5'5", (arrived 5 years ago)
Jacob Lutz, John Phillip De Haas Philadelphia City PA 7/26/1780, 16
    91 days, Tuesday, 300 dollars, (relatives live nearby)
William Newman Luxley, Robert Wright Monmouth NJ 1/10/1776, English 25 farmer
    9 days, Tuesday, 10 dollars, 5'9-10",
Matthias Luyker, Brian Wilkinson Philadelphia City PA carver 12/25/1755, German 16
    20 days, Friday, 1.5 pounds, short, (relatives live nearby)
James Lyis, Margaret Lowe Talbot MD 3/27/1746, Irish weaver
    5 pounds,
Thomas Lynagh, William Ellis Cecil MD 10/2/1746, Irish C
    12 days, Saturday, 1.5 pounds, (lately arrived)
John Lynch, Unlisted Name 7/5/1786, Irish 30
    7 days, Wednesday, 20 dollars, 5'8",
Thomas Lynch, John Yoder Philadelphia PA 7/9/1747, Irish 20
    4 days, Sunday, 3 pistoles,
Thomas Lynch, William Ramsey Chester PA 2/16/1769, 20
    1.5 pounds, 5'8",
Philip Lynn, Henry Skiles Lancaster PA 4/29/1756, German 24
    4 pounds, 5'4",
Joseph Lyon, Thomas Overend Philadelphia City PA 11/8/1750, Irish 20 heel-maker
    3 pounds, 5'7",

Joseph Lyon, Joseph Sinclar Philadelphia City PA heel-maker 2/20/1753, Irish 22 heel-maker
    2 days, Tuesday, 2 pounds, short, (2nd escape)
Peter Lyon, William Allen Chester PA 5/17/1764, Irish 20
    9 days, Tuesday, 2 pistols, 5'7", (arrived last fall)
Robert Lyon, Jacob Lemmon Baltimore MD 6/9/1784, Scot fuller C
    33 days, Saturday, 8 dollars, 5'6", (lately arrived)
James Lyons, James Kennedy Chester PA 8/6/1767, Irish 25
    4 days, Sunday, 2.5 pounds, 5'9-10",
Joseph Lyons, Joseph Sinclar Philadelphia City PA heel-maker 9/14/1752, Irish
    3 days, Monday, 3 pounds, (arrived 2 years ago)
William Lyons, Joshua Fisher Philadelphia City PA 6/15/1769, Irish fuller
    8 days, Wednesday, 5'5", (ran from ship)
Philip Macall, Robert Holiday Chester PA 7/28/1737, Irish 24
    4 days, Sunday, 1.5 pounds, middle,
Daniel Macarty, Jacob Hagie Philadelphia PA papermaker 5/30/1751, Irish-American 17 A
    3 days, Monday, 2 pounds, 5',
Daniel Macarty, Jacob Hagie Philadelphia PA papermaker 7/11/1751, Irish-American 17 (2nd esc) A
    3 days, Monday, 1.5 pounds, 5',
Daniel Macarty, Jacob Hagie Philadelphia PA papermaker 10/10/1751, Irish-American 17 (3rd esc) A
    2 days, Tuesday, 1.5 pounds, 5',
Daniel Macarty, Benjamin Corson Bucks PA 4/10/1755, Irish-American 21 (4th escape) A
    4 days, Sunday, 1 pound, 5'8",
Dennis Macarty, David Linsey Bucks PA 7/30/1741, Irish 30
    6 days, Friday, 2 pounds, middle,
Sheeley Macarty, William Hitchman Cecil MD 9/20/1750, Irish 36
    10 days, Monday,
Matthew MacChoon, Mary Harvey New Castle DE 9/14/1774, English 15
    1.5 pounds, (arrived last April)
Bernard MacClue, Rebecca Leech Philadelphia PA 8/4/1748, Irish 16
    6 days, Friday, 5 pounds, 5',
Alexander MacCoy, Patrick Dovan Anne Arundel MD 8/15/1745, Scot 30
    24 days, Monday, 1.5 pounds, middle,
Samuel MacCoy, Michael Hutchinson Bucks PA tailor 11/23/1752, American 19 A
    3 days, Monday, 4 pounds,
Alexander MacDonald, Robert Ritchie Chester PA 11/3/1763, Scot 26 pewterer
    1 pound, 5'8", (lately arrived)
Daniel MacDonald, Patrick Brown Hunterdon NJ 6/8/1749, Irish 19
    11 days, Sunday, 3 pounds, short,
Donald MacDonald, William Ellis Cecil MD 10/2/1746, Irish
    12 days, Saturday, 1.5 pounds,
Donald Macdonald, William Ellis Cecil MD 10/2/1746, Irish C
    12 days, Saturday, 1.5 pounds, (lately arrived)
Nicholas MacDonnell, Nicholas Rogers Philadelphia City PA 9/17/1730, Irish 23 baker
    3 days, Monday, 2 pounds, middle,
John MacGarvey, Thomas Jacob Cecil MD 8/6/1747, weaver
    1 pound, middle,
John MacGuire, John Phillips Kent MD 3/26/1730, Irish
    11 days, Sunday, 2 pounds, middle,
Patrick MacGuire, Samuel John Atlee Lancaster PA 1/10/1771, Irish 21
    5 days, Saturday, 1 pound, 5'8",
Patrick MacGuire, Samuel John Atlee Lancaster PA 4/25/1771, Irish 21 (2nd escape)
    7 days, Thursday, 1 pound, 5'7-8",
Edward MacGunnigan, William Armour New Castle DE 9/25/1746, Irish 22
    14 days, Thursday, 1.5 pounds, short,
John MacHafee, Lancelot Martin Bucks PA 9/21/1738, Irish 20
    4 days, Sunday, 2 pounds, short,
Alexander MacHaham, Daniel Jappie Philadelphia City PA ship captain 8/27/1747, Irish 25
    6 days, Friday, 1.5 pounds, (ran from ship)
John Machlin, Isaac Pinn Chester PA sadler 3/7/1781, A
    16 days, Monday, 1 spanish dollar, 5'4-5",
Morice Machony, John Alison Lancaster PA 4/19/1770, Irish 19
    9 days, Tuesday, 3 pounds, 5'9",
Agnes MacKay, Jared Graham Lancaster PA 11/24/1768,
    7 days, Thursday, 6 dollars,
Jane MacKelanen, Moses Hewes Philadelphia City PA 12/23/1729,
    10 days, Monday, 1 pound, middle,

James MacKelliek, Patrick Henry Lancaster PA 6/8/1749, Irish 29 weaver
    25 days, Sunday, 3 pistoles, short,
Westlock MacKenny, Peter Bard Philadelphia City PA 1/21/1746, 32 carpenter L
    45 days, Monday, 3 pounds, middle,
John MacKenzy, Peter Cuff Philadelphia City PA 6/1/1732, Scot 30 soldier
    2 pounds, middle,
Ann Mackey, Alexander Feasey 5/5/1763, Irish 30
    22 days, Wednesday, six pence,
Ann Mackey, David Ray Lancaster PA 11/7/1792, Irish 20
    56 days, Wednesday, 4 dollars, 5'5-6", (lately arrived)
Anne Mackey, Jared Graham Lancaster PA 5/3/1770, Irish 18
    9 days, Tuesday, 4 dollars,
John Mackey, Robert Ritchie Chester PA 11/3/1763, Scot 19 sailor
    1 pound, 5'6", (lately arrived)
Nancy Mackey, Robert Smith 7/12/1775, Irish L
    14 days, Thursday, 1 pound,
William MacKinney, Daniel O'Nel Gloucester NJ 3/27/1746, American L
    3 pounds, middle,
John Mackmaman, Samuel Richardson Bucks PA 3/29/1729, Irish
    11 days, Sunday, 3 pounds, short,
Mary Macknamara, Aquila Jones Philadelphia City PA 7/7/1773, American 10 L
    6 days, Friday, 1 pound,
Thomas Mackon, William Harrison Burlington NJ 6/17/1736, 24 weaver
    2 pounds, middle,
Alexander MacLane, James English Monmouth NJ 5/6/1731, Irish 20
    2 pounds, short,
Barney MacMahon, Charles Elliot Salem NJ 8/14/1776, Irish 15
    2 pounds,
John MacMullen, Enos Lewis Philadelphia PA 8/15/1745, Irish 17
    3 days, Monday, 2 pounds,
Neal MacNeal, John Matlack Gloucester NJ farmer 3/22/1729, Irish
    2 pounds,
William MacQueen, Robert Ritchie Chester PA 11/3/1763, Scot 21 sailor
    1 pound, 5'9", (lately arrived)
James MacQuier, Benjamin Bradford Cecil MD doctor 6/4/1747, Irish
    27 days, Friday, 1 pound, 5'6",
John MacQuire, James Terry Philadelphia City PA 9/28/1752, Irish
    4 days, Sunday, 3 pounds, 5'10",
Patrick MacQuire, Thomas Fletcher Philadelphia PA 6/18/1747, Irish
    4 days, Sunday, 2 pounds, middle,
Daniel Macraw, Charles Dick Fredericksburg VA 10/9/1746, Scot
    67 days, Sunday, 2 pistoles, 5'2",
Mary MacRoy, Elias Grosjean Philadelphia PA ironworks 6/11/1767, Irish 20
    7 days, Thursday, 3 pounds, middle,
John MacWhan, Katherine Child Philadelphia City PA 9/20/1750, merchant
    1 day, Wednesday, short,
Dennis Madden, Joseph Tate Lancaster PA pastor 6/14/1750, Irish 25 soldier L
    3 pounds, 5'9",
Michael Madden, John Livezey Philadelphia PA 1/29/1794, 18 A
    9 days, Monday, 0.06 dollars,
William Madden, Philip Backen Lancaster PA 7/27/1774, American 26 gaol sale L
    5 pounds, 6',
Elizabeth Maddock, John Galbreath Philadelphia City PA shopkeeper 7/12/1759,
    6 days, Friday, 3 pounds,
Nicholas Magahey, William Woodward Hunterdon NJ 8/13/1752, Irish
    4 days, Sunday, 3 pounds, 5'5", (has a wife)
Philip Maganaty, George McCullough Lancaster PA 7/31/1766, Irish 17
    7 days, Thursday, 2 pounds, 5'5-6", (arrived this summer)
John Magaragill, Isaac Smith Accomack VA 6/22/1738, Irish 25 tailor
    11 days, Sunday, 6 Virginia pounds,
Abraham Magee, Michael Hutchinson Bucks PA tailor 9/14/1749, Irish 24 tailor
    4 days, Sunday, 4 pounds, middle,
Abraham Magee, Philip Marot Burlington NJ 10/18/1750, Irish 25 tailor (2nd escape)
    4 days, Sunday, 2 pounds, middle,
Charles Magee, Evan Evans Chester PA 4/20/1785, Irish butcher
    3 days, Sunday, 3 pounds, 5'6",

James Magee, John Shugert Cecil MD 5/8/1760, Irish cooper
   26 days, Saturday, 3 pounds, 5'8",
Samual Magee, Abraham Yarnall New Castle DE 1/6/1763, 13 shoemaker A
   1 pound,
Sarah Magee, John Walker Chester PA 9/12/1765, 25
   1 pound,
Henry Magg, Justinean Fox Philadelphia City PA 12/15/1790, tailor A
   33 days, Friday, (has 3 years 2 months left to serve)
Ever Magines, Joseph Wilson Chester PA 8/2/1770, Irish 22 weaver
   8 days, Wednesday, 1.5 pounds, (arrived 2 days ago)
Edward Maginnis, Andrew Richman Gloucester NJ 9/6/1775, Irish 20
   4 dollars, 5'8",
Charles Maguire, John Reilly Frederick MD 9/18/1755, Irish 23
   8 days, Wednesday, 2 pistoles, 5'9",
Turrence Magwigin, William Allen Burlington NJ 1/28/1755, Irish 27
   2 days, Tuesday, 2 pounds, 5'6",
Turrence Magwigin, William Allen Burlington NJ 9/4/1755, Irish 27 (2nd escape)
   5 days, Saturday, 3 pounds, 5'6",
John Mahaffey, James Bennet Chester PA 11/2/1774, Irish 19
   8 days, Wednesday, 2 pounds, 5'7", (lately arrived)
John Mahany, John Pricket Philadelphia City PA 1/10/1740, 22
   2 days, Tuesday, 1.5 pounds, (purchased the day before from Capt. Atwood)
Thomas Mahar, Thomas Lewis Chester PA 7/9/1752, Irish
   10 days, Monday, 3 pounds, middle,
John Maher, Joshua Fisher Philadelphia City PA 6/15/1769, Irish gentleman's servant
   8 days, Wednesday, 5'5", (ran from ship)
Paul Mahon, Simon Shirlock Philadelphia City PA shipwright 9/3/1747, Irish 24 sawyer
   5 days, Saturday, 5 pounds, middle,
Cornelius Mahoney, Jacob Shinn Burlington NJ 8/2/1775, Irish
   4 dollars, 5'6-7",
John Mahoney, Henry Howard Baltimore MD 10/13/1784, Irish 26
   92 days, Tuesday, 20 pounds, 5'7",
John Mahony, William Webb Harford MD 8/7/1776, Irish 23 C
   72 days, Tuesday, 16.5 dollars, 5'10",
Joseph Mahony, Edward Broadfield Philadelphia PA 9/27/1764, Irish 19
   6 days, Friday, 1 pound, 5'4", (lately arrived)
James Mahoon, John Wilkins Jr Gloucester NJ 8/23/1775, 19
   8 days, Wednesday, 1 pound, 5'6",
Rachel Mahorne, Matthias Keene Philadelphia PA 12/14/1752, Irish 25
   6 days, Friday, 1.5 pounds, tall,
John Maine, Robert Ford St Mary's MD 7/13/1738, English
   112 days, Saturday, 5 Maryland pounds,
Christopher Major, Thomas Bourtchier Philadelphia City PA shoemaker 9/13/1750, English 25
   6 days, Friday, 1.5 pounds, 5'8",
Christopher Major, Matthias Holstein Philadelphia PA 1/29/1751, English 26 (2nd escape)
   9 days, Tuesday, 2 pounds, tall,
Edward Major, Richard Pearne Philadelphia PA miller 7/21/1737, English gardener
   2 pounds, short,
William Makee, William Nelson New Castle DE 9/15/1773,
   26 days, Saturday, 5'6", (ran from ship)
Patrick Makferson, James Whithill Lancaster PA 7/7/1743, Irish 50 soldier
   8 days, Wednesday, 1 pound,
Christian Henry Malchowff, Unlisted Name Philadelphia City PA 4/6/1796, German 26 tailor
   10 days, Sunday, 7 dollars, 5'9",
William Malice, James Hinchman Gloucester NJ 9/22/1779, American 18 A
   27 days, Thursday, 40 dollars, 5'2-3",
Peggy Mallen, John Singleton Chester PA 6/29/1758,
   14 days, Thursday, 1.5 pounds, 5',
John Malliby, Levi Pownall Lancaster PA 12/24/1788, A
   15 days, Tuesday, 0.03 pounds, 5'6",
John Charles Mallin, John Dickenson Salem NJ 11/10/1773, German butcher
   4 days, Sunday, 5'6-7",
Thomas Malloy, James Hockley Chester PA 5/19/1763, Irish 27
   11 days, Sunday, 3 pounds, 5'5",
James Malone, Thomas Willcox Chester PA papermaker 7/20/1738, Irish 18
   8 days, Wednesday, 3 pounds, short,

John Malone, Nehemiah Baker Chester PA 8/1/1751, Irish 16
   3 days, Monday, 1.5 pounds,
John Malone, John Sewell Kent MD 9/26/1765, Irish 20 C
   3 pistols, 5'7",
James Maloney, John Gourley Bucks PA 9/5/1751, Irish 20
   6 days, Friday, 1.5 pounds, short,
Timothy Maloney, Fretwell Wright Burlington NJ 8/1/1745, Irish 20
   3 pounds, short,
John Malony, James Clark Chester PA 5/9/1771, Irish 23
   7 days, Thursday, 3 dollars, 5'10",
No Name Man, Moses Ward Gloucester NJ 2/28/1738, English
   4 days, Sunday, 2 pounds, middle,
No Name Man, Thomas Shee Baltimore MD 8/23/1739, cooper
   25 days, Sunday, 5 pounds, middle,
No Name Man, John Searle Philadelphia City PA ship captain 9/14/1738, Irish 22
   1 pound, middle,
No Name Man, Robert Robb York PA 9/1/1763, Irish 30
   96 days, Saturday, 3 pounds, 5'6",
No Name Man, James Graham Chester PA 8/18/1763, Irish 20 weaver
   16 days, Tuesday, 1.1 pounds, 5'6", (arrived 4 weeks ago)
No Name Man, Henry Fagundas Philadelphia City PA 5/16/1765, German 25 shoemaker (ran before)
   5 days, Saturday, 3 pounds, middle,
No Name Man, Robert Slater New Castle DE 8/15/1765, Irish tanner
   4 days, Sunday, 2.5 pounds, 5'3-4",
No Name Man, William Bennet Baltimore MD 9/12/1765,
   11 days, Sunday, 1 pound, 5'7",
No Name Man, Philip Calvin Baltimore MD 3/2/1769, Irish 18
   13 days, Friday, 5 pounds, 5'5",
No Name Man, Robert Maxwell Chester PA 11/24/1768, English
   3 pounds, (arrived 5 years ago)
No Name Man, John Jacob Muckle Lancaster PA 10/18/1770, Irish 29
   5 pounds, 5'2-3",
No Name Man, William Weathers Cecil MD 8/16/1770, Irish 25
   1 pound, 5'4-5",
No Name Man, David Vandyke Philadelphia PA 5/15/1766, Irish shoemaker
   3 days, Monday, 1.5 pounds, 5'6",
No Name Man2, David Vandyke Philadelphia PA 5/15/1766, Irish
   3 days, Monday, 1.5 pounds, 5'6",
No Name Man, Thomas Pusey New Castle DE 3/29/1770, 23
   1 pound, 5'7",
No Name Man, Joseph Vanneman Salem NJ 9/13/1775, English 23 shoemaker (ran before)
   31 days, Monday, 4 dollars, 5'5-6",
No Name Man, Christopher Dietrick Gloucester NJ 11/17/1773, Irish 28
   21 days, Thursday, 1 pound,
No Name Man, Reinhard Canmer Philadelphia City PA brewer 5/31/1775, German
   10 days, Monday, 2 pounds, 5'5",
No Name Man, Jacob Lemmon Harford MD 10/19/1774, Irish 24
   14 days, Thursday, 2 pounds, 5'11", (has been in the colonies before)
No Name Man, Conrad Schitz Philadelphia PA 2/28/1771, Irish 18 A
   0.05 pounds, 5'5",
No Name Man, Robert Roberts Kent MD 6/14/1764, English blacksmith C
   11 days, Sunday, 2.5 pounds,
No Name Man, Thomas McCool Baltimore MD 10/30/1760, C
   2 pounds, 5'6",
No Name ManA, James Wroth Kent MD 6/23/1768, C
   5 pounds,
No Name ManB, Oliver Hastings Kent MD 6/23/1768, 40 C
   5 pounds,
No Name ManC, John Curbuc Kent MD 6/23/1768, 40 C
   5 pounds,
Thomas Manahan, George Ross Lancaster PA 3/29/1759, 11
   3 days, Monday, 1 pound, (enticed away by his father)
William Mangles, John Leath Philadelphia City PA 8/23/1753, English 27 sailor
   6 days, Friday, 3 pounds, 5'10",
Edward Mankeen, James Young Salem NJ 8/26/1762, 19 tailor
   2 pounds, 5'8",

Ebenezer Manlove, John Gordon Kent DE 8/2/1764, 19 A
   10 dollars, 5'4",
William Manly, James Braddock Talbot MD 11/8/1775, English 31 sawyer C
   18 days, Sunday, 3 pounds, 5'8",
William Manly, James Braddock Talbot MD 5/15/1776, English 32 sawyer (2nd escape) C
   11 days, Sunday, 2 pounds, 5'7",
Catherine Mannaughan, James Teas New Castle DE 10/26/1774, Irish 30
   44 days, Tuesday, 1 pound, short,
John Mannaughan, James Teas New Castle DE 10/26/1774, Irish 35
   44 days, Tuesday, 1 pound, 5'2",
James Mansfield, Stephen Vidal Philadelphia City PA schoolmaster 5/7/1741, 18
   7 days, Thursday, 2 pounds, short,
Samuel Mansfield, Samuel Smith Salem NJ 6/11/1772, German 40
   29 days, Wednesday, 3 pounds, 6', (relatives live nearby)
Johannes Manskul, John Harrison Berks PA 12/31/1754, 19
   6 days, Friday, 1 pound, middle,
Thomas Manson, Matthias Laybolt Philadelphia City PA 8/1/1765, 16 A
   6 days, Friday, 6 dollars, 5'6",
Benjamin Manuel, William Hunter Chester PA 5/15/1755, American 30 L
   33 days, Saturday, 2 pounds, 5'4",
Bryan Maquod, Jacob Hilman Gloucester NJ 7/31/1766, Irish 20
   27 days, Friday, 2 pounds, 5'2",
John Mara, Samuel Gilpin Cecil MD 6/6/1771, Irish 20
   8 days, Wednesday, 3 pounds, 5'8",
Michael Mara, Abraham Barns St Mary's MD 7/13/1738, Irish 25 turner
   112 days, Saturday, 5 Maryland pounds, short,
Michael Margatroyd, William Gough Queen Anne's MD 1/6/1730,
   9 days, Tuesday, 2 pounds, middle,
James Marier, Hance Hamilton York PA 10/10/1751, Italian
   8 days, Wednesday, 2 pistoles, short,
John Maris, James Graham Chester PA 8/18/1763, 27
   16 days, Tuesday, 1.1 pounds, 5'7",
David Marker, John Banning Kent DE 8/9/1770, American 21 carpenter L
   22 days, Wednesday, 6 dollars, 5'9",
John Markland, Hugh Gaine NY 8/12/1772, 16 A
   15 days, Wednesday, 2 pounds,
John Marks, Casper Michenfelder Lancaster PA 12/28/1774, German 17 cooper A
   16 days, Tuesday, 4 dollars, 5'3",
John George Marks, Adam Gebhard Northampton PA 12/7/1785, German 17
   9 days, Monday, 5 pounds, tall, (arrived last fall)
Zedekiah Marlin, Richard Mount Hunterdon NJ 11/8/1764, 18
   2 pounds, 5'6",
John Marling, John Welsh Baltimore MD ironworks 8/28/1755, 22 farmer C
   18 days, Sunday, 3 pounds, 5'10",
James Maroney, Samuel Knox York PA 11/18/1772, Irish 21
   36 days, Wednesday, 12 dollars, 5'11",
Patrick Marra, Thomas Archer Baltimore MD 8/19/1756, Irish 22 glover
   2 pounds, 5'8",
John Marren, Joseph Cockran Cecil MD 9/8/1763, 22 weaver L
   about 2 months ago, 3 pistoles, 5'6",
James Marrington, Edward Voss King & Queen VA 11/29/1764, English brickmaker
   2.5 pounds, 5'5",
Mary Marrington, Edward Voss King & Queen VA 11/29/1764, Irish 30
   2.5 pounds,
John Marrow, William Kelley New Castle DE 4/12/1764, Irish 21
   13 days, Friday, 2 pounds, 5'10",
Thomas Marrow, John Kennedy York PA 5/15/1766, 22
   10 days, Monday, 2 pounds, 5'5",
Catherine Marsh, Peter Denny Queen Anne's MD 9/6/1770, English 22
   20 days, Friday, 4 dollars, middle,
John Marsh, John Robert Holliday Baltimore MD 5/16/1771, C
   8 days, Wednesday, 3 pounds, 5'5",
John Marshal, Isaac Foreman Burlington NJ 7/29/1742, English
   4 days, Sunday, 2 pounds,
John Marshal, Isaac Foreman Burlington NJ 9/22/1743, English (2nd escape)
   11 days, Sunday, 3 pounds, tall,

Edward Marshall, Giles Knight Bucks PA 9/6/1770, Irish 17
    24 days, Monday, 1 pound, (arrived last fall)
John Marshall, Michael Minier 9/12/1792, 15 A
    3 days, Sunday, 2 dollars,
Thomas Marshall, Andrew Leake Sommerset PA 12/12/1754, Scot
    5 pounds, middle,
William Marshall, Isaac Cox Kent DE 6/13/1771, A
    29 days, Wednesday, 8 dollars, 5'8",
Ambrose Martin, Robert Drake Bucks PA 12/11/1793, A
    10 days, Sunday, 0.03 pounds, 5'5-6",
David Martin, Martin Shugart York PA 8/31/1785, French 20 cordwainer
    4 dollars, 5'7-8",
James Martin, Rynar Tyson Philadelphia PA 6/25/1761, Irish 25 L
    3 pounds, 5'6",
James Martin, John Hopkins Gloucester NJ 8/18/1763, Irish 27 (2nd escape) L
    4 days, Sunday, 3 pounds, 5'6",
John Martin, Frederick Baker Philadelphia City PA 3/1/1770, Scot 22 baker
    11 days, Sunday, 8 dollars, 5'6-7",
Jonathan Martin, Henry Crosby 9/20/1770, 18 (ran before) A
    10 days, Monday, 2 pounds, short,
Mary Martin, Isaac Tyson Philadelphia PA 6/2/1763, Irish 20
    2 days, Tuesday, 1 pound,
Oliver Martin, John Wilcocks Philadelphia City PA ship captain 11/15/1759, 23 A
    1 day, Wednesday, 3 pounds, 5'7",
Peggy Martin, James Whitehead Philadelphia City PA workhouse-keeper 12/29/1773, Scot 17
    24 days, Monday, 2 pounds, 5', (arrived this fall)
Richard Martin, Andrew Cochran Cecil MD 5/26/1784, 21 shoemaker
    8 days, Tuesday, 4 dollars, 5'4-5",
Robert Martin, Robert Bell Philadelphia City PA bookseller 11/8/1780, 15 A
    93 days, Monday, 200 dollars,
Thomas Martin, Richard Dennis New Castle DE 4/9/1767, 25 A
    2 pounds, 5'6",
William Martin, Henry Glasford Chester PA 6/19/1746, Irish 20 miller
    4 days, Sunday, 2.5 pounds, 6',
William Martin, Job Ruston Chester PA 8/13/1747, Irish 21 miller (2nd escape)
    5 days, Saturday, 3 pounds, tall,
William Martin, Thomas Pim Chester PA 12/21/1774, Irish 40
    6 dollars, 5'9-10", (arrived last summer)
John Martingle, Henry Baker Frederick MD 1/5/1774, sadler
    20 dollars, 5'5",
John Mashman, Job Haines Chester PA 4/12/1775, American 16 L
    9 days, Tuesday, 2.5 pounds,
Andrew Mason, James Lowther Philadelphia City PA 10/7/1772,
    5 days, Saturday,
Richard Mason, Robert Miller Bucks PA 6/11/1767, English 16 sailor
    early June, 8 dollars, 5'6-7", (use to the sea)
Thomas Mason, William Runsney Lancaster PA 4/3/1755, Irish 23 L
    18 days, Sunday, 3 pounds, 5'5",
Adam Massacre, Hance Hamilton York PA sheriff 10/10/1751, German-American 28 farmer L
    8 days, Wednesday, 3 pistoles, 5'10",
Matthias Masterson, Henry William Stiegal Lancaster PA glassmaker 4/3/1766, Irish painter
    12 days, Saturday, 15 dollars, 5'3",
Joseph Mathas, Joseph Kelly Monmouth NJ 3/6/1740, American 24 weaver L
    4 days, Sunday, 3 pounds, middle,
Philip Matks, John Raser Philadelphia City PA 3/29/1775, German-Jew
    4 days, Sunday, 3 pounds, 5'5",
Charles Matthew, Jacob Ommersetter 7/4/1765, 18 A
    4 days, Sunday, 1 pound, 5'6",
Francis Matthews, John Lewden Chester PA 6/27/1765, English 16
    8 dollars,
Jacob Matthews, Samuel Snowden Anne Arundel MD ironworks 7/18/1765, 28 carpenter
    30 days, Tuesday, 10 pounds, 6', (imported)
John Matthews, James Baxter Cecil MD ironworks 12/13/1739, C
    13 days, Friday, 2.5 pounds, small,
Patrick Matthews, Thomas Fletcher Philadelphia PA 6/18/1747, Irish
    4 days, Sunday, 2 pounds, short,

Benjamin Matthewson, Robert Mattockes Gloucester NJ 6/8/1769, 22 farmer
    8 days, Wednesday, 2 pounds, 5'10",
William Matthewson, William Clarke ship captain 7/8/1742, Scot L
    32 days, Sunday, 1 pound,
Charles Matthias, Daniel Levan Berks PA 4/19/1759, German 17
    240 days, Tuesday, 4 pounds, short,
Henry Daniel Matthias, Unlisted Name Philadelphia City PA 4/6/1796, German 24
    10 days, Sunday, 7 dollars, 5'8",
John Matthias, Benjamin Williams Bucks PA 8/16/1764, English
    7 days, Thursday, 2 pounds, 5'6",
John Matthias, Benjamin Williams Bucks PA 12/27/1764, English (2nd escape)
    14 days, Thursday, 2 pounds, 5'6",
John Henry Matthias, Unlisted Name Philadelphia City PA 4/6/1796, German 28 hair-dresser
    10 days, Sunday, 7 dollars, 5'10",
Jacob Matz, Elizabeth Smith Philadelphia PA 12/13/1753, German 15
    9 days, Tuesday, 1 pound,
James Maxwell, James Passmore Chester PA 7/8/1795, 19 shoemaker A
    10 days, Sunday, 10 dollars, 5'6-7",
Edward May, Josiah Halstead Monmouth NJ 4/28/1763, English
    16 days, Tuesday, 5 pounds, 5'4",
George May, Bernard Rapp Philadelphia PA 12/11/1766, German 22 smith
    9 days, Tuesday, 3 pounds, 5', (lately arrived)
John May, John Kerr Bucks PA 2/8/1775, Irish 20
    10 days, Monday, 1.5 pounds, 5'8",
John May, John Wilkinson Bucks PA 6/7/1775, Irish 20 (2nd escape)
    15 days, Wednesday, 2 pounds, 5'8-9",
Patrick May, Joseph Decow Hunterdon NJ 9/24/1741, Irish
    4 days, Sunday,
Thomas May, Peter Grubb Lancaster PA ironworks 2/2/1743, English 30
    10 days, Monday, 2.5 pounds,
Edward Maybe, Jacob Hugg Gloucester NJ 11/28/1754, English 22
    9 days, Tuesday, 2 pounds, 5',
Edward Maybe, Jacob Hugg Gloucester NJ 9/4/1755, English 23 (2nd escape)
    3 days, Monday, 2 pounds, short,
John Mayer, Philip Neiss Bucks PA 8/13/1788, German 25 miller
    20 days, Thursday, 8 pounds, 5'5-6",
Thomas Mayfield, William Smith York PA 9/22/1773, American L
    10 days, Monday, 2 pounds, 5'4-5",
John Maylam, Daniel Oliver Boston MA perkemaker 4/12/1753, 19
    25 days, Sunday, 20 dollars,
John Maynard, John Lewis Gloucester VA 6/15/1738, 26 bricklayer
    51 days, Tuesday, 1 pistole, tall,
Morgan McAnally, Thomas England Philadelphia City PA tallow-chandler 4/25/1754,
    1.5 pounds, 5',
William McAnalty, Anthony Whitely New Castle DE 5/30/1754, Irish 23
    15 days, Wednesday, 1 pound,
Robert McAnaly, John Leath Philadelphia City PA 11/15/1753, Irish 32
    41 days, Friday, 2 pounds, 5'7",
Patrick McAnelly, Davis Bevan Chester PA 9/6/1770, Irish
    17 days, Monday, 4 dollars, 5'5",
Daniel McAnira, Richard Smith Salem NJ 9/29/1773,
    3 pounds, 5'8",
Daniel McAnitinie, Michael Finley York PA 1/2/1772, Irish 21
    18 days, Sunday, 2 pounds, 5'8",
Patrick McAnnaly, William Edwards Chester PA 5/5/1768, Irish 25
    17 days, Monday, 3 pounds, 5'6",
John McAnnelly, John Musgrove Frederick MD 10/22/1767, Irish 25 school teacher
    20 days, Friday, 5 pounds, 5'8-10", (has relatives nearby)
Thomas McAtee, David Kennedy Chester PA 7/8/1742, 30 weaver
    8 days, Wednesday, short,
Dennis McAuliff, Jacob Shoemaker Philadelphia City PA blacksmith 3/24/1752, Irish blacksmith
    7 days, Thursday, 2 pounds, 5'4",
Dennis McAvoy, Benjamin Elliot Huntingdon PA 9/10/1788, Irish 24
    15 days, Tuesday, 8 dollars, 5'8-9",
John McAvoy, John Taylor Lancaster PA 6/12/1755, Irish 20
    11 days, Sunday, 2 pounds, 5'9",

Daniel McBird, John Rowan Chester PA 8/17/1749, weaver
    18 days, Sunday, 1.5 pounds,
Daniel McBride, David Watson Lancaster PA 6/20/1771, Irish 24
    4 days, Sunday, 3 pounds, 5'10-11",
Hugh McBride, James Moore Lancaster PA blacksmith 8/11/1763, Irish 18
    4 dollars, 5'2",
James McBride, James Moore Chester PA storekeeper 9/20/1750, Irish 40
    7 days, Thursday, 3 pounds, 6',
James McBride, Derick Barcalow Monmouth NJ 11/30/1774, Irish 25
    11 days, Sunday, 3 pounds, 5'7-8", (arrived last spring)
John McBride, Thomas Euthorp Cecil MD 4/23/1752, Irish
    4 days, Sunday, 4 pounds, short,
John McBride, Thomas Ebtharp Cecil MD 7/16/1752, Irish (2nd escape)
    6 days, Friday, 2 pounds, short,
John McBride, Thomas Harry Chester PA cooper 1/26/1764, Irish 23 A
    5 days, Saturday, 3 pounds, 5'6",
John McBride, Thomas Harry Chester PA cooper 7/5/1764, Irish 23 (2nd escape) A
    11 days, Sunday, 2 pounds, 5'5",
Thomas McBride, William Ross Lancaster PA 3/8/1775, Irish 24
    5 days, Saturday, 8 dollars, 5'6", (arrived last spring)
Philip McBronggan, Alexander Steuart Cecil MD 10/29/1761,
    14 days, Thursday, 3 pounds, short,
James McCabe, Philip Dougherty Chester PA 4/17/1776, Irish 40 gaol sale L
    8 dollars, 5'5-6", (arrived 5 years ago)
John McCabe, Archibald Hamilton Salem NJ 10/25/1753, Irish 23 tailor
    9 days, Tuesday, 3 pounds, 5'8",
William McCabe, William Smith Baltimore MD 3/14/1771, Irish 21
    54 days, Saturday, 20 dollars,
Barney McCaddem, William Cathar Cecil MD 7/5/1770, 22 flaxhackler
    97 days, Friday, 2 pounds, 5'4-5",
Hugh McCage, John Miller Lancaster PA 9/5/1771, Irish 16 cooper
    10 days, Monday, 2 pounds, 5'3", (arrived 1 year ago)
William McCall, John Nelson Philadelphia City PA 7/18/1745, Scot 40 carpenter
    12 days, Saturday, 1 pound, tall,
Edward McCallagan, Patrick McGonegal New Castle DE 12/22/1773, Irish 30
    112 days, Thursday, 5 pounds, 5'7",
Dennis McCallin, James Todd ironworks 1/30/1772, Irish 19
    7 days, Thursday, 3 pounds, 5'8",
Hugh McCallion, Andrew Crips New Castle DE 9/5/1771, 20 shoemaker A
    17 days, Monday, 4 dollars, 5'8-9",
Thomas McCallon, Christopher Postgate 10/3/1734, 19 tailor
    2 days, Tuesday, 1 pound, short,
John McCan, Matthew Hand Philadelphia City PA 10/18/1775, Irish 24 cabinetmaker
    120 days, Wednesday, 10 dollars, 5'5-6",
Nicholas McCan, Archibald McElroy Philadelphia City PA 12/24/1767, Irish 25 barber
    3 days, Monday, 8 dollars, 5'6", (arrived last fall)
William McCan, John Bull Philadelphia PA 7/9/1772, Irish 30
    Jan. 1770, 5 pounds,
Michael McCane, George Read New Castle DE 4/16/1761, Irish 16
    19 days, Saturday, 2 pistoles,
James McCann, Thadeus D'Adamousky Philadelphia PA starchmaker 11/17/1784, 16
    9 days, Monday, 1 dollar,
John McCann, George Richey Chester PA 4/26/1775, 22
    16 days, Tuesday, 4 dollars, 5'7",
Thomas McCann, John Harris Baltimore MD 12/6/1770, Irish 25
    57 days, Wednesday, 6 dollars, 5'8-9",
Patrick McCans, Samuel Tolbert Philadelphia PA 3/27/1766, Irish 22
    (is handcuffed)
Hugh McCaron, Rees Morgan Chester PA 3/19/1761, Irish 23 miller
    2 pounds, middle,
Charles McCarter, Thomas Thomas New Castle DE 3/8/1739, Scot 37
    5 days, Saturday, 1.5 pounds, short,
Dennis McCarter, Malcom McKnown Lancaster PA 11/19/1767, Irish 35 tinker
    18 days, Sunday, 5 pounds, 5'3-4",
John McCarter, John Cooper York PA 7/16/1772, Irish millwright
    17 days, Monday, 5'8-9",

Anne McCarthy, David Marple Bucks PA 11/29/1770, Irish 25
    7 days, Thursday, 2 pounds, short,
Carthy McCarthy, William Bond MD 9/11/1740, Irish 28 sailor
    18 days, Sunday, 3 pounds, middle,
George McCartney, Daniel Bates Gloucester NJ 7/4/1751, English 19
    3 days, Monday, 2 pounds, short,
Michael McCartney, James Hamilton Chester PA 12/7/1752, Irish tailor
    17 days, Monday, 5 pounds, 5'7",
Alice McCarty, Unlisted Name New Castle DE 11/13/1766, Irish 35 C
    15 days, Wednesday,
Barnaby McCarty, Richard Richison Chester PA 4/18/1754, Irish 46
    3 days, Monday, 1.5 pounds, 5',
Darby McCarty, Thomas Pointen 12/22/1763, Irish 25
    1.5 pounds, 5'6",
Dennis McCarty, William Taite Northumberland VA 5/30/1765, Irish blacksmith C
    29 days, Wednesday, 3 pounds, 5'5",
James McCarty, Thomas Martin Chester PA 1/29/1751, Irish 21 weaver
    2 pounds, short,
James McCarty, Jacob Housser Lancaster PA 12/13/1764, Irish 20
    4 dollars, 5'4",
James McCarty, William Snow Anne Arundel MD ship captain 2/15/1770, Irish
    1 pound, 5'6", (ran from ship)
John McCarty, William Ross York PA 2/28/1776, Irish 19
    15 days, Wednesday, 8 dollars, 5'7", (arrived last June)
Timothy McCarty, Reuben Thomas Chester PA 9/3/1767, Irish 19
    15 days, Wednesday, 1.5 pounds, 5'3-4",
William McCarty, Thomas Bull Chester PA ironworks 11/23/1785, Irish 20 drummer
    9 days, Monday, 1.5 pounds, 5'5-6",
John McCaulesd, Adam McNelly Bucks PA 4/4/1751, Irish 18
    7 days, Thursday, 2 pounds, short,
John McCay, Robert Porter Cecil MD 9/11/1776, Scot 25 sailor
    10 days, Monday, 8 dollars, 5'6",
William McCay, James West 4/19/1750,
    18 days, Sunday, 3 pounds, short,
James McCib, John Zimberman Montgomery PA 4/25/1787, Irish 30
    18 days, Saturday, 3 pounds, 5'10",
Bernard McCindred, Daniel Lippincot Burlington NJ 3/29/1764, Irish 16
    13 days, Friday, 5 pounds, (arrived 6-7 months ago)
James McClachan, William Fullerton Lancaster PA 11/27/1755, Irish
    6 days, Friday, 3 pounds, middle,
William McClachry, Joseph Graisbury Philadelphia City PA 4/6/1774, English 21 tailor
    2 days, Tuesday, 10 dollars, short,
Daniel McClain, William Denny Chester PA 9/18/1766, Scot 22
    19 days, Saturday, 1.5 pounds, 5'7",
Patrick McClane, William Selthridge Sussex NJ 10/1/1741, Irish
    12 days, Saturday, 1.5 pounds,
John McClary, Robert Allison Chester PA 10/27/1763, Irish 20
    10 days, Monday, 1.5 pounds, 5'6",
John McClaughlin, Peter Bard Burlington NJ ironworks 8/20/1752, Irish 35
    1.5 pounds, middle,
Daniel McClay, John John Chester PA 11/17/1768, Scot
    14 days, Thursday, 4 dollars, 5'6",
James McClean, Thomas Lawson 8/20/1752, tailor
    6 days, Friday,
John McClean, James Lattimer New Castle DE 3/5/1767, American 18 A
    12 days, Saturday, 2 pounds, middle,
Peter McClean, John Blacklige Philadelphia PA 9/2/1762, 30
    4 days, Sunday, 1 pound,
Peter McClean, John Lewis Cecil MD 7/22/1756, Irish
    7 days, Thursday, 2 pounds, 5'4", (use to the sea)
Roger McClean, Nathaniel Marcer Chester PA 3/27/1793, 17 tailor A
    15 days, Tuesday, 0.003 pounds, 5'4-5",
William McClellan, William Graham Chester PA 3/3/1768, Irish 20
    7 days, Thursday, 2 pounds, 5'8-9",
Jean McClellen, James Walker New Castle DE 9/6/1753, Irish
    11 days, Sunday, 1 pound, short,

Margaret McClenny, Henry Clark Philadelphia City PA 3/7/1738, Irish 40
    1 day, Wednesday, 1 pound,
William McClery, Robert Pyle Chester PA 10/2/1766, Irish 20 weaver
    11 days, Sunday, 5 pounds, 5'7",
Arthur McClosky, Robert Powell Chester PA 4/23/1752, Irish 25 L
    3 days, Monday, 1 pound, middle,
Arthur McClosky, Robert Powell Chester PA 5/17/1753, Irish 26 (2nd escape) L
    2 days, Tuesday, 1.5 pounds, middle,
Arthur McClosky, Robert Powell Chester PA 9/20/1753, Irish 26 (3rd escape) L
    3 days, Monday, 1.5 pounds, middle,
Catherine McClue, Robert Alison Cecil MD 8/10/1749, C
    54 days, Saturday, 3 pounds, short,
Patrick McClusky, James Gordon Baltimore MD 8/4/1773, 25 C
    38 days, Monday, 3 pounds, 5'6",
Edward McColgan, Patrick McConnegal New Castle DE 3/7/1771, Irish 32
    25 days, Sunday, 3 pounds, 5'6",
John McColhem, William Noblit Chester PA 6/7/1744, Irish 26
    14 days, Thursday, 3 pounds,
James McCollister, William Tennis Montgomery PA 8/20/1788, Irish-American 22 shoemaker A
    9 days, Monday, 4 dollars, 5'4-5",
Margaret McCollister, James Bennett Chester PA 5/20/1742, 25
    1 day, Wednesday, 1.25 pounds, short,
Archibald McCollom, John Magee Bucks PA 11/15/1786, 18
    15 days, Tuesday, 1 dollar,
Thomas McColly, Anthony Miller Lancaster PA 5/30/1771, American L
    18 days, Sunday, 3 pounds, 5'5",
William McComan, Andrew Miller Chester PA 3/4/1756, Irish 19
    8 days, Wednesday, 7 pounds, 5'6",
John McCommon, David Dowlin Montgomery PA 5/4/1791, Irish 21
    12 days, Friday, 0.03 pounds, 5'8",
Elizabeth McConegal, Caleb Armitage Philadelphia PA 9/27/1775, Irish 20
    7 days, Thursday, 1 pound,
William McConnell, Barzilla Ridgway Burlington NJ 12/22/1784, Irish 17
    12 dollars, 5'2-3",
William McConway, William Denny Chester PA 5/3/1764, Irish 21
    2 pounds, 5'2",
Dennis McCordy, Elizabeth Fury 8/24/1766, Irish cordwainer
    275 days, Tuesday, 2 pounds,
James McCorestan, George Crow Chester PA 11/16/1769, Irish 22 sailor
    28 days, Thursday, 2 pounds, 5'7",
Catherine McCormack, Jeremiah Barnard Chester PA 9/3/1794, 16
    1.25 pounds,
William McCormack, Elijah Cozens Gloucester NJ 4/26/1786, Irish 18 tailor
    83 days, Thursday, 16 dollars,
Charles McCormick, Abraham Holmes Lancaster PA 6/12/1766, Irish 16
    17 days, Monday, 4 pounds, 5'4",
Charles McCormick, Abraham Holmes Lancaster PA 10/27/1768, Irish 18 (2nd escape)
    14 days, Thursday, 2 pounds, 5'8-9",
Charles McCormick, Abraham Holmes Lancaster PA 1/2/1772, Irish 21 (3rd escape)
    29 days, Wednesday, 4 dollars,
Cornelius McCormick, David Fleming Chester PA 11/9/1774, Irish 18
    1 pound,
Henry McCormick, Richard Evans Chester PA 7/18/1751, Irish L
    8 days, Wednesday, 1.5 pounds, short,
James McCormick, John Crawford York PA 1/2/1772, Irish 27
    18 days, Sunday, 2 pounds, 5'6",
John McCormick, Benjamin Davis Philadelphia PA 7/10/1746, Irish 35
    3 pounds,
John McCormick, Evan Griffith Chester PA 7/12/1770, Irish 40
    5 days, Saturday, 4 dollars, 5'10",
John McCormick, William Eldridge Cumberland NJ 8/31/1769,
    10 days, Monday, 2 pounds,
Mary McCormick, Glover Hunt Philadelphia City PA 9/18/1760, Irish 16
    39 days, Sunday, 4 dollars, short,
Maxwell McCormick, William Greighton Lancaster PA 7/16/1752, Irish 19 weaver (ran before)
    14 days, Thursday, 2 pounds, 5'7",

James McCornet, John Fuller Baltimore MD 6/26/1740, Scot 26
    16 days, Tuesday, 1 pound,
Sampson McCotter, James Fullton Philadelphia City PA 5/22/1766, Irish blacksmith
    2 pounds, 5'6", (was in the navy)
Thomas McCoun, Thomas Wynne Philadelphia PA 5/20/1736, Irish 22 weaver
    14 days, Thursday, 2 pounds,
Peter McCourt, James McKee New Castle DE 7/26/1775, 17
    9 days, Tuesday, 3 dollars, 5'4",
Daniel McCown, Isaac Dutton Delaware PA 4/11/1792, Irish 18
    3 pounds, 5'6-8",
James McCown, Andrew Boggs Lancaster PA 4/14/1784, Irish
    10 dollars, 5'10", (arrived last fall)
John McCoy, Thomas Carney Salem NJ 11/30/1749, Irish 17
    204 days, Monday, 5 pounds, short,
John McCoy, Thomas Wisnart 9/17/1761, Irish 18
    1.5 pounds, 5'7",
John McCreary, Thomas Money Cecil MD 7/19/1750, 24 C
    4 days, Sunday, 0.75 pounds, middle,
Mary McCreary, Thomas Money Cecil MD 7/19/1750, 47 C
    4 days, Sunday, 0.75 pounds,
William McCreary, William Ball Philadelphia City PA 11/8/1764, Irish 22
    13 days, Friday, 3 pounds, 5'8", (arrived Sept. 8th)
Richard McCree, Robert McKey Philadelphia PA 10/18/1750, Irish 23
    4 days, Sunday, 3 pounds, 5'6",
Francis McCue, Charles Harah Lancaster PA 1/2/1772, Irish 30
    18 days, Sunday, 1 pound, 5'8", (arrived 4 years ago)
Patrick McCue, Adam Williamson New Castle DE 8/2/1775, English
    end of May, 3 pounds, 5'4-5",
Robert McCuley, John Singleton New Castle DE 7/14/1763, Irish soldier
    5 days, Saturday, 3 pounds, 6', (arrived last May)
Arthur McCullough, John Black Chester PA 12/13/1753, Irish 18
    4 days, Sunday, 2 pounds, 5'6",
Arthur McCullough, John Black Chester PA 3/12/1754, Irish 18 (2nd escape)
    7 days, Thursday, 2 pounds, 5'6",
David McCullough, John Wells Philadelphia PA 7/17/1755, American 17 L
    7 days, Thursday, 2 pounds, 5'4",
John McCullough, Adam Menely Bucks PA 11/15/1750, Irish
    9 days, Tuesday, 2 pistoles, short,
John McCullough, Jacob Patterson New Castle DE 9/23/1762, Irish
    34 days, Friday, 8 dollars, 5'9",
John McCullough, Hugh Newell Burlington NJ 1/15/1767, Irish 18
    2 pounds, 5'6",
Robert McCully, Samuel Porter New Castle DE 7/18/1765, 25 gaol sale L
    24 days, Monday, 4 dollars, 5'7",
Thomas McCully, William Skiles Lancaster PA 7/4/1771, Irish 23
    8 days, Wednesday, 3 pounds, 5'5",
James McCurry, Philip Davis Cumberland PA 9/28/1752, 18 (ran before)
    34 days, Friday, 1 pound,
John McCutchin, John Stinson Philadelphia City PA 11/7/1754, Scot 25 tailor
    14 days, Thursday, 3 pounds, 5'10",
James McCutchon, John Long Chester PA 4/22/1762, Irish 19
    6 days, Friday, 2 pounds,
Catherine McDaniel, Henry Cowen Lancaster PA 8/12/1772,
    11 days, Sunday, 2 pounds,
Daniel McDaniel, John Horner Hunterdon NJ 11/2/1749, Irish 20
    37 days, Tuesday, 5 pounds, 5'6",
Edward McDaniel, Thomas Bartholomew Philadelphia City PA tavern-keeper 2/20/1753, Irish 20
    2 days, Tuesday, 2 pounds, tall,
Garret McDaniel, Joseph Brick 4/16/1752,
    4 pounds, tall, (may be just a thief)
George McDaniel, James Pryor Chester PA 8/18/1757, English 26 (2nd escape)
    9 days, Tuesday, 3 pounds, 5'10",
George McDaniel, John Hanley Chester PA 5/8/1755, English 24 (ran before)
    25 days, Sunday, 1.5 pounds, 5'8",
Hugh McDaniel, Thomas Harrison Philadelphia City PA 5/31/1775, American 30 farmer L
    about 2 years ago,

James McDaniel, James Martin New Castle DE 2/25/1755, Irish
   30 days, Tuesday, 2 pounds,
John McDaniel, William Roe Chester PA 7/28/1737, Scot 24
   4 days, Sunday, 1.5 pounds, tall,
John McDaniel, Thomas Thornbrough Lancaster PA 9/6/1750, English 35 mason
   3 pounds, middle,
John McDaniel, Isaac Waterman Philadelphia PA 10/13/1773, American 17 L
   44 days, Tuesday, 4 dollars, 5'3-4",
Matthew McDaniel, Margaret Jackson Burlington NJ 3/6/1740, Irish 21 gaol sale L
   6 days, Friday, 3 pounds, middle,
Michael McDaniel, Robert Ackin Cecil MD 12/14/1774, Irish 22 (ran before)
   8 dollars, 5'5", (wears an iron collar)
Nicholas McDaniel, James Isaiah Ross Dutche NY 11/21/1751, Irish 20
   5 pounds, 5'10",
Randal McDaniel, Timothy Scarth Philadelphia PA tanner 6/15/1738, Irish 20
   11 days, Sunday, 2 pounds, middle,
Reynolds McDaniel, Nathaniel Giles Lancaster PA ironworks 10/28/1762, Irish 30
   17 days, Monday, 5 pistoles, 5'8",
George McDaniels John Hanley Chester PA 12/19/1754, English 23
   12 days, Saturday, 1.5 pounds, 5'7",
John McDeed, John Pyle Chester PA 4/10/1766, Irish 21
   3 pounds, 5'5-6",
Catherine McDennal, Henry Cowan Lancaster PA 7/25/1771, Irish 20
   7 days, Thursday, 2 pounds,
Catherine McDermond, William Chevers New Castle DE 7/28/1773, 15
   2.5 pounds, (arrived July 12th last, ran from ship)
John McDermont, Paul Ralston New Castle DE 8/7/1766, Irish 25
   11 days, Sunday, 3 pounds, 5'6",
John McDermont, Paul Ralston New Castle DE 4/21/1768, Irish 27 (2nd escape)
   11 days, Sunday, 2 pounds, 5'6",
Catherine McDermot, William Nelson New Castle DE 9/15/1773,
   26 days, Saturday, (ran from ship)
Michael McDermot, Daniel Quigley Burlington NJ 3/28/1734, 25
   1 pound, short,
Terence McDermot, Joshua Baker Lancaster PA 6/29/1738, Irish 35 distiller
   16 days, Tuesday, 1.5 pounds, middle,
Jane McDole, George Lesur Philadelphia PA 10/6/1773, Irish 17 (pregnant)
   3 days, Monday, 2 pounds, 5',
Brian McDonal, Caleb Hartman Lancaster PA 11/23/1774, Irish 20 tailor
   36 days, Wednesday, 4 dollars, short, (arrived this fall)
Alexander McDonald, Captain Hinton Philadelphia City PA ship captain 11/21/1751, Irish sawyer
   1 pound, (ran from ship)
Arthur McDonald, Francis Jordon Bucks PA 2/10/1742, Irish 21
   2 pounds, middle,
Arthur McDonald, Thomas Ewing Philadelphia City PA 9/1/1763, 26
   11 days, Sunday, 5 pounds, 5'9",
Catherine McDonald, Henry Cowan Lancaster PA 10/21/1772, Irish
   7 days, Thursday, 1.5 pounds, 5'1",
Colin McDonald, Fletcher Gray Philadelphia City PA 11/18/1772, Scot 36 tailor
   5 pounds, 6', (ran from ship)
Daniel McDonald, John Miller Northampton PA 3/28/1765, Scot 25
   11 days, Sunday, 4 pounds, 5'6",
Daniel McDonald, James Bringhurst 10/13/1763, 16 sailor A
   4 days, Sunday, 2.5 pounds, 5'5", (use to the sea)
Donald McDonald, William Miller Northampton PA 5/16/1765, Scot 25 shoemaker
   60 days, Sunday, 5 pounds, 5'6",
Edmund McDonald, Thomas Evans Bucks PA 6/27/1751, Irish 35
   4 days, Sunday, 2 pounds, short,
Felix McDonald, David Jones Frederick VA ironworks 4/12/1764, 22 weaver
   2.5 pounds, 5'4",
Hugh McDonald, Archibald Thomson Philadelphia PA 8/15/1771, Irish 35
   10 days, Monday, 4 dollars, 5'5",
James McDonald, John Valentine Philadelphia PA 5/17/1750, Irish 24 hired L
   7 days, Thursday, 3 pounds,
James McDonald, Isaac Wayne Chester PA 1/6/1773, Irish 28 sailor hired L
   5 days, Saturday, 2.1 pounds, 5'3-4",

James McDonald, Samuel Vanleer Chester PA 6/30/1773, Irish 28 sailor hired (2nd escape) L
    7 days, Thursday, 1.5 pounds, 5'3-4",
John McDonald, David Dewar Philadelphia City PA ship captain 12/26/1752, Scot 24 baker
    1 pound, 5'6", (ran from ship)
John McDonald, William Glenn Lancaster PA 5/31/1775, Irish 20
    12 days, Saturday, 2 pounds, 5'9-10",
John McDonald, John Fleming York PA 10/12/1774, Scot
    5 pounds, 5'6",
Margaret McDonald, John Baus Philadelphia City PA tavern-keeper 3/10/1763, Irish 27
    15 days, Wednesday, 2 pounds,
Patrick McDonald, George Moore Lancaster PA 7/14/1773, Irish 22 (ran before)
    10 days, Monday, 2 pounds, 5'8",
Reynold McDonald, Robert Miller Lancaster PA 10/1/1747, 26
    16 days, Tuesday, 3 pounds, 6',
Robert McDonald, John Anderson Lancaster PA 5/22/1776, Irish 17
    12 days, Saturday, 4 dollars, 5'5-6",
William McDonald, Patrick Doral Anne Arundel MD 2/12/1745, Scot 30
    21 days, Thursday, 2 pounds, middle,
William McDonald, Robert Bail New Castle DE 1/26/1769, 30
    11 days, Sunday, 1.5 pounds, 5'5",
William McDonald, Henry Schnaderle Lancaster PA 10/10/1771, Irish 18
    46 days, Sunday, 3 pounds, 5'6-7",
John McDonall, John Olivar Burlington NJ 2/15/1775, Irish 20 painter
    30 days, Tuesday, 8 dollars, 5'5",
Hugh McDonanald, Abraham Kentzing 7/19/1770, 27 soldier
    18 days, Sunday, 2 pounds, 5'8",
Richard McDonnald, Andrew Todd Chester PA 2/20/1766, Irish 20
    5 days, Saturday, 5 pounds, 5'7",
Alexander McDonnaugh, Abraham Matlack Burlington NJ 5/10/1764, Irish 24
    4 days, Sunday, 5 pounds, (arrived last fall, has a brother nearby)
Bryan McDonnel, Robert Carr Hunterdon NJ 8/9/1739, 20
    4 days, Sunday, 1.5 pounds, middle,
John McDonnel, James Moorehead Lancaster PA 5/18/1774, Irish
    4 dollars, 5'6",
Patrick McDonnel, John Hanly Chester PA 5/21/1747, Irish 28 L
    8 days, Wednesday, 2 pistoles, short,
Alexander McDonnell, Samuel Massey Queen Anne's MD 7/16/1752, Irish 22 sawyer
    11 days, Sunday, 2 pistoles, 5'6",
Anne McDonnell, James Holliday Baltimore MD 3/26/1772, Scot 40
    3 pounds, (has a 3 year old child)
Elizabeth McDonnell, Joseph Kelly 5/9/1765, 30 gaol sale L
    168 days, Thursday, 1 pound,
John McDonnell, Barney Daily Kent MD 9/15/1763, 15 tailor
    24 days, Monday, 1.5 pounds, 4'6",
Thomas McDonough, Robert Siminton Lancaster PA 3/13/1750, Irish 21
    9 days, Tuesday, 2.5 pounds,
Dennis McDowell, Roger Kirk Chester PA 11/6/1740, 34
    3 days, Monday, 1 pound,
Henry McDowell, Johnathon McKell Philadelphia PA 9/3/1767, Irish 20
    6 days, Friday, 2 pounds, 5'7",
James McDowell, William Lewis 4/24/1755,
    25 days, Sunday, 4 pistoles, short,
John McDowell, George Hunter Chester PA 2/9/1769, Irish 18
    10 days, Monday, 2.5 pounds, short,
Nathaniel McDowell, John Strawbridge Cecil MD 5/12/1763, Irish 30 spinning-wheel-maker
    11 days, Sunday, 3 pounds, 5'8",
William McDowell, Jacob Bell Philadelphia City PA shoemaker 7/29/1772, 19 A
    7 days, Thursday, 1.5 pounds, 5'6",
Mary McElwrath, James Maxwell Lancaster PA 12/15/1773, Irish 19
    1.5 pounds, middle,
John McEnery, Ezekiel Griffith Chester PA 12/13/1770, 22 wool comber
    9 days, Tuesday, 7 dollars, 5'7-8",
Nicholas McEntire, Samuel Ralston New Castle DE 7/17/1746, Irish 17
    10 days, Monday, 1 pound, short,
Roger McEvoy, Humphry Brooks Baltimore MD 6/14/1770, C
    10 days, Monday, 1.5 pounds, 5'8-9",

John McFaddin, Alexander Johnston Chester PA 1/16/1772, Irish
   22 days, Wednesday, 2 pounds, 5'6-7",
James McFall, Nathaniel Bowser Philadelphia City PA tailor 4/5/1750, Irish 45
   15 days, Wednesday, 3 pounds, short,
Neal McFall, William McConcky Monmouth NJ 9/5/1751, Irish 45
   12 days, Saturday, 3 pounds, middle,
Neil McFall, James Barclay Bucks PA 7/3/1755, Scot 18
   6 days, Friday, 2 pounds, middle,
Daniel McFarland, John Evans Montgomery PA 11/23/1791, 18
   4 days, Saturday, 0.5 pounds, 5'6-7",
Doncan McFebrich, William Parkhill Chester PA 5/28/1772, weaver A
   2 pounds,
Robert McFee, John Hawthorn New Castle DE 7/26/1744, Irish 22 cooper
   8 days, Wednesday, 2 pounds, short,
James McFilie, Andrew McDowell Chester PA 12/4/1760, Irish 20
   9 days, Tuesday, 3 pounds, 5'8",
James McGarrel, Jonas Seely Berks PA 2/27/1753, Irish
   9 days, Tuesday, 2 pounds, middle,
Thomas McGawn, Marmaduke Cooper Gloucester NJ 5/28/1788, Irish 17
   2 days, Monday, 4 dollars,
Dennis McGee, Amor Chandler Chester PA 10/9/1766, Irish 24 blacksmith
   4 days, Sunday, 2 pounds,
Dennis McGee, Amor Chandler Chester PA 10/4/1770, Irish 28 blacksmith (2nd escape)
   7 days, Thursday, 10 dollars, 5'7-8",
Sarah McGee, Barzillai Coat Burlington NJ 4/30/1777, Irish-American 23 L
   10 days, Monday, 8 dollars, 5'7",
William McGee, William Boyd Chester PA 5/2/1751, Irish 18
   7 days, Thursday, 2 pounds, short,
William McGee, William Dunwodie Chester PA 8/5/1756, 19
   18 days, Sunday, 1.5 pounds,
John McGhee, Samuel Reed Salem NJ 1/24/1749, 20
   20 days, Friday, 2 pounds, middle,
John McGill, Lawrence Salter Burlington NJ ironworks 4/10/1776, Irish 32
   19 days, Saturday, 1.5 pounds, 5'10",
Michael McGillaughlin, Thomas Stewart Cecil MD 7/2/1741, Irish 20
   3 days, Monday, 1 pound,
Robert McGinney, Michael Masser Lancaster PA 8/7/1776, Irish 18 tanner
   9 days, Tuesday, 5'5", (arrived 1 year ago)
Robert McGinney, Michael Masser Lancaster PA 4/2/1777, Irish 19 tanner (2nd escape)
   10 days, Monday, 10 dollars,
John McGinnis, James Cloyd Chester PA 1/1/1755, Irish 22
   3 days, Monday, 1 pound, 5'6",
Michael McGinnis, Clement Cardiff New York NY ship captain 10/15/1761, Irish 17
   11 days, Sunday, 8 dollars, (ran from ship)
Thomas McGinnus, Joseph Wilkinson Chester PA 4/10/1760, Irish
   2 pounds, (was in the army)
Grace McGittigan, James Wallace 12/1/1763, Irish 25
   52 days, Monday, 4 dollars, middle, (arrived last March)
Charles McGlacbon, Charles White Philadelphia City PA 4/23/1741, Scot carpenter L
   4 days, Sunday, 2.5 pounds, tall,
John McGlaughlin, John Atkinson Jr Bucks PA 12/20/1764, Irish 50
   15 days, Wednesday, 1.5 pounds, 5'6",
John McGlaughlin, Robert Robb Northumberland PA 6/23/1773, Irish 25 shoemaker
   22 days, Wednesday, 8 dollars, 5'6-7",
John McGlaughlin, Robert Robb Northumberland PA 8/18/1773, Irish 25 shoemaker (2nd escape)
   13 days, Friday, 4 dollars, 5'8",
John McGlaughton, William Young Philadelphia City PA 2/11/1762, Irish 30 footman
   8 days, Wednesday, 1.5 pounds, short,
Bryan McGlew, John Vernor Lancaster PA 1/10/1749, Irish 18
   12 days, Saturday, 4 pounds, 5'4",
Amos McGloughlin, Vincent Gilpin New Castle DE 8/9/1764, 18
   2 pounds, 5'6",
Neal McGonnagle, Joseph Jeffries York PA 5/3/1775, Irish 25
   6 dollars, 5'4-5",
John McGork, James Molesworth Philadelphia City PA 11/23/1774, Irish
   3 pounds, 5'6", (arrived last Dec.)

Michael McGorman, Andrew Barr Chester PA 10/30/1776, Irish 15
    7 days, Thursday, 4 dollars, 5'4-5",
Thomas McGouran, Elisha Hughes Chester PA 10/23/1766, Irish 30
    10 days, Monday, 6 pounds,
Michael McGowan, Barclay & Mitchell Philadelphia City PA 3/15/1775, Irish 17
    8 days, Wednesday, 3 pounds, 5', (lately arrived)
Francis McGowen, Sellwood Griffin 3/19/1761, Irish
    11 days, Sunday, 1 pound, 5'4", (use to the sea)
James McGrady, Samuel Cleneay New Castle DE 4/5/1764, Irish 20
    4 dollars, 5'4",
James McGrady, Benjamin Hegeman Somerset NJ 4/10/1766, Irish 24 (2nd escape) L
    16 days, Tuesday, 2.5 pounds, short, (has 3 years left to serve)
John McGragh, William Rumsey Cecil MD 4/14/1737, American 24 L
    46 days, Sunday, 5 pounds,
James McGraugh, Robert Massey Stafford VA 7/5/1744, Irish
    19 days, Saturday,
John McGraugh, James Love Lancaster PA 8/15/1754, Irish 24
    4 days, Sunday, 2 pounds, 6',
John McGraw, Amos Garrett Lancaster PA ironworks 9/20/1753, Irish 28 butcher
    5 days, Saturday, 4 pistoles, 6',
Nicholas McGray, John Dabbin Philadelphia City PA blacksmith 5/14/1741, Irish 26
    4 days, Sunday, 5 pounds,
John McGregor, Benjamin Bartholomew Jr Chester PA 5/31/1775, Scot 20
    14 dollars, 5'6-7",
Duncan McGriger, Edward Drugan Kent MD 4/16/1752, Scot 19
    4 pistoles,
John McGuigan, William Scott York PA 8/3/1769, 18
    2 pounds, 5'5",
John McGuigen, James Patterson Lancaster PA 5/3/1764, Irish 36
    18 days, Sunday, 2 pounds, 5'6",
Daniel McGuigin, Aaron Hall Philadelphia City PA 12/9/1772, Irish 30 weaver
    8 days, Wednesday, 3 pounds, 5'8",
Bartholomew McGuire, George Enderkin Chester PA 11/23/1749, Irish 24 L
    4 days, Sunday, 5 pounds,
Bartholomew McGuire, Thomas Evans Chester PA 3/20/1750, Irish 24 (2nd escape) L
    4 days, Sunday, 4 pounds, 5'6", (arrived 10 years ago)
Bartholomew McGuire, Francis Graham New Castle DE 1/29/1751, Irish 25 (3rd escape) L
    9 days, Tuesday, 2 pounds,
Dennis McGuire, Evan Evans Chester PA 11/19/1767, Irish 18 sailor
    6 days, Friday, 3 pounds, 5'8",
Francis McGuire, William Patterson Lancaster PA 10/20/1773, Irish 16
    43 days, Wednesday, 4 dollars, 5',
Hugh McGuire, William Hicks Philadelphia City PA 9/28/1769, Irish 19
    3 days, Monday, 3 pounds, 5'6-7",
James McGuire, Roger North Philadelphia PA 8/20/1752, Irish 25 currier
    3 days, Monday, 3 pounds,
John McGuire, John Addis Bucks PA 3/9/1758, 18
    3 days, Monday, 1 pounds, short,
John McGuire, John Boucther Philadelphia PA 11/16/1774, Irish 27
    2 pounds, 5'5-6",
John McGuire, George Taylor Monmouth NJ 5/10/1750, Irish 30 L
    30 days, Tuesday, 5 pounds, 6',
Michael McGuire, John Abbitt York PA 3/19/1751, 18
    2 pounds,
Nicholas McGuire, Caleb Perkins New Castle DE 4/5/1739, Irish 40 (ran before)
    5 days, Saturday, 2 pounds,
Patrick McGuire, James Bennett Chester PA 5/20/1742, 21
    1 day, Wednesday, 1.25 pounds,
Patrick McGuire, John Bleakley Philadelphia City PA 6/4/1741, Irish 22
    1 pound,
Patrick McGuire, Thomas Wills Chester PA 3/27/1750, Irish 17
    2 pounds, short,
Patrick McGuire, Patrick Archbold Chester PA 8/30/1759, cooper A
    11 days, Sunday, 2 pistoles, 5'5",
Thomas McGuire, John Fulton Chester PA 5/8/1793, 19 hatter A
    70 days, Wednesday, 10 dollars, 5'9",

William McGuire, Joseph Reyner Chester PA 10/26/1732, Irish shoemaker
    1 pound, short,
Charles McGuoan, Stephen Atkinson Lancaster PA 5/9/1765, Irish 20
    11 days, Sunday, 5 pounds,
Michael McGuyer, Susannah McLaughlin Cecil MD 5/21/1767, English
    23 days, Tuesday, 2 pounds, 5',
Philip McGuyre, Elijah Stinson Bucks PA 4/7/1784, Irish 19
    12 days, Friday, 5'9-10", (arrived last fall)
Thomas McHarge, Hussey & Fitzgerald Philadelphia City PA 4/16/1752, Scot tailor
    8 days, Wednesday, 3 pounds, middle,
James McHoney, John Singleton Chester PA 6/29/1758,
    14 days, Thursday, 1.5 pounds, 5'6",
Patrick McIlroy, Joseph Johnson Philadelphia PA 9/6/1770, Irish 21
    11 days, Sunday, 3 pounds, 5'9-10",
John McIlvaine, Christian Ginther Lancaster PA 6/4/1761, 19 potter A
    39 days, Sunday, 4 pounds,
Eleanor McIndoe, John Fox Chester PA 5/28/1777, 14 A
    13 days, Friday, 8 dollars, (relatives live nearby)
Daniel McInniry, Richard Smith Jr Salem NJ 10/13/1773, Irish
    10 dollars, 5'8",
William McIntire, William Moore Berks PA 7/17/1793, Irish 18
    10 days, Sunday, 6 dollars, 5'1-2",
Edward McKaehill, Andrew Ledlie Berks PA 8/18/1784, Irish 16
    14 days, Wednesday, 12 dollars, 5'4-5", (arrived last fall)
Archibald McKaghan, John Foulks Lancaster PA tanner 4/9/1747, Irish
    4 days, Sunday, 2 pounds, middle,
John McKahan, Robert Armstrong Lancaster PA 6/21/1759, American 18 L
    72 days, Tuesday, 1 pound, short,
Hugh McKain, Conrad Boner Frederick MD 12/1/1773, Irish tailor
    30 days, Tuesday, 10 pounds, 5'4",
Richard McKane, Boston Shull Salem NJ 5/1/1776, 25 gaol sale L
    6 days, Friday, 4 dollars, 5'3-4",
Joseph McKay, Peter Dillon Philadelphia City PA ship captain 8/20/1783, Irish 24 wheelwright
    3 days, Sunday, 5'7", (ran from ship)
Joug McKeake, John Miller Lancaster PA 11/17/1773, Irish 19
    17 days, Monday, 4 dollars,
Daniel McKeddie, Benjamin Duvall Caroline VA 7/7/1748, Scot 18
    34 days, Friday, 1 pistole, short,
James McKeen, Thomas Folwell Gloucester NJ 10/29/1783, 17 tailor
    15 days, Tuesday, 12 dollars, 5'4",
John McKenally, John Leaths Philadelphia City PA 10/11/1753, 32
    6 days, Friday, 1.5 pounds, 5'7",
Charles McKennan, Thomas Marshall Chester PA 11/22/1739, Irish 24 (2nd escape)
    4 days, Sunday, 2 pounds, middle,
Charles McKennan, Thomas Marshall Chester PA 6/28/1739, Irish 24
    3 days, Monday, 2 pounds, middle,
Michael McKenney, Alexander McIntosh Kent MD 12/18/1766, Irish 26 L
    19 days, Saturday, 1 pistole, 5'5",
Peter McKenney, William Sardiner Chester PA ironworks 5/5/1743,
    3 pounds, short,
James McKever, John Stapler New Castle DE 12/9/1772, American 18 L
    7 days, Thursday, 3 pounds, 4'5",
Katherine McKew, John Gill Gloucester NJ 10/14/1742, Irish
    52 days, Monday, 3 pounds, middle,
Margaret McKew, Bernard Hudley Lancaster PA 12/13/1764, 19
    26 days, Saturday, 1 pound,
Neal McKew, David Jones Berks PA 5/22/1766, Irish 19
    6 days, Friday, 2 pounds, 5'6",
Thomas McKew, William Denny Cumberland PA 1/24/1765, Irish soldier L
    18 days, Sunday, 1.5 pounds, short,
John McKindry, Lewis Roberts Philadelphia PA 8/11/1763, Irish 17
    9 days, Tuesday, 1.5 pounds, 5'2",
James McKinley, James Clayton Kent DE 4/23/1761, American 22 L
    10 days, Monday, 2 pistoles. 5'6",
Margaret McKinney, John Hanna Chester PA 7/3/1766, 15
    10 days, Monday, 1 pound,

Martin McKinney, Robert McConner Cumberland PA 11/14/1771, 25
    83 days, Friday, 3 pounds, 5'5-6",
Daniel McKinzey, Philip Price 7/17/1782, Scot 20
    14 days, Wednesday, 3 pounds, 5'6",
Daniel McKneel, William Woodside Philadelphia City PA ship captain 8/2/1750, Irish sailor A
    14 days, Thursday, 4 pounds, short,
James McKnight, Patrick Hart New Castle DE 8/26/1772, 35 soldier
    3 pounds, 5'7",
James McKnight, John Crosby Chester PA 8/18/1763, Irish 30 shoemaker L
    9 days, Tuesday, 3 pounds, 5'6",
Patrick McKogh, Amos Alexander Cecil MD 5/14/1767, Irish 20 cooper
    12 days, Saturday, 1.5 pounds, 5'5", (arrived last fall)
Frederick McKowne, William Miller Lancaster PA 4/13/1774, Irish 18
    13 days, Friday, 2 pounds, 5'4",
Peter McLane, John Meas Lancaster PA 8/20/1761, Irish 30
    9 days, Tuesday, 5 pounds, 5'7",
John McLarty, Robert Allison Chester PA 8/2/1764, Irish 19
    5 pounds, 5'6",
Charles McLaughlin, Edward Graham Cumberland PA 10/14/1772, Irish tailor
    9 days, Tuesday, 2.5 pounds, 5'5",
Hugh McLaughlin, Robert Stewart Lancaster PA 6/8/1749, Irish
    10 days, Monday, 3 pounds, 5'8",
Hugh McLaughlin, John Gibbons Lancaster PA 2/25/1762, Irish 40
    15 days, Wednesday, 2 pounds, 5'6",
Hugh McLaughlin, Edward Crosby Lancaster PA 11/23/1774, cooper A
    3 pounds, 5'6", (already served out the term to pay for his passage)
James McLaughlin, Jacobus Hines New Castle DE 9/12/1754, Irish 19
    18 days, Sunday, 2 pounds, 5'6",
James McLaughlin, Jacobus Hines New Castle DE 6/26/1755, Irish 20 (2nd escape)
    42 days, Thursday, 2 pounds, 5'6",
James McLaughlin, William Foott New Castle DE 6/20/1771, 22 cooper
    8 days, Wednesday, 8 dollars, 5'8",
John McLaughlin, Joseph Alison Chester PA 11/16/1752, Irish
    7 days, Thursday, 2 pounds, 5'7",
John McLaughlin, Amos Grandine Philadelphia PA 4/25/1754, butcher
    30 days, Tuesday, 2 pounds, middle,
John McLaughlin, Peter Bard Burlington NJ ironworks 3/27/1753, Irish 35 sawyer
    2 pounds, short,
Michael McLaughlin, Alexander Hill Salem NJ 7/19/1753,
    4 days, Sunday, 3 pounds, 5'6",
Paddy McLaughlin, John Chestnut Bucks PA 8/16/1753, Irish
    3 days, Monday, 1.5 pounds, 5',
Patrick McLaughlin, William Montgomery Lancaster PA 8/20/1761, Irish 27
    2 pounds, 5'6",
Patrick McLaughlin, Thomas Robinson New Castle DE 9/10/1788, Irish 28
    9 days, Monday, 4 dollars, 5'10",
Sarah McLaughlin, William Hamilton Philadelphia City PA wigmaker 11/2/1758, Irish 18
    44 days, Tuesday, 2 pounds, (arrived 3 months ago)
William McLeary, Lodowick Ligget Chester PA 8/29/1765, Irish weaver
    3 days, Monday, 3 pounds, 5'8",
Martha McLoud, John Zell Philadelphia PA 8/10/1774, Scot 18
    30 days, Tuesday,
Farrel McLoughlan, Henry Hockley Chester PA ironworks 8/21/1740, Irish 35
    4 days, Sunday, 2 pounds, middle,
Catherine McLoy, Robert Smith Chester PA 6/6/1765, Irish 23
    22 days, Wednesday, 2 pounds,
Hugh McMahan, David Smith Philadelphia City PA 5/9/1754, 40 cooper
    13 days, Friday, 1.5 pounds, 5'10",
John McMahon, Samuel Boyer NY butcher 4/29/1742, Irish 25 butcher
    11 days, Sunday, 3 pounds, short,
John McMahon, Mary Williams Frederick MD 6/12/1776, Irish-American 20 soldier L
    355 days, Friday, 5 pounds, 5'5-6",
Richard McManemen, John Buffington Chester PA 1/2/1753, Irish
    8 days, Wednesday, 2 pounds, short, (has been in the colonies before)
James McManua, Alexander Lowery Lancaster PA 4/18/1765, Irish 18
    13 days, Friday, 3 pounds, 5'7",

Brian McManus, Joseph Thomson Chester PA 9/30/1736, 36
    7 days, Thursday, 2 pounds, short,
John McMechen, Robert Adams Chester PA 10/18/1750, Irish 25
    4 days, Sunday, 1 pound, short,
Thomas McMewee, John Mountain 9/27/1770, Irish 23
    2 pounds, 5',
Robert McMinn, Joseph Burr Bucks PA 6/21/1786, Irish 17
    3 days, Sunday, 8 dollars, 5'8",
John McMiskell, James McLure Cumberland PA 3/29/1775, Scot 18
    2 pounds, 5'6",
John McMullan, James Murdock Chester PA 11/5/1767, 24
    9 days, Tuesday, 6 dollars, 5'4-5",
William McMullan, Clement Humphreys 7/5/1770, Irish 19
    4 days, Sunday, 4 dollars, 5'8-9",
Dennis McMullen, William Montgomery Chester PA 8/3/1774, Irish 22
    5 days, Saturday, 4 dollars, 5'10",
Dennis McMullen, Robert Lamborn Chester PA 10/5/1774, Irish 22 (2nd escape)
    31 days, Monday, 4 dollars, 5'10", (arrived last May)
John McMullen, James Crawford Lancaster PA 9/21/1774, Irish 40
    8 dollars, 5'7-8",
Catherine McMullin, Anthony Hull Philadelphia City PA 5/24/1764, Irish 35
    2 pounds,
James McMullin, John Enos New Castle DE 2/5/1777, Irish 17
    7 days, Thursday, 3 dollars, 5'6-7",
John McMullin, Jonathan Morris Chester PA 6/21/1764, Irish 16
    5 days, Saturday, 1 pound,
John McNamara, Zachariah Nieman Philadelphia PA 7/19/1770, Irish 17
    9 days, Tuesday, 2 pounds, 5'5-6",
Michael McNamara, John Seely Baltimore MD 8/19/1756, Irish 22 C
    2 pounds, 5'8",
Cormick McName, James Hamilton Lancaster PA 9/9/1772, 28 L
    14 days, Thursday, 6 dollars, 5'5",
Catherine McNamee, Robert Miller Lancaster PA 10/1/1747, 34
    16 days, Tuesday, 2 pounds,
John McNeal, Benjamin Weatherby Chester PA 7/6/1749, Irish 24
    8 days, Wednesday, 2 pounds, (served some time in Talbot)
Francis McNealis, William Smith Lancaster PA 4/18/1754, Irish 25
    5 pounds, 5'10",
Francis McNealis, William Smith Lancaster PA 6/20/1755, Irish 26 (2nd escape)
    6 days, Friday, 2 pounds, 5'10", (wears an iron collar)
Francis McNealis, William Smith Lancaster PA 10/9/1755, Irish 26 (3rd escape)
    4 days, Sunday, 2 pounds, 5'10", (arrived 8 to 10 years ago)
Patrick McNealy, Jonathan Vaughn Talbot MD ironworks 9/29/1763, Irish
    23 days, Tuesday, 1.5 pounds, middle,
Thomas McNeely, Amos Alexander Cecil MD 5/14/1767, Irish 20 cooper
    12 days, Saturday, 1.5 pounds, 5'5", (arrived last May)
William McNeely, Isaac Hilbert Jr Chester PA 12/24/1783, Irish 19
    10 days, Sunday, 5'10-11",
Charles McNeil, Presley Blackiston Philadelphia City PA 11/10/1773, Scot 28 shoemaker
    2 days, Tuesday, 5 pounds, 5'7-8", (arrived 2 months ago, but has been in colonies before)
John McNeil, Edward Matthews Philadelphia City PA 1/22/1756, Irish drummer
    35 days, Thursday, 3 pounds, middle,
Laughlin McNeil, William Clifton Philadelphia City PA 12/22/1773, Irish nailer
    8 dollars, 5'6",
John McNelis, Richard Jones Chester PA 9/15/1784, Irish 18
    2 pounds, 5'5-6",
John McNemare, Peter Downey Philadelphia City PA 8/13/1747, Irish 25
    15 days, Wednesday, 3 pounds, 5'4",
Philip McNickal, William Richey Chester PA 10/26/1774, Irish 28 weaver
    55 days, Friday, 8 dollars, (arrived this year)
James McNut, Thomas Brown Chester PA 1/27/1773, 20 cooper A
    32 days, Sunday, 0.5 pounds,
Charles McOnagel, Morgan Evans Lancaster PA 4/14/1743, Irish 20
    16 days, Tuesday, 1.5 pounds,
Owen McOwen, Henry Howard Baltimore MD 10/13/1784, Irish 27
    92 days, Tuesday, 20 pounds, 5'8",

Henry McPeak, William McIlvaine Philadelphia City PA merchant 4/5/1759, Irish 16
    11 days, Sunday, 2 pounds, 5'1", (has 5.5 years to serve)
Michael McPhaddin, William Rice Bucks PA 8/24/1785, Irish 26 weaver
    3 days, Sunday, 6 dollars, 5'9",
Catherine McPherson, Robert Whitehill Lancaster PA 12/1/1768, Irish 25
    14 days, Thursday, 4 dollars,
Daniel McPherson, Peter Reeve 10/7/1762, Scot 15
    14 days, Thursday, 1 pound, short,
James McQuaid, Thomas Parvin Chester PA 7/31/1755, Irish
    10 days, Monday, 2 pounds,
Morris McQuaid, Seth Lippincott Burlington NJ 7/10/1776, Irish 18
    2 days, Tuesday, 8 dollars, 5'7",
David McQuatto, Samuel Nutts Chester PA ironworks 1/6/1737, Scot hammerman L
    3 pounds, short,
John McQue, James Colgan Kent DE 9/2/1762, Irish 22
    4 pounds, 5'5",
Alexander McQuilen, John Harley Chester PA 10/18/1775, Irish 20
    3 days, Monday, 8 dollars, 5'8-9",
Thomas McQuire, Peter Worrial Lancaster PA 4/8/1742, Irish C
    2 pounds, short,
Danial McShane, Jacob Stern Sussex NJ ironworks 3/12/1772,
    8 dollars, 5'10",
Edward McSurely, Nathaniel Ring Chester PA innholder 5/28/1761, Irish 29
    2 pounds, 5'3", (has travelled alot)
Edward McSurely, Nathaniel Ring Chester PA innholder 5/6/1762, Irish 30 (2nd escape)
    17 days, Monday, 3 pounds, 5'5",
Grace McSwain, Manaseth Logue Cecil MD 4/21/1748, Irish 25
    8 days, Wednesday, 2 pounds, short,
Thomas McSwine, William Wright Lancaster PA 3/12/1740, 20
    254 days, Sunday, 2 pounds,
Owen McVey, Hugh Coupland Baltimore MD 6/9/1748, Irish 23 laborer C
    18 days, Sunday, 2 pounds, (arrived 20 months ago)
Brian McWhenney, John Miles Northumberland PA 11/29/1775, Irish
    102 days, Sunday, 8 dollars, 5'9", (lately arrived)
Andrew McWhiney, James Morrison Lancaster PA 2/22/1775, Irish 16
    1.5 pounds, 5'6-7", (arrived last fall)
William McWhorter, Michael Rankin New Castle DE 7/25/1771, Scot 19
    16 days, Tuesday, 2 pounds, 5'5", (arrived this month, has relatives nearby)
James McWilliam, Daniel Evans Bucks PA 9/20/1775, American 18 L
    15 days, Wednesday, 4 dollars, 5'6",
John McWorthir, George Stern New Castle DE 3/20/1776, American 16 L
    31 days, Monday, 3 dollars,
John Meach, Joseph Miller 8/21/1776, English 19
    7 days, Thursday, 5 dollars, 5'7-8",
John Meagher, John Steelman Cape May NJ 8/3/1769,
    10 days, Monday, 5 pounds, 5'5",
John Meahan, Jacob Lemmon Cecil MD 12/20/1770, Irish 21 leather-dresser
    11 days, Sunday, 3 pounds, 5'7-8",
John Mealey, Benjamin Bradford Cecil MD doctor 6/4/1747, Irish 40
    27 days, Friday, 1 pound,
Edward Means, Joseph Miller 3/1/1764, 30 sailor
    2 pounds,
Daniel Meansey, Curtis Grubb Lancaster PA ironworks 7/21/1768, Scot 30
    10 days, Monday, 2 pounds, 5'6-7",
Philip Meany, David Eckhoff Chester PA 5/1/1755, French
    12 days, Saturday, 1.5 pounds, 5',
William Mearns, Isaac Whitelock Lancaster PA 8/16/1750, English 30 mason
    3 pounds, tall,
Thomas Mecan, Robert Evans Cecil MD 8/3/1769, Irish 17
    16 days, Tuesday, 1.5 pounds, 5',
William Mecan, John Bull Philadelphia PA 1/11/1770, Irish
    4 dollars,
Christiana Mechell, Marcus Hoanecker Philadelphia PA 5/26/1757, German 35
    16 days, Tuesday, 4 pounds,
Thomas Meclene, Samuel Beall Jr Frederick MD ironworks 7/3/1766, Irish
    13 days, Friday, 3 pounds,

Roger Medin, John Pass Burlington NJ 9/4/1746, Irish
    2.5 pounds, middle,
David Meek, Samuel Beall Jr Frederick MD ironworks 5/19/1768, Scot 24 schoolmaster
    54 days, Saturday, 5 pounds, 5'8-9", (arrived last fall)
Tobias Meek, John Gill Gloucester NJ 7/10/1755, German 22
    6 days, Friday, 5 pounds, middle,
Neal Megloughin, Nathaniel Ring Chester PA innholder 7/20/1738, 40 L
    8 days, Wednesday, 3 pounds,
Edmund Megound, Samuel Barnes Cumberland PA 8/1/1751, Irish 40
    about 6 weeks ago, 1 pound, short,
Thomas Megraw, John Vansant Kent MD 7/27/1769, Irish soldier
    17 days, Monday, 10 dollars, 5'10",
Samuel Mehary, David Sterret Lancaster PA 4/3/1793, 17 miller A
    17 days, Sunday, 6 pounds, 5'9",
Peter Mehler, David Shaffer Philadelphia City PA 6/27/1771, American 25 waggoner L
    7 days, Thursday, 3 pounds, 6',
Arnold Melchizedeck, William Dewees Philadelphia PA 10/2/1729,
    22 days, Wednesday, 1 pound, middle,
Hannah Meldrum, James Edmondston Chester PA 9/21/1752,
    20 days, Friday, 2 pounds, 5'2",
Lawrence Mellow, Robert McConnell Lancaster PA 7/4/1765, French 22
    4 days, Sunday, 2 pounds, 5',
Melen Mellow, Henry Hoffman Chester PA 11/28/1792, 19 wheelwright A
    10 dollars, 5'6",
John Melone, William Brown Lancaster PA 6/18/1794, Irish 16
    6 dollars, 5',
John Melony, William Miller Chester PA 5/31/1764, Irish
    4 days, Sunday, 1 pound,
Peter Mennel, Daniel Lippincott Jr Burlington NJ 8/9/1770, German 18
    4 days, Sunday, 3 pounds, 5',
Melchor Mennig, Jacob Wentz Philadelphia PA 7/19/1753, German 25
    9 days, Tuesday, 2 pounds, short,
Francis Mens, Joseph Bell Philadelphia City PA 5/6/1756, Irish 25 schoolmaster
    1 day, Wednesday, 1.5 pounds,
Frances Mercer, Richard Carsan New Castle DE 5/27/1756, Irish 22
    7 days, Thursday, 1.5 pounds, 5'6",
William Meredith, Joshua Pancoast Philadelphia City PA 7/7/1768, 18 carpenter A
    3 days, Monday, 4 dollars, 5'6",
John Merk, Mary Black Burlington NJ 5/9/1771, German 19
    12 days, Saturday, 6 dollars, 5'5", (relatives live nearby)
William Merone, Augustine Stillman Philadelphia City PA 9/6/1750, 17 shoemaker A
    2 days, Tuesday, 1 pound,
James Merratty, Daniel Kelly Philadelphia PA 8/12/1736, Irish 40
    17 days, Monday, 2 pounds,
Edward Merriot, William Brown Queen Anne's MD 3/31/1757, 50 joiner C
    25 days, Sunday, 3 pistoles, 5'4",
James Merrison, Valentine Rinchart Somerset NJ 6/6/1771, 22 L
    15 days, Monday, 3 pounds, 5'6",
James Merron, Thomas McCaghry Middlesex NJ 8/24/1766, Irish
    2 pounds, 5'4",
Christian Mertle, Willing & Morris Philadelphia City PA merchants 2/23/1774, German
    14 days, Thursday, 1.5 pounds, 5', (lately arrived, ran with wife)
John Clode Mesha, James Hankinson Monmouth NJ 5/22/1755, French
    3 days, Monday, 3 pounds, 5'6",
Andrew Mets, Benjamin Powell 5/26/1773, German 18
    22 days, Wednesday, 4 dollars, 5'3-4",
Christian Metz, Mark Bird Berks PA ironworks 4/21/1773, German 46 miller
    16 days, Tuesday, 3 dollars, 5'9-10",
George Metzner, Philip Jacob Irlon Culpepper VA potash-trade 3/20/1766, German
    5 pounds, 5'6", (arrived 1.5 years ago)
Frederick Meyer, John Pannebacker Berks PA 3/8/1775, German 30 school teacher
    87 days, Sunday, 4 dollars, 5'8-9",
Anna Meyers, Charles Ferguson Philadelphia City PA shipwright 7/6/1774, German 25
    3 days, Monday, 3 pounds, 5'4-5",
Patrick Michaley, Alexander Snodgrass Lancaster PA 1/16/1772, Irish
    21 days, Thursday, 4 dollars, (lately arrived)

Philip J Michell, John Brown Philadelphia City PA 5/23/1771, German 24
    4 days, Sunday, 8 dollars, 5'4", (arrived 10 months ago)
Anna Catherina Michtder, William Snowden Hunterdon NJ 11/3/1757, German 26
    14 days, Thursday, 1.5 pounds, (has a small girl)
Dorothy Mickle, Israel Lawrence Salem NJ 11/22/1764, Irish 20
    9 days, Tuesday, 2 pounds, 5'2",
Aaron Middleton, Isaac Pearson Burlington NJ 11/16/1732, English 26 clockmaker
    12 days, Saturday, 2 pounds, short,
Richard Middleton, Richard Clayton Chester PA 3/1/1729, English
    2.5 pounds, short,
Thomas Middleton, Joseph Oldham Philadelphia City PA 9/8/1748, Irish nailer
    1.5 pounds,
Christopher Mier, Hugh Linn Chester PA 2/6/1753, German 45
    15 days, Wednesday, 2 pounds,
Margaret Mier, Henry Hockman Bucks PA 6/26/1766, German 17
    0.05 pounds,
John Milben, Matthew Grier Bucks PA 2/2/1769, Irish 20
    4 days, Thursday, 4 pounds, 5'6-7",
John Milburn, Thomas Lawson VA ironworks 9/23/1762, 30 forge carpenter L
    28 days, Thursday, 10 pounds, 5'10",
Juliana Milcahee, Anthony Fortune Philadelphia City PA 9/25/1776, 30
    0 days, Thursday, 0.03 pounds, (has 3 month old child)
William Mileham, Edward Price Philadelphia PA 3/22/1775, American 18 L
    10 days, Monday, 4 dollars, 5'6",
Bartholomew Miles, Henry Cooper Burlington NJ 6/25/1747, Irish 26
    4 days, Sunday, 2.5 pounds, 5'6",
Francis Miles, George Ege York PA ironworks 7/23/1777, English 20
    10 days, Monday, 20 dollars, 5'5-6",
Nicholas Miles, James Gibson Cumberland PA 8/15/1771, Irish
    3 pounds,
John Miligen, Joshua McDowell New Castle DE 8/27/1767, Irish 26
    10 days, Monday, 6 pounds, 5'8",
George Millar, Robert Lewis New Castle DE 11/21/1754, German 25 stocking-weaver
    5 days, Saturday, 3 pounds, tall,
John Millar, Robert Newcom Talbot MD 3/27/1746, Scot 30 cooper
    5 pounds,
William Millard, Peter Browne Philadelphia City PA 10/3/1745, 20
    2 days, Tuesday, 2 pounds, middle,
Robert Millby, Lawrence Washington Philadelphia City PA 9/22/1748, Irish weaver C
    6 days, Friday, 5 pounds, 5'10",
Barbara Miller, Christian Jung Philadelphia PA 8/27/1777, German 14
    12 days, Saturday, 3 pounds,
Daniel Miller, Lazarus Pine 5/17/1753, Irish 40
    4 days, Sunday, 1.5 pounds, 5'8",
George Miller, Valentine Brown Philadelphia City PA locksmith 4/19/1780, A
    10 days, Sunday, 100 dollars,
Griffel Miller, Edmund Peers NY 5/27/1736, Scot 20 maid
    2 pounds,
Jacob Miller, Christian Cramer Philadelphia City PA 6/11/1772, German 18 baker
    25 days, Sunday, 1 pound, 5',
James Miller, Philip Hinkel Chester PA 5/11/1774, Irish 26
    3 days, Monday, 3 pounds, 5'10",
John Miller, John Wray Chester PA 12/20/1753, Irish 17
    2 pounds, (wears an iron collar)
John Miller, Francis Dudley Burlington NJ 5/8/1755, German 19
    11 days, Sunday, 3 pounds, 5'7",
John Miller, John Bell Chester PA 8/31/1758, 20
    2 pounds, 5'8",
John Miller, John Bell Chester PA 5/3/1759, 20 (2nd escape)
    9 days, Tuesday, 2 pounds, 5'8",
John Miller, John Van Lasche Chester PA 6/30/1773, German-Jew 16
    3 days, Monday, 3 pounds, 4'5-6",
John Miller, Casper Deel Lancaster PA 8/21/1776, German-Jew 19 (2nd escape)
    8 dollars, 4'10",
John Christian Miller, Stephen Van Cortlandt NJ 4/15/1756, German 18 baker
    28 days, Thursday, 3 pounds, 5'10",

Lewis Miller, Andrew Sprowle Norfolk VA 8/28/1755, cooper
   5 pistoles, 5'8",
Michael Miller, Leonard Stoneburner Philadelphia PA 12/22/1757, German 20 baker
   6 days, Friday, 2 pounds, 5'6",
Michael Miller, John Foulke Bucks PA 12/23/1762, 16
   7 days, Thursday, 5 pounds,
Peter Miller, Bernhard Dritel Philadelphia PA 8/16/1770, French 30
   4 days, Sunday, 1 pound, 5',
Peter Miller, John Staufer Lancaster PA 4/19/1775, German 18
   19 days, Saturday, 5'2",
Philip Peter Miller, Nicholas Seidel Philadelphia PA 2/7/1776, German
   3 pounds, 5'5",
Thomas Miller, George Boyd Lancaster PA 10/25/1753, Welsh 20
   3 pounds, 5'8",
Thomas Miller, George Boyd Lancaster PA 6/27/1754, Welsh 21 (2nd escape)
   1 pound, 5'8",
William Miller, Levin Whealin 5/24/1775, 23
   6 days, Friday, 4 dollars, 5'10",
William Miller, Daniel Hughes Frederick MD ironworks 10/5/1774, 30
   16 days, Tuesday, 3 pounds, 5'10", (has been in the colonies before)
William Miller, Andrews & Postlethwaite 2/1/1732, 45 L
   43 days, Wednesday, 2 pounds, middle,
Arthur Millholland, James Adams Chester PA 9/6/1739, 30 Indian-trader L
   38 days, Monday, 3 pounds, middle,
Thomas Milliner, John Howard Baltimore MD ironworks 7/5/1764, 20 C
   5 pounds, 5'4",
Lorange Millo, Isaac Richardson Lancaster PA 10/3/1765, French 27
   11 days, Sunday, 1 pound, 5'5-6",
Daniel Mills, George Aston Chester PA 9/11/1746, English tanner
   17 days, Monday, 3 pounds, middle,
Hezekiah Mills, Robert Toms Philadelphia City PA 7/22/1736, English 14 tailor
   7 days, Thursday, 2 pounds, short,
John Mills, William Crosthwaite Philadelphia City PA perukemaker 10/27/1737, 18
   2 pounds, middle,
John Mills, Joseph Shepard Salem NJ 7/5/1744, Irish 21
   1 pound,
Robert Mills, Samuel Hanson Charles MD 11/16/1774, Irish 22 gardener
   3 pounds, (arrived last Sept.)
Joseph Millwater, Daniel Davis Chester PA 4/25/1734, 40
   5 days, Saturday, 3 pounds, short,
Samuel Milson, John Anderson Lancaster PA 11/16/1769, English
   0.75 pounds,
Timothy Minchan, William Simpson Philadelphia City PA 10/10/1754, Irish 20
   8 days, Wednesday, 2 pounds, 5'5",
John Mines, Peter Hall 5/12/1743, Irish 20 blacksmith
   17 days, Monday, 1.5 pounds, middle,
Hance Michael Ming, Joseph Howell Philadelphia City PA tanner 10/9/1755, German 26
   4 days, Sunday, 3 pounds, 5'4",
Hans Michael Minolt, John Davis Chester PA 5/29/1755, German 18
   32 days, Sunday, 3 pounds, (father lives nearby)
Cornelius Minthorn, Nathaniel Wilson 5/11/1791, nailer A
   10 days, Sunday, 0.05 pounds,
Ebenezer Mirit, William Shephard Philadelphia PA 5/17/1764, American 25 L
   11 days, Sunday, 3 pounds, 5'10",
Henry Misener, Christopher Curfess Philadelphia City PA 7/9/1772, German 40
   5 pounds,
James Mitchel, John Orr Philadelphia PA 11/12/1730, 28 cooper
   6 days, Friday, 4 pounds, middle,
John Mitchel, Robert Story Philadelphia PA 12/15/1737,
   10 days, Monday, 2.5 pounds,
Philip Mitchel, Henry Neff Lancaster PA 2/10/1773, 20
   3 pounds, 5',
Richard Mitchel, John Lovering Cecil MD 7/5/1750, 30
   12 days, Saturday, 2 pistoles, short,
Thomas Mitchel, John Parvin Berks PA 4/23/1777, 20
   42 days, Thursday, 0.05 pounds, 5'3-4",

John Mitchell, Michael Graham Chester PA 10/3/1771, 17 gaol sale L
 15 days, Wednesday, 4 dollars, 5'6",
Patrick Mitchell, James Lestrange Salem NJ 8/20/1747, Irish 22
 7 days, Thursday, 3 pounds, short,
Patrick Mitchell, Andrew Ball Salem NJ 6/16/1748, Irish 23 (2nd escape)
 1 day, Wednesday, 3 pounds, short,
Philip Mitchell, Joseph Luckens Philadelphia City PA innholder 1/23/1766, 15
 1 pound,
Philip Mitchell, Joseph Luckens Philadelphia City PA innholder 4/2/1767, 16 (2nd escape)
 32 days, Sunday, 0.25 pounds,
Robert Mitchell, Conyngham & Nesbitt New Castle DE merchants 9/1/1784, Irish weaver
 8 days, Tuesday, 3 pounds, 5'10", (ran from ship)
Edward Mitchem, John Metcalfe Baltimore MD 5/10/1753, 40 schoolmaster C
 March, 6 pounds, 5', (has been in the colonies for some time)
Samuel Moate, Symour Hood Philadelphia City PA ship captain 5/17/1770, English 16 A
 0.08 pounds, (apprenticed to the ship)
John Jacob Moder, James Mason Salem NJ 2/9/1774, German 17
 9 days, Tuesday, 1.5 pounds,
Anna Louisa Moesler, Christian Young Philadelphia PA 9/26/1787, German 25
 29 days, Tuesday, 8 dollars, 5'2-3",
Benjamin Moffet, Christopher Martin Philadelphia PA caulker 8/3/1785, 18 caulker A
 2 days, Monday, 4 dollars,
Benjamin Moffet, Christopher Martin Philadelphia PA caulker 8/2/1786, 19 caulker (2nd escape) A
 3 days, Sunday, 0.03 pounds,
Daniel Mohegan, William Attwood Philadelphia City PA ship captain 10/23/1740, 25
 4 days, Sunday, 1.5 pounds, short,
David Moles, David Wilson Chester PA 9/1/1790, Irish
 14 days, Wednesday, 6 dollars, 5'6", (arrived 6 years ago)
John Moll, William Lux Baltimore MD 4/18/1754, English 30 C
 3 pounds, (arrived April 1753)
William Mollen, Thomas Worrall Chester PA 7/17/1766, 20
 7 days, Thursday, 1.5 pounds, 5'6",
Michael Molloy, John Boyle Philadelphia City PA 6/29/1769, Irish 21
 11 days, Sunday, 3 dollars, 5'8-9", (ran from ship)
Bartley Moloy, Thomas Pim Chester PA 10/7/1772, Irish 23
 8 days, Wednesday, 4 pounds, 5'8-9",
Edward Monday, John Worthington Dorsey York PA 9/30/1772, English 30
 12 days, Saturday, 1.5 pounds, 5'5",
John Monday, John Read Lancaster PA 3/16/1769, Irish
 17 days, Monday, 3 pounds, 5'4",
Michael Monday, Mordecai Evans Philadelphia PA 3/28/1771, Irish 18
 5'8", (has 7 months left to serve)
Timothy Money, Benjamin Randolph Philadelphia City PA cabinetmaker 11/22/1770, Irish sawyer
 9 days, Tuesday, 6 dollars, 5'8",
James Monk, Michael Earle Cecil MD 4/30/1752, American 30 sailor L
 13 days, Friday, middle,
Alexander Monro, Jonas Metsger Lancaster PA 9/5/1771, Irish
 4 dollars, 5',
George Monrow, John Brown Gloucester NJ 6/25/1752, Scot 30
 3 days, Monday, 3 pounds, 5'9",
George Monrow, William Roberts Salem NJ 5/9/1751, Irish 30 soldier
 1 pound,
Hugh Montgomery, John Kell Philadelphia City PA 7/7/1748, 20
 25 days, Sunday, 5 pounds,
John Montgomery, Nathan Sheppard Philadelphia City PA 8/23/1764, 25
 11 days, Sunday, 2.5 pounds, 5'8", (use to the sea)
Margaret Montgomery, Francis Johnston Philadelphia City PA 7/13/1785, Irish 18
 7 days, Wednesday, 8 dollars, 5'3-4",
Mary Montgomery, John Heap 9/3/1777, Irish
 90 days, Friday, 20 dollars,
William Moody, Joseph Duer Bucks PA 11/30/1752, English tailor
 4 pounds, short, (has been in the navy)
George Moone, Joseph Feinauer Philadelphia City PA 7/28/1773, English 21
 8 days, Wednesday, 3 pounds, 5'3-4",
Michael Mooney, Alexander McIntosh Kent MD 12/18/1766, Irish 28 L
 19 days, Saturday, 1 pistole, 6',

William Mooney, Brian Wilkinson Philadelphia City PA carver 4/5/1749, Irish 20 carver
    39 days, Sunday, 3 pounds, little,
John Moor, Clayton Levick Kent DE 4/12/1764, English 45
    25 days, Sunday, 2 pounds,
John Moor, Joshua Bunting Burlington NJ 10/25/1775, Irish 25
    4 dollars, 5'10",
Roger Moor, William Walker Bucks PA 7/7/1743, Irish 23
    3 days, Monday, 5 pounds,
William Moor, Heslop & Blair Fredericksburg VA 1/30/1772, English farmer C
    76 days, Friday, 15 dollars, 5'9-10",
Ambrose Moore, William Fullerton Lancaster PA 9/13/1750, Irish 19
    1 pound, short, (lately arrived)
Christopher Moore, Jeremiah Persol Chester PA 11/13/1755, Irish cooper
    4 days, Sunday, 2 pounds, 5'8",
Daniel Moore, Jonathan Coutes Chester PA 2/26/1777, Irish 20
    59 days, Monday, 4 dollars, 5'6",
Fanny Moore, Jacob Waggoner Philadelphia PA 3/26/1777, 35
    11 days, Sunday, 0.05 pounds,
George Moore, John Parrish Philadelphia City PA 5/1/1776, English 24 brushmaker
    61 days, Saturday, 4 dollars, 5'10",
James Moore, Thomas Harris Hunterdon NJ 6/9/1748, Irish 22
    11 days, Sunday, 2 pounds, middle,
John Moore, Thomas Robertson Chester PA 12/26/1752, 24 weaver
    8 days, Wednesday, 2 pounds, short,
John Moore, Thomas Robertson Chester PA 10/4/1753, 25 weaver (2nd escape)
    10 days, Monday, 2 pounds, short,
John Moore, John Inglis Philadelphia City PA 9/26/1751, Irish 20 ropemaker
    5 days, Saturday, 2 pounds, 5'8",
John Moore, James Hamilton Lancaster PA 5/26/1763, Irish
    16 days, Tuesday, 3 pounds,
John Moore, Andrew Boyd Lancaster PA 2/24/1763, Irish 30
    7 days, Thursday, 2 pounds, 5'8",
John Moore, Joseph Bell Philadelphia City PA 9/29/1763, Irish 37 carpenter
    6 days, Friday, 2 pounds, 5'6",
John Moore, Robert Way Chester PA 9/1/1768, Irish 20 blacksmith
    4 days, Sunday, 3 pounds, 5',
John Moore, John Hider Jr Gloucester NJ 12/9/1772, Irish 18
    3 days, Monday, 5 pounds, 5'10",
John Moore, William Rankin York PA 10/4/1764, American 18 carpenter A
    18 days, Sunday, 2 pounds, 5'6",
Joseph Moore, James Keemer Philadelphia PA 7/18/1751, Irish
    5 days, Saturday, 1.5 pounds, short,
Margaret Moore, John Hanna Chester PA 7/3/1766, 21
    10 days, Monday, 1 pound,
Mary Moore, Adam Jordan Bucks PA 8/27/1752, Irish
    6 days, Friday, 3 pounds, middle,
Patrick Moore, Daniel Hopewell Burlington NJ 10/9/1760, Irish 22
    21 days, Thursday, 3 pounds, 5'8",
Peter Moore, Michael Baldridge Chester PA 9/4/1776, Irish 21
    3 days, Monday, 2 pounds, 5'8",
William Moore, John Park Chester PA 12/22/1737, 20
    7 days, Thursday, 1 pound, short,
William Moore, Charles Moore 12/3/1761, 19 hatter A
    5 days, Saturday, 1.5 pounds, 5'9",
William Moore, Jonathan Robeson Philadelphia PA 5/18/1785, 18 blacksmith A
    1 day, Tuesday, 6 dollars, 5'6-7",
William Moore, Joseph Money Berks PA 8/23/1753, Irish 30 butcher L
    2 pounds, 5'6",
William Moore, Philip Welsh Burlington NJ 9/13/1753, Irish 30 butcher (2nd escape) L
    1.5 pounds, 5'6",
Andrew Moorehead, Robert Moore Philadelphia City PA joiner 4/9/1767, 17 A
    21 days, Thursday, shop shavings,
Barnut Moran, John Paul Chester PA 4/18/1754, German 40
    23 days, Tuesday, 2 pounds, 5'7",
Mary Moran, Charles Mothesby Baltimore MD 9/15/1763, Irish 56
    32 days, Sunday, 2 pounds,

Robert Morchel, John Miller Northampton PA 3/28/1765, Irish 19
 11 days, Sunday, 4 pounds, 5'10",
James Mordox, Henry Sparks Gloucester NJ 7/6/1738, Irish 60 blacksmith
 4 days, Sunday, 2 pounds,
John More, Robert Ford St Mary's MD 7/13/1738, Irish
 112 days, Saturday, 5 Maryland pounds, tall,
Thomas Moreland, Samuel Johnston Lancaster PA 5/6/1762, Irish 17 weaver
 25 days, Sunday, 3 pounds,
Bryant Morgan, Arthur Lee Kent MD 4/23/1747, Irish 40
 4 days, Sunday, 1 pound, short,
Cicely Morgan, Samuel Floyd Chester PA 3/29/1775, Irish
 16 days, Tuesday, 4 dollars,
Darby Morgan, Robert Lamboth Chester PA 8/27/1741, Irish 19
 3 days, Monday, 1 pound,
Edward Morgan, Samuel Nutts Chester PA ironworks 6/5/1740, tailor
 45 days, Monday, 1 pistole, middle,
Evan Bradbury Morgan, John O'Brian Philadelphia City PA 6/29/1769, American 16 A
 38 days, Monday, 0.08 pounds, 5',
Hugh Morgan, John Forest Chester PA 9/5/1754, Irish 22 weaver
 8 days, Wednesday, 2 pounds, 5'6",
James Morgan, Patrick Renalds Burlington NJ 5/16/1751, English 27 wheelwright
 2 pistoles, 5'8",
James Morgan, Richard Carelton New Castle DE 10/8/1794, 19 tailor
 57 days, Tuesday, 8 dollars, 5'3-4",
John Morgan, Owen Evans Philadelphia PA 6/9/1737, Welsh 24
 4 days, Sunday, 2 pounds, tall,
John Morgan, Thomas Pryor Bucks PA 4/27/1749, Irish 18
 6 days, Friday, 2 pounds,
John Morgan, Jeremiah Manning Middlesex NJ 8/31/1774, Irish 21
 4 dollars, 5'4",
John Morgan, Jeremiah Manning Middlesex NJ 8/9/1775, Irish 22 (2nd escape)
 17 days, Monday, 5 dollars, 5'5",
John Morgan, William Carson New Castle DE 12/15/1773, Irish
 3 pounds, 5'7-8",
Richard Morgan, Francis Batten Gloucester NJ 8/30/1753, Welsh
 37 days, Tuesday, 1.5 pounds, short,
William Morgan, William Williams Philadelphia PA 11/1/1739, English 29
 4 days, Sunday, 2 pounds, tall,
William Morgan, Henry Fagen Chester PA 6/13/1745, English 37 (2nd escape) L
 2 days, Tuesday, 3 pounds, middle,
William Morgan, Henry Fagen Chester PA 1/21/1746, English 37 (3rd escape) L
 13 days, Friday, 2 pounds, middle,
William Morgan, Abel James Philadelphia PA 4/13/1769, Welsh 25 mason
 11 days, Sunday, 3 pounds, 5'8",
John Morne, Daniel McBride New Castle DE 2/9/1774, Irish 20
 10 days, Monday, 1 pound, 5'2",
Thomas Morrah, Archibald Mickle Gloucester NJ 11/27/1755, Irish 20
 3 days, Monday, 2 pounds, 5'6",
Eleanor Morris, Lydia Morgan Philadelphia City PA 1/2/1753, Irish 23
 6 days, Friday, 2 pounds, middle,
Elizabeth Morris, Robert Montgomery Philadelphia PA 10/18/1750, English 24
 4 days, Sunday, 3 pounds, middle,
Elizabeth Morris, John Robinson Philadelphia PA 3/5/1751, English 24 (2nd escape)
 12 days, Saturday, 1 pound,
James Morris, Jacob Starn Sussex NJ ironworks 10/8/1767, 35
 May, 1.5 pounds, 5'6",
James Morris, Edmund Hollingshead Burlington NJ 5/29/1776, English
 9 days, Tuesday, 4 dollars, 5'8",
James Morris, Joshua Piercey Jr Chester PA 7/30/1794, American 17 A
 24 days, Sunday, 16 dollars, 5'7-8",
John Morris, Archibald Ritchie VA 3/21/1765, English 35 groom
 6 days, Friday, 5 pounds, 5'10", (arrived last summer)
Margaret Morris, William Cowen Cumberland PA 3/6/1782, American 15 L
 134 days, Tuesday, 3 dollars,
Pierce Morris, William Patterson Lancaster PA 8/18/1773, Irish 23
 29 days, Wednesday, 2 pounds, 5'7",

Thomas Morris, Rapahannock Company Baltimore MD 9/3/1747, Irish 35 C
    2 pistoles, middle, (lately arrived)
Allen Morrison, Henry Neils 3/23/1774, Scot 20
    20 dollars, 5'6", (arrived last summer)
Edward Morrison, William Pennell Chester PA 5/26/1773, Irish 22
    3 days, Monday, 5 dollars, 5'9",
John Morrison, Thomas Graves Salem NJ 9/1/1763,
    3 days, Monday, 3 pounds, 5'6",
John Morrison, William Snute Cumberland NJ 7/28/1763, Irish 30
    10 days, Monday, 2 pounds, 5'8",
John Morrison, Robert Robb York PA 1/5/1764, Irish 30 (2nd escape)
    5 pounds, 5'8",
John Morrison, William McClean Chester PA 11/29/1770, weaver
    14 days, Thursday, 3 pounds, 5'9-10",
John Morrison, John Sharp Chester PA 9/16/1772, Irish 22
    8 dollars, 5'10-11", (arrived 2 weeks ago)
John Morrison, Jonathan Stathem Cumberland NJ 7/2/1761, 30 gaol sale L
    2 pounds, short,
Lot Morrison, John Kirkpatrick Chester PA 8/13/1752, Irish 40
    6 days, Friday, 4 pounds,
Matthew Morrison, John Taylor New Castle DE 2/26/1754, Irish 23
    9 days, Tuesday, 2 pounds, short,
Matthew Morrison, John Rambo Gloucester NJ 5/8/1766, Irish 35 (2nd escape) L
    44 days, Tuesday, 5 pounds, 5'5",
James Morrow, Andrew Crawford Philadelphia PA 9/10/1783, Irish 20
    3 days, Sunday, 8 dollars, 5'7",
John Morrow, Thomas Moody New Castle DE 10/15/1767, Irish 20
    14 days, Thursday, 5 pounds, 5'10",
Patrick Morrow, Robert McGrew York PA 10/12/1774, Irish 22
    38 days, Monday, 2 pounds, 5'7",
John Morton, John Richey Bucks PA 9/20/1739, Scot 24
    7 days, Thursday, 2 pounds, (lately arrived)
Thomas Morton, Absalom Chrisfield Kent MD 5/14/1777, English
    9 days, Tuesday, 10 dollars, 5'5",
Charles Mosely, Ralph Perkenson Philadelphia City PA 6/28/1739, butcher
    51 days, Tuesday,
Catherine Moserin, Christian Derrick Philadelphia PA 3/23/1774, German
    11 days, Sunday, 1 pound, 5',
Charles Anthony Moss, James Vansant Bucks PA 3/5/1777, German
    4 dollars, 5'7",
Heziekiah Moss, David Thomas Bucks PA 12/17/1767, American 20 shoemaker L
    4 days, Sunday, 8 dollars,
James Mosson, Amos Strickland Bucks PA sheriff 8/1/1751, Irish 23 skinner
    2 days, Tuesday, 1.5 pounds,
James Mosson, Amos Strickland Bucks PA sheriff 9/19/1751, Irish 23 skinner (2nd escape)
    9 days, Tuesday, 1.5 pounds,
James Moulton, Flora Dorsey Baltimore MD 4/18/1765,
    11 days, Sunday, 2 pounds, 5'7",
William Mourton, Thomas Barr New Castle DE 7/31/1740, Irish 23
    11 days, Sunday, 1.5 pounds, middle,
Jacob Mowser, Jonathan Davis Chester PA 1/10/1760, German 17
    11 days, Sunday, 2.5 pounds, 5'6", (father lives nearby)
John Moyers, Joseph Dean Bucks PA 9/7/1774, German 35
    11 days, Sunday, 4 dollars, 5'6-7",
Nicholas Moyse, Henry William Stiegal Lancaster PA ironworks 9/29/1768, English 35 sailor
    19 days, Saturday, 2 pistoles, 5'4",
Francis Muchely, John Richard Philadelphia PA 11/2/1774, German
    3 pounds, 5'8-9",
Mary Muckleroy, Samuel Lippincott Burlington NJ 4/16/1748, Irish maid
    3 pounds, middle,
Benjamin Mucklewain, Caleb Atkinson Burlington NJ 7/20/1796, 19 A
    11 days, Saturday, 3 pounds, 5'10-11", (use to the sea)
John Muckmenmom, Matthias Boatman Philadelphia PA tavern-keeper 10/6/1763,
    5 days, Saturday, 2.5 pounds, 5'5",
Robert Muir, John Cameron New Castle DE 11/22/1753, Scot 19 tailor
    2 pounds,

James Muirhead, Isaac Lemon Lancaster PA 1/24/1749, Irish
    9 days, Tuesday, 3 pounds, (lately a servant)
John Mulhall, Timothy Dargen Prince William VA 9/11/1735, Irish
    168 days, Thursday, 2.5 pounds, short,
Hugh Muligan, William Smith York PA 12/22/1763, 16
    14 days, Thursday, 3 pounds, 5'4",
Daniel Mulk, George Fosler Bucks PA 7/4/1787, German baker
    11 days, Saturday, 6 dollars,
Richard Mullanic, Joshua Owings Baltimore MD 2/16/1769, Irish 45 C
    10 days, Monday, 7 pounds, 5'7-8", (wears an iron collar)
Andrew Mullen, John Kirlin Berks PA 8/9/1775,
    10 days, Monday, 8 dollars,
Christina Mullen, Joseph Spencer Philadelphia PA 11/10/1790, 16
    27 days, Thursday, 2 dollars, short,
Daniel Mullen, Peter Broades Philadelphia PA 1/2/1766, Irish 16
    7 days, Thursday, 1 pound, 5'5",
Margaret Mullen, George McCullough Lancaster PA 5/20/1756, Irish 40
    22 days, Wednesday, 2 pounds, short,
Patrick Mullen, Samuel Sharp Chester PA 4/17/1766, Irish 20 hatter
    11 days, Sunday, 1.5 pounds, 5'6-7",
Patrick Mullen, Samuel Sharp Chester PA 7/16/1767, Irish 21 hatter (2nd escape)
    10 days, Monday, 1.5 pounds, short,
Simon Mullguion, Robert Dryburgh 6/11/1767, Irish 24 tailor (2nd escape)
    2 pounds, 5'6", (lately arrived)
Simon Mullguion, Robert Dryburgh 11/13/1766, Irish 23 tailor
    18 days, Sunday, 2 pounds, 5'5", (lately arrived)
Richard Mullharron, James Wallace Philadelphia City PA 6/17/1762, Irish
    7 days, Thursday, 2 pounds, 5'4",
James Mullin, Mary Miller Philadelphia PA 9/18/1776, 15
    1 pound,
John Mullin, Joseph Smith 12/6/1745, Irish 17 sailor A
    9 days, Tuesday, 2.5 pounds, short,
William Mullin, Charles Walker Bucks PA 9/4/1776, Irish 16
    1 pound, 5'5",
William Mullin, Thomas Worrall Chester PA 2/6/1766, American 20 L
    10 days, Monday, 2 pounds, 5'7",
William Mullin, Thomas Worrall Chester PA 7/17/1766, American 20 (2nd escape) L
    7 days, Thursday, 1.5 pounds, 5'6",
Harper Mullins, Isaac Norris Philadelphia City PA merchant 10/23/1740, English painter
    11 days, Sunday, 3 pounds, middle,
Matthew Mulloan, Jonathan Potts Philadelphia PA 9/16/1742, Irish 20
    5 days, Saturday, 3 pounds, short,
Hugh Mulvehill, David Clement New Castle DE 6/28/1753, Irish C
    4 days, Sunday, 3 pounds, 5'6",
John Mulveney, William Long Franklin PA 7/5/1786, Irish 25 weaver L
    68 days, Friday, 5 pounds, 5'8-9",
Catherine Mum, George Leib Philadelphia PA tanner 11/24/1773, German
    31 days, Monday, 3 pounds, 5',
John Munday, Robert Fulton Lancaster PA 6/2/1768, Irish laborer
    4 days, Sunday, 4 dollars, 5'7",
James Mundle, Robert Lewis Chester PA 10/4/1744, 20
    1 day, Wednesday, 2.5 pounds, short,
James Munks, Robert Mills Cecil MD 9/28/1774, 25 collier L
    33 days, Saturday, 4 dollars, 5'2",
James Munn, John Gilks Baltimore MD 10/9/1755, English joiner
    4 pistoles, (lately arrived)
Anne Munro, Edward Duffield Philadelphia PA 7/24/1776, Scot 18 (pregnant)
    65 days, Tuesday, 1 pound, short,
Jeffe Munrow, Joshua McDowell Chester PA 5/21/1761, American 19 L
    14 days, Thursday, 3 pounds, 5'11",
Morgan Murfey, David Lawell Bucks PA 10/17/1751, Irish
    8 days, Wednesday, 3 pounds, 5'8",
Thomas Murfy, Joshua Bunting Burlington NJ 11/30/1774, Irish 19
    8 days, Tuesday, 8 dollars, 5'6-7",
Thomas Murfy, Joshua Bunting Burlington NJ 3/8/1775, Irish 19 (2nd escape)
    5 days, Saturday, 5'6",

Thomas Murland, Samuel Johnston Lancaster PA 4/15/1762, Irish 17
2 pounds,
Cornelius Murley, William Noble Chester PA 7/8/1742, Irish 39
2 pounds,
Daniel Murphey, Simon Wilmer Kent MD 6/25/1752, Irish sawyer C
2 pounds, 6',
Dennis Murphey, Benjamin Aritage Jr Philadelphia City PA 11/25/1772, Irish nailer
2 pounds, 5'9-10", (lately arrived, has 3.5 years to serve)
James Murphey, Andrew Stephen Lancaster PA 12/3/1767, Irish
16 days, Tuesday, 2 pounds, 5'10",
James Murphey, John Willmott Baltimore MD 7/15/1756, American 34 farmer L
32 days, Sunday, 5 pounds, (ran with wife who is pregnant)
John Murphey, John Scott Morris NJ 5/30/1754, Irish 28 schoolmaster
156 days, Thursday, 2 pounds, middle,
John Murphey, Amos Strickland Bucks PA sheriff 4/11/1751, Irish 25
4 days, Sunday, 3 pounds, short,
John Murphey, Thomas Atkinson Berks PA 6/1/1774, Irish 18
21 days, Thursday, 2 pounds, 5'4",
John Murphey, Valentine Liebheart York PA 5/31/1775, Irish 19 (2nd escape)
12 pounds, 5'3-4",
John Murphey, John Patterson Fairfax VA 8/28/1760, Irish 28 joiner C
31 days, Monday, 20 pounds, 5'4",
Lawrence Murphey, Jeremiah Clement Chester PA hatter 5/14/1730, Irish weaver
37 days, Tuesday, 8 pounds, middle,
Philip Murphey, Jonas Chambers Cecil MD 5/4/1769, Irish coppersmith L
3 pounds, 5'7-8",
Bartholomew Murphy, Thomas Levis Chester PA 9/13/1770, Irish 18
4 days, Sunday, 4 dollars, 5'6",
Bartholomew Murphy, Thomas Levis Chester PA 3/31/1773, Irish 21 (2nd escape)
4 days, Sunday, 1 pound, 5'6-7", (arrived 5.5 years ago)
Daniel Murphy, David Lewrlin New Castle DE 5/25/1769, Irish 27
30 days, Tuesday, 3 pounds, 5'5',
Dennis Murphy, David Vandyke Philadelphia PA 5/15/1766, Irish cooper
3 days, Monday, 1.5 pounds, 5'6",
Edward Murphy, Abraham Robinson Baltimore MD 10/25/1770, weaver
18 days, Sunday, 2 pounds, 5'4",
Edward Murphy, William Snow Anne Arundel MD ship captain 2/15/1770, Irish
1 pound, 5'8", (ran from ship)
Edward Murphy, John Deaver Baltimore MD 11/9/1769, Irish blacksmith
11 days, Sunday, 5 pounds, 5'5",
Garret Murphy, Samuel Henry Philadelphia City PA 8/24/1769, Irish 24
11 days, Sunday, 20 dollars, 5'8",
James Murphy, Samuel Soumain Philadelphia City PA goldsmith 8/1/1754, Irish 28 tailor
4 days, Sunday, 1 pound, tall,
James Murphy, James Finley Berkeley VA 5/17/1775, Irish 30
10 days, Monday, 8 dollars, 5'9",
Morgan Murphy, Reas Thomas New Castle DE 7/13/1749, Irish 20
2 pounds, middle,
Robert Murphy, William Branson Berks PA ironworks 9/13/1744, Irish 19
2 days, Tuesday, 5 pounds, short,
Alexander Murray, Joseph Wharton Jr Philadelphia City PA 8/21/1766, Scot 17
3 days, Monday, 1.5 pounds, 5'3", (ran from ship)
Bryan Murray, Stephen Jenkins Philadelphia PA 9/11/1746, Irish 24
12 days, Saturday, 1 pound,
Carlent Murray, Francis Rogers Philadelphia City PA ship captain 2/14/1765, Irish 21
1.25 pounds, 5'6", (ran from ship)
James Murray, Edward Hughes Lancaster PA 8/11/1768, Irish
8 days, Wednesday, 4 dollars, 5'5-6", (arrived 2 years ago)
James Murray, William Campbell Bedford VA 6/4/1772, Irish 28
31 days, Monday, 4 pounds, 5'2-3",
James Murray, Hugh Jeffery Harford MD 9/21/1774, Irish 40
8 days, Wednesday, 8 dollars, 5'5", (arrived August 1773)
Michael Murray, Robert Coleman Philadelphia PA ironworks 9/28/1774, Irish 19
2 pounds, 5'2", (arrived last spring)
Michael Murray, Edward Stevenson Frederick MD 5/28/1767, Irish C
14 days, Thursday, 5 pounds, 5'8",

William Murray, Peter Footman Somerset MD 10/10/1765, Irish
   28 days, Thursday, 4 pounds, 5'6", (brother lives nearby)
Martha Murrey, William Hannum Chester PA 5/11/1774, 23
   22 days, Wednesday, 1 pound,
Roger Murrey, Patrick Reynolds Burlington NJ 8/3/1738, 28
   6 days, Friday, 2 pounds, middle,
Benjamin Murry, Curtis Grubb Lancaster PA ironworks 7/21/1768, English plaisterer
   10 days, Monday, 2 pounds, 5'7-8",
Lewis Murry, William Stacy Baltimore MD 8/2/1775, Irish cooper
   13 days, Saturday, 5 pounds, 5'10",
Mary Musgrove, Thomas Chappell 12/13/1786, 17
   0.03 pounds
Johan Jeremiah Myah, Josiah Halstead Monmouth NJ 2/26/1756, German 21 blacksmith
   5 days, Saturday, 3 pounds, 5'4",
Anna Christiana Elizabeth Myer, Samuel Lewis Chester PA 12/27/1775, German 20 (ran before)
   (no other information)
Hans George Myer, Jacob Duche 6/20/1754, German 17
   26 days, Saturday, 3 pounds, 5',
John Michael Myer, Reuben Hains Philadelphia City PA 10/22/1783, German 35 brewer
   2 days, Monday, 8 dollars, 5'9-10", (lately arrived)
Philip Myers, Aylmer Grevill Philadelphia City PA 9/12/1745, American L
   277 days, Sunday, 2 pounds, short,
Christian Nagle, Michael Withers Lancaster PA 9/7/1796, German 25 tailor
   1 day, Tuesday, 20 dollars,
Barney Nahan, Thomas King Lancaster PA 10/30/1766, Irish 28
   141 days, Wednesday, 2 pounds, 5'7-8",
No Name, Thomas Smith New Castle DE shopkeeper 9/26/1732,
   5 days, Saturday, 1 pound, middle,
No Name, Armstrong Smith Philadelphia City PA shipwright 10/8/1730,
   3 days, Monday, 1 pound,
No Name, Henry Smith Lancaster PA 11/24/1737, Welsh 18
   6 days, Friday, 3 pounds,
No Name, Joseph Jackson Bucks PA 7/24/1732,
   15 days, Wednesday, 1 pound, middle,
No Name, Thomas Carr Baltimore MD 3/25/1742, English 26 weaver
   11 days, Sunday, 4 pounds, short, (arrived 8 months ago)
No Name, Thomas Tyler 8/27/1747, 18
   3 pounds,
No Name, John Jones Lancaster PA sheriff 8/30/1750, German
   1 pound,
No Name, Colin Ferguson Kent MD 5/23/1754, 20
   11 days, Sunday, 0.25 pounds,
No Name, Isaac Whitelock Lancaster PA 7/25/1751, Irish 18
   2 pistoles, short,
No Name, Isaac Whitelock Lancaster PA 7/25/1751, English 23 tanner
   2 pistoles, middle,
No Name, Rudolph Sauter Chester PA 6/5/1755, German 14
   8 days, Wednesday, 2 pounds,
No Name, Abel Shepherd Cumberland NJ 1/22/1794, 17
   15 days, Tuesday, 4 dollars, short,
No Name, Sarah Massey Queen Anne's MD 3/15/1759, Welsh 15 C
   1 pistole,
No Name, Charles Miller New Castle DE 8/14/1746, English brassfounder C
   5 pounds,
Elizabeth Nangel, Abel Rees Chester PA 6/5/1776, Irish 19
   3 dollars, short, (arrived last August)
Thomas Nangle, John Winder Jr Philadelphia PA 8/1/1765, Irish
   1.5 pounds, 5'5",
Godfrey Nather, Jacob Slosser Culpepper VA potash-trade 3/20/1766, German
   5 pounds, 5'6", (arrived 1.5 years ago)
Robert Naylor, John Parker Bucks PA joiner 3/13/1730, 20
   2 pounds, short,
Robert Naylor, John Parker Bucks PA joiner 8/20/1730, 20 (2nd escape)
   4 days, Sunday, 2 pounds, short,
Dennis Neal, Daniel Walker Chester PA 9/7/1732, Irish 19
   10 days, Monday, 2 pounds, tall,

Lawrence Neal, John Townsend Chester PA 8/24/1769, Irish 24
    4 days, Sunday, 2.5 pounds, 5'8",
Mary Neal, James Hicklin New Castle DE 8/8/1754, Irish 20
    2 pounds,
Valentine Neal, Jacob Warrick Monmouth NJ 6/27/1745, Irish
    4 days, Sunday, 2 pounds,
John Neale, Stephen Onion Baltimore MD ironworks 4/2/1747, Irish 28 C
    9 days, Tuesday, 3 pounds,
Francis Nealis, James Allison Philadelphia City PA 9/24/1748, 18
    15 days, Wednesday, 1 pound,
Daniel Neall, Daniel O'Nell Gloucester NJ 3/27/1746, Irish 28
    3 pounds,
Patrick Neall, John Holmes York PA 4/18/1765, 28
    16 days, Tuesday, 4 pounds, 5'8", (use to the sea)
John Nealy, Amor Chanbler Chester PA 10/9/1766, Irish 20
    4 days, Sunday, 2 pounds, 5'6",
Bryan Neary, Robert Allison Chester PA 12/10/1767, Irish 19
    4 days, Sunday, 10 pounds, 5'10",
Bryan Neary, Robert Allison Chester PA 5/19/1768, Irish 19 (2nd escape)
    16 days, Tuesday, 1 pound, 5'10",
Elizabeth Neason, Joseph Beals Philadelphia City PA drayman 4/19/1753, German
    8 days, Wednesday, 1 pound,
John Neblinger, Philip Hall Philadelphia City PA 9/26/1765, German 30 butcher
    11 days, Sunday, 3 pounds,
John Neel, John Maxwell Lancaster PA 4/27/1785, Irish 20 cooper
    6 dollars, 5'7",
John Neeles, Richard Jones Chester PA 6/1/1785, Irish 20
    23 days, Monday, 10 dollars, 5'6-7", (arrived last summer)
David Neeper, William Montgomery Lancaster PA 3/2/1773, Irish weaver
    3 dollars, 5'6",
Simon Neil, John McCreary Lancaster PA 7/19/1770, Irish 20
    10 days, Monday, 5'4",
John Neill, Robert Greaves 5/26/1784, Irish
    10 days, Sunday, 8 dollars, 5'9-10", (lately arrived)
Alexander Nelson, Edmund Farrel Philadelphia City PA tanner 7/3/1732, Irish 24
    1 day, Wednesday, 2 pounds, middle,
Alexander Nelson, Edmund Farrel Philadelphia City PA tanner 3/22/1733, Irish 24 (2nd escape)
    8 days, Wednesday, 3 pounds, middle,
John Nelson, John Jones Lancaster PA breeches-maker 7/28/1768, Irish 21 A
    5 dollars, 5'6-7",
John Nelson, Benjamin Rogers Baltimore MD 8/20/1761, 30 gardener C
    11 days, Sunday, 1 pound, (arrived this summer)
Michael Neugant, James Riddle Philadelphia PA 7/21/1773, 20 tailor
    4 dollars, 5'7",
Francis Nevel, Solomon Ridgway Burlington NJ 4/13/1769, Irish
    3 days, Monday, 4 dollars, 5'10",
Francis Nevill, Samuel Sykes Burlington NJ 1/28/1768, Irish 20 wool comber
    4 pounds, 5'8",
Patrick Nevin, John Vancleave Baltimore MD 6/30/1773, Irish 25
    11 days, Sunday, 2 pounds, 5'4",
Adam Newbecker, John Miller Chester PA 10/16/1755, German 26
    18 days, Sunday, 1 pound, short, (has 3 years left to serve)
George Peters Newcomb, William Griffie Cecil MD 2/9/1769, Irish
    18 days, Sunday, 3 pounds, 5'4",
John Newcomb, Thomas Blair Hunterdon NJ 1/7/1752, Irish 22
    9 days, Tuesday, 2 pounds, 5'9",
Mary Newel, Stophel Longstreet Bucks PA 10/10/1751, Welsh 22
    2 pounds,
Amos Newfer, John Williamson Chester PA 3/8/1786, 18 A
    2 pounds, 5'6",
Thomas Newlan, Timothy Green Lancaster PA 2/14/1765, Irish
    2 pounds, 5'5",
John Newland, John Hance New Castle DE 4/21/1748, Irish 26
    3 pounds, middle,
Andrew Newman, Charles Jenkins Philadelphia City PA 3/17/1763, Irish
    5 days, Saturday, 3 pounds, 4'3",

Benjamin Newport, Abraham Judah Philadelphia City PA 10/21/1762, English 35 bookkeeper L
    4 pounds,
Sarah Newton, John Patterson Philadelphia City PA 12/7/1796, 7
    77 days, Wednesday, 0.06 dollars,
George Ney, Henry Hill 5/4/1785, German 20
    3 days, Sunday, 3 pounds, 5'6-7", (arrived 6 weeks ago)
John Nibel, Peter Wick Philadelphia City PA 9/27/1775, German 21 tailor
    8 dollars, 5'8-9",
Henry Francis Nible, Amor Grubb New Castle DE 4/17/1776, German 20
    15 days, Wednesday, 8 dollars, 5'6-7",
Henry Francis Nible, Amor Grubb New Castle DE 7/3/1776, German 20 (2nd escape)
    10 days, Monday, 8 dollars, 5'6-7",
William Nicholas, William Jones Philadelphia PA 5/23/1751, English 30
    4 days, Sunday, 2 pounds,
John Nicholls, Moses Rankin Philadelphia City PA ship captain 5/22/1755, Irish 24 joiner
    8 days, Wednesday, 2 pounds, 5'8",
Joseph Nicholls, William Comagys Kent MD 8/28/1755, English 25
    11 days, Sunday, 1 pound,
Samuel Nicholls, William Smith Queen Anne's MD 8/31/1758, English 23
    18 days, Sunday, 1.5 pounds, middle,
Walter Nicholls, William Johnson Baltimore MD 11/28/1754, English 30 C
    18 days, Sunday, 1.33 pounds, 5'7", (arrived March 1754)
Abington Nichols, Adam Stephens Frederick VA doctor 10/25/1750, American L
    5 pistoles,
William Nichols, John Parry Chester PA 5/25/1738, English 34 brickmaker
    6 days, Friday, 2 pounds, middle, (newly arrived but has been in America before)
John Nicholson, Anthony Wilkinson Philadelphia City PA 6/20/1734, 27 carver L
    6 days, Friday, 3 pounds, middle,
Michael Nicholson, John Huber Philadelphia City PA baker 8/18/1773, Irish 18
    5 weeks ago, 2 pounds, 5'6",
Nicolas Nicholson, Walter Sterling PhiladelphiaCity PA ship captain 10/10/1754, English 30 carpenter
    6 days, Friday, 5 pounds, 5'7",
William Nickle, John Beemer Hunterdon NJ 4/20/1774, German 24 soldier
    23 days, Tuesday, 5 pounds, 5'7-8",
John Nicks, Joseph Watkins Anne Arundel MD ironworks 7/22/1762, English 25 C
    8 days, Wednesday, 4 pounds, 6', (arrived in 1760)
John Nicolls, Robert Maghee Middlesex NJ 5/24/1770,
    12 dollars, short, (arrived 7 years ago)
Francis Niell, Joseph Burr Jr Burlington NJ 10/11/1775, Irish 20
    5 days, Saturday, 12 dollars, 5'5",
Edward Niggarly, Asher Woolman Burlington NJ 3/10/1784,
    20 days, Thursday, 3 pounds, 5'9-10",
William Niners, William Snow Anne Arundel MD ship captain 2/15/1770, English
    1 pound, 5'8", (ran from ship)
John Nixon, Mounce Keen Salem NJ 12/6/1764, 24
    25 days, Sunday, 2 pounds,
Peggy Nixon, James Mercer Lancaster PA 8/12/1772,
    7 days, Thursday, 3 dollars,
Thomas Nixon, John McClellen Burlington NJ 11/9/1796, 17 A
    4 days, Saturday, 2 dollars,
William Nixon, John Daniel Chester PA 8/21/1755, Irish
    4 days, Sunday, 1.5 pounds, 5'6",
John Noah, James Roberts Chester PA blacksmith 11/21/1751, Welsh 14
    7 days, Thursday, 2 pounds,
John Noah, Aubrey Harry Chester PA 1/8/1754, Welsh 16 (2nd escape)
    13 days, Friday, 1.5 pounds, 5'5",
Digory Noal, William Campbell Frederick MD 9/6/1775, English gaol sale L
    5 pounds, 6',
Roger Noble, Robert Miller Chester PA 6/18/1741, English 30
    2 days, Tuesday, 1.5 pounds, short,
George Nock, Levy Marks Philadelphia City PA tailor 8/13/1767, American 21 tailor A
    2 pounds,
Roger Noland, Mounce Keen Salem NJ 3/28/1751, Irish
    9 days, Tuesday, 2.5 pounds, middle, (went on Cape Breton expedition)
Philip Nold, Benjamin Kendall Philadelphia City PA 3/19/1767, German 30 L
    11 days, Sunday, 8 dollars, 5'6",

John Noles, Andrew Kennedy Philadelphia City PA 10/22/1783, Irish 18
   3 days, Sunday, 10 dollars, 5'5-6", (lately arrived)
Bernard No Name, William Foster Burlington NJ 4/26/1764, Irish 19
   3 days, Monday, 3 pounds, 5'2",
Catherine No Name, James Smith York PA 9/6/1753, Irish 30
   16 days, Tuesday, 3 pounds,
Charles No Name, Joseph Chavier Queen Anne's MD 3/27/1766, English 35 weaver C
   11 days, Sunday, 2 pounds, short,
Dennis No Name, Ebenezer Brown Gloucester NJ 1/1/1745, Irish 25
   10 days, Monday, 2 pounds, middle,
Elizabeth No Name, William Windsor Frederick VA 9/21/1758, Welsh C
   46 days, Sunday, 2 pistoles,
John No Name, William Evans NJ ironworks 7/4/1771, 21
   12 days, Saturday, 5 pounds, 5'4-5",
Michael No Name, John Femel PhiladelphiaCity PA baker 12/13/1748, German 25
   4 days, Sunday, 3 pounds, 4'9",
John Nonn, Thomas Bradford 2/5/1794, German 20 printer
   23 days, Monday, 15 dollars, 5'10", (lately arrived)
John Noon, Thomas Beat 12/10/1761, 25 C
   11 days, Sunday, 2.5 pounds, 5',
William Noonan, John Hoopes Chester PA 8/24/1769, Irish 26
   4 days, Sunday, 2.5 pounds, 5'7",
William Noreliff, John Gilks Baltimore MD 10/9/1755, English 30 ship carpenter
   4 pistoles, 5'10",
Anna Maria Norman, William Williams Baltimore MD ironworks 10/23/1746, German C
   157 days, Monday, 5 pounds, middle,
John Norman, Thomas Stedham Caroline MD 11/30/1774, 16
   2 pounds,
John Norman, Henry Good Lancaster PA ironworks 9/18/1776, English
   14 days, Thursday, 5 pounds, 5',
B John Normand, Benjamin Cooper Sussex NJ ironworks 3/19/1761, 25
   21 days, Thursday, 5 pistoles, 5'10",
John Norris, William Smith Philadelphia City PA shoemaker 6/11/1730, 24
   5 pounds, middle,
Joseph Norris, John Rees Philadelphia PA 5/2/1751, American 30 L
   8 days, Wednesday, 3 pounds, short,
Patrick Norris, Charles Clendinen Lancaster PA 2/16/1769, Irish 23 cooper
   6 days, Friday, 5 pounds, 5'6",
Patrick Norris, Charles Vallaly Berks PA 7/10/1766, Irish 30 L
   6 days, Friday, 5 pounds, 5'5",
William Norris, Edward Stevenson Frederick MD 3/12/1772,
   4 pounds, 5'4-5",
Robert Norry, James Mackey Philadelphia City PA 5/7/1741, Irish 20 pewterer
   263 days, Sunday, 3 pounds,
Thomas North, Francis Phillips Baltimore MD ironworks 1/8/1767, 30 wheelwright C
   11 days, Sunday, 10 pounds, 5'9-10",
James Norton, Isaac Mather Philadelphia PA 2/26/1777, 18 A
   24 days, Monday, 0.20 pounds, 5'7-8",
Katey Norton, Robert Fulton Lancaster PA 7/7/1763, Irish 25
   11 days, Sunday, 3 pounds, (arrived last fall)
James Nower, Aquila Hall Baltimore MD 9/26/1771, bricklayer
   5 pounds, 5'6-7",
John Nowland, John Jackson Cecil MD doctor 8/29/1745,
   1 pound,
Patrick Nowler, Caleb Lippincott Burlington NJ 5/24/1786, Irish 19
   5 days, Friday, 5 dollars, 5'6-7",
John Nugent, Captain Hinton Philadelphia City PA ship captain 11/21/1751, English wheelwright
   1 pound, (ran from ship)
Michael Nugent, Thomas Tobin Hunterdon NJ 6/8/1774, Irish 30
   45 days, Monday, 8 dollars, 5'9",
Philip Null, John Potts 6/17/1756, German
   8 days, Wednesday, 1.5 pounds,
Casper Nuyne, Joseph Pennock Chester PA 5/24/1775, German 45
   2 pounds, 5'9",
Michael O'Baro, Rees Price Chester PA 6/19/1746, Irish 20
   4 days, Sunday, 2.5 pounds,

Francis O'Brian, William Gibson Lancaster PA 6/21/1770, 26 L
    10 days, Monday, 2 pounds, 5'9",
James O'Brian, John Crawford Bucks PA 2/13/1766, Irish 25 ship carpenter
    5 pistoles, 5'4",
James O'Brian, John Wallace Kent MD 9/26/1765, Irish 30 C
    36 days, Wednesday, 2 pounds, 5'10",
John O'Brian, Griffith Jones Chester PA 6/30/1773, Irish 23
    3 days, Monday, 2.5 pounds, 6'1",
William O'Brian, Abraham Shreve Salem NJ 2/22/1775, Irish 28 L
    336 days, Tuesday, 20 dollars,
John O'Brien, Legh Master Frederick MD ironworks 9/19/1771, Irish 26
    19 days, Saturday, 6 pounds, 5'8",
Mark O'Brion, Alexander Davis Baltimore MD 9/21/1774, Irish 25 shoemaker
    46 days, Sunday, 10 pounds, 5', (his wife went with him)
Catherine O'Bryan, John Ashford Cecil MD 5/24/1750, Irish 30 C
    17 days, Monday, 1 pound, middle,
Connor O'Bryan, Bryan Connolly Cecil MD 5/17/1753, Irish 25
    12 days, Saturday, 5 pounds, 5'4",
James O'Bryan, Edward Worrell Kent MD 3/11/1755, Irish weaver
    13 days, Friday, 3 pistoles, short,
James O'Bryan, John Ashford Cecil MD 5/24/1750, Irish 22 C
    17 days, Monday, 1 pound, 5'6",
John O'Bryan, John Monrow Burlington NJ 10/6/1768, Irish 35 shoemaker
    6 days, Friday, 10 pounds, 5'6",
Mary Ann O'Bryan, John Firth Salem NJ 11/5/1767, Irish 17
    6 days, Friday, 3 pounds, short,
Rose O'Bryan, Jacob Kaiser Philadelphia City PA tailor 6/25/1767, Irish 16
    2 pounds, 4'9",
Rose O'Bryan, Unlisted Name 10/19/1769, Irish 18 (2nd escape)
    11 days, Sunday, 2 pounds, (ran off with a man)
Terence O'Bryan, John White Lancaster PA 1/5/1774, Irish (female)
    24 days, Monday, 3 pounds, 5'6",
Patrick O'Caden, John Prosser New Castle DE 8/2/1744, Irish 25
    46 days, Sunday, 1 pound, 5'4",
Manus O'Cannon, John Simpson Philadelphia PA 8/7/1776, Irish 30
    5 dollars, 5'5",
Charles O'Conner, Marein Flick Philadelphia PA 9/13/1770, Irish biscuit baker
    11 days, Sunday, 2 dollars, 5'6",
Mary O'Dannel, Dennis Cunrads Philadelphia PA 5/25/1749, Irish 22
    10 days, Monday, 1 pound, short,
Laughlin O'Dennysey, William Moore New Castle DE 3/24/1747, Irish 30
    11 days, Sunday, 3 pounds, 6',
Owen O'Donelly, William Anderson 9/3/1730, Irish 26 brickmaker
    2.5 pounds,
James O'Donnally, William Blair Chester PA 1/15/1740, 18
    2 days, Tuesday, 2 pounds, middle,
Con O'Donnell, Benjamin Thornburgh Frederick VA 6/4/1772, Irish 35
    25 days, Sunday, 5 pounds, 5'8",
Richard O'Donovan, W. Yates Frederick MD 9/28/1774, Irish 22
    3 pounds, 5'11", (arrived Sept. 19, 1772)
Brian O'Dougherty, James McDowell Chester PA 11/23/1769, sailor
    1 pound, 5'4",
Roger O'Dougherty, John Elder Lancaster PA 2/11/1755, Irish
    12 days, Saturday, 2.5 pounds,
Patrick O'Durish, David Sheerer Chester PA 7/31/1746,
    11 days, Sunday, 3 pounds,
Owen O'Gublin, James Warstall Philadelphia City PA 7/12/1780, 18 A
    4 days, Saturday, 50 dollars,
Patrick O'Hagen, Robert Young Cecil MD 3/13/1753, Irish 30
    11 days, Sunday, 2 pounds, 6',
Patrick O'Hara, Richard Baker Chester PA 9/13/1775, Irish 19
    3 days, Monday, 6 pounds, 5'8",
Patrick O'Hara, Richard Baker Chester PA 7/17/1776, Irish 20 (2nd escape)
    9 days, Tuesday, 3 dollars, 5'7-8",
Patrick O'Hara, Robert Young 8/6/1747, A
    1 day, Wednesday, 2.5 pounds, 5'9",

Edward O'Harah, William McPherson Lancaster PA 6/29/1774, Irish 19 (ran many times before)
    12 days, Saturday, 3 dollars, 5'6-7", (arrived 4 years ago)
Catherine O'Harra, Moses MacIlvaine Lancaster PA 6/25/1747, Irish
    9 days, Tuesday, 2 pounds, (arrived 10 months ago)
Mary O'Harra, William Hanna Lancaster PA tavern-keeper 6/11/1767,
    1 pound, short,
Patrick O'Kean, Matthew McClung Lancaster PA 7/7/1773, Irish 20
    3 pounds, 6',
Teddy O'Lanshahin, Joseph Gavin Philadelphia City PA shoemaker 8/4/1748, Irish 21 shoemaker
    11 days, Sunday, 3 pounds,
Daniel O'Mullen, James Huston Philadelphia City PA 12/26/1765, 15
    4 days, Sunday, 2 pounds,
Bryan O'Murry, Joseph McFarlan Bucks PA 10/6/1748, Irish
    7 days, Thursday, 2 pounds, 5'6",
Charles O'Neal, James Yates Jr Bucks PA 2/29/1732,
    162 days, Monday, 3 pounds, short,
Charles O'Neal, Alexander Johnston Chester PA 2/5/1756, Irish
    11 days, Sunday, 1.5 pounds,
Charles O'Neal, John Lewden New Castle DE 8/23/1775, Irish 20
    11 days, Sunday, 3 pounds, 5'8-9",
Fernando O'Neal, Joshua Baker Lancaster PA 1/10/1738, 30
    26 days, Saturday, 1.5 pounds, middle,
Jim O'Neal, Benjamin Humphrey Philadelphia City PA scythesmith 12/15/1763, Irish 19
    4 days, Sunday, 5 pounds, 5'5",
John O'Neal, John McCadden Philadelphia City PA ship captain 9/2/1762, Irish 18 tailor
    2 pounds, 5'7", (ran from ship)
John O'Neal, Samuel Lightfoot Chester PA 12/4/1760, 18
    13 days, Friday, 3 pounds, middle,
John O'Neal, David Rose Philadelphia City PA 9/16/1762, 20 (2nd escape)
    16 days, Tuesday, 5'7",
John O'Neal, Mark Elliot Jr New Castle DE 8/23/1775, Irish 28
    10 days, Monday, 8 dollars, 5'7-8", (arrived last June)
John O'Neal, James Dye Salem NJ 4/19/1775, Irish 28 weaver
    17 days, Monday, 5'6",
John O'Neal, Lawrence Salter Burlington NJ ironworks 1/25/1775, Irish 23
    9 days, Tuesday, 10 dollars, 5'8-9",
John O'Neal, Henry Snevely Lancaster PA 8/10/1769, Irish-American 16 L
    1.5 pounds,
Mary O'Neal, John Hayes Chester PA 9/22/1763,
    11 days, Sunday, 2.5 pounds,
Owen O'Neal, Andrew Lycan Philadelphia PA 12/4/1766, Irish 23 weaver
    3 days, Monday, 3 pounds, 5'8-9",
Con O'Neel, Peter Menkrns Cecil MD 6/14/1753, Irish 40
    42 days, Thursday, 2 pounds,
Arthur O'Neil, William Mansell Chester PA 9/16/1795, Irish 16
    9 days, Monday, 6 dollars, 5'5-6",
Charles O'Neil, Patrick McSherry York PA 5/9/1765, Irish 25 sailor
    11 days, Sunday, 3 pounds, 5'5", (arrived last summer, use to the sea)
Hugh O'Neil, John Huey New Castle DE 10/18/1739, Irish 30
    3 days, Monday, 2 pounds, 6',
James O'Neil, John McClellan Philadelphia City PA 10/27/1784, Irish tanner
    5'7-8", (ran from ship)
Patrick O'Neil, Mark Connors Philadelphia PA 2/26/1751, Irish 19
    5'6",
Connel O'Nelis, Thomas Strawbridge Chester PA 5/7/1772, Irish 18
    10 days, Monday, 1.5 pounds, 5'6-7",
Thomas O'Shochany, Joseph Richardson Philadelphia PA 3/23/1769, Irish 30
    11 days, Sunday, 5 pounds, 5'6-7", (arrived several years ago)
John O'Skullion, Alexander McPherson Chester PA 5/19/1784, Irish
    10 days, Sunday, 3 pounds, 5'7",
James Oag, John Malcolm Philadelphia City PA sailmaker 5/6/1762, Scot
    14 days, Thursday, 8 dollars, 5'6",
William Oak, Thomas Talbot Baltimore MD 8/7/1766, 22 C
    18 days, Sunday, 20 dollars, 5'7", (lately arrived)
Catherine Elizabeth Ochlier, Frederick Giffer Lancaster PA 11/20/1755, German 14
    10 days, Monday, 3 pounds, (father took her away)

Michael Odigh, John Potts 6/17/1756, German smith
    8 days, Wednesday, 1.5 pounds,
Thomas Offinton, Robert Givins Cecil MD 9/18/1755, Irish 21
    8 days, Wednesday, 2 pounds, middle,
Joseph Ogin, John Lloyd Philadelphia PA 12/10/1783, 15
    8 days, Tuesday, 4 dollars,
William Ogleby, Isaac Knight Philadelphia PA 7/5/1775, 17
    3 days, Monday, 6 dollars, 5'8-9",
Michael Ohuangst, Nicholas Hess Philadelphia City PA 6/11/1772, 19 A
    3 days, Monday, 5 pounds, 5'7",
Mary Olden, George Wall Jr Philadelphia City PA 8/13/1783, 15 A
    6 weeks ago, 1 dollar,
John Olford, Aaron Brian Burlington NJ 4/27/1774, American L
    7 days, Thursday, 5 pounds, 5'6",
Edward Olive, Alexander Morgan Gloucester NJ 10/20/1748, Irish 18
    1 pound,
Christopher Oliver, Samuel Osbourne Chester PA 12/27/1739, English 20 weaver
    4 days, Sunday, 2 pounds,
Griffith Oliver, John Gracey Chester PA 7/10/1755, Welsh 21
    3 days, Monday, 1.5 pounds, middle, (arrive 1 month ago)
John Oliver, William Lynch Philadelphia PA 8/6/1741, Irish 25
    10 days, Monday, 3 pounds, middle,
Thomas Oliver, Abraham Holmes Lancaster PA 1/2/1772, Irish
    29 days, Wednesday, 4 dollars, 5'7",
Edward Olliff, Alexander Morgan Gloucester NJ 2/6/1750, Irish 19
    2 pounds,
Dennis Oloug, Archibald Beard New Castle DE 9/16/1736,
    10 days, Monday, 2 pounds,
Nancy Olphut, John Schneider Berks PA 9/12/1792, Irish 17
    21 days, Wednesday, 4 dollars, middle, (lately arrived)
Samuel Onerthrow, Thomas Masterman 6/24/1762, 15 A
    11 days, Sunday, 0.25 pounds,
Thomas Onion, Samuel Yarnell Chester PA 6/1/1738, English bellows-maker
    29 days, Wednesday, 1 pound, middle,
Andrew Opperman, Ferdinand Facundus Philadelphia City PA surgeon 5/17/1764, German 29 soldier A
    10 days, Monday, 2 pounds, 5'3",
Maria Dorothy Ordessin, Paul Gaspard Breton Philadelphia City PA 9/21/1785, German 40
    102 days, Saturday, 3 pounds, 5'1-2", (lately arrived)
Joseph Orin, Daniel Mercer Philadelphia City PA 1/14/1746, 16
    7 days, Thursday, 1.5 pounds,
Thomas Orpin, Samuel Wilson Chester PA 4/11/1771, English 23
    3 pounds, 5'8",
Hugh Orr, John Rankin Chester PA 2/20/1772, Irish 28 L
    4 pounds, 5'8-9",
John Orr, Isaac Gleave Chester PA 6/10/1756, Irish 17
    3 days, Monday, 1.5 pounds, 5'3", (arrived 3.5 years ago)
Matthias Ortman, Peter Hassenclever EJ ironworks 6/12/1766, German 24 miner
    14 days, Thursday, 5 pounds, 5'6", (under a 3 year 4 month contract, imported)
John Osborn, John Maffett Chester PA 11/8/1753, Irish 20
    11 days, Sunday, 2 pounds,
William Osbourne, Nathan Rigbie Cecil MD 8/17/1749, English 22
    21 days, Thursday, 5 pounds, tall,
William Osier, John Bull Philadelphia PA 6/2/1768, American 45 L
    3 pounds, 5'6-8",
William Ossman, David Rees Bucks PA 10/6/1757, 20
    7 days, Thursday, 1.5 pounds, 5'4",
John Ottoway, Richard Sparks Salem NJ 3/31/1763, English 50
    7 days, Thursday, 1.5 pounds, 5'4",
John Oulden, Peter Cheesman Gloucester NJ 4/28/1773, Irish
    4 days, Sunday, 3 pounds, 5'4",
John Oulton, Charles Carroll Baltimore MD ironworks 6/21/1753, English 24 C
    19 days, Saturday, 4 pistoles, middle,
John Oulton, Charles Carroll Baltimore MD ironworks 3/26/1754, English 25 (2nd escape) C
    9 days, Tuesday, 4 pistoles, middle,
John Oulton, Charles Carroll Baltimore MD ironworks 9/12/1754, English 25 (3rd escape) C
    12 days, Saturday, 1 pound, short, (wears a steel collar, arrived 4 years ago)

Thomas Ounges, James Baldwin Philadelphia PA 4/23/1741, Irish
    4 days, Sunday, 2.5 pounds, short, (arrived last fall)
Barbara Overkirken, Marmaduke Cooper Gloucester NJ 7/12/1775, German 18
    32 days, Sunday, 10 pounds, 4'10",
Henry Overkirken, Marmaduke Cooper Gloucester NJ 7/12/1775, German 27
    32 days, Sunday, 10 pounds, 5',
Thomas Overrington, Samuel Hilldruf Anne Arundel MD 7/14/1743, 27 tanner L
    23 days, Tuesday, 3 pounds, short,
Thomas Overton, Michael Lawrless 6/16/1743, 30 weaver C
    8 days, Wednesday, 3 pounds, middle,
Edward Owen, Robert Roberts Philadelphia PA 4/12/1739, Irish 17
    2 days, Tuesday, 1.5 pounds, middle,
George Owen, Samuel Swift Philadelphia PA 8/23/1770, English 30 joiner
    14 days, Thursday, 5 pounds, 4'8-10",
John Owen, Amos Griffith Philadelphia PA 3/26/1754, Welsh 24
    3 days, Monday, 1.5 pounds, 5'10",
Christopher Owens, Robert Wallace Lancaster PA 6/29/1769, Irish 20
    38 days, Monday, 3 pounds, tall,
Elizabeth Owens, Benjamin Wallace 7/6/1774, Irish
    11 days, Sunday, 4 dollars,
John Owens, Alexander McClister Chester PA 1/13/1763, Irish 19
    32 days, Sunday, 1.5 pounds, 5'8",
John Owens, Jacob Lemmon Baltimore MD 11/17/1784, Irish 23 laborer
    5 pounds, 5'8-9", (lately arrived)
Simeon Owens, John Lukens surveyor 5/3/1764, Irish 14
    31 days, Monday, 3 pounds,
Thomas Owens, Nathan Dorsey Anne Arundel MD 10/1/1767, Irish 20
    15 days, Wednesday, 10 pounds, 5'8-9",
William Owens, Thomas Callender Philadelphia City PA 9/9/1772, American 16 A
    76 days, Friday, 0.25 pounds, (apprentice to ship)
Margaret Owings, Joseph Bentley Chester PA 7/24/1776, Irish
    7 days, Thursday, 1.5 pounds, 5'6",
Thomas Owings, John Deaver Baltimore MD 11/26/1767, Irish 25 plaisterer
    10 days, Monday, 10 pounds,
Timothy Packom, Evan Jones Kent DE 4/12/1733, blacksmith
    4 days, Sunday, 5 pounds, tall,
Charlotte Page, Joseph Ashton 8/4/1790, 15
    8 days, Tuesday, 0.03 pounds,
Edward Pain, Samuel Hale Philadelphia City PA potter 6/20/1734, potter
    7 days, Thursday, 5 pounds, middle,
Jane Pain, John Roe Queen Anne's MD 4/23/1752, English 20
    1 pound,
John Painter, Jeremiah Sheredine Baltimore MD ironworks 6/13/1765, English 30 C
    18 days, Sunday, 5 pounds, 5'8-10",
Thomas Painter, Alexander Cowan Harford MD 9/21/1774, English 30
    3 pounds, 5'6-7",
Henry Paiton, Jacob Comegys Kent MD 5/28/1767, English 22 sailor C
    3 pounds, 5'6", (use to the sea)
John Pall, John Robert Holliday Baltimore MD 5/16/1771, C
    8 days, Wednesday, 3 pounds, 5'10",
Catherine Palmer, John James Jr Bucks PA 8/20/1764, Scot 29
    5 pounds, 5',
David Palmer, Samuel Renick Cumberland PA 11/24/1773, 22 A
    62 days, Friday, 4 dollars, 5'6",
John Palmer, Sarah Davis Chester PA 4/18/1771, Irish 17
    6 days, Friday, 4 dollars, 5'1",
William Palmer, Unlisted Name Philadelphia PA ironworks 6/11/1747, Irish 18
    23 days, Tuesday, 2 pistoles, short,
William Palmer, Henry Lawrence Chester PA 6/4/1752, American 21 L
    2 days, Tuesday, 3 pounds, middle,
William Palmer, Henry Lawrence Chester PA 9/27/1753, American 22 weaver (2nd escape) L
    3 days, Monday, 3 pounds, middle,
George Palmore, Benjamin Armitage Bucks PA 3/22/1729, English 33
    3 days, Monday, 2 pounds, middle,
John Pancake, William Rigby 10/23/1776, 18 A
    8 days, Wednesday, 1 pound, 5'5",

John Pankes, George Hooke York PA 6/27/1751, German
    9 days, Tuesday, 4 pounds, 6',
Bastian Panner, John Bishop Berks PA 4/17/1766, (took his wife also)
    8 days, Wednesday, 5 pounds, short,
John James Papineau, James Richard Baltimore MD 10/9/1746, French 45 cooper 5',
Charles Parker, John Glen Cumberland PA 7/19/1770, Irish 18
    8 dollars, 5'6-8",
Charles Parker, John Glen Cumberland PA 6/13/1771, Irish 19 (2nd escape)
    4 dollars, 5'6", (arrived 4 years ago)
John Parker, Thomas Green Chester PA 7/8/1731, 20
    4 days, Sunday, 3.5 pounds, short,
John Parker, Robert Hart Cecil MD 12/20/1753, Irish
    7 days, Thursday, 3 pounds, 5'6",
Mary Parker, William Thompson Baltimore MD 12/23/1772, English 23 C
    13 days, Friday, 5 pounds,
Benjamin Parkinson, Edward Norris Baltimore MD 8/17/1769, English 20 C
    40 days, Saturday, 3 pounds, 5'6-8",
George Parks, Samuel Hurford Philadelphia City PA 8/6/1747, 17
    4 days, Sunday, 2 pounds, short,
George Parks, Christiana Jaquet New Castle DE 8/26/1772, Irish 20
    3 pounds, 5'8",
John Parks, Joseph Parx Chester PA 8/20/1767,
    35 days, Thursday, 6 pounds, 5'6",
Richard Parks, John Welsh Baltimore MD ironworks 10/18/1770, English basketmaker C
    mid-June, 5 pounds,
William Parnes, Hugh Coulter Philadelphia City PA 4/28/1748, sailor L
    8 days, Wednesday, 5 pistoles, 6',
Jacob Parrot, Hugh Jones Cecil MD 5/17/1750, English 20 footman C
    1 day, Wednesday, 1 pound, short,
Jacob Parrot, Hugh Jones Cecil MD 5/21/1752, English 22 footman (2nd escape) C
    43 days, Wednesday, 2 pounds, short,
Jacob Parrot, Otho Othoson Cecil MD 3/27/1753, English 23 footman (3rd escape) C
    10 days, Monday, 1 pound, short,
John Parry, Richard Parker Philadelphia City PA tailor 5/21/1752, Welsh
    11 days, Sunday, 4 pounds, 5'6",
Richard Parson, Charles Whitelock Cecil MD 4/4/1771, English 23
    9 days, Tuesday, 5 pounds, 5'7",
John Parsons, Samuel Galloway Anne Arundel MD 7/6/1774, English 24 shoemaker
    19 days, Saturday, 4 pounds, 5'7-8",
John Parsons, Alexander Campbell Dumfries VA 11/18/1772, Irish 20 laborer
    11 days, Sunday, 7 pounds, 6', (arrived 3 weeks ago)
John Parsons, V. Deaton Anne Arundel MD 6/16/1743, English 30 C
    31 days, Monday, 3 pounds, short,
John Parsons, V. Deaton Anne Arundel MD 11/3/1743, English 30 (2nd escape) C
    45 days, Monday, 3 pistoles, short,
Stephen Parstow, William Cox Middlesex NJ 7/17/1732, English 21 blacksmith
    16 days, Tuesday, 2 pounds, middle,
Stephen Parstow, William Cox Middlesex NJ 7/25/1734, English 22 blacksmith (2nd escape)
    6 days, Friday, 1.5 pounds,
George Partington, John Eicholtz Lancaster PA 7/9/1767, English 30 blacksmith
    19 days, Saturday, 3 pounds, 5'6-7",
John Partridge, Evan Price Lancaster PA 3/11/1735, American 17 sailor L
    2 pounds, tall,
John Jacob Pass, John Taylor Lancaster PA 8/30/1753, German miller
    5 pounds, 5'4",
John Passanban, William Edwards Baltimore MD 11/23/1769, 40 C
    23 days, Tuesday, 5 pounds, 5'8-9", (lately arrived)
Richard Pater, William Ogborn 8/16/1764, American 30 carter L
    29 days, Wednesday, 2 pounds, 5'7",
James Paterson, Francis Graham New Castle DE 10/1/1747, 25 blacksmith
    12 days, Saturday, 2 pounds, middle,
James Patience, William Ross Philadelphia City PA 9/24/1767, Scot shoemaker
    11 days, Sunday, 1 pound, 5'4",
Robert Patrick, Henry Bitting Bucks PA 10/31/1771, Irish 17
    29 days, Wednesday, 2.5 pounds,

Alexander Patterson, Timothy Grunon Cecil MD 9/4/1746, 18 tailor
    18 days, Sunday, 2 pounds, short,
James Patterson, William McMullin Philadelphia City PA 8/4/1773, Irish 26 carpenter
    17 days, Monday, 2 pounds, 5'9", (arrived 7 years ago)
John Patterson, William Philips Philadelphia City PA ship captain 11/19/1747, Irish 22 blacksmith
    6 days, Friday, 1 pound,
John Patterson, John Davis Chester PA doctor 1/10/1771, Irish distiller L
    6 days, Friday, 2 pounds, 5'5",
Thomas Patterson, David Sproat Philadelphia City PA 7/6/1774, Scot 18 A
    2 pounds, 5'8", (apprenticed to the Brig Commerce)
William Patterson, Nicholas Bayard NY 6/25/1747, Irish 23
    3 pounds, 5'7",
William Patterson, Henry Reynolds New Castle DE 12/13/1770, American 16 cooper L
    1 pound,
William Patterson, John Stapler New Castle DE 12/9/1772, American 18 cooper (2nd escape) L
    7 days, Thursday, 5 pounds, 4'5",
Jonathan Paul, Christopher Heroesheimer Philadelphia PA 3/11/1795, 19 blacksmith A
    10 days, Sunday, 5 pounds, 5'7-8",
Richard Payne, John McAdow Baltimore MD 4/6/1774, English 25
    11 days, Sunday, 8 dollars, 5'5",
William Payne, William Ennalls Dorchester MD 5/1/1766, English sawyer
    33 days, Saturday, 5 pounds, 5'8", (arrived in 1764, use to the sea)
John Peacock, Henry Moliere Philadelphia PA 3/21/1792, 17 A
    Aug. 1990, 1 dollar, 4'6",
John Peak, James Vaux Montgomery PA 5/9/1792, English 28 bellowsmaker
    8 dollars, 5'4",
Benjamin Pearce, Edward Rummey Anne Arundel MD 8/16/1744, English 30 C
    39 days, Sunday, 3 pounds sterling, tall,
George Pearce, William Jenkins Baltimore MD 10/10/1754, English 40 C
    7 days, Thursday, 1 pistole, (arrived Aug. 1752)
Joseph Pearce, Thomas Gilbert Philadelphia City PA 2/6/1766, English 23
    2 days, Tuesday, 1 pound, 5'6",
Richard Pearce, Robert Roberts Kent MD 6/14/1764,
    11 days, Sunday, 2.5 pounds,
John Pearsly, Richard Swanwick Chester PA 8/28/1776, Irish
    3 days, Monday, 10 pounds, 5'7-8",
Joseph Pearson, Daniel Hains Lancaster PA 6/22/1769, English 19
    19 days, Saturday, 3 pounds, 5'5",
Ross Pearson, William Griffitts Philadelphia City PA 11/15/1753, Irish 19
    10 days, Monday, 1 pound, 5',
Samuel Pearson, Hugh Lindsay Philadelphia City PA carpenter 10/22/1747, Irish 19 A
    3 days, Monday, 1 pound,
Thomas Pearson, James Braddock Talbot MD 5/15/1776, English 19 sawyer C
    11 days, Sunday, 2 pounds, 5'6",
John Peasly, Richard Swanwick Philadelphia PA 8/30/1775, Irish
    12 days, Saturday, 16 dollars,
Samuel Peason, Patrick Ogilly tailor 9/13/1750, 17 tailor A
    14 days, Thursday, 2 pounds, 5'4",
John Andrew Peats, William Lawrence Philadelphia PA 9/9/1789, German 30 tailor
    10 days, Sunday, 4 dollars,
Dennis Pehan, Joseph Keas Bucks PA 10/18/1764, Scot 30
    26 days, Saturday, 5 pounds, 5'4",
William Peineburg, Jacob Miller WJ 6/15/1769, German 45
    10 days, Monday, 3 pounds, 5'4",
John Peirce, Symour Hood Philadelphia City PA ship captain 5/17/1770, Welsh
    1.5 pounds, 5'6",
Susan Pelan, John Vanderen 9/1/1784, Irish
    17 days, Sunday, 6 dollars,
William Penafee, Mordicai Miller 8/21/1776, English 23
    7 days, Thursday, 5 dollars, 5'9",
Henry Pencor, Abraham Dehaven Philadelphia PA innholder 8/10/1758, German 23
    3 pounds, 5'3", (was a wagon driver in the army)
Philip Pendergraft, Jonathan Wainwright Philadelphia City PA 10/17/1754, Irish 24 hatter
    5 days, Saturday, 3 pounds, 5',
John Pendergrass, Edward Hopkins New Castle DE carpenter 8/20/1747, Irish 20
    4 days, Sunday, 3 pounds,

John Penemore, James Franklin Baltimore MD ironworks 3/8/1764, C
    13 days, Friday, 5 pounds, 6',
Joseph Penick, Thomas Rutland Anne Arundel MD 6/1/1769, 23 C
    28 days, Thursday, 4 dollars, 5'8",
Robert Pennce, Thomas Marsh Kent MD 3/6/1760, English 50 carpenter C
    8 days, Wednesday, 1.5 pounds, 5', (lately arrived)
William Pennel, James Prowell Chester PA 7/23/1752, English 37 carpenter
    8 days, Wednesday, 5 pounds, 5'3",
William Pennell, John Malcolm Philadelphia City PA sailmaker 7/15/1756, Irish sailmaker A
    12 days, Saturday, 6 pistoles,
Benjamin Penny, James Smith Baltimore MD ironworks 5/7/1772, English 35 plummer
    72 days, Tuesday, 4 pounds, 5'5",
Rebecca Catherina Pepper, Caleb Musgrove Lancaster PA 7/8/1756, German 36
    18 days, Sunday, 1.5 pounds,
John Pepperedine, Philip Croney Queen Anne's MD 4/16/1752, American L
    about 2 years ago, 1.5 pounds, middle,
George Perepoint, Samuel Cosh Queen Anne's MD 3/22/1764, 35
    10 dollars,
Robert Perkinson, Richard Baily Philadelphia City PA weaver 4/1/1736, 30 weaver
    6 days, Friday, 2 pounds,
Lawrence Perkley, Brian Wilkinson Philadelphia City PA carver 3/26/1754, German 40 carver
    9 days, Tuesday, 5 pounds, (arrived last fall)
William Perlin, Joseph Hugg Gloucester NJ 7/21/1763, English 19 soldier L
    5 days, Saturday, 3 pounds, 5'2",
Henry Pero, Jacob Renno 6/16/1773, American 21 L
    75 days, Saturday, 1.05 pounds, 5',
Eleanor Perrel, James Davis Chester PA 6/4/1772, 14
    30 days, Tuesday, 1 pound, short,
Edward Perry, John Wilson Baltimore MD 3/26/1767, English
    11 days, Sunday, 2 pounds,
Elizabeth Perry, Cornealius Van Horne Monmouth NJ 4/27/1738, English 20
    11 days, Sunday, 2.5 pounds, middle,
Jack Perry, John Miller Lancaster PA 7/19/1775, Irish 18
    10 days, Monday, 3 pounds, 5'2",
James Perry, Samuel Dorsey Jr Baltimore MD ironworks 9/20/1775, 28 C
    32 days, Sunday, 3.75 pounds, 5'6",
Abraham Peters, Buckler Bond Harford MD 1/10/1771, English 24 C
    8 days, Wednesday, 3.5 pounds, 5'9",
Abraham Peters, Buckler Bond Harford MD 5/3/1775, English 28 (2nd escape) C
    39 days, Sunday, 3 pounds, 5'9",
John Peterson, Joseph Nabb Queen Anne's MD 5/12/1773, German shoemaker
    5 pounds,
John Peterson, William Dewees Philadelphia PA 4/13/1774, German
    7 days, Thursday, 1.5 pounds, 4'6", (arrived last fall)
John Peterson, Terence Heaheelman Lancaster PA tavern-keeper 7/3/1776, German 16
    19 days, Saturday, 4 dollars,
Mary Peterson, Adam Williams Philadelphia PA 7/20/1758, English-American 22 L
    9 days, Tuesday, 1 pound,
Peter Peterson, Matthias Landenberger Philadelphia City PA 5/18/1769, 19 A
    3 days, Monday, 0.03 pounds, 5'7",
Swain Peterson, Hugh Coulter Philadelphia City PA 4/28/1748, sailor L
    8 days, Wednesday, 5 pistoles,
John William Petre, Thomas Parry Berks PA 6/26/1776, German 28 drummer
    10 days, Monday, 5 dollars, 5'2-3",
Elizabeth Catherine Petter, George Kastner Philadelphia PA 9/25/1755, German 22
    6 days, Friday, 1.5 pounds,
John Petty, Michael Earle Cecil MD 9/4/1755, English 38 tanner
    2 pistoles, 5'6",
David Pew, Hinson Wright Queen Anne's MD 3/20/1750, English 36
    9 days, Tuesday, 2 pounds, middle,
Owen Pharley, George Smith Baltimore MD 11/1/1764, Irish 20 weaver
    28 days, Thursday, 1.5 pounds, 5'6",
Jacob Phaskel, Moses Quinby Hunterdon NJ 9/7/1796, 18
    11 days, Saturday, 20 dollars, 5'7",
William Phegan, James Little Philadelphia PA 8/26/1772, Irish 22
    13 days, Friday, 2 pounds, 5'5-6", (arrived 5 weeks ago)

Edward Phelps, Thomas Smyth Kent MD 7/22/1756, 22 C
  2 pistoles, 5'10",
Margaret Philips, John Eglinton Gloucester NJ 12/1/1748, 30
  6 days, Friday, 2 pounds, middle,
Robert Philips, Thomas Marshall Philadelphia City PA cooper 2/25/1755, Irish 22 cooper A
  2 days, Tuesday, 1.5 pounds, 5'6",
William Philips, William Kindell Kent MD 12/21/1758, Welsh
  11 days, Sunday, 1 pistole, 5'9",
Abel Phillips, Henry Comeley Philadelphia PA 4/30/1730, 24
  5 days, Saturday, 2.5 pounds,
Patrick Phillips, Joseph Brinton Chester PA 5/15/1776, Irish 16
  6 days, Friday, 1.5 pounds, short,
William Phillips, Cornelius Hains New Castle DE 6/20/1771, 19 sailor
  12 days, Saturday, 2 dollars, 5', (use to the sea)
Stephen Phipps, Charles Allen Kent MD 6/6/1771, English 50 tailor
  11 days, Sunday, 2.5 pounds, 5'7",
Patrick Phlaugherty, Bryan Connor Chester PA 7/25/1754, Irish 23
  13 days, Friday, 4 pounds, 5'9",
Asa Piatt, John Green Northampton PA 7/13/1796, 19 joiner A
  18 days, Saturday, 14 dollars, 5'6",
Elsa Picke, William Mattingly Baltimore MD 10/30/1740, 35 C
  19 days, Saturday, 5 pounds, middle,
Rachel Pickerin, Matthias Kerlin Chester PA tavern-keeper 12/23/1746, English 30
  15 days, Wednesday, 2 pounds, (has a 6 month old child)
John Pickson, Jeremiah Sheredine Baltimore MD ironworks 7/7/1763, English 40 C
  10 days, Monday, 5 pounds, 5'5",
Isaac Pidgeon, Richard Shoemaker Philadelphia PA 11/18/1772, 17
  11 days, Sunday, 2 pounds, 5'6",
Francis Lawrence Pidginett, Joseph Bell Burlington NJ ironworks 7/5/1775, Portugese
  10 days, Monday, 5 dollars, 5'7-8",
Francis Lawrence Pidginett, Joseph Ball Burlington NJ ironworks 9/11/1776, Portugese (2nd esc)
  16 days, Tuesday, 8 dollars, 5'7-8",
Robert Pierce, Mary Hunter Kent DE 9/24/1761, English 48 sawyer
  end of Aug., 5 pounds, short, (has been several years in this country)
John Piercy, John Simkin New Castle DE 8/22/1751, C
  4 days, Sunday, 1 pound, (is handcuffed)
William Piers, Levi Hollingsworth Philadelphia City PA 1/2/1772, English 20 conveyor
  10 days, Monday, 6 pounds, 5'9-10",
Stephen Pike, Cornelius Hains New Castle DE 9/19/1771, 20 (2nd escape) A
  10 days, Monday, 1.5 pounds, 5'1",
Stephen Pike, Cornelius Hains New Castle DE 6/14/1770, 18 A
  9 days, Tuesday, 0.5 pounds,
Charles Piller, Philip Miller Baltimore MD 3/27/1776, Scot barber
  21 days, Thursday, 8 dollars, 5'3", (arrived 3 months ago)
John Pimpel, Anthony Grove tailor 4/27/1769, German-American 18 tailor A
  18 days, Sunday, 2 pounds, 5'5",
Isaac Pinkeney, David Gorsuch Baltimore MD 10/17/1771, 35 sailor C
  18 days, Sunday, 25 dollars, 5'8-9",
George Pinshen, Cornelius Daily Queen Anne's MD 8/28/1766, Irish cooper
  2 pounds, short,
John Pinter, Valentine Bryant Hunterdon NJ 4/2/1761, German 27 cooper
  18 days, Sunday, 2 pounds, 5'7",
Peter Piper, Samuel Gilbert Berks PA 7/24/1782, 20 A
  31 days, Sunday, 0.03 pounds, 5'6",
William Pissrom, Alexander Rutherford Philadelphia City PA shoemaker 7/3/1760, 19 A
  3 days, Monday, 2 pounds, 5'5",
William Pitrekin, Charles Rass Philadelphia City PA 12/26/1754, 16 A
  12 days, Saturday, 0.5 pounds, short,
William Pitt, William Young Jr Baltimore MD 7/28/1773, 47 tallow-chander C
  17 days, Monday, 2 pounds, 6', (arrived 4 weeks ago)
David Pitts, Samuel Hodson New Castle DE ship captain 6/25/1741, English nailer
  6 days, Friday, 1 pound, short, (ran from ship)
John Pitts, Thomas O'Bryan Queen Anne's MD 8/18/1757, sailor
  18 days, Sunday, 5'6",
Philip Andrew Pitzler, Frederick Stone Lancaster PA 8/1/1754, German 28 sadler
  4 days, Sunday, 4 pounds, 5'4",

John Platfoot, Thomas Clark New Castle DE 8/10/1774, English
    4 days, Sunday, 2 pounds, 5'5",
James Plato, Archibald Ritchie VA 3/21/1765, English 33 gardener
    6 days, Friday, 5 pounds, (arrived last summer)
John Platt, Adam Williamson New Castle DE 8/2/1775, English
    21 days, Thursday, 1 pound,
John Platt, Charles Carroll Baltimore MD ironworks 11/30/1752, English 37 husbandman C
    18 days, Sunday, 4 pistoles, middle,
John Plaun, Thomas Stewart Augusta VA 4/11/1765, Scot 45 bookbinder
    25 days, Sunday, 5 pounds, 5'4", (arrived last fall)
Catherine Plimlen, Peter Lerur Lancaster PA 6/30/1757, German 18
    20 days, Friday, 1 pound,
Thomas Plunket, Philip Becker Lancaster PA 9/29/1773, 18 shoemaker A
    10 days, Monday, 12 dollars, 5'3.5",
Benjamin Poet, Edward Wyatt Philadelphia City PA tailor 8/30/1739, German 16 A
    4 days, Sunday, 1.5 pounds,
John Pollard, Edward Stevenson Frederick MD 3/12/1772, 25
    4 pounds, 5'6-7",
Joseph Pollard, Jacob Pollard 5/14/1767, 19 A
    19 days, Saturday, 0.5 pounds, 5'5",
Johannes Polluck, Matthew Clarkson NY 12/9/1736, German 20
    33 days, Saturday, 3 pounds, (arrived last mid-Sept.)
Edward Ponting, Johnathon Roberts Queen Anne's MD 4/27/1769, English 25 shoemaker C
    30 days, Tuesday, 2.5 pounds, 5'6-7", (arrived Nov. 1768)
Joseph Pool, Thomas Bleamy Baltimore MD 5/30/1771, English 35 hatter C
    29 days, Wednesday, 2 pounds, 5'4",
William Pool, Samuel Kennedy Chester PA doctor 7/7/1768, 34 tailor
    13 days, Friday, 3 pounds, (has been a solider)
Richard Poole, Jeremiah Sheredine Baltimore MD ironworks 7/7/1763, English 35 C
    10 days, Monday, 5 pounds, 5'4",
Richard Poore, John Blackwood Gloucester NJ fuller 9/15/1743, Irish
    7 days, Thursday, 2 pounds, short,
Catherine Pope, Richard Cheyney Chester PA 5/19/1773, Irish 20
    3 days, Monday, 1 pound, 5'2-3",
Alexander Porter, James Boyd Chester PA 2/2/1785, Irish 20
    9 days, Monday, 10 dollars, 5'9-10",
James Porter, William Brigden Lancaster PA 7/17/1776, 18
    22 days, Wednesday, 3 dollars, 5'8",
John Porter, Edward Cook Cumberland PA 7/16/1767, Scot 19 weaver
    17 days, Monday, 5 pounds, 5'4", (use to the sea)
Mary Porter, Arthur Foster Lancaster PA 4/24/1746,
    30 days, Tuesday, 2 pounds, short,
Robert Porter, Daniel Crawford Chester PA 7/23/1752, Irish
    2 days, Tuesday, 1.5 pounds, 5'7",
Ephraim Pote, John Doyl 11/4/1756, 19 A
    244 days, Friday, 3 pounds, 5'5",
Henry Potter, James Cawley Baltimore MD ship captain 8/9/1750, Irish 30 C
    32 days, Sunday, 4 pounds, (lately arrived)
John Peter Pouel, Joshua Lampeter Philadelphia City PA tanner 10/2/1776, 16 A
    1 pound,
George Powell, Francis Harris Philadelphia City PA 11/8/1764, English 20 (ran before)
    11 days, Sunday, 2 pounds, (lately arrived)
George Powell, Hugh Coulter Philadelphia City PA 4/28/1748, sailor L
    8 days, Wednesday, 5 pistoles,
John Powell, Robert Lewis New Castle DE 8/20/1747, Irish 20
    4 days, Sunday, 3 pounds,
Nathanial Powell, R. Grisham Kent MD 7/6/1769, English 30 C
    10 days, Monday, 10 dollars,
William Powell, Thomas Ludlam Cape May NJ 5/9/1771, 30 soldier L
    5 pounds, 5'4",
Charles Power, George Patten Chester PA 7/21/1768, Irish 18 sadler
    31 days, Monday, 1 pound, 5'6",
Francis Power, Herman Vansant Bucks PA 8/14/1766, Irish 21
    3 pounds, 5'6", (was in the navy)
Philip Power, James Pullock Cumberland PA 9/5/1765, barber
    10 days, Monday, 5 pounds, 5'8",

Samuel Powis, Michael Thomas Talbot MD 7/15/1762, 23
    2 pounds, 5'7",
John Prat, Flora Dorsey Baltimore MD 12/28/1769, 25 C
    14 days, Thursday, 3 pounds, 6',
Cornelius Pratt, Thomas Wilson Philadelphia PA 7/10/1776, Irish 25
    4 days, Sunday, 1 pound, 5'2",
Patty Pratt, Nathan Collens Philadelphia PA 2/5/1777, Irish 16
    47 days, Saturday, 2 pounds,
Joseph Pratton, Joseph Yeats Philadelphia City PA tavern-keeper 5/17/1764, English 22
    4 days, Sunday, 3 pounds,
Abraham Praul, James No Name Philadelphia PA 12/15/1763, 18 shipwright A
    1,085 days, Thursday, 2 pounds, 5'10",
John Pray, Frederick Bicking Philadelphia City PA papermaker 7/9/1761, 17 A
    3 days, Monday, 2 pounds, short,
Catherine Preden, James Broon New Castle DE 9/29/1757, Irish
    6 days, Friday, 1 pound, short,
William Prees, John Seale Queen Anne's MD 6/1/1769, 50 C
    18 days, Sunday, 1 pound, 5'6-7",
John Prengel, William Hutson Salem NJ 7/10/1776,
    6 days, Friday, 8 dollars, 5'2",
John Preston, George Shoemaker Philadelphia City PA 12/10/1767, English 30 blacksmith
    7 days, Thursday, 2 pounds, 5'8", (lately arrived)
Thomas Preston, James Moore Baltimore MD 8/22/1771, Irish 24
    11 days, Sunday, 2.5 pounds, 5'9",
Thomas Preston, Crispin Pearson Bucks PA 6/28/1775, English 23 (2nd escape)
    45 days, Monday, 8 dollars,
Thomas Preston, Crispin Pearson Bucks PA 10/5/1774, English 22
    7 days, Thursday, 4 dollars, 5'5",
Richard Prestwood, Alexander Lawson Baltimore MD ironworks 4/20/1749, English 40 C
    1.5 pounds, middle,
David Price, Thomas Nixon Kent DE 7/24/1746, American 24 L
    14 days, Thursday, 2 pounds, short,
Elizabeth Price, Joseph Thackery Gloucester NJ 3/27/1740, Irish 23
    2 pounds,
John Price, Thomas Ratlidge 8/26/1762, English 24
    22 days, Wednesday, 10 dollars, 5'7",
John Price, John McCulagh Chester PA 4/12/1786, Welsh-German 40 L
    4 dollars, 6',
Rice Price, Robert Roberts Kent MD 4/26/1764, English C
    15 days, Wednesday, 8 dollars,
Richard Price, Edmund Briggs Bucks PA 8/30/1744, English
    1 pound, middle,
Samuel Price, Andi McBay New Castle DE 4/30/1767, wool comber L
    2 pounds,
Thomas Price, Larkin Randall Baltimore MD 11/8/1770, English 30 tailor C
    10 dollars, 5'10",
William Price, Samuel Coles Gloucester NJ 10/13/1748, English 19
    10 days, Monday, 2 pounds, middle,
William Price, John Dorbin Cecil MD 6/3/1762, 40
    21 days, Thursday, 2 pounds, 5'9",
William Price, James Wilson New Castle DE 9/13/1764, 42 (2nd escape)
    2.5 pounds,
William Pride, John Leeth Philadelphia City PA ship captain 7/30/1752, Irish
    5'8", (ran from ship, has been in colonies before)
Richard Priest, Solomon Holton Queen Anne's MD 5/19/1763, English 20 C
    1.1 pounds sterling, 5'6",
Joseph Priestman, Jacob Lemmon New Castle DE 3/17/1768, 24 breeches-maker
    9 days, Tuesday, 3 pounds, 5'5",
Joseph Prior, George Brown Baltimore MD 4/15/1742, American 28 L
    24 days, Monday, 7 pounds, tall,
John Pritchard, Charles Foreman Kent MD 5/24/1750, English
    2 pounds, short,
Rees Pritchard, Anthony Cunard Philadelphia PA 8/17/1738, 30
    4 days, Sunday, 1.5 pounds,
Richard Pritchard, James McKnight Lancaster PA Ferryman 1/8/1751, Welsh 27
    9 days, Tuesday, 3 pounds, middle,

Walter Pritchet, Henry Neill Philadelphia City PA 7/3/1766, Irish tailor
    5 pounds, 5'7", (lately arrived)
Winford Pritchet, Henry Neill Philadelphia City PA 7/3/1766, Irish stay-maker (female)
    5 pounds, short, (wife to Walter Pritchet, lately arrived)
David Proctor, Hugh Bowes Philadelphia City PA ship captain 11/10/1768, Scot
    10 pounds, (arrived 1 year ago)
Mary Proctor, William Sterritt Chester PA 1/3/1771, Irish 25 mantuamaker
    25 days, Sunday, 4 dollars, middle, (arrived over 2 years ago)
Edward Proger, James McIlvaine Sussex NJ 7/9/1752, English 20 tailor
    2 pounds, 5'6",
William Prosser, Thomas Witherill Jr Burlington NJ 1/2/1753, 18 shoemaker A
    3 days, Monday, 2 pounds, 5'8",
Elizabeth Prugelin, Christopher Sower Philadelphia PA printer 2/10/1773, German 26
    7 days, Thursday, 0.25 dollars,
Simon Puch, Captain Crymer Baltimore MD ship captain 8/18/1763, English 28 C
    10 days, Monday, 1 pistole, 5'5",
John Pugh, Benjamin Betterton Philadelphia City PA 7/22/1742, 18 cooper A
    1 pound,
William Pullen, John White Philadelphia City PA 8/31/1738, English 21
    4 days, Sunday, middle,
James Pummell, Thomas Green Philadelphia City PA 2/28/1749, American A
    1 pound, (has 2 years to serve)
David Punch, Issac Rees Philadelphia PA 4/5/1739, Irish 19 weaver
    34 days, Friday, 1.5 pounds, middle,
David Punch, Isaac Rees Philadelphia PA 8/21/1740, Irish 20 weaver (2nd escape)
    4 days, Sunday, 1 pound, middle,
Edward Purcell, Hugh Patrick Lancaster PA 4/10/1746, 20
    15 days, Wednesday, 5 pounds,
Peter Purcell, Cornelius Stidham New Castle DE 8/21/1766, Irish weaver
    9 days, Tuesday, 3 pounds, 5'3", (lately arrived)
Richard Purchase, Thomas Harrison Anne Arundel MD ironworks 9/12/1765, English 30 C
    25 days, Sunday, 5 pounds, 5'5", (arrived Nov. 1763)
John Purday, Robert All 10/30/1766, Irish 27 soldier (took his wife)
    1 pound, 5'9", (arrived 6 weeks ago)
John Purfield, John McCall Bucks PA 11/17/1748, Irish 35 tailor
    4 days, Sunday, 1.5 pounds, 5'8",
James Purnel, Samuel Worthington Philadelphia PA 4/30/1730, 30
    5 days, Saturday, 2.5 pounds, short,
Daniel Pursel, Richard Osburn Loudoun VA 9/7/1774, Irish wool comber
    4 pounds, 5'8",
John Pursley, George Cunningham Cumberland PA 8/17/1774, Irish 23
    17 days, Monday, 3 pounds, 5'7-8",
William Que, Manasses Woods Bucks PA 5/8/1740, Irish
    7 days, Thursday, 2 pounds, short,
Philip Queen, John Hay Lancaster PA 8/23/1764, Irish 14
    2 pounds,
John Quelch, Jacob Lemmon Cecil MD 12/20/1770, Irish 19 breeches-maker
    11 days, Sunday, 3 pounds, 5'6-7",
Robert Quick, Thomas Boyer Kent MD 9/26/1765, English 40 C
    36 days, Wednesday, 2 pounds, 5'6-7",
Hugh Quin, John Graham Chester PA 3/19/1772, Irish 15
    19 days, Saturday, 2 pounds, (arrived 1 year ago)
James Quin, William McClure Philadelphia City PA 6/29/1774, Irish 19 tailor
    7 days, Thursday, 4 dollars, 5'4-5", (arrived this spring)
John Quin, Robert Dixon Queen Anne's MD 12/8/1784, Irish 21 (ran before)
    17 days, Sunday, 3 pounds, 5'11",
Patrick Quin, Hugh Bowes Philadelphia City PA ship captain 5/11/1769, Irish 37
    4 days, Sunday, 3 pounds, 5'6-7",
Patrick Quin, Samuel Owings Baltimore MD 6/16/1773, Irish 40 (2nd escape)
    11 days, Sunday, 7.5 pounds, 5'5",
Sophia Quinn, James Nevill Philadelphia PA 10/1/1783, 17
    8 days, Tuesday, 0.06 Spanish dollars,
William Quirk, Peter Sutter Philadelphia City PA 7/27/1769, Irish
    4 days, Sunday, 1.5 pounds, (lately arrived)
Henry Raby, Henry Martin Philadelphia City PA 4/28/1784, Irish
    5 days, Friday, 5'6",

John Racener, John Risdon Burlington NJ 1/9/1772, American 22 L
    10 days, Monday, 12 dollars, 5'8",
Christopher Racer, Joseph Engle Burlington NJ 7/25/1771, German 19
    7 days, Thursday, 1.5 pounds, 5'3-4",
John Rachford, John Houseman Kent DE 10/26/1738, English
    22 days, Wednesday, 5 pounds,
Henry Radmont, Walter Thetford New Castle DE 6/14/1744,
    15 days, Wednesday, 3 pounds,
Henry Raffardy, Joseph Batholomew Chester PA 11/3/1743, Irish 22
    4 days, Sunday, 1.5 pounds, middle,
William Ragan, Joseph Harlen Chester PA 8/18/1743,
    4 days, Sunday, 1 pound, middle,
Elizabeth Rainey, Joseph Jackson Monmouth NJ 10/6/1763, Irish 17
    6 days, Friday, 1.5 pounds, short, (lately arrived)
Paul Rairdon, Zadoch Street Salem PA 7/27/1796, Irish
    20 days, Thursday, 8 dollars, 5'8-9",
William Ralston, Thomas White Chester PA 8/3/1769, Irish 19
    11 days, Sunday, 4 pounds, 5'4", (arrived 3 years ago)
William Ralstone, James Adams Bucks PA 5/11/1785, Irish weaver
    4 days, Saturday, 3 pounds, 5'7-8",
Henry Ramsey, Amos Griffith Philadelphia PA 3/26/1754, 18
    3 days, Monday, 1.5 pounds, 5'11",
James Ramsey, John Nidy Lancaster PA 4/30/1772,
    17 days, Monday, 5 pounds, 5'3-4",
William Ramsey, William Davidson Philadelphia City PA 6/12/1746, sailor L
    3 pounds, 5'9",
James Randles, Robert Blain York PA 11/30/1774, Irish 16 butcher
    28 days, Thursday, 8 dollars, 5'2-3",
Andrew Rankin, Samuel Martin Chester PA 3/13/1776, Irish 18
    10 days, Monday, 8 dollars, 5'4",
George Rankin, James Wilson New Castle DE 9/13/1764, Irish 35
    2.5 pounds, 5'7", (arrived 10 months ago, but was in the colonies before)
Thomas Rankin, Thomas Rutherford Frederick VA sheriff 8/27/1747, 30 C
    5 pounds, 5'9", (not a new arrival)
William Rankin, John Hutchinson Middlesex NJ 7/30/1767, Irish 20 shoemaker
    3 pounds,
Patrick Rannahan, David Rankin Chester PA 10/2/1766, Irish 24 weaver
    2 pounds, 5'7", (has relatives nearby)
Edward Rannels, William Bird Philadelphia PA 6/21/1744, Irish 21
    1.5 pounds,
Henry Rap, George Schneider Philadelphia PA 7/26/1775, German 18
    10 days, Monday, 4 dollars, 5'4",
Daniel Raredon, John Hall New Castle DE 7/3/1760, Irish 24 L
    2 pounds, short,
William Ratchford, Daniel McNeill Lancaster PA 1/30/1753, Irish 25
    2 pounds, 5'10",
Jane Ratcliff, Richard Cox 8/26/1762, English
    12 days, Saturday, 1.5 pounds,
John Ratcliffe, Joseph Drinker Philadelphia City PA 12/4/1760, 17 A
    4 days, Sunday, 1 pound, 5'6",
Jane Rattlife, Henry Hendrickson Gloucester NJ 7/24/1760, 16
    1 day, Wednesday, 1 pound, short,
Alexander Rauch, John Peters 5/4/1785, German 25
    3 days, Sunday, 3 pounds, (arrived 6 weeks ago)
Thomas Raw, Jonathan Chapman Baltimore MD ironworks 7/30/1747, English 26 C
    45 days, Monday, 5 pounds, tall,
Thomas Raw, Nathan Chapman Stafford VA ironworks 4/16/1748, English 27 (2nd escape) C
    6 days, Friday, 2 pistoles, tall, (was in Baltimore)
John Rawlings, William Fitzhugh Calvert MD 7/24/1766, English butcher
    2.5 pounds, 5'6",
James Ray, Joseph Rogers Chester PA 10/17/1745, Irish 18
    11 days, Sunday, 1.5 pounds,
James Ray, John Stokes Bucks PA 11/24/1748, Irish 21 (2nd escape)
    8 days, Wednesday, 2 pounds, short,
Peter Ray, James Thompson Lancaster PA 10/14/1772, Irish 22
    1 pound, 5'10",

John Raymer, William Walker Stafford VA 7/26/1744, English 35 blacksmith C
    28 days, Thursday, 4 pistoles,
James Rea, Jost Dubs Berks PA ironworks 4/2/1747, Irish 19
    18 days, Sunday, 2 pounds, short,
Edward Reace, Thomas Slipper Kent MD 3/12/1751,
    9 days, Tuesday, 1 pound, 5',
Ann Read, William Mecum Salem NJ 7/20/1785, Irish 16
    10 days, Sunday, 3 dollars, short,
Catherine Read, Alexander Johnston Chester PA 2/5/1756, Irish (with 14 month old child)
    11 days, Sunday, 1.5 pounds, tall,
James Read, William Ball Philadelphia PA 11/2/1774, Irish 23 mason
    3 days, Monday, 10 dollars, 5'9-10", (arrived last July)
John Read, Daniel Gritt Chester PA 2/13/1766, Irish 16
    9 days, Tuesday, 1 pound, 5',
John Read, Edward Bosman Baltimore MD 7/20/1769, English 24 C
    10 days, Monday, 8 dollars, 5'8", (arrived July 1, 1769)
John Read, James Franklin Baltimore MD ironworks 4/4/1771, English 26 (2nd escape) C
    12 days, Saturday, 20 dollars, 5'8-9",
Joseph Read, David Fulton Philadelphia City PA 7/21/1773, Irish 50
    7 days, Thursday, 8 dollars, 5'6-7", (lately arrived)
Robert Read, James Perigo Baltimore MD 4/13/1774, Scot 22
    7.5 pounds, 5'9",
Thomas Read, Michael Masser Lancaster PA 8/7/1776, Irish 20 tanner
    9 days, Tuesday, 5'8", (arrived 1 year ago)
Thomas Read, Michael Masser Lancaster PA 4/2/1777, Irish 20 tanner (2nd escape)
    10 days, Monday, 10 dollars,
William Read, Joshua McDowell Chester PA 8/4/1768, English 25 wagonmaker
    11 days, Sunday, 3 pounds,
Matthew Reading, Samuel Nutts Chester PA ironworks 6/5/1740,
    45 days, Monday, 1 pistole, middle,
Sarah Reading, William Rudderow Burlington NJ 9/30/1762,
    1.5 pounds, 5'2",
Gregory Readington, Samuel Mendenhall Chester PA 4/12/1750, Irish 20 corker
    4 days, Sunday, 2 pounds, 5'10",
Stephen Rean, Joseph Chambers York PA 1/1/1767,
    about 2 years ago, 2 pounds, 5'5",
George Rear, Unlisted Name Chester PA 11/13/1776, German 19
    8 days, Wednesday, 3 pounds, 5'8",
John Reardon, Philip Syng Philadelphia PA 9/4/1776, Irish 25
    6 days, Friday, 8 dollars, 5'10",
William Reardon, William Clayton Chester PA 12/10/1745, Irish 25 L
    20 days, Friday, 2 pounds,
William Reardon, William Reynolds Chester PA 12/16/1746, Irish 26 gaol sale (2nd escape) L
    5 days, Saturday, 2 pistoles, short,
William Reardon, William Moore Chester PA 6/4/1747, Irish 27 (3rd escape) L
    4 days, Sunday, 5 pounds, short,
Daniel Reaverdy, William Graham Bucks PA 11/8/1750, 18 weaver
    3 pounds, 5'8",
James Red, John Cannon Baltimore MD 3/13/1766, Irish 22 shoemaker
    17 days, Monday, 2.5 pounds, 5'10",
John Reddy, Jonathan Tatnal Philadelphia PA 1/4/1732, Irish farmer
    2 pounds, tall,
Lawrence Reddy, Richard Osburn Loudoun VA 9/7/1774, Irish
    4 pounds, 5'6",
William Redford, Abraham Whitaker Baltimore MD 8/16/1770, English 25
    11 days, Sunday, 2.5 pounds, 5'7",
John Redgrave, Henry Taulbird 5/26/1763, 17 weaver A
    29 days, Wednesday, 0.5 pounds, 5'8",
Edward Rediken, Thomas Mershon Hunterdon NJ 9/8/1743, Irish 22 weaver
    3 pounds, middle,
Henry Redman, James Campbell 9/5/1751, 24
    short,
Patrick Redman, Samuel Dorsey Jr Anne Arundel MD ironworks 10/18/1775, Irish 24
    11 days, Sunday, 8 pounds, 5'6",
Thomas Redmon, John Edwards Salem NJ 5/26/1743, Irish 25
    13 days, Friday, 3 pounds, middle,

Andrew Redmond, Legh Master Frederick MD ironworks 9/19/1771, Irish 30 turner
    19 days, Saturday, 6 pounds, 5'10-11",
Francis Redrige, Joseph Cox Burlington NJ ironworks 7/10/1776, Spanish
    17 days, Monday, 5 dollars, 5'5-6",
Rachael Reece, Joseph West Chester PA 3/4/1795,
    23 days, Monday, 0.03 pounds, (has 2 years 7 months left to serve)
Jonathan Reed, Edward William Boston MA currier 8/18/1737, Irish 32 currier
    199 days, Monday, 5 pounds,
Lewis Reed, George Read New Castle DE 3/24/1768, German 30 (ran with wife) L
    2 pistoles, 4'4-5",
Michael Reed, Jacob Jeanes Montgomery PA 11/2/1785, Irish 20
    3 days, Sunday, 3 dollars, 5'10-11",
Casper Reel, Ludwig Meckelbourg Philadelphia City PA 5/28/1761, German 19 (ran before) A
    17 days, Monday, 4 pounds,
Hotman Reel, Benton Davis Chester PA 6/10/1756, German 12
    32 days, Sunday, 1 pound, 4'2",
Evan Rees, Benjamin Reynolds Chester PA 7/30/1783, American 18 A
    3 days, Sunday, 3 pounds, tall,
John Rees, Phineas Roberts Philadelphia City PA 4/11/1751, 19 cooper A
    4 days, Sunday, 2 pounds, short,
William Reeves, Thomas Trevees Baltimore MD 7/19/1770, 27 C
    8 days, Wednesday, 1.5 pounds, 5'5", (lately arrived)
Timothy Regan, William Marshall Chester PA 9/12/1751, Irish 20
    4 days, Sunday, 1 pound, 5'3",
James Reid, Samuel Faires Bucks PA 3/27/1740, Scot fuller
    25 days, Sunday, 3 pounds, middle,
John Reid, Cornelius Daily Queen Anne's MD 1/2/1766, Irish 22
    2 pounds, 5'6", (arrived Feb. 1763)
John Reid, Cornelius Daily Queen Anne's MD 7/10/1766, Irish 22 (2nd escape)
    last June, (imported)
Jacob Reiley, Gabriel Dolbow Gloucester NJ 8/24/1774, American 26 L
    8 days, Wednesday, 1 pound, 5'8-9",
Thomas Reiley, Joseph Tatnall New Castle DE 9/13/1775, 30 miller
    3 days, Monday, 5'6",
James Reily, William Selthridge Sussex NJ 10/1/1741, Irish 30 weaver
    12 days, Saturday, 1.5 pounds,
James Reily, Samuel Large WJ 3/17/1752, American 16 L
    9 days, Tuesday, 2 pounds,
John Reily, Bernard Preston Jr Baltimore MD 4/12/1770, Irish 35 C
    17 days, Monday, 3 pounds, 5'9",
Lawrence Reily, James Williams Chester PA 12/25/1755, Irish 26
    37 days, Tuesday, 3 pounds, 5'10",
Miles Reily, Robert Miller Lancaster PA 12/10/1751, Irish 17
    7 days, Thursday, 2 pounds, middle,
Joseph Reine, Francis Dudley Burlington NJ 5/8/1755, English 19
    11 days, Sunday, 3 pounds, 5'7",
Maximus Remberger, Solomon Brumfield Berks PA 6/16/1773, German 20
    8 dollars, 5'7-8",
Bastian Remus, Joseph Williams Philadelphia PA 5/10/1753, German 40 miller
    2 days, Tuesday, 2 pounds, short,
John Reney, Josiah Hibberd Chester PA 4/16/1777, Irish 19
    4 dollars,
David Renney, John Colley Philadelphia City PA 7/26/1775, Scot 20 tailor
    3 pounds, 5'6",
Margaret Repsher, Paul Gaspard Breton Philadelphia City PA 9/21/1785, German-American 12 L
    13 days, Thursday, 2 pounds, 4',
Richard Revenscrafft, Jacob Mayer Philadelphia City PA 11/17/1773, Irish
    4 days, Sunday, 1 pound, short,
George Rex, William Downing Lancaster PA 3/16/1785, 19 miller A
    10 days, Sunday, 6 dollars, 5'9",
Bryan Reyley, Jacob Sharpless Chester PA 2/12/1754, Irish
    16 days, Tuesday, 5 pounds, 5'6",
Andrew Reynell, Daniel Brodhead Bucks PA 7/28/1763, German-American 22 blacksmith L
    10 pounds, 5'7",
Catherine Reynen, John Spence Philadelphia City PA 9/11/1766, German 21
    32 days, Sunday, 1 pound, short,

Humphrey Reynolds, John Parry Chester PA 10/19/1732, English 22
    7 days, Thursday, 2 pounds, short,
James Reynolds, Benjamin Humphreys Philadelphia City PA scythesmith 10/3/1765, Irish 29
    4 days, Sunday, 5 pounds, 5'6",
James Reynolds, Samuel Morrison Lancaster PA 4/5/1770, Irish 20
    4 days, Sunday, 3 pounds, 5'7-8",
James Reynolds, John Bull Baltimore MD 4/12/1770, Irish 26 C
    17 days, Monday, 3 pounds, 5'8",
Patrick Reynolds, Joshua Baker Lancaster PA 6/29/1738, Irish 30
    16 days, Tuesday, 1.5 pounds, short,
Patrick Reynolds, James Bryson Baltimore MD 9/29/1784, Irish 19
    13 days, Thursday, 15 pounds, 5'5-6",
Richard Reynolds, John Blackledge Philadelphia PA 6/14/1775, English 19
    4 dollars, 5'6",
Mary Anne Reyt, Andrew Mitchell Chester PA 7/2/1767, German 40
    9 days, Tuesday, 5 pounds, (wife to Peter Reyt)
Peter Reyt, Andrew Mitchell Chester PA 7/2/1767, German 27
    9 days, Tuesday, 5 pounds,
Richard Rhoads, Thomas Jones Baltimore MD 7/12/1764, 26 bricklayer C
    11 days, Sunday, 5 pounds, 5'6",
William Rhoads, John Roberts Philadelphia PA 5/31/1764, 17 tailor A
    1.5 pounds,
James Rian, Robert Beverlin Kent MD 10/3/1754, 23
    7 days, Thursday, 2 pounds, 5'3",
Lochlan Rian, Emory Sudler Kent MD 12/31/1767,
    17 days, Monday, 5 pounds, 5'8",
Daniel Rice, William Shipley 1/23/1772, 17
    4 weeks ago, 1 pound, 4'10",
John Rice, Robert King Lancaster PA 7/23/1777, 17 A
    40 days, Saturday, 6 dollars, 5'5-6",
Samuel Rice, Joshua McDowell Chester PA 3/28/1765, Irish 45 wool comber gaol sale L
    15 days, Wednesday, 6 pounds, 5'11",
Samuel Rice, James Popham New Castle DE 4/23/1767, Irish 47 wool comber (2nd escape) L
    7 days, Thursday, 5'10",
Jacob Rich, Frederick Bicking Philadelphia City PA papermaker 2/19/1761, 18
    24 days, Monday, 1 pound, 5',
Francis Richard, James McLacklen Kent MD 7/7/1763, English 45 blacksmith C
    19 days, Saturday, 3 pounds, 6',
George Richard, Jacob Fox Hunterdon NJ 1/24/1765, 15 A
    10 days, Monday, 2 pounds, 4'7",
Edward Richards, James Riddle Philadelphia PA 9/6/1770, tailor
    11 days, Sunday, 2 pounds, 5'2-3",
George Washington Richards, Thomas Claypole Salem NJ 3/19/1794, 17 cordwainer A
    6 pounds, 5'5",
Stephen Richards, Denton Jacques Frederick MD ironworks 7/24/1776, English 28 C
    24 days, Monday, 5 pounds, 5'5-6",
Thomas Richards, Jacob Comegys Kent MD 4/7/1768, Welsh C
    9 days, Tuesday, 2 pounds, 5'8",
William Richards, Daniel Melford Gloucester NJ 10/12/1796, 17 A
    3 days, Sunday, 0.06 dollars, 5'8-9",
James Richardson, William Blair Philadelphia City PA 9/4/1760, Irish 28 weaver
    8 days, Wednesday, 2 pounds, 5'3", (has a brother nearby)
Joseph Richardson, Philip Yarnal Chester PA 9/7/1732, Irish 18
    8 days, Wednesday, 1.5 pounds, short,
Robert Richardson, Michael Lang Philadelphia City PA 5/22/1766, Scot
    15 days, Wednesday, 3 pounds, 5'5",
William Richardson, Anthony Hooper Gloucester NJ 12/22/1773, 17
    6 days, Friday, 1 pound, 4'8-9",
William Richardson, Nicholas Hofaker Lancaster PA 3/12/1772, English 20 chimneysweep L
    about 3 months ago, 5'4",
William Richardson, Curtis Grubb Lancaster PA ironworks 11/4/1772, English 20 chimsweep (2nd esc) L
    16 days, Tuesday, 2 pounds, 5'4-5",
William Richardson, Giles Lovering Salem NJ 12/22/1773, English 22 chimneysweep (3rd esc) L
    8 days, Wednesday, 1 pound, 4'8-9",
William Richardson, Isaac Reign Salem NJ 4/27/1774, English 22 chimneysweep (4th escape) L
    10 days, Monday, 4 dollars, 5'4-5",

William Richardson, Isaac Reign Salem NJ 12/21/1774, English 23 chimneysweep (5th escape) L
    140 days, Thursday, 2 dollars,
Daniel Richman, Cornelius Austin Salem NJ 9/5/1792, 19 blacksmith A
    31 days, Sunday, 0.03 pounds, 5'6-8",
John Richman, John Vorhees Monmouth NJ 7/7/1763, 20
    5 days, Saturday, 3 pounds, 5'10",
Matthew Richmond, John Smith Lancaster PA 1/22/1751, Irish 24
    43 days, Wednesday, 1 pound, short,
Samuel Richy, James Read New Castle DE 9/10/1783, American gaol sale L
    6 days, Thursday, 16 dollars, 5'8-9",
Thomas Rickaly, Charles Green Baltimore MD 7/14/1743, 26 C
    10 days, Monday, 5 pounds, middle,
William Riddle, Oliver Brooks Salem NJ 7/18/1792, 20 A
    3 days, Sunday, 4 dollars, 5'5-6",
John Michael Rider, Hugh Blackwood Salem NJ 7/16/1767, German 21
    11 days, Sunday, 4 dollars, 5'7",
James Ridgely, John Deaver Baltimore MD 10/1/1767, Irish
    15 days, Wednesday, 10 pounds, tall,
John Ridgway, Nathaniel Grubb Chester PA 5/12/1748, English 35
    1 day, Wednesday, 5 pounds, middle,
Anthony Rietz, Henry Klein Philadelphia City PA 3/15/1748, German 20
    10 days, Monday, 2 pounds, 5', (has 1.5 years left to serve)
Thomas Rieve, Jacob Hederick York PA 7/17/1776, English 20
    28 days, Thursday, 5 pounds, 5'2",
John Rigar, Lieutenant Shute Cumberland NJ 3/18/1762, German 26
    3 pounds, 5'3",
John Rightorn, John Kent MD Ironworks 4/22/1762, 40 C
    30 days, Tuesday, 5 pounds, 5'8",
Zacheriah Rigton, Conrad Smith Baltimore MD 9/15/1763, German-American 20 A
    19 days, Saturday, 5 pounds,
Eleaner Riley, John Hill Chester PA 6/14/1786, Irish 20
    3 days, Sunday, 6 dollars, 5'4",
John Riley, Moses Irving Lancaster PA 7/31/1766, Irish 22
    7 days, Thursday, 2 pounds, 5'9", (arrived this summer)
John Riley, Evan Lewis Chester PA 4/11/1771, Irish 17
    8 dollars, 5'10",
Timothy Riley, Joseph Baker Chester PA 8/2/1744, Irish 30
    1.5 pounds, short,
Thomas Rilland, James Work Lancaster PA 1/11/1759, American 30 shoemaker L
    32 days, Sunday, 2 pistoles, 5'6",
Charles Rine, William Kreeg PA 1/3/1776, German mason A
    8 days, Wednesday, 5 pounds, 5'9", (2 years left to serve, father lives in York PA)
Patrick Rine, John Wilson Lancaster PA 12/15/1773, 17
    16 days, Tuesday, 4 dollars,
John Rinn., George Wood Bedford PA 12/22/1773, Irish 40
    Sept., 4 dollars, 5'8",
John Christian Rister, John Marshall Philadelphia City PA 10/17/1771, German tailor
    3 pounds, 5'6", (was a soldier)
Samuel Rittenhouse, Michael Ziegler Montgomery PA tanner 10/28/1789, 19 tanner A
    10 days, Sunday, 5 pounds, 5'10",
Catherine Roach, Charles Moor Philadelphia City PA hatter 3/27/1740, 22
    about 35 days ago, 1.5 pounds,
Edmund Roach, Robert Lewis Chester PA 10/4/1744, 16
    1 day, Wednesday, 2.5pounds, short,
Edward Roach, Thomas Brown Lancaster PA brickmaker 4/5/1750,
    18 days, Sunday, 3 pounds, short,
Elizabeth Roach, Robert Wakely Philadelphia City PA 9/19/1754, Irish 22
    13 days, Friday, 1.5 pounds, middle, (lately arrived)
John Roach, Andrew Read Burlington NJ ironworks 9/1/1743, Irish 20 sadler
    2 pounds,
Patrick Roach, Josiah Carpenter 11/22/1753, Irish 18
    3 days, Monday, 1 pound, (arrived this spring)
Robert Roach, John Needham Bucks PA 8/4/1768, Irish 17
    4 days, Sunday, 1 pound,
Tom Roach, Benjamin Humphrey Philadelphia City PA scythesmith 12/15/1763, Irish 19
    4 days, Sunday, 5 pounds, 5'5",

Sarah Robbins, Henry Williams Frederick MD 4/14/1773, English 25 C
   314 days, Thursday, 20 dollars, 5'2",
William Robbins, James Elliot Delaware PA 10/15/1794, 19
   16 days, Monday, 10 dollars, 5'8",
John Robert, Joseph Likens Philadelphia PA 11/18/1772, 17 blacksmith A
   11 days, Sunday, 2 pounds, 5'6-7",
Abel Roberts, Owen Brooke Chester PA 10/1/1783, 17 A
   30 days, Monday, 0.03 pounds, 5'6",
Daniel Roberts, Richard James Kent DE 5/27/1736,
   5 pounds, (oldest son)
Elizabeth Roberts, Richard Sanderson Chester PA 5/17/1764, Irish 23
   1 pound, (lately arrived)
Evan Roberts, Abraham Dehaven Philadelphia PA innholder 9/6/1750, Welsh 25 shoemaker
   5 days, Saturday, 5 pounds, middle,
Evan Roberts, Joseph Chavier Queen Anne's MD 6/6/1765, English 33 C
   1.5 pounds, 5',
Evan Roberts, Joseph Chavier Queen Anne's MD 3/27/1766, English 34 (2nd escape) C
   11 days, Sunday, 2 pounds,
John Roberts, Richard James Kent DE 5/27/1736,
   5 pounds, (younger son)
John Roberts, Douglas Cambell Philadelphia PA ironworks 2/4/1752, 20
   11 days, Sunday, 2 pounds,
Robert Roberts, Richard James Kent DE 5/27/1736, 30
   5 pounds, (father)
Thomas Roberts, Ann Amos widow 7/3/1735, Welsh 22
   10 days, Monday, 2 pounds,
William Roberts, Peter Presly Northumberland VA 12/21/1738, English 23 shoemaker C
   39 days, Sunday, 3 pistoles,
William Roberts, Thomas Harrison Anne Arundel MD ironworks 6/18/1767, Welsh 26 C
   early June, 3 pounds, 5'9",
James Robertson, John Haines Philadelphia City PA joiner 4/29/1742, Scot 25 joiner
   24 days, Monday, 3 pounds,
James Robertson, Job Fallows Chester PA 8/19/1772, Irish 24 L
   10 days, Monday, 3 pounds, 5'6-7",
John Robertson, John Robert Holliday Baltimore MD 8/15/1771, 14 C
   22 days, Wednesday, 1.5 pounds, 4',
Nancy Robertson, William Heston Bucks PA 11/9/1785, Irish 22 (pregnant)
   8 days, Tuesday, 3 dollars, 5'2",
Richard Robertson, Nicholas Hieus Lancaster PA hatter 8/23/1764, Irish 20 hatter
   3 pounds, 5'5",
Charles Robeson, Peter Custer Montgomery PA 5/25/1796, 18
   16 days, Monday, 20 dollars, 5'7",
David Robeson, John Taylor Chester PA 7/19/1770, American 18 L
   7 days, Thursday, 2 pounds, 5'6",
John Robeson, Alexander Lowery Lancaster PA 8/17/1769, Irish 22
   2 pounds, 5'6",
John Robeson, John Hopkins Lancaster PA 3/19/1788, 16
   180 days, Friday, 2 dollars,
Malcolm Robeson, James Davis Philadelphia City PA 6/19/1746, Scot
   42 days, Thursday, 1 pound, short,
Samuel Robins, John Denton Hunterdon NJ 7/25/1771, 19 A
   108 days, Monday, 16 dollars, 5'6",
Agnes Robinson, William Heston Bucks PA 9/6/1786, Irish (female with 2 month old child)
   26 days, Friday, 0.03 pounds,
Andrew Robinson, Peter Dicks Chester PA 2/26/1751, Irish 20
   9 days, Tuesday, 3 pounds, middle, (arrived last summer)
James Robinson, Samuel McCall Philadelphia PA 6/15/1749, Scot 37
   12 days, Saturday, 3 pounds, (lately arrived)
James Robinson, Patrick Berret Lancaster PA 1/31/1765, Irish 30
   3 pounds, 5'6",
James Robinson, John Clark New Castle DE 7/5/1764, 35 soldier L
   56 days, Thursday, 12 dollars,
John Robinson, Thomas Rogers Chester PA 4/30/1741, Irish 18 weaver
   4 days, Sunday, 2 pounds, middle,
John Robinson, John Michael Philadelphia City PA 7/25/1754, 24 wigmaker
   13 days, Friday, 2 pounds, 5'9",

John Robinson, John Strawbridge Cecil MD 10/20/1768, English 22
    4 days, Sunday, 7 dollars, (arrived 3 weeks ago)
John Robinson, David Davis Winchester VA 2/6/1772, Irish 18
    35 days, Thursday, 5 pounds, short, (wears an iron collar)
John Robinson, John Creiner Lancaster PA brassfounder 4/3/1776, 22
    45 days, Monday, 20 dollars, 5'4",
Joseph Robinson, George Hargroves Baltimore MD 8/20/1752, Scot tailor
    49 days, Thursday, 2 pounds,
Matthew Robinson, William Robinson Chester PA 9/14/1774, 17 A
    17 days, Monday, 1 pound, 5',
Patrick Robinson, Patrick Dougherty Cecil MD 11/14/1754, 26 shoemaker
    2 pounds, 5'8",
Philip Robinson, James Allison Chester PA 6/18/1761, Irish 27
    11 days, Sunday, 1 pound, short,
Richard Robinson, Patrick Sim Prince George MD doctor 7/31/1735, tailor
    15 days, Wednesday, 8 pounds, short,
Thomas Robinson, Francis Farron Lancaster PA 5/19/1757, 18 chimneysweep
    6 weeks ago, 1 pound, 5',
Thomas Robinson, Daniel Pocock Baltimore MD 8/6/1752, English 30 C
    18 days, Sunday, 4 pistoles, tall,
Thomas Robson, Isham Randolph Philadelphia City PA ship captain 4/16/1748, sailor L
    2 pounds, 5'6",
Mary Roch, James Dunlap Salem NJ 9/2/1756, Irish 22
    13 days, Friday, 1.5 pounds,
John Roche, James Moore Chester PA storekeeper 11/30/1749, Irish
    23 days, Tuesday, 2 pounds, 5'6",
Henry Rock, John Henderson Monmouth NJ 12/15/1743, weaver
    2 pounds, tall,
John Rock, Owen Hugh Chester PA 12/22/1773, Welsh 17
    2 pounds, 5'6-7", (arrived Nov. 13, 1772)
Owen Rodgers, George McDowell Philadelphia City PA 9/20/1770, Irish 35
    6 dollars, 5'7",
Emanuel Rodrigues, Joseph Ball Burlington NJ ironworks 9/11/1776, Spanish 30
    16 days, Tuesday, 8 dollars, 5'6-7",
James Roe, Owen Owen Philadelphia City PA 6/20/1734, Irish 18
    2 days, Tuesday, 2 pounds, short,
James Roe, Owen Owen Philadelphia City PA 9/19/1734, Irish 18 (2nd escape)
    3 days, Monday, 2 pounds,
James Roe, Collin Ferguson Kent MD 4/3/1766, 35 tailor C
    2.5 pounds,
John Roe, Thomas Lindley Philadelphia City PA blacksmith 9/17/1730, 24 blacksmith
    3 days, Monday, 2 pounds,
John Roe, Thomas Lindley Philadelphia City PA blacksmith 5/4/1732, 25 blacksmith (2nd escape)
    5 days, Saturday, 1 pound,
Patrick Roe, Caleb Pierce Chester PA 7/12/1786, Irish 20 tailor
    3 days, Sunday, 8 dollars, 5'6-7", (arrived 10 months ago)
Thomas Roger, Christopher Huddy Philadelphia City PA ship captain 5/28/1741, 21 tailor
    6 days, Friday, 1.5 pounds, tall, (ran from ship)
Thomas Roger, James Franklin Baltimore MD ironworks 3/15/1775, English 30 C
    5 pounds, 5'10-11",
Abraham Rogers, James Reppeth Queen Anne's MD 4/20/1758, English 30 C
    22 days, Wednesday, 2 pounds, 5'8",
Grace Rogers, John Jacques New Castle DE 9/20/1759, Irish 30
    63 days, Thursday, 2 pounds, middle,
Grace Rogers, John Jacques New Castle DE 6/12/1760, Irish 31 (2nd escape)
    28 days, Thursday, 1.5 pounds, middle,
Hugh Rogers, Thomas Rigden Prince George MD 10/20/1773, Irish 21 carpenter
    5 pounds, 5'6-7", (arrived 1 year ago)
James Rogers, Conyngham & Nesbitt Philadelphia City PA merchant 10/3/1765, Irish 22 cutler
    2 pounds, 5'6", (ran from ship)
Margaret Rogers, Alice Dodd Philadelphia City PA 10/26/1752, American 14 A
    1 pound, tall,
Robert Rogers, James Williamson, Calvert MD 8/18/1737, carpenter
    5 pounds, short,
Sarah Rogers, Hugh Poulk Queen Anne's MD 1/2/1766, English breeches-maker C
    short,

Sarah Rogers, Hugh Poulk Queen Anne's MD 7/10/1766, English breeches-maker (2nd escape) C June, 2 pounds,
Stephen Rogers, Thomas Debroachbroom Queen Anne's MD 4/28/1768, English 30
  2 pounds, 5'6",
Thomas Rogers, Andrew Crawford Philadelphia PA 12/26/1752, Irish wigmaker
  9 days, Tuesday, 2.5 pounds, 5'11",
Thomas Rogers, James Bleake Kent MD 10/13/1757, English 25 C
  2 pistoles, 5'8",
John Rogharty, Hugh Patrick Lancaster PA 4/10/1746, 20
  15 days, Wednesday, 5 pounds,
John Rolf, Joseph Pemberton Jr Philadelphia City PA grazier 8/2/1775, English
  17 days, Monday, 4 dollars, 4'10",
John Rolison, David Davis Winchester VA 6/11/1772, Irish 18
  59 days, Monday, 3 pounds, short,
William Ronane, Joseph Hargrave Philadelphia PA 8/7/1735, 24
  3 days, Monday, 2 pounds, middle,
John Roney, John Jackson Cecil MD doctor 8/29/1745, Irish
  1 pound,
John Roney, John Cuthbert Chester PA 8/9/1744, Irish
  3 days, Monday, 2 pounds, short,
Thomas Roney, John Baldwin Cecil MD 8/29/1745, Irish 23
  1 pound,
William Roney, Moses Black Lancaster PA 10/11/1753, Irish 23
  8 days, Wednesday, 3 pounds, 5'6",
James Rood, Abraham Williams Philadelphia PA 9/4/1755, Irish 25
  5 days, Saturday, 1 pound,
Michael Roof, Joshua Shreve Burlington NJ 11/17/1773, German
  3 days, Monday, 6 dollars, (lately arrived)
Abraham Rooker, Benjamin Barton Philadelphia City PA chairmaker 8/16/1753, chairmaker
  3 days, Monday, 2 pounds, middle,
William Rooker, Joseph Lacey Chester PA 4/28/1773, 15
  9 days, Tuesday, 6 dollars, 5',
Bryan Rooney, Paul McNaught Chester PA 4/10/1766, Irish 24
  7 days, Thursday, 2 pounds, 5'9",
Henry Roosin, Leonard Vanfossen Montgomery PA 7/6/1796, 19 A
  16 dollars, 5'7",
Peter Rose, Benjamin Dawson St Mary's MD 8/23/1764, English painter
  92 days, Wednesday, 4 pistoles, middle,
George Rosenberger, Francis West Cumberland PA 6/11/1772, German 29
  3 pounds, 5'8-9", (arrived 5 months ago)
John Ross, John Mitchell Fredericksburg VA 10/9/1746, Scot
  67 days, Sunday, 2 pistoles,
John Ross, David Hacket Chester PA 5/8/1755, Irish 20
  8 days, Wednesday, 1.5 pounds, 5'6",
John Ross, William Brown Queen Anne's MD 7/26/1770, C
  16 days, Tuesday, 3 pounds, 6'4",
Jonathan Ross, Jacob Ritter Philadelphia PA 4/12/1770, 24 blacksmith A
  17 days, Monday, 1.5 pounds,
George Michael Rossmiller, George Dudt Northampton PA 2/18/1768,
  26 days, Saturday, 5 pounds, 5'4",
Conrad Rothhass, George G Woelpper Philadelphia City PA 2/1/1792, German 23 butcher
  3 days, Sunday, 3 pounds,
Thomas Roughman, Henry Bower York PA 9/15/1768,
  1.5 pounds,
Hugh Rouke, Joseph Grove Philadelphia PA 7/29/1742, Irish 18
  4 days, Sunday, 5 pounds, tall,
James Roult, David Davis Chester PA 6/30/1737, Irish 15 weaver
  7 days, Thursday, 1 pound, middle,
Robert Rouze, Roger Hiffernan Philadelphia City PA chocolate-grinder 3/25/1755, Irish 21
  6 days, Friday, 1.5 pounds, 5'9",
Dennis Rowan, John Blackburn Lancaster PA 11/23/1755, Irish 20
  16 days, Tuesday, 2 pounds, 5'8",
William Rowan, William Sutton New Castle DE 12/30/1762, English blacksmith L
  2 pounds, 5'6",
John Rowney, John Read Cecil MD 7/10/1755, Irish 22
  9 days, Tuesday, 3 pounds, tall,

Michael Royan, Joseph Mays Lancaster PA 5/25/1774, Irish
    13 days, Friday, 3 pounds, 5'5-6",
Dennis Roynane, Mark Alexander Baltimore MD 8/16/1770, Irish
    11 days, Sunday, 5 pounds, middle,
Robert Rozemon, John Jones Jr Bucks PA 8/14/1776, English 18
    2 pounds, 5',
Jacob Rozencrants, Henry Rees Philadelphia PA 9/27/1786, German 30 baker
    8 days, Tuesday, 7 dollars, 5'6", (arrived 1 year ago)
Edward Ruble, Gabriel Coppner Salem NJ 9/8/1757, Irish carpenter gaol sale L
    6 days, Friday, 2 pistoles, 5'5",
John Ruchan, James Richardson Chester PA 11/13/1755, Irish 22 mason L
    6 days, Friday, 2 pounds, 5'6",
Joseph Rudsdel, John Hallowell Philadelphia City PA shoemaker 9/11/1776, English
    0.5 pounds, 5',
Joseph Rue, William Baker Bucks PA 8/28/1746, 19 shoemaker A
    4 days, Sunday, 2 pounds, middle,
Joshua Rue, John Lewis Kent MD 5/7/1772, American 17 millwright A
    4 dollars, 5'6",
Lewis Rue, Anthony Wright Philadelphia City PA shoemaker 9/22/1773, 17 A
    4 dollars, 5'4",
Abraham Ruker, Benjamin Barton Philadelphia City PA chairmaker 3/6/1753, Irish 24
    2 days, Tuesday, 2 pounds, 5'6",
Thomas Rumford, Henry Guest Salem NJ 4/17/1782, 18 A
    17 days, Sunday, 8 dollars, 5',
Peter Rundles, Samuel Kennedy Chester PA doctor 3/5/1777, Irish 15
    8 dollars, 5'2",
Peter Runey, James Thompson Lancaster PA 6/14/1770, Irish 20 (2nd escape)
    7 days, Thursday, 2 pounds, 5'10",
Peter Runey, James Thompson Lancaster PA 3/22/1770, Irish 20
    13 days, Friday, 2 pounds, 5'10",
Thomas Russel, Justus Rubenkam Bucks PA 10/4/1786, 20 A
    9 days, Monday, 0.03 pounds, 5'7",
William Russel, John Junkens Cumberland PA 6/23/1768, 22 pipemaker
    3 pounds, 5'9",
James Russell, William Fitzhugh Calvert MD 7/24/1766, English baker
    2.5 pounds, 5',
William Russell, Sutton Burgan Kent MD 6/20/1751, English physician
    3 pounds, middle,
James Ruth, Charles Clunn Salem NJ 9/27/1780, 11 A
    25 days, Saturday, 1 dollars,
Jane Rutliff, Joseph Kemble Philadelphia PA 5/5/1763, 17
    9 days, Tuesday, 3 pounds,
John Rutter, Philip Yost Montgomery PA 8/1/1787, 19 wheelwright A
    13 days, Thursday, 8 dollars,
Daniel Ryan, John Hackett Chester PA 11/14/1745, Irish 26
    21 days, Thursday, 2 pounds,
Dennis Ryan, John Miller Lancaster PA 2/2/1748, Irish 18
    3 days, Monday, 3 pounds, middle,
James Ryan, James McLachlan Kent MD 8/22/1754, Irish
    8 days, Wednesday, 1.5 pounds,
John Ryan, John Williamson Chester PA fuller 7/3/1740, Irish 18
    8 days, Wednesday, 3 pounds, middle,
John Ryan, Thomas Ebtharp Cecil MD 10/31/1745, Irish 21
    4 days, Sunday, 5 pounds, short,
John Ryan, Amos Garrett Baltimore MD 5/14/1747, Irish 23 (2nd escape)
    10 days, Monday, 1.5 pounds, short,
John Ryan, Seth Pancoast Chester PA 3/31/1773, Irish 20
    4 days, Sunday, 1.5 pounds, 5'8-9", (arrived 10 months ago)
John Ryan, Jacob Bear Lancaster PA 9/30/1772, Irish 20 cooper
    11 days, Sunday, 5'10", (has 1 year to serve)
John Ryan, Curtis Grubb Lancaster PA ironworks 9/1/1773, Irish 17
    22 days, Wednesday, 7 dollars, 5'9-10",
John Ryan, Caleb Parry Philadelphia PA 5/29/1776, Irish 17
    8 dollars, 5'6-7", (has 4 years left to serve)
John Ryan, Cornelius Devenny New Castle DE 11/19/1767, Irish 30 gaol sale L
    23 days, Tuesday, 2.5 pounds, 5'6-7",

Michael Ryan, Francis Dawes Baltimore MD 9/29/1784, Irish 20 shoemaker
    13 days, Thursday, 15 pounds, 5'6",
Richard Ryan, Morris Cones New Castle DE 3/4/1762, 30
    14 days, Thursday, 5 pounds, 6',
Richard Ryan, William Vogan Lancaster PA weaver 12/6/1759, Irish
    6 days, Friday, 3 pounds, 5'10",
Thomas Ryan, Henry Bishop New Castle DE 3/28/1751, Irish 22
    9 days, Tuesday, 1.5 pounds, 5'6",
Thomas Ryan, Henry Bishop New Castle DE 9/12/1751, Irish 22 (2nd escape)
    4 days, Sunday, 1.5 pounds, 5'6",
Thomas Ryan, Carsan & Barclay & Mitchell Philadelphia City PA 9/18/1766, Irish 21
    9 days, Tuesday, 2 pounds, 5'9", (ran from ship, lately arrived)
William Ryan, Robert Williamson Philadelphia City PA ship captain 9/25/1740, shoemaker
    6 days, Friday, 1 pounds, (elderly)
William Ryan, Robert McFelly Lancaster PA 7/16/1752, Irish 24 tailor
    3 pounds, 5'8",
William Ryan, John Singleton York PA 12/22/1763, Irish 50
    46 days, Sunday, 2 pounds, 5'7", (arrived last summer)
Bryan Ryley, George Walker Chester PA 1/28/1746, Irish 18
    4 days, Sunday, 1 pound, short,
John Ryley, John Michener Philadelphia PA 11/3/1748, Irish 20
    4 days, Sunday, 3 pounds, middle,
Edward Rylot, Edward Stevenson Frederick MD 3/12/1772, 27
    4 pounds, 5'6-7",
John Ryne, Thomas Morton Burlington NJ 6/1/1769, Irish 22
    2 pounds, 5'6-7",
John Ryon, Curtis Grubb Lancaster PA ironworks 6/28/1775, Irish 20
    9 days, Tuesday, 6 dollars, 5'10-11",
Richard Sadler, William Buckland Anne Arundel MD 4/20/1774, Irish 35
    18 days, Sunday, 5 pounds, 5'9-10",
Benjamin Sagers, Aweray Richardson Baltimore MD 9/6/1775, English blacksmith C
    10 pounds, 5'11",
Dennis Salmon, Mary Grubb Chester PA 4/14/1768, Irish 21 schoolmaster
    8 days, Wednesday, 10 pounds, 5'7-8",
George Salmon, Nathan Chapman Stafford VA ironworks 4/16/1748, Scot 23
    6 days, Friday, 2 pistoles, middle,
Thomas Saltar, Rowland Evans Philadelphia PA 5/1/1776, English gardener
    9 days, Tuesday, 3 pounds, middle,
Samuel Salter, Alexander Lawson Baltimore MD ironworks 4/3/1746, C
    5 pounds, short,
Thomas Salter, Benjamin Meve Cecil MD 12/23/1772, American 42 L
    20 days, Friday, 2 pounds, 6',
Elizabeth Samford, Jeremiah JB Lancaster PA 8/26/1756, Irish 34
    mid-July, 1 pistole,
Edward Sampson, Joseph Wright Lancaster PA tailor 8/26/1742, 23 tailor
    9 days, Tuesday, 2 pounds,
John Sandels, Michael Earle Cecil MD 4/17/1766, English 28 (ran before) C
    8 days, Wednesday, 5 pounds,
William Sanders, William Pennell Chester PA 6/6/1765, English 22
    3 pounds, 5'9",
Joseph Sandimont, Joseph Hayes Chester PA 7/10/1732, 19 glover
    2 pounds, middle,
William Sandorn, Thomas Barnsley Bucks PA 8/14/1766, English 18
    3 pounds, 5'5",
James Sanns, George Wells Philadelphia City PA shipwright 4/24/1760, Irish 23 A
    2 days, Tuesday, 2 pounds, 5'7",
Anne Saul, Samuel Glarson Chester PA 7/19/1770, Irish 22
    39 days, Sunday, 5 dollars, middle, (arrived 2 years ago)
Richard Saunders, Christopher Ruth Queen Anne's MD 6/27/1754, English 20
    8 days, Wednesday, 2.5 pounds,
George Saunderson, Nathaniel Potts 10/10/1751, English 19
    11 days, Sunday, 2 pounds,
Joseph Savage, Roger Coleman Kent MD 3/12/1751,
    9 days, Tuesday, 1 pound, 5'8",
Patrick Savage, Henry Weaver Lancaster PA 4/25/1771, Irish 25
    10 days, Monday, 5 pounds,

Richard Savage, Joseph Kelly Bucks PA 6/4/1747, Irish 25
    11 days, Sunday, 2 pounds,
Zenus Savige, John Hide Philadelphia City PA 7/23/1783, 16 A
    3 pounds,
Anne Sawyer, Anne Milton Kent MD 10/13/1757, English (pregnant)
    1 pistole, short,
Charles Sawyer, Thomas Price Anne Arundel MD 4/20/1774, English 21 bricklayer C
    14 days, Thursday, 5 dollars, 5'7-8",
Michael Sax, Barnard Stroup Northampton PA 4/15/1756, German 15
    5 days, Saturday, 2 pounds, middle,
George Say, Henry Stiegal Berks PA ironworks 5/9/1765, joiner
    17 days, Monday, 2 pistoles, (arrived last fall)
Patrick Scandlon, William Dunwodie Chester PA 10/13/1768, Irish 19
    9 days, Tuesday, 2 pounds,
John Scanlan, Samuel Carson Philadelphia City PA 8/18/1773, Irish wool comber
    25 days, Sunday, 3 pounds, 5'4", (lately arrived)
Timothy Scannell, William Spafford Philadelphia City PA 7/28/1748, Irish
    1 pound, short,
Henry Schaeffer, Peter Hassenclever EJ ironworks 6/12/1766, German 38 miner
    14 days, Thursday, 5 pounds, 5'6", (under a 3 year 4 month contract, imported)
John Godippe Schammer, Amos George Philadelphia PA 7/26/1775, German 21 tanner
    3 days, Monday, 2.5 pounds, 5'6-7",
Augustus Schatton, Wallace & Donaldson Philadelphia City PA 11/17/1784, German
    2.5 pounds, 5'8", (ran from ship)
Cornelius Schawn, Michael Willcox Dorchester MD 1/26/1774, American L
    20 days, Friday, 2 pounds, 5',
Alexander Scheetz, Christopher Robins 10/31/1751, German
    4 pounds,
Nicholas Schendler, Matthew Ray Philadelphia PA 6/5/1755, German 17
    4 days, Sunday, 5 pounds, short,
John Erhard Schlagel, William Oakford Salem NJ 5/28/1767, German 30
    11 days, Sunday, 1.5 pounds, 5'7",
Henry Schoup, John Jones Philadelphia PA 5/28/1772, German 20 tanner
    4 days, Sunday, 12 dollars, 6',
Zechariah Schub, Joseph Kenderdine Philadelphia PA 5/29/1755, German 16
    10 days, Monday, 2 pounds, 5',
John Christian Schur, Peter Heisler 2/15/1792, German 19
    103 days, Friday, 4 dollars, 5'4",
Johan Schuter, Jasper Poleson New Castle DE 5/3/1753, German 48
    10 days, Monday, 1.5 pounds, middle,
John Christopher Schutts, Caleb Evans Philadelphia City PA blacksmith 8/16/1759, German
    3 pounds, 5'6",
George Schwartz, Lewis Klotz Northampton PA 5/27/1762, American 17 A
    10 pounds, tall,
Thomas Scoffield, Nathan Hoopes Chester PA 9/6/1753, English 40 weaver
    3 days, Monday, 2 pounds, 5'10",
John Scollay, Robert McConaughy Chester PA 4/5/1770, Scot school teacher
    31 days, Monday, 5 pounds, 5'7-8",
Andrew Scott, Phillip Moore Delaware PA 11/23/1791, 20
    4 dollars, 5'6-7",
Evans Scott, Smith Bowen 3/23/1796, 17
    8 dollars,
Henry Scott, Andrew McDowell Chester PA 8/18/1763, 25 weaver
    66 days, Monday, 3 pounds, 5'10",
Jane Scott, Alexander Johnston Chester PA 8/1/1765, Irish 20
    2 pounds, middle, (imported)
Jennet Scott, John Baldwin Chester PA 9/2/1772, Irish 20
    14 days, Thursday, 4 dollars, middle,
Robert Scott, John Kirkpatrick Chester PA 8/13/1752, 30
    6 days, Friday, 4 pounds, middle,
Samuel Scotten, Benjamin Bradford Cecil MD doctor 5/7/1741, English 20
    5 days, Saturday, 1 pound,
Hannah Dorothy Scouss, James Sexton Monmouth NJ 8/23/1759, German
    2 pounds,
John Scully, John Boyle Philadelphia City PA 6/29/1769, Irish 21
    11 days, Sunday, 3 dollars, 5'8", (ran from ship)

Henry Seabrand, James Gillespie Lancaster PA 12/12/1754, German 30
   3 pounds, 5'10",
Samuel Searson, Francis Phillips Baltimore MD ironworks 1/8/1767, 29 wheelwright C
   11 days, Sunday, 10 pounds, 5'9",
Richard Sebley, William Hemphill New Castle DE 6/1/1769, English woman's heel-maker
   16 days, Tuesday, 2.5 pounds, 5'4",
John Sedimon, Lodowick Debler Philadelphia PA 12/27/1739, German 17
   8 days, Wednesday, 3 pounds, middle,
William Seers, Boaz Boyce New Castle DE 6/6/1751, 20 weaver A
   1 pound,
Michael Seitz, John Baus Philadelphia City PA tavern-keeper 3/17/1768, German 40
   21 days, Thursday, 3 pounds,
Sarah Sembler, Nathaniel Grubb Chester PA 11/18/1736, English 25
   11 days, Sunday, 2 pounds, short,
Arthur Sennet, Thomas Reading Hunterdon NJ 6/11/1767, Irish 19 sailor
   12 days, Saturday, 2 pounds, 5'4-5",
Robert Sentry, Daniel Cook Cecil MD 11/30/1732,
   4 days, Sunday, 3 pounds, tall,
Matthew Serone, Joseph Bell Burlington NJ ironworks 7/5/1775, French 28
   10 days, Monday, 5 dollars, 5'7-8",
Lewis Seybell, Frederick Detz Philadelphia City PA 8/13/1767, 18 tailor A
   3 dollars, 5'6-7",
George Seymour, Joseph Watkins Anne Arundel MD ironworks 7/22/1762, English 50 C
   7 days, Thursday, 4 pounds, 6', (arrived in 1759)
George Seymour, Joseph Watkins Anne Arundel MD ironworks 9/23/1762, English 50 (2nd esc) C
   4 pounds, 6', (arrived in 1759)
Christian Shade, George Evans Philadelphia PA 12/15/1763,
   5 days, Saturday, 3 pounds, 5'7",
Elizabeth Shae, Thomas Johnson Worcester MD 7/16/1788, Irish 26
   65 days, Monday, 1.5 pounds, 5'4", (wife to John Shae)
John Shae, Thomas Johnson Worcester MD 7/16/1788, Irish 30
   65 days, Monday, 1.5 pounds, 5'6-7",
Henry Shafter, John Chamberlin New Castle DE 1/3/1749, English shoemaker
   27 days, Friday, 1.5 pounds,
Daniel Shanahan, Matthew McCling Lancaster PA 5/10/1775, Irish 24
   10 days, Monday, 4 dollars, 5'7-8",
James Shank, David Thomson Philadelphia City PA shipbuilder 9/4/1766, English 20 A
   4 days, Sunday, 5 pounds, 5'4',
Edward Shannahon, Bryan O'Mara Philadelphia City PA 3/1/1775, Irish 19 barber
   9 days, Tuesday, 4 dollars, 5'4", (arrived last fall)
Edward Shannon, Valentine Honey Queen Anne's MD 6/28/1753, Irish 22
   15 days, Wednesday, 1.5 pounds, 5'8",
James Shannon, Benjamin Jackson Philadelphia City PA 6/21/1759, Irish 18
   14 days, Thursday, 5 pounds, 5'6",
John Shannon, John King Philadelphia City PA 12/2/1762, English
   2 pounds, 5'10",
John Shannon, Benjamin Reynolds Chester PA 5/1/1776, Irish 16
   16 days, Tuesday, 3 dollars, 5'6",
William Shannon, John Shellenberg Lancaster PA 8/17/1769, Irish 24 L
   7 days, Thursday, 8 dollars, 5'8-9", (arrived 4 years ago)
Andrew Sharp, James Hill Chester PA 6/16/1784, Irish 18 blacksmith
   210 days, Tuesday, 10 dollars, 5'4-5", (arrived last fall)
Joseph Sharp, William Downs Gloucester NJ 6/9/1768, 18 A
   2 pounds, 5'10",
Margaret Sharp, Jacob Bough Chester PA 9/3/1777, 13
   29 days, Wednesday, 6 dollars,
Thomas Sharp, William Smithson Harford MD 5/3/1775, English 15
   39 days, Sunday, 3 pounds, 5'3",
Robert Sharpless, Thomas Harris Queen Anne's MD 7/1/1756, Irish
   mid-May, 5 pounds, 5'10",
Jacob Sharrots, Joseph Few Chester PA 10/5/1758, German 17
   8 days, Wednesday, 1.5 pounds, short,
Tobias Shaubhut, William Wood Philadelphia City PA tailor 11/15/1786, German 25 tailor
   3 days, Sunday, 4 dollars, 5'7", (lately arrived)
Alexander Shaw, William Turner Philadelphia PA 9/25/1776, Scot 18
   4 dollars,

Ann Shaw, Isaac Taylor Chester PA 6/4/1772,
  30 days, Tuesday, 1 pound,
Henry Shaw, Richard Osburn Loudoun VA 9/7/1774, Irish shoemaker
  4 pounds,
John Shaw, Richard Sparks Salem NJ 3/31/1763, 16
  7 days, Thursday, 1.5 pounds,
Margaret Shaw, Anthony Hull Philadelphia City PA 4/21/1763, 40
  11 days, Sunday, 1 pound,
Timothy Shaw, Daniel Hughes Frederick MD ironworks 8/3/1774, Irish 35 C
  15 days, Wednesday, 3 pounds, 5'5", (arrived 1 month ago)
Matthew Shea, David Davis Philadelphia PA 9/25/1766, Irish 18
  4 days, Sunday, 2 pounds, 5'3",
Adam Frederick Sheaffer, Phillip Hahn Montgomery PA 7/7/1790, German 23
  10 days, Sunday, 10 dollars, 5'6", (arrived 20 months ago)
John Shealine, Joseph Jenkins Lancaster PA 8/19/1772, Irish 21
  5 pounds, 5'7-8",
James Shearer, Thomas Cummins Chester PA 8/15/1787, Irish 25
  9 days, Monday, 6 dollars, 5'6", (lately arrived, been in the colonies before)
John Shee, William Bell Chester PA 8/26/1772, Irish 45
  18 days, Sunday, 5 pounds, 5'6-7",
Richard Shee, Robert Way Chester PA 4/26/1770, Irish 40
  4 days, Sunday, 3 pounds, 5'8-10",
James Sheeby, David Morgan Lancaster PA 8/29/1771, Irish
  3 pounds, 5'7-8", (lately arrived)
John Sheehan, Samuel Means New Castle DE 2/4/1768, Irish 18
  4 days, Sunday, 3 pounds, 5'8", (arrived last fall)
John Sheehan, William Clenrey New Castle DE 3/28/1771, Irish 20 (2nd escape)
  27 days, Friday, 4 dollars, 5'10-11",
Patrick Sheeren, Joseph Johnson Philadelphia PA 2/27/1766, Irish 23 school teacher
  8 days, Wednesday, 1.5 pounds, 5'3-4",
Patrick Sheeren, Barnard Criet Philadelphia City PA 5/1/1766, Irish 23 school teacher (2nd escape)
  8 days, Wednesday, 3 pounds, 5'3-4",
John Sheerlock, Alexander Lawson Baltimore MD ironworks 5/29/1746, Irish 25
  8 days, Wednesday, 3 pounds, 5'8",
Robert Sheils, Peter Presly Northumberland VA 12/21/1738, English 26 gardener C
  39 days, Sunday, 3 pistoles,
John Sheldon, John Forwood Baltimore MD 1/6/1773, English 30 nailer C
  162 days, Wednesday, 2 pounds, 6',
John Sheller, William Eckhar 10/6/1773, German chimneysweep
  11 days, Sunday, 6 pounds, 6'2", (arrived this year)
John William Shelock, Isaac Budd Burlington NJ 8/20/1777, German 30
  15 dollars, 5'8-9",
John Shelton, John Downs Queen Anne's MD 2/18/1762, English 25 L
  26 days, Saturday, 1 pound, short,
Mary Shemfessel, Lewis Farmer Philadelphia City PA 6/4/1772, German 17
  0.1 pounds, 5',
John Shepard, Thomas Elliot Baltimore MD 10/17/1765, English 30 C
  42 days, Thursday, 1 pound, 5'10",
Jane Shepherd, Michael Swoope York PA 10/5/1774, Irish 19
  9 days, Tuesday, 1 pound, 5'5-6",
Jane Shepherd, Michael Swoope York PA 7/19/1775, Irish 20 (2nd escape)
  27 days, Friday, 1.5 pounds,
Jane Shepherd, Jacob Double York PA 7/31/1776, Irish 21 (3rd escape)
  31 days, Monday, 3 pounds, 5'3",
William Sheppard, Unlisted Name Philadelphia City PA 9/11/1766, Irish 18
  6 days, Friday, 1.5 pounds, 5'4-5", (arrived last spring)
Benjamin Shepperd, James Haldawe 4/15/1762, 18 (ran before) A
  22 days, Wednesday, 2 pounds, 5'9",
Nathaniel Shepperd, Jonathan Malsbary Burlington NJ 12/28/1774, American 25 L
  9 days, Tuesday, 4 dollars, 5'4",
John Sherff, William Connell Philadelphia City PA 8/23/1775, German 26 cabinetmaker
  21 days, Thursday, 5'8-9", (arrived last fall)
John Sheridan, George Flemming Lancaster PA 7/3/1760, Irish 28
  8 days, Wednesday, 5 pounds, 5'11",
Thomas Sheridan, John Manning Dorchester MD 12/23/1772, Irish 19
  10 days, Monday, 6 dollars, 5'8-9",

Matthew Sherone, Joseph Ball Burlington NJ ironworks 9/11/1776, French 30 shoemaker (ran before)
    16 days, Tuesday, 8 dollars, 5'7-8",
Patrick Sherradon, Caleb Cowsland Chester PA 10/6/1737, Irish 26
    15 days, Wednesday, 5 pounds, tall, (arrived 3 months ago)
William Sherrett, Peter Lawrence Philadelphia City PA 8/6/1747, A
    4 days, Sunday, 2 pounds,
Henry Sherwood, Charles Ridgely Jr Baltimore MD ironworks 7/23/1752, 23 tailor
    13 days, Friday, 2.5 pounds, middle,
Tobias Shewen, James Steel 5/27/1736, 23
    9 days, Tuesday, middle,
Donald Shields, John McCullough Lancaster PA 10/25/1775, Irish 18
    50 days, Wednesday, 1 pound, 5'5-6",
John Shields, Samuel McAlbany Chester PA 9/2/1742, Irish
    4 days, Sunday, 2 pounds,
John Shields, John Dorsey Anne Arundel MD 9/13/1770, Scot 30 C
    31 days, Monday, 20 dollars, 5'8-9",
Patrick Shields, Theophilus Alexander Cecil MD 10/31/1754, Irish 20
    11 days, Sunday, 2 pounds, (arrived 6 weeks ago)
John Shimmin, William Smith Philadelphia City PA 9/27/1775, 15 A
    6 days, Friday, 0.05 pounds,
Mary Shingleton, Jane Davis 6/22/1774, 17
    8 days, Wednesday, 0.25 pounds,
Gamahiel Shinn, Benjamin Gibbs Jr Philadelphia City PA 9/18/1755, 17 A
    4 days, Sunday, 1 pistole, 5'5",
Michael Shiram, William Smith Cumberland PA 10/9/1755, German 30 nailsmith
    about 2 months ago, 2 pistoles, 5'5",
Rueben Shoar, Manasses Woods Bucks PA 5/8/1740, English 22
    7 days, Thursday, 2 pounds, short,
Matthew Shoe, Daniel Davis Philadelphia PA 10/11/1764, Irish 17
    10 days, Monday, 2.5 pounds, 5'2",
Richard Shoe, Joseph Mitchell Philadelphia City PA merchant 3/20/1766, Irish 26 baker
    end of Oct., 6 dollars,
John Shoemaker, Valentine Hagner Philadelphia City PA cooper 7/2/1761, German-American 16 A
    5 days, Saturday, 5 pounds,
Thomas Sholl, William Pott Berks PA 11/24/1763, German 23
    11 days, Sunday, 2 pounds, 5'9", (lately arrived)
Timothy Shoogle, Joseph Bond Bucks PA 12/10/1741, Irish 16
    9 days, Tuesday, 1 pound, short,
John Shoppley, Marmaduke Tilden Kent MD 6/7/1750, American shoemaker L
    3 pounds, tall,
Catherine Short, William Anderson Philadelphia City PA 3/29/1786, 18
    8 dollars,
William Shorter, John Righter Philadelphia PA 8/21/1776, English 19 sailor
    38 days, Monday, 1.5 pounds, 5'4-5", (use to the sea)
Benjamin Shotton, Thomas Smyth Kent MD 7/22/1756, shoemaker (ran 2 times before) C
    2 pistoles, 5'8",
George Shriner, Michael Brand Philadelphia PA 11/16/1749, German 22
    15 days, Wednesday, 4 pounds, short,
Benjamin Shriver, John Gorgas Philadelphia PA 12/27/1786, 20 A
    24 days, Sunday, 0.1 pounds, 5'7-8",
John George Shubart, Conrad Haass 10/5/1785, German 30 baker
    3 days, Sunday, 3 pounds, 5'4-5",
John Shupaid, John Brown Cecil MD 12/15/1757, English 23 gardener
    24 days, Monday, 2 pounds, 5',
John Henry Sickman, John Potts 9/5/1751, German
    1.5 pounds,
William Siddon, Elijah Weed 7/18/1765, 17 shoemaker A
    29 days, Wednesday, 6 dollars, 5'5",
Michael Siebenlist, Lewis Farmer Philadelphia PA 4/9/1794, German 19
    17 days, Sunday, 30 dollars, 5'6",
Christian Signetz, Joseph Cauffman Philadelphia City PA 9/4/1776, German 45 butcher L
    3 days, Monday, 2 pounds, 5'4",
George Silchnitter, Conrad Wagner Philadelphia PA 7/23/1777, German 14
    4 dollars,
Jacob Silcocks, Jacob Myers Baltimore MD 3/14/1771, English 21 C
    5 pounds, 5'7",

William Siltz, Samuel Flower Philadelphia City PA 8/24/1769, German 17 driver
    4 days, Sunday, 1.5 pounds, 5'6",
William Silvene, Kinvin Wreth Kent MD 8/27/1752, English
    2.5 pounds, short,
Joseph Simmonds, John Boham Lancaster PA 12/26/1752, English 20 brickmaker
    (no other information)
Thomas Simmonds, Charles Christie Baltimore MD 7/10/1755, English
    11 days, Sunday, 3 pistoles, 6', (use to the sea)
Isaac Simmons, Jacob Kaiser Philadelphia City PA tailor 7/21/1768, English shoemaker
    1 pound, 5', (use to the sea)
Isaac Simmons, Michael Righterbook Philadelphia PA 12/22/1768, English 19 shoemaker (2nd esc)
    2.5 pounds, 5',
John Simmons, Daniel Harkens York PA 2/15/1775, English 25
    12 days, Saturday, 8 dollars, 5'6-7",
Joseph Simmons, Joseph Hackney Burlington NJ 4/2/1752, Irish 18
    25 days, Sunday, 2 pounds, middle,
Joseph Simmons, Thomas Davis Cecil MD 7/12/1753, 19
    8 days, Wednesday, 5 pounds, short,
Thomas Simmons, John Ensor Jr Baltimore MD 4/25/1765, English 27 C
    10 pounds, 5'8",
William Simmons, Edward Parrish 8/31/1758, English 30 bricklayer
    9 days, Tuesday, 5 pounds, 5'8",
John Simms, John Howard Anne Arundel MD 10/28/1742, 30 C
    32 days, Sunday, 3 pounds,
Edwards Simons, William Fisher 7/19/1753, buttonmaker
    2 pounds, 6',
Henry Simons, Conrad Kotts Hunterdon NJ 12/3/1767, Irish tailor
    13 days, Friday, 4 dollars, 5'6",
Mary Simonton, Isaac Tremble Chester PA 2/15/1775, Irish 26
    17 days, Monday, 1 pound, 5'3-4",
George Simpson, Corbin Lee Baltimore MD ironworks 7/9/1767, Scot
    19 days, Saturday, 20 pistoles, 5',
John Simpson, John Lloyd Chester PA 9/21/1774, Irish 19
    8 days, Wednesday, 2 pounds, 5'8-9",
John Simpson, Benjamin Lloyd Philadelphia City PA 12/14/1774, Irish 19 (2nd escape)
    9 days, Tuesday, 3 dollars, 5'8-9",
Samuel Simpson, Joseph Cobourn Chester PA 7/30/1767, 12
    44 days, Tuesday, 1 pound,
Thomas Simpson, James Ager Baltimore MD 4/26/1764, English
    17 days, Monday, 2 pounds, 5'8",
Thomas Simpson, Thomas Maybury Philadelphia PA 7/26/1775, English 18 shoemaker
    8 days, Wednesday, 3 pounds, 5',
William Harrison Simpson, Benjamin Rambo Gloucester NJ 7/29/1772, 19 joiner A
    8 days, Wednesday, 4 dollars,
James Sims, Mathias Vanhorne Burlington NJ 1/7/1755, 40
    19 days, Saturday, 3 pounds, tall,
John Sims, Robert Moorehead Lancaster PA 4/13/1774, Irish-American 18 L
    13 days, Friday, 2 pounds, 5',
John Sims, James Moorehead Lancaster PA 5/18/1774, Irish-American 18 (2nd escape) L
    4 dollars, 5',
William Sims, Thomas Beare Philadelphia City PA ship captain 12/19/1752, Scot 25
    1.5 pounds, 5'4", (use to the sea)
Alexander Simson, Thomas Stewart Augusta VA 4/11/1765, Scot 45 bookbinder
    2 pounds, short,
John Simson, Benjamin Lloyd Philadelphia City PA 3/8/1775, Irish 19
    9 days, Tuesday, 1 pound, 5'7-8",
William Simson, Archibald Home Hunterdon NJ 12/2/1742, 30
    5 days, Saturday, 2 pounds, short,
James Singeword, Benjamin Tasker Baltimore MD ironworks 5/15/1760, English 30 C
    18 days, Sunday, 4 pounds, middle, (arrived this year)
Philip Sinloup, John Potter Chester PA 4/11/1754, German 40
    4 days, Sunday, 2 pounds, 5'6",
John Size, Bartholomew Tims Chester PA 1/31/1760, 17 weaver
    2 pounds, 5'6",
Charles Skaddock, Samuel Hanson Charles MD 7/8/1742, 26 C
    67 days, Sunday, 3 MD pounds, tall,

William Skanlon, Thomas Clark New Castle DE 11/12/1741, Irish 20
    9 days, Tuesday, 1.5 pounds, tall,
Dennis Skeban, Robert Taylor Hunterdon NJ 4/6/1769, American 27 millwright L
    40 days, Saturday, 5 pounds, 5'8",
Ann Skilling, Robert Gordon Hall 9/6/1775, Irish
    11 days, Sunday, middle, (lately arrived)
John Skinner, Jonathan Stout Monmouth NJ 9/18/1755, English shoemaker
    26 days, Saturday, 2 pounds, 6',
Elizabeth Skit, Daniel Prichard Bucks PA 11/2/1728,
    2 pounds, short,
Michael Slainey, John White Baltimore MD 9/26/1751, Irish miller
    19 days, Saturday, 10 pounds,
John Slater, Samuel Levis Chester PA 12/6/1775, English 18
    25 days, Sunday, 1 pound, 5'4",
Patrick Slavin, John Kerlin Chester PA 3/6/1760, Irish
    6 days, Friday, 2 pounds, short,
John Sleighuff, Jacob Stroun Philadelphia PA 6/11/1794, 17 wheelwright A
    3 days, Sunday, 4 dollars, 5'5",
Patrick Slevan, David Scott Cumberland PA 8/13/1752, Irish 25
    10 days, Monday, 3 pistoles, 5'6",
Margaret Sliter, David Elder Cecil MD 5/21/1761, English 28
    2.5 pounds,
Elizabeth Slomage, John Butler Bucks PA 3/8/1759, German (7 months pregnant)
    66 days, Monday, 5',
Betty Slone, William Read New Castle DE 2/17/1773, Irish 20
    15 days, Wednesday, 1 pound, middle,
Michael Slusser, Jacob Gongaware Northampton PA constable 9/14/1791, tailor
    6 pounds, 6'6",
Christopher Slyder, Solomon Stockdale Baltimore MD 6/27/1765, American 35 L
    4 pounds, 5'6",
John Slye, John Graham Chester PA 6/23/1768, American 37 L
    12 days, Saturday, 3 pounds, 5'6",
Timothy Smally, Thomas Jurey Kent MD 6/11/1772, English 35
    25 days, Sunday, 1.5 pounds, 4'10",
James Smart, Thomas Johnson Baltimore MD 1/20/1757, C
    18 days, Sunday, 1.5 pounds, 5'6", (arrived 6 months ago)
William Smart, William Ditto Baltimore MD 8/22/1771, English 22 waggoner C
    18 days, Sunday, 1.5 pounds,
Andrew Smith, Robert Horner Charles MD 5/19/1748, (rebel)
    18 days, Sunday, 2.5 pounds, 5'4",
Ann Smith, Thomas Stalker Philadelphia PA 10/9/1760, German
    34 days, Friday, 1.5 pounds, (mother lives in Philadelphia)
Benjamin Smith, John Summerl Salem NJ 6/2/1773, tailor
    3 days, Monday, 1.5 pounds,
Betsy Smith, Jacob Bunner Philadelphia City PA 8/9/1775, English 17
    4 days, Sunday, 2 dollars,
Catherine Smith, Thomas Smith Lancaster PA ironworks 12/2/1762, Irish 25
    2 pounds, middle,
Catherine Smith, John Ellis Berks PA 10/1/1767, Irish 24
    17 days, Monday, 1.5 pounds, short,
Charles Smith, Peter Grubb Lancaster PA ironworks 2/2/1743, English 20 blacksmith
    10 days, Monday, 2.5 pounds, middle,
Christian Smith, William Lawrence Gloucester NJ 6/23/1773, German
    6 days, Friday, 5 pounds, 5'2-3",
Clement Smith, Daniel Thomas Philadelphia PA 6/8/1796, 18 A
    15 days, Tuesday, 10 dollars, 5'7-8",
Constart Smith, Joseph Harker Gloucester NJ 7/30/1794, American 20 A
    4 days, Saturday, 6 dollars, 5'7-8",
Cornelius Smith, John Milegan York PA 6/21/1759, L
    9 days, Tuesday, 5 pounds, 5'8",
David Smith, Jedediah Allen Salem NJ 3/10/1773, 20
    7 days, Thursday, 2 dollars, 5'7-8",
Edward Smith, James Chambers Charles MD 11/6/1760, L
    5'6",
George Smith, John Baldwin Chester PA 4/23/1730, 21
    4 days, Sunday, 5 pounds, middle,

George Smith, James Ager Baltimore MD 4/26/1764, English
    17 days, Monday, 2 pounds, 6',
George Smith, William Prosser Salem NJ 12/27/1786, shoemaker
    2 days, Monday, 20 dollars, 5'6",
George Smith, Ellis Gill Northumberland VA 12/1/1743, Irish 45 blacksmith C
    108 days, Monday, 10 pistoles, 5'6",
Henry Smith, William Buckley Bucks PA 12/12/1754, English
    4 days, Sunday, 2 pounds, short, (arrived last fall)
Henry Smith, William Peters Chester PA 8/8/1765, English 24 wheelwright
    4 days, Sunday, 3 pounds, 5'7-8",
Henry Smith, William Peters Chester PA 5/15/1766, English 25 wheelwright (2nd escape)
    11 days, Sunday, 5 pounds, 5'7-8",
Henry Smith, William Peters Chester PA 4/7/1768, English 26 wheelwright (3rd escape)
    8 days, Wednesday, 10 pounds, 5'7-8",
Henry Smith, Andrew Ball Cecil MD 3/5/1761, German wagon driver gaol sale L
    17 days, Monday, 2 pistoles, 5'4",
James Smith, William Moode Philadelphia City PA 9/28/1752, 24 shoemaker
    4 days, Sunday, 3 pounds, short,
James Smith, James Black Chester PA 8/5/1756, Irish 20
    4 days, Sunday, 4 dollars, 5'6",
James Smith, James Hanna Lancaster PA 7/6/1774, Irish 28
    8 dollars, 5'4",
James Smith, John Gibson York PA 6/4/1772, English 25 barber
    22 days, Wednesday, 2 pounds, 5'6-7",
James Smith, George Stake York PA 8/11/1773, English 26 barber (2nd escape)
    10 days, Monday, 5 pounds, 5'6-7",
James Smith, Robert Carson Philadelphia City PA 11/16/1774, English wool-dyer
    15 days, Wednesday, 8 dollars, 5'6-8",
James Smith, William Kille Gloucester NJ 3/24/1763, American 22 hired L
    8 days, Wednesday, 5 pounds, 5'10",
James Smith, William Rush Philadelphia City PA blacksmith 8/16/1753, nailer L
    3 days, Monday, 3 pounds,
John Smith, John Naylor Philadelphia City PA 7/7/1743, English nailer
    5 days, Saturday, 3 pounds, 5'8",
John Smith, William Thomas Lancaster PA 6/16/1743, 19
    4 days, Sunday, 5 pounds,
John Smith, John Diemer Philadelphia PA 5/3/1750, Irish 22
    1 day, Wednesday, 2 pounds,
John Smith, William Paterson Chester PA 4/19/1750, Irish 23
    4 days, Sunday, 2 pounds, middle,
John Smith, William Jones Chester PA 2/16/1769, 34
    8 days, Wednesday, 1.5 pounds, 5'6-7",
John Smith, William Paxon Bucks PA 11/3/1773, English
    15 days, Wednesday, 3 pounds, 6',
John Smith, William Gregory Queen Anne's MD 5/10/1775, 22
    66 days, Monday, 5'9",
John Smith, William Waugh York PA 9/8/1773, English soldier
    15 days, Wednesday, 2.5 pounds, 5'8",
John Smith, Thomas Lancaster Philadelphia PA 7/7/1773, Irish 25
    6 days, Friday, 1.5 pounds, 5'2-3",
John Smith, Richard Osburn Loudoun VA 9/7/1774, Irish
    4 pounds, 5'7",
John Smith, William Brown Cumberland PA 8/28/1776, English 30 carpenter
    1.5 pounds,
John Smith, Thomaszin Ellzey Fairfax VA 9/7/1774, English 25 sailor C
    47 days, Saturday, 80 dollars, 6',
John Smith, Andrew Bozorth Burlington NJ 4/26/1764, Irish gaol sale L
    11 days, Sunday, 3 pounds, 5'10",
John Smith, Thomas Temple Chester PA 12/1/1773, 23 L
    11 days, Sunday, 3 pounds, 5'10", (was in the navy)
Johnathan Smith, James Pennell Chester PA 6/2/1779, 25
    3 days, Sunday, 50 dollars, 5'11",
Joseph Smith, Jacob Hindman Talbot MD 3/27/1746, Irish 22 weaver
    5 pounds, middle,
Joseph Smith, Thomas Harris Lancaster PA 5/21/1752, English 35 barber
    9 days, Tuesday, 2 pounds, middle,

Joseph Smith, Benjamin Mason Philadelphia PA 7/21/1768, 18
   4 days, Sunday, 0.5 pounds, 5'6",
Joseph Smith, Fielding Lewis Frederick VA 8/30/1775, Scot 26 painter
   23 days, Tuesday, 10 dollars, 6',
Joseph Smith, Joseph Donaldson NJ 1/27/1763, 18 A
   7 days, Thursday, 5'2",
Joseph Smith, Isham Randolph Philadelphia City PA ship captain 4/16/1748, sailor L
   2 pounds, 5'7",
Lawrence Smith, James Crouch York PA 6/11/1761, Irish
   1.75 pounds, 5'5",
Margaret Smith, Thomas Whiteside Chester PA 2/23/1774, Irish
   34 days, Friday, 4 dollars, (arrived last summer)
Mary Smith, Robert Wakely Philadelphia City PA 9/19/1754, English 20
   13 days, Friday, 1.5 pounds, tall, (lately arrived)
Mary Smith, Robert Bradshaw Lancaster PA 9/5/1754, American 17 (pregnant) L
   49 days, Thursday, 1.5 pounds,
Maurice Smith, Richard Sedgwick Cecil MD 10/31/1751, Irish 20 wigmaker
   9 days, Tuesday, 2 pounds, 5'10",
Michael Smith, Hermanus Orner Philadelphia PA 1/28/1762, German-American 15 L
   22 days, Wednesday, 1 pound,
Nathaniel Smith, Joseph Newbold Burlington NJ 10/10/1765, 28
   10 days, Monday, 3 pounds, 5'10",
Patrick Smith, Thomas Bryarly Baltimore MD 10/20/1768, Irish
   4 days, Sunday, 1.5 pounds, 5'4-5",
Richard Smith, Samuel Allen Burlington NJ 4/25/1765, Irish 19
   1 pound,
Richard Smith, Peter Massey Kent MD 8/28/1755, English 21
   11 days, Sunday, 1 pound, tall,
Richard Smith, Ephrain Howard Anne Arundel MD 8/9/1764, English 20 C
   5 pistoles, 5'6",
Robert Smith, Samuel Garrison Salem NJ 8/8/1771, Irish 18
   5 days, Saturday, 4 dollars, short,
Robert Smith, Joshua Bunting Burlington NJ 4/4/1771, English 18
   8 days, Wednesday, 10 dollars, 5'7-8",
Samuel Smith, John Singleton New Castle DE 4/30/1767, Irish 34
   2 pounds, 5'7", (arrived last fall)
Samuel Smith, Francis Phillips Baltimore MD ironworks 10/1/1767, 22 barber
   mid-August, 2 pounds, 5'3-4",
Samuel Smith, John Patton Berks PA ironworks 8/4/1784, American 20 A
   10 days, Sunday, 3 pounds, 5'7",
Thomas Smith, Joseph Decow Hunterdon NJ 9/24/1741, currier
   4 days, Sunday, 3 pounds, middle,
Thomas Smith, Joseph Decow Hunterdon NJ 12/17/1741, currier (2nd escape)
   3 days, Monday, 3 pounds, middle,
Thomas Smith, Humphrey Carson Queen Anne's MD 5/2/1771, English 17 weaver
   16 days, Tuesday, 2 pounds, 5'2",
William Smith, Joseph Wharton Jr Philadelphia City PA 8/21/1766, English 18
   3 days, Monday, 1.5 pounds, 5'4", (ran from ship)
William Smith, John Logan Lancaster PA 8/14/1766, English 45
   2 pounds, 5'8",
William Smith, James Morgan Bucks PA ironworks 11/27/1766, English 26
   3 pounds, 5'4-5",
William Smith, Moses Yamans Sussex NJ ironworks 5/26/1773, English
   6 days, Friday, 3 pounds, 5'9", (has a wife and 2 children)
William Smith, George Smith Bucks PA 6/16/1790,
   Dec. 1789, 7 dollars,
William Smith, John Dorsey Anne Arundel MD 7/2/1761, Irish 20 C
   101 days, Monday, 10 pistoles,
William Smith, Joshua Owings Baltimore MD 2/16/1769, English 30 C
   10 days, Monday, 7 pounds, 6',
William Smith, Abraham Darington Chester PA 4/7/1763, American 25 L
   5 days, Saturday, 5 pounds, 6',
William Smithes, John Bailey Chester PA 4/6/1769, English 19
   7 days, Thursday, 8 dollars, 5'5",
Cornelius Snell, Jonathan Ingham Bucks PA 8/31/1774, German 24 sailor
   9 days, Tuesday, 2 pounds, 5'7-8", (use to the sea)

Leena Snell, Jonathan Ingham Bucks PA 8/31/1774, German 23
  9 days, Tuesday, 2 pounds, short, (wife to Cornelius Snell)
Richard Snell, Jacob Roberts Gloucester NJ 9/11/1776, English 17
  6 dollars, 5'3-4",
Philip Sobst, Caleb Newbold WJ 10/23/1776, 15
  8 dollars,
Anthony Socer, Archibald Wright Kent MD 6/13/1771, Portugese
  12 days, Saturday, 4 dollars, 5'9",
Andrew Socket, James Riggs Anne Arundel MD 4/25/1765, 19
  16 days, Tuesday, 2 pounds, 5'10",
Jacob Solard, John Grandon 11/30/1758, 16 tailor A
  3 pounds,
Timothy Somers, William Watson Philadelphia City PA shipwright 6/16/1737, Irish 27
  0 days, Thursday, 3 pounds, middle,
Leonard Sommet, Jacob Greff Philadelphia City PA 7/23/1752, German 23
  8 days, Wednesday, 4 pounds, 5'8",
Ann Sorby, Joseph Fred Chester PA 10/16/1766, Irish 21
  27 days, Friday,
John Soulsby, James Walkera Anne Arundel MD ironworks 7/27/1769, Scot C
  11 days, Sunday, 5 pounds, (arrived June 1769)
William South, Richard Foote Stafford VA 7/5/1744, Irish 24 school teacher C
  19 days, Saturday, 1 pistole, middle, (arrived 18 months ago)
Lawrence Soward, Thomas Shipley Chester PA 6/20/1745, Irish 20 (ran before)
  4 days, Sunday, 2.5 pounds,
Marsh Sowerbutts, David Benfield Harford MD 10/5/1774, English sawyer
  10 days, Monday, 10 pounds, 5'9-10",
Baltus Spackholtz, William McKnight Monmouth NJ 8/8/1754, German 25 miller
  3 pounds, middle,
William Spaggs, Thomas Williams Philadelphia City PA hatter 7/12/1739, English 33
  4 days, Sunday, 1.5 pounds, short,
William Sparkes, Isaac Ashley Kent MD 7/23/1747, English 40 butcher C
  2 pounds,
Rebecca Spear, John Brown Chester PA 11/25/1772,
  73 days, Monday, 6 dollars,
Euronemus Speese, Mark Bird Berks PA ironworks 5/24/1764, German forgeman
  19 days, Saturday, 5 pounds, 5'5",
John Spence, Adam Cook Salem NJ 6/20/1771, English 27
  9 days, Tuesday, 2 pounds, 6'3",
James Spencer, Thomas Lee VA 8/20/1747, 27 C
  46 days, Sunday, 5'8",
John Spencer, John Douglas MD ironworks 9/14/1769, 25
  25 days, Sunday, 1.5 pounds,
Joseph Spencer, James Baxter Cecil MD ironworks 12/13/1739, English 30 C
  13 days, Friday, 2.5 pounds,
Sarah Spencer, Joseph Gibbons Jr Chester PA 11/13/1766, Irish 20
  4 days, Sunday, 2 pounds, middle,
George Frederick Spier, Thomas Yardley Bucks PA 11/1/1775, German 40
  3 days, Monday, 3 pounds, 5'8-9",
George Frederick Spier, Garret Broadhead Northampton PA 7/3/1776, German 40 (2nd escape)
  14 days, Thursday, 8 dollars, 5'7-8",
Lorance Spoller, William Purvine Augusta VA 8/21/1766, German 16
  73 days, Monday, 10 pounds, 5'5",
William Sprage, John Thornton Philadelphia City PA 7/12/1775, English 26 shoemaker
  15 days, Wednesday, 3 pounds, 5'4",
John Sprague, Robert Bass 8/19/1772, English 20
  8 days, Wednesday, 5 pounds, 5'6",
William Springate, Daniel Chamier Baltimore MD 7/4/1771, Welsh gardener C
  11 days, Sunday, 5 pounds, 5'4",
William Springer, Job Garretson Baltimore MD ironworks 7/12/1775, 23 gardener C
  10 days, Monday, 5 pounds,
Joseph Sprout, Joseph Nicholson Jr Kent MD 12/18/1766, 22 C
  2 pounds, 5'9",
John Spurflew, Simon Edgell Philadelphia City PA pewterer 5/10/1739, English 30 copperrefiner
  9 days, Tuesday, 1 pound, (lately arrived)
Joshua Sreave, George Spence Burlington NJ 1/22/1767, German-American 18 L
  3 pounds, 5'9-10",

John Stacey, Hugh Durborow Philadelphia City PA chairmaker 9/6/1753, 17 A
    4 days, Sunday, 1.5 pounds, short,
Jonathan Stacy, John McCadlough Philadelphia City PA cooper 9/6/1753, 18 A
    4 days, Sunday, 1.5 pounds,
James Stafford, James Byrne Philadelphia City PA 12/6/1764, Irish 18
    14 days, Thursday, 1 pound,
Thomas Stafford, Henry Owens Anne Arundel MD 9/24/1767, Irish 21 C
    3 pounds, tall,
Augustine Stahl, John Robinson New Castle DE 6/21/1753, German 23 mason
    11 days, Sunday, 3 pounds, 5'6",
Jacob Staine, James Child 2/5/1761, German L
    6 days, Friday, 3 pounds, 5'9", (relatives live nearby)
Christain Frederic Staites, John Vance Cumberland PA 4/12/1775, German 18 wagon driver
    5 pounds, 5'8",
John Stall, John Bringhurst Philadelphia PA 8/20/1761, 18 A
    12 days, Saturday, 5 pounds, 5'6",
Alexander Stamper, Abraham Sailor 4/5/1753, English 24
    4 days, Sunday, 3 pounds, 6',
John Standly, John Patrick Chester PA 7/6/1749, Irish L
    9 days, Tuesday, 3 pounds, 5'7",
Catherine Stanford, Zachary Stugars York PA 10/17/1754, Irish 30
    4 days, Sunday, 1.5 PA pounds,
Sanderson Stanford, James Smith York PA 9/6/1753, English
    16 days, Tuesday, 3 pounds, 5'10",
Sanderson Stanford, Zachary Stugars York PA 10/17/1754, English (2nd escape)
    4 days, Sunday, 1.5 PA pounds, 5'10",
John Stanton, Benjamin Bravard Cecil MD 2/20/1772, Irish 17
    6 days, Friday, 1.5 pounds, 5'8-9",
William Stanton, William Harvey Baltimore MD 7/11/1765, C
    18 days, Sunday, 2 pounds,
Conrad Starkel, Leonard Melchior Philadelphia City PA tavern-keeper 6/11/1767, German 19
    11 days, Sunday, 5 pounds, 5'6", (lately arrived)
William Starkey, John Hulme Bucks PA 12/17/1794, 17 A
    19 days, Friday, 8 dollars, 5'8",
John Starr, Nathaniel Chew Chester PA ship captain 6/20/1751, German
    16 days, Tuesday, 5 pistoles, (ran from ship)
David Steadman, Armstrong Smith Philadelphia City PA shipwright 5/22/1735, Irish 35
    6 days, Friday, 1 pound, tall,
John Stedham, Solomon Smith Salem NJ 7/8/1762,
    12 days, Saturday, 5 pounds, 5'6",
Samuel Stedler, Henry Stedler Philadelphia City PA 1/13/1773, German 19 potter A
    133 days, Thursday, 5 pounds, 5'6-7",
Alexander Steel, James Agnow Philadelphia City PA 10/30/1740, Irish
    11 days, Sunday, 1 pound, tall,
Alexander Steel, Hugh Kelly New Castle DE 9/26/1751, Irish 19 soldier
    10 days, Monday, 2 pounds,
James Steel, William Pennell Chester PA 4/26/1750, American 22 L
    5 pounds, middle,
John Steel, John Craig Bucks PA innkeeper 11/23/1758, English 40 gaol sale L
    7 days, Thursday, 2 pounds, 5'7",
John Steel, Joseph Morrison Lancaster PA 2/5/1754, English sailor L
    8 days, Wednesday, 3 pounds, 5'5",
James Steell, William Pennell Chester PA 6/8/1749, American 22 L
    3 days, Monday, 3 pounds, middle,
Joseph Steell, William Oakford Salem NJ 7/18/1751, 28
    6 days, Friday, 2 pounds, middle,
John Henry Steinfeifer, Yost Seessee Berks PA 4/7/1779, German 19
    7 days, Wednesday, 100 dollars, 5'6-7",
Francis Steits, John Vance Cumberland PA 11/27/1776, Geman 18
    5 pounds, 5'7-8",
Peter Stell, David Thomson Philadelphia City PA shipbuilder 9/4/1766, Scot 19 A
    4 days, Sunday, 5 pounds, 5'4",
Francis Stemeas, Stephen Harlon Chester PA 9/4/1755, German 30
    23 days, Tuesday, 2 pounds, short,
Jacob Stenger, Richard Wistar Philadelphia City PA 4/19/1770, German 18
    10 dollars, 5'8",

Joseph Stennard, John Gosling Gloucester NJ 3/14/1765, 37
    last May, 3 pounds,
Margaret Stephens, John Prietly Bucks PA 11/1/1770, English 19
    4 days, Sunday, 5 pounds, middle,
Michael Stephens, Thomas Harrison Philadelphia City PA 9/2/1772, French 22 tailor
    10 days, Monday, 15 dollars, 5'7-8",
Richard Stephens, William Ware Cecil MD 7/8/1756, English horse-cutter
    24 days, Monday, 3 pounds, tall,
Johann Dewald Stesse, Robert Paul Bucks PA 8/24/1774, German 19   (ran 3 times before)
    7 days, Thursday, 3 pounds, 5'2-3", (arrived 1 year ago)
Cornelius Stevens, William Attmore Philadelphia City PA 6/7/1750, 18 joiner A
    4 days, Sunday, 2 pounds, tall,
John Stevens, Captain Hinton Philadelphia City PA ship captain 11/21/1751, Irish
    1 pound, (ran from ship)
Richard Stevens, John Ducker Anne Arundel MD 1/27/1763, German tailor C
    30 days, Tuesday, 10 pounds, 5'8",
Andrew Stevenson, Samuel Cauldwell Lancaster PA 9/6/1753, Scot
    2 pounds, 5'5",
Jamiman Stevenson, John Ross Philadelphia City PA 1/1/1761, English 20
    3 pounds,
Jenny Stevenson, John Dunlap 12/17/1783, Irish 21
    2 days, Monday, 5 pounds, tall, (arrived 9 weeks ago)
Hugh Steward, Samuel Hart Hunterdon NJ 4/23/1752, A
    4 days, Sunday, 2 pounds, middle,
John Steward, James Eldridge Chester PA 12/8/1748, Irish 16
    10 days, Monday, 1.5 pounds, tall,
Martha Steward, Jeffrey Hodnett Philadelphia PA 1/25/1759, Irish 18
    4 days, Sunday, 2 pounds,
Robert Steward, Leonard Keffer Morris NJ 12/20/1748, Irish hired L
    12 days, Saturday, 3 pounds, middle,
William Steward, John Hamilton Chester PA 9/5/1765, Irish 22
    7 days, Thursday, 2 pounds,
William Steward, John Hamilton Chester PA 12/5/1765, Irish 22 (2nd escape)
    8 days, Wednesday, 2 pounds, 5'10",
William Steward, William Melchior Chester PA 1/22/1767, Irish 23 (3rd escape)
    36 days, Wednesday, 2.5 pounds, 5'10",
Abraham Stewart, Isaac Zane Philadelphia City PA 4/11/1754, English 19
    4 days, Sunday, 5 pounds, middle,
James Stewart, William Ferguson Monmouth NJ 11/8/1770, Irish
    54 days, Saturday, 1.5 pounds, 5'7",
James Stewart, John Henderson Philadelphia City PA nailmaker 11/10/1790, 18 nailmaker A
    63 days, Wednesday, 5 dollars, 4'10",
Michael Stewart, John Glen Cumberland PA 12/12/1771, Irish 35 soldier
    199 days, Monday, 4 dollars, 5'5",
William Stewart, Robert Adams Chester PA 10/18/1750, Irish 17
    4 days, Sunday, 1 pound, middle,
William Stewart, Thomas Gilpin Kent MD 10/14/1762, 25 soldier L
    9 days, Tuesday, 3 pounds, short,
Jonathan Stickwood, William Goodwin Baltimore MD 9/14/1769, English 21 C
    16 days, Tuesday, 5 pounds, 5'8-9",
Jacob Stier, Charles Bouman 6/20/1792, German 20 butcher
    3 days, Sunday, 4 dollars, 5'8-9",
Isaac Still, John Mackey Chester PA 3/6/1776, 16
    2 pounds, 5'8",
Godfried Stinehever, Valentine Hofman Philadelphia City PA 8/11/1784, German 20 A
    6 dollars, 5',
Anne Carrola Stockey, Robert Gelton Boston MA 3/16/1747, English 25
    65 days, Tuesday, 1 pound,
William Stogdell, William Scott Philadelphia City PA 10/26/1758, English 29 tailor
    2 days, Tuesday, 2 pounds, 5'8", (lately arrived, was in the navy)
David Stogdin, David Ayers Cumberland NJ 12/10/1794, 18 A
    14 days, Wednesday, 4 dollars,
Johannes Stohr, Wallace & Donaldson Philadelphia City PA 11/17/1784, German
    2.5 pounds, 5'7", (ran from ship)
John Stokes, Samuel Holiday Cumberland PA 10/26/1769, Irish 19
    24 days, Monday, 1.5 pounds, 5'7",

John Stokes, Samuel Holiday Cumberland PA 6/7/1770, Irish 20 (2nd escape)
    25 days, Sunday, 2 pounds, 5'7-8",
Godfrey Stone, Charles Ridgely Jr Baltimore MD ironworks 9/26/1765, German 35 C
    58 days, Tuesday, 4 pounds, 6',
Peter Stone, John Duncan Bucks PA 1/8/1794, German 19
    11 days, Saturday, 10 dollars, 5'4-5",
John Stoner, Jacob Beam Lancaster PA 3/10/1768, German blacksmith
    3 pounds, 5'6",
George Storey, Joseph Bonsall Chester PA 10/30/1776, Irish 20
    3 days, Monday, 4 dollars, 5'5-6",
Elizabeth Stormer, Elizabeth Weekes Philadelphia City PA shopkeeper 2/9/1748, German 15
    3 days, Monday, 3 pounds, tall,
John Story, Joseph Caldwell Kent DE 3/14/1765, 20 schoolmaster
    40 days, Saturday, 2 pounds,
Benjamin Strattin, Joseph Bates Burlington NJ 6/9/1784, blacksmith A
    30 days, Monday, 3 pounds, 5'7-8",
Ann Strawbridge, Benjamin Armitage Philadelphia City PA 4/14/1743, Irish 20
    44 days, Tuesday, 1 pound, middle,
William Stretch, Frederick Busard Chester PA 9/8/1768, Irish 20
    9 days, Tuesday, 3 pounds, tall,
Thomas Stringer, Francis Phillips Baltimore MD ironworks 9/15/1768, 25 C
    16 days, Tuesday, 3 pounds, 5'6",
William Stringer, Thomas Blair Hunterdon NJ 5/15/1755, 22
    11 days, Sunday, 1 pound, 5'7",
Valentine Strong, Alexander Crukshank Philadelphia City PA shoemaker 7/6/1749, Irish 20
    2 pounds,
Valentine Strong, William Spear Lancaster PA 6/21/1750, Irish 21 (2nd escape)
    2.5 pounds, 5'6",
Frantz Strother, Alexander Hamilton Philadelphia City PA merchant 7/24/1755, German 16
    22 days, Wednesday, short,
Abraham Stuages, John Stille Philadelphia City PA 4/13/1769, 19 tailor A
    6 days, Friday, 5 pounds, 5'6",
James Stuart, Benjamin Taylor Chester PA 2/1/1775, Scot 22 clerk
    12 days, Saturday, 8 dollars, 5'8-9",
Mary Stuart, George Chrisman Philadelphia PA 1/10/1776, English
    2 pounds, 5'2",
Thomas Stuart, Edward Parker Chester PA 6/18/1767, Irish 30
    2 pounds, 5'8",
William Stuart, William Moode Philadelphia City PA 3/11/1746, Irish 37 shoemaker
    5 days, Saturday, 3 pounds, short,
William Stuart, William Moode Philadelphia City PA 5/15/1746, Irish 37 shoemaker (2nd escape)
    9 days, Tuesday, 5 pistoles, 5',
William Stuart, William Gaa Philadelphia City PA barber 1/16/1753, Irish 22
    17 days, Monday, 3 pounds, 5'7",
William Stuart, Andrew Caldwell Lancaster PA 10/22/1767, Irish 20
    19 days, Saturday, 1.5 pounds, 5'9",
Catherine Stutner, John McCarter Lancaster PA 4/1/1756, German 60
    38 days, Monday, 1.5 pounds,
Mary Stutner, John Lingfield Lancaster PA 4/1/1756, German 16
    38 days, Monday, 1.5 pounds,
John Sudwell, John Lawrence Burlington NJ 11/29/1759, English
    4 days, Sunday, 3 pounds,
Maria Suffyah, Joseph Foster Philadelphia PA 4/15/1756, German 17
    1 pound, short,
Florence Sulavon, Andrew Litle Lancaster PA 3/10/1773, Irish 20 sailor (male)
    8 days, Wednesday, 2 pounds, 6',
Florence Sulavon, Andrew Litle Lancaster PA 6/16/1773, Irish 20 sailor (2nd escape)
    2 days, Tuesday, 4 dollars 5'10",
Daniel Sulivan, Joshua Pierce Chester PA 7/26/1775, 19
    3 pounds, 5'8-9",
John Sulivan, Stephen Hoopes Chester PA 11/1/1739, Irish 25
    4 days, Sunday, 1.25 pounds, short,
Andrew Sullivan, Lleweling Davis Chester PA 10/22/1741, Irish 21
    3 days, Monday, 1.5 pounds,
Cornelius Sullivan, James Patterson Lancaster PA 6/28/1764, Irish
    1.5 pounds, (lately arrived, ran from ship)

Cornelius Sullivan, John Roberts Burlington NJ 4/21/1748, Irish 20 L
  3 days, Monday, 5 pounds, middle,
Cornelius Sullivan, John Roberts Burlington NJ 6/2/1748, Irish 20 (2nd escape) L
  3 days, Monday, 3 pounds, middle,
Cornelius Sullivan, Joseph Biddle Burlington NJ 6/23/1748, Irish 20 (3rd escape) L
  9 days, Tuesday, 2 pounds, middle,
Cornelius Sullivan, Joseph Biddle Burlington NJ 8/31/1749, Irish 21 (4th escape) L
  2 days, Tuesday, 2 pounds, middle,
Daniel Sullivan, Mahlon Stacy Burlington NJ ironworks 8/12/1736, 25
  2 pounds, tall,
Daniel Sullivan, Samuel Smith Anne Arundel MD 8/8/1745, Irish 30 carpenter
  30 days, Tuesday, 3 pounds, middle,
Daniel Sullivan, Joseph Wood Cecil MD 10/11/1750, Irish weaver
  11 days, Sunday, 3.5 pounds, middle, (lately arrived)
Daniel Sullivan, Thomas Batten Gloucester NJ 6/19/1776, 35
  3 days, Monday, 2 pounds, 5'8",
Francis Sullivan, Alexander Wilson Lancaster PA 7/23/1772, 20 weaver
  18 days, Sunday, 2 pounds, 5'6-7", (arrived 2 years ago)
Francis Sullivan, Alexander Wilson Lancaster PA 6/16/1773, 21 weaver (2nd escape)
  11 days, Sunday, 5 pounds, 5'6-7", (arrived 2 years ago)
Jeremiah Sullivan, John Logue New Castle DE 9/12/1751, 22
  4 days, Sunday, 1 pound, middle,
Mary Sullivan, Thomas McMollin Chester PA 3/26/1745, Irish 20
  15 days, Wednesday, 0.5 pounds,
Patrick Sullivan, John Moor Chester PA 10/31/1751, Irish 50
  4 days, Sunday, 3 pounds, 5'10",
Samuel Sullivan, Benjamin Gibbs Jr Philadelphia City PA 9/18/1755, 17 A
  4 days, Sunday, 1 pistole, 5'2",
John Sullivane, Isaac Handy Somerset MD 11/24/1768, Irish
  about 4 weeks ago, 4 pounds, 5'9", (lately arrived)
John Sundberry, Michael Montgomery Chester PA 10/6/1768, Swedish 22
  18 days, Sunday, 3 pounds, 5'8",
William Sunderland, John Bunting Burlington NJ 9/7/1738, English 20
  7 days, Thursday, 2 pounds, middle,
John Surman, Rowland Evans Philadelphia PA 9/2/1756, Irish 22
  4 days, Sunday, 1.5 pounds, 5'5",
Margaret Suthward, John Anderson Lancaster PA 4/18/1754, English 18
  2 pounds,
James Sutton, Burroughs Abit Gloucester NJ 10/17/1771, 19 A
  12 days, Saturday, 2.5 pounds, 5'9-10",
John Swaine, William McDowell Cumberland PA 4/17/1766, 20
  2 pounds, 5'4",
James Swainey, Robert Kirkwood New Castle DE 9/28/1774, Irish 24
  10 days, Monday, 8 dollars, 5'7-8", (lately arrived)
Hannah Swainy, James David Chester PA 11/24/1748, Irish L
  25 days, Sunday, 2.5 pounds, short, (arrived 7 years ago)
John Swam, Joseph Foreman Monmouth NJ 9/26/1745, American 25 L
  8 days, Wednesday, 3 pounds, short,
John Swam, Joseph Foreman Monmouth NJ 7/3/1746, American 26 (2nd escape) L
  7 days, Thursday, 3 pounds, short,
Andrew Swarts, Miles Evans Philadelphia PA 8/21/1755, German miller
  11 days, Sunday, 1.5 pounds,
John Swayney, James Barnes Chester PA 3/27/1753, Irish 35
  3 pounds,
George Sweeney, John Wilcocks Philadelphia City PA ship captain 10/5/1749, Irish 20
  11 days, Sunday, 2 pounds, middle,
Richard Sweftman, Samuel Simpson Philadelphia PA 11/7/1771, 16 shoemaker A
  11 days, Sunday, 2 pounds, tall,
James Sweney, Stephen Mendenhall New Castle DE 11/27/1766, 18
  9 days, Tuesday, 3 pounds, 5'6-7",
John Sweney, Benjamin Davis Chester PA 4/13/1785, Irish tailor
  3 days, Sunday, 5 dollars, 5'6",
Rachel Swigg, William Smith Queen Anne's MD 8/31/1758, English 50
  18 days, Sunday, 1.5 pounds, middle,
Hannah Swinburn, Peter Garson NY 8/24/1774,
  3 dollars,

Henery Katy Swingos, John Harpes Philadelphia City PA 1/9/1766, German 29
    1 pound, (lately arrived)
Edward Swinny, John Thomas Philadelphia PA 9/5/1751, Irish weaver
    6 days, Friday, 2 pounds, 5'8",
Edward Swinny, John Peters Philadelphia City PA ship captain 10/8/1747, L
    middle,
Henry Switzer, James Jones Jr Philadelphia PA 7/26/1775, German 45 shoemaker
    3 days, Monday, 2.5 pounds, 5'9-10",
William Symonds, William Russell Baltimore MD 8/30/1770, 25 barber C
    9 days, Tuesday, 4 pounds, 5'5", (lately arrived)
John Taft, Samuel Bunting Bucks PA 10/8/1730, 35 weaver
    7 days, Thursday, 2 pounds, middle,
Peter Tailen, Godfrey Deal Philadelphia PA shopkeeper 10/13/1768, German 13
    29 days, Wednesday, 4 dollars,
Henry Talbot, Captain Morrison Baltimore MD 9/29/1763, Irish
    11 days, Sunday, 1.5 pounds, middle,
John Talifero, Stephen Hollingsworth Philadelphia City PA cordwainer 4/16/1730,
    2 days, Tuesday, 1.5 pounds, short,
Israel Tallman, Richard Allen Philadelphia City PA 8/13/1788, American 16 chimneysweep L
    4 dollars, (mother is an Indian)
Thomas Tamerlane, Charles Blake Philadelphia City PA 6/18/1730, East-Indian 23 rigger L
    3 days, Monday, 2 pounds, short,
John Tanner, Benjamin Chapman Bucks PA 12/14/1796, 19 miller A
    24 days, Sunday, 0.07 dollars, 5'7-8",
Terrence Taring, Abraham Holmes Lancaster PA 11/1/1775, Irish 24
    23 days, Tuesday, 8 dollars, 5'6-7",
Stephen Tashhire, David Davis Berks PA 6/18/1772, French 30
    7 days, Thursday, 2 pounds, 5'7-8",
Benjamin Taylor, Christopher Adle Philadelphia PA 8/21/1766, English 16
    8 days, Wednesday, 1.5 pounds,
Claudius Taylor, Edward Bonsall Philadelphia City PA 6/6/1765, Irish 23 A
    11 days, Sunday, 3 pounds, 5'6",
David Taylor, George Hogeland Bucks PA 9/1/1763, 25
    4 days, Sunday, 3 pounds, 5'4",
Edward Taylor, Patrick Lynch Cecil MD 12/21/1774, Irish 21
    1 pound, 6',
Elizabeth Taylor, James Clemson Lancaster PA 3/28/1771, English 23
    14 days, Thursday, 2 pounds, 5'6", (has lived some time in the colonies)
James Taylor, William Longwill Cecil MD 9/1/1768, Irish 18
    14 days, Thursday, 2 pounds, 5'3",
John Taylor, Benjamin Davis Chester PA 6/16/1743,
    about 2 months ago, 1.25 pounds, short,
John Taylor, John Adamson 6/25/1752, Irish 18 weaver
    2 days, Tuesday, 1.5 pounds, short,
John Taylor, James Stephens Philadelphia City PA biscuit baker 9/23/1762, English 30
    8 days, Wednesday, 1.5 pounds, 5'3",
John Taylor, Henry Spling Philadelphia City PA 1/24/1776, shoemaker
    3 days, Monday, 3 pounds, (was a soldier)
John Taylor, Neal Smirkey 11/22/1764, 19 A
    11 days, Sunday, 1 pound, 5'6",
Lewis Taylor, William Shallcross Bucks PA 2/19/1767, Irish
    10 days, Monday, 1.5 pounds, 5'6",
Robert Taylor, Samuel Ankram Lancaster PA 9/19/1765, 25
    14 days, Thursday, 5 pounds, 5'10",
Samuel Taylor, John McCalion Chester PA 12/3/1783, 23
    20 days, Thursday, 3 dollars, 5'7-8",
Thomas Taylor, John Bull Philadelphia PA 7/9/1772, Irish 23
    7 days, Thursday, middle,
Thomas Taylor, Joseph Gavin Philadelphia City PA shoemaker 2/5/1767, shoemaker L
    1.5 pounds, short,
William Taylor, John Caunan Burlington NJ 11/9/1752, English
    34 days, Friday, 2 pounds, 5'6",
William Taylor, John Davis Lancaster PA 4/4/1751, English 20
    4 days, Sunday, 2 pounds,
William George Tear, Benjamin Blyth Cumberland PA 7/13/1769, English
    17 days, Monday, 3 pounds, middle,

Henry Tedder, Jacob Giles Baltimore MD 10/25/1753, English gardener
    11 days, Sunday, 5 pounds, 5'8",
Hendrick Tedman, Cornelius Bogart tavern-keeper 7/30/1752, German
    11 days, Sunday, 3 pounds,
James Teeple, Benjamin Harris Somerset NJ 9/5/1765, 19 shoemaker A
    19 days, Saturday, 6 pounds, 5'7",
John Teernam, Robert Mack New Castle DE 7/5/1770, Irish
    9 days, Tuesday, 10 dollars, 5'8",
George Temple, John McClain Lancaster PA 1/17/1771, 18 A
    10 days, Monday, 1.5 pounds, 5'9-10", (indented in 1770)
John Tendeu, Richard Clayton Chester PA 5/12/1768, French 18 A
    12 days, Saturday, 4 dollars, 5'5",
Abraham Tennis, Elias Thomas Bucks PA 10/19/1769, 19 tanner A
    5 days, Saturday, 2.5 pounds, 5'8",
Lawrence Tensle, Arthur Vankirk Middlesex NJ 7/22/1756, German carpenter
    11 days, Sunday, 3 pounds, 5'4",
George Terret, John Needham Philadelphia City PA 11/6/1746, Irish weaver
    3 days, Monday, 2 pounds, middle,
John Test, Josiah Miller Salem NJ 9/16/1795, 14
    3 days, Sunday, 8 dollars,
Charles Tew, William Kansey Kent MD 7/17/1760, English 25 C
    10 days, Monday, 2 pistoles, 5'8",
Mose Tharp, Edward Hill Philadelphia PA 5/2/1751, American 21 L
    13 days, Friday, 1 pound, 6',
Leray Theogore, William Adams Baltimore MD 8/4/1768, French 19 barber
    3 pounds, 5'5-6", (lately arrived)
Richard Thetford, Joshua Lord Gloucester NJ 4/19/1764, Irish 15
    8 dollars, 5'4", (arrived 5 months ago)
Richard Thetford, Joshua Lord Gloucester NJ 6/12/1766, Irish 17 (2nd escape)
    9 days, Tuesday, 2 pounds, 5'5-6",
Philip Thiebout, Michael Bower Philadelphia City PA 2/14/1776, German 25 butcher
    16 days, Tuesday, 3 pounds, 5'10",
Catherine Thillen, Michael Croll Philadelphia PA 9/8/1773, German 21
    12 days, Saturday, 2 dollars, (has 6 years to serve)
Daniel Thomas, Peter Hunter Chester PA 5/31/1770, Irish-American 21 L
    11 days, Sunday, 5 pounds, middle,
David Thomas, George Leib Philadelphia PA tanner 10/23/1776, Welsh 14
    2 days, Tuesday, 8 dollars,
Evan Thomas, Daniel Smith Philadelphia City PA 7/20/1774, Welsh 24 waiter
    10 days, Monday, 6 dollars, (arrived 6 weeks ago)
George Thomas, William Carmichael Kent MD 8/17/1774, English 19
    9 days, Tuesday, 6 dollars, 5'1",
George Thomas, George Temple Queen Anne's MD 10/4/1775, English 20 (2nd escape)
    24 days, Monday, 5 pounds, 5'4-5",
Henry Thomas, Thomas Cocky Baltimore MD 9/10/1761, 37 C
    5 pistoles, 5'10",
Henry Thomas, William Ler Chester PA 3/6/1776, American 19 cordwainer A
    22 days, Wednesday, 6 dollars, 5'9-10",
James Thomas, Joseph Mitchell Philadelphia City PA merchant 3/20/1766, English 20 baker
    end of Oct., 6 dollars, 5',
James Thomas, Thomas Lewis Chester PA 5/15/1760, tailor A
    12 days, Saturday, 1.5 pounds, 5'8",
John Thomas, Alexander MacKelroy Bucks PA 6/12/1766, English 45 carpenter
    14 days, Thursday, 2 pounds, 5'8", (use to the sea)
Meredith Thomas, Charles Young Baltimore MD 6/30/1773, Irish 20
    21 days, Thursday, 6 dollars, 5'6", (lately arrived)
William Thomas, John Holland Chester PA 5/21/1747, English 20
    4 days, Sunday, 3 pounds, short,
William Thomas, William Carmichael Kent MD 8/17/1774, English 17
    9 days, Tuesday, 6 dollars, 5'1",
William Thomas, George Temple Queen Anne's MD 10/4/1775, English 18 (2nd escape)
    24 days, Monday, 5 pounds, 5'4-5",
William Thomas, Mathias Larny Chester PA 12/15/1743, English 14 tailor A
    21 days, Thursday, 1 pound,
William Thomas, Mathias Larny Chester PA 11/21/1745, English 16 tailor (2nd escape) A
    4 days, Sunday, 1 pound, middle,

William Thomas, Alexander Stuart Cecil MD 9/18/1755, English 20 C
   10 days, Monday, 2 pistoles, 5'6", (arrived 6 weeks ago)
Alexander Thompson, Edward Rees Chester PA 3/23/1769, 18
   30 days, Tuesday, 1 pound, 5'2-3",
Edward Thompson, Andrew Pearce Cecil MD 8/29/1765, English 29 C
   8 days, Wednesday, 2 pounds, (lately arrived)
Edward Thompson, Henry Ward Pearce Cecil MD 4/17/1766, English 30 (2nd escape) C
   8 days, Wednesday, 5 pounds, 6',
James Thompson, Edmund Conoly Chester PA 11/3/1748, Irish weaver
   4 days, Sunday, 2 pounds,
James Thompson, John Roberts Philadelphia PA 5/29/1776, American 19 L
   4 dollars, 5'5-6",
John Thompson, William Childs Philadelphia City PA ship captain 8/1/1745,
   5 days, Saturday, 5'8", (ran from ship)
John Thompson, James Edmondston Chester PA 9/21/1752,
   20 days, Friday, 2 pounds, 5'3", (use to the sea)
John Thompson, Richard Dobson Cecil MD 4/29/1762, 18 (took his wife also) A
   3 pounds, 5'4",
John Thompson, Job Kimsey Gloucester NJ 6/4/1794, 18 A
   80 days, Sunday, 6 dollars, 5'3-4",
Joseph Thompson, David Lawrence Chester PA 9/26/1751, Irish 22
   2 pounds, middle,
Patrick Thompson, Conyngham & Nesbitt Philadelphia City PA merchants 6/14/1764, Irish 24 chandler
   4 days, Sunday, 5'10", (ran from ship)
Patrick Thompson, Archibald Gardiner Philadelphia City PA 7/10/1766, Irish 26 chandler (2nd esc)
   3 days, Monday, 1.5 pounds, 5'8",
Rebecca Thompson, John McKee Lancaster PA 1/23/1782, 35
   96 days, Friday, 0.03 pounds,
Richard Thompson, Peter Whitner Montgomery PA 1/16/1793, Irish tailor
   7 days, Wednesday, 4 dollars, 5'6-7",
William Thompson, James Gibson Cumberland PA 9/5/1765, tailor
   10 days, Monday, 2 pounds, 5'10",
William Thompson, William Hoffman Baltimore MD 3/19/1767, English 30 joiner
   5 pounds, 5'4",
William Thompson, John Eunuch Kent MD 6/19/1766, Welsh 19
   11 days, Sunday, 1 pound, 5',
William Thompson, Mounce Keen NJ 1/4/1792, 18
   3 days, Sunday, 4 dollars, 5'7-8",
William Thompson, Thomas Harris Chester PA 8/1/1787, English
   3 days, Sunday, 4 dollars, 5'8",
William Thompson, William Long Franklin PA 7/5/1786, 22
   68 days, Friday, 5 pounds, 5'7-8",
William Thompson, Abraham Jarrett Baltimore MD 11/12/1767, 30 confectioner C
   last July, 4 dollars, tall,
William Thompson, John Sparling Burlington NJ 7/6/1749, American L
   3 pounds, short,
William Thompson, Thomas Barr York PA 6/9/1763, 30 peddler L
   14 days, Thursday, 5 pounds, middle,
James Thomson, William Bodly Chester PA 3/8/1775, 35 carpenter
   10 days, Monday, 6 dollars, 5'7-8",
William Thomson, John Marlet Sussex NJ 2/25/1755, Irish
   1.5 pounds, 5'8",
George Thornton, Thomas Bull Chester PA ironworks 11/23/1785, Irish 23 fifeplayer
   9 days, Monday, 1.5 pounds, 5'7-8",
Margaret Thornton, Ephraim Pennington York PA 8/9/1775, Irish 19
   21 days, Thursday, 8 dollars,
Thomas Thornton, John Starr Chester PA 10/12/1752,
   5 pounds, middle,
Henry Thorton, Amos Strickland Bucks PA sheriff 7/23/1747,
   9 days, Tuesday, 2 pounds,
Joseph Thorton, Francis Allen Cecil MD 4/8/1756, C
   1.5 pounds, short,
Matthew Tiers, John McCalla Philadelphia City PA 6/30/1768, English 27 tailor
   4 days, Sunday, 3 pounds, 5'5-6", (arrived last fall)
Matthew Tiers, John McCalla Philadelphia City PA 1/10/1771, English 30 tailor (2nd escape)
   13 days, Friday, 2 pounds, 5'5-6",

Charles Tilden, Andrew Jolley New Castle DE 5/26/1743, 16 A
    1 pound,
John Tillis, Morton Morton Chester PA 3/24/1773, American L
    9 days, Tuesday,, 2 pounds, 5'7",
Matthew Tinks, John McCalla Philadelphia City PA 11/15/1770, English 30 tailor (ran before)
    18 days, Sunday, 2 pounds, 5'5-6",
Charles Tippin, William Reynolds Anne Arundel MD 11/15/1775, gardener
    11 days, Sunday, 5 pounds,
Thomas Tipping, Benjamin Dorsey Frederick MD 9/20/1770, Welsh 40 C
    7 pounds, 5'7-8", (arrived July 1770)
George Tippins, William Bordley Kent MD 8/1/1771,
    5 pounds, short,
George Titloff, Joseph Miller Lancaster PA 12/4/1782, German 24 soldier L
    14 days, Wednesday, 4 dollars, 5'3-4",
Sarah Tivy, Peter Jaquet Jr New Castle DE 8/31/1785, Irish 25
    6 days, Thursday, 16 dollars,
Richard Tobine, Curtis Grubb Lancaster PA ironworks 9/6/1764, Irish 25 joiner
    14 days, Thursday, 10 dollars, 5'10", (was in the army)
Thomas Tolbot, William Newman 5/14/1767,
    14 days, Thursday, 1 pound, 5'8",
John Tombleson, Samuel Passmore Cecil MD 5/15/1755, English 27
    11 days, Sunday, 5 pounds, 6',
Michael Tomil, Derrick Clever Berks PA 6/5/1760, German 16
    67 days, Sunday, 2 pounds,
John Tomlins, John Lewis Gloucester VA 6/15/1738, 26
    51 days, Tuesday, 1 pistole, tall,
Thomas Tomlinson, William Bond MD 9/11/1740, English 28 tailor
    18 days, Sunday, 3 pounds, short,
Patrick Tommins, Robert Holiday Chester PA 7/28/1737, Irish 18
    4 days, Sunday, 1.5 pounds, middle,
Hannah Tompson, Unlisted Name 10/8/1741, English
    1 pound,
Smith Tomson, John Lamborn Chester PA 9/1/1768, Scot 18 barber
    4 days, Sunday, 3 pounds, 5',
William Tone, William Carter Philadelphia City PA 8/24/1769, 16 shoemaker A
    12 days, Saturday, 3 dollars, 5',
Margaret Tonner, Michael Crider Lancaster PA 10/17/1765, German 22
    19 days, Saturday, 1 pound,
Daniel Tonney, David Frost Bucks PA 8/24/1785, Irish 17
    3 days, Sunday, 6 dollars, 5'6-7",
William Tonry, Thomas Humphreys Philadelphia PA 1/17/1776, 19 A
    10 days, Monday, 8 dollars, 5'7-8",
Patrick Tool, Job Coles Gloucester NJ 3/29/1786, Irish 19
    3 days, Sunday, 2 pounds, 5'6",
David Toole, John Robert Holliday Baltimore MD 8/15/1771, Irish 24 C
    22 days, Wednesday, 1.5 pounds, 5'4-5",
David Toole, John Robert Holliday Baltimore MD 8/10/1774, Irish 27 (2nd escape) C
    36 days, Wednesday, 20 pounds, 5'5-6",
Terrence Toole, George Rice Jones Philadelphia City PA butcher 2/7/1740, Irish butcher
    4 days, Sunday, 2 pounds, short,
John Tootbill, Thomas Stedham Caroline MD 11/30/1774, 22
    2 pounds, 5'4-5",
Thomas Tottan, Andrew Borell New Castle DE 7/1/1762, 15
    5 days, Saturday, 1 pistole, 4'6",
George Townly, Reese Meredith Philadelphia City PA 7/31/1740, English 23 carpenter
    11 days, Sunday, 2 pounds,
George Townly, William Maugridge Philadelphia City PA joiner 10/23/1740, English 23 carpenter
    11 days, Sunday, 3 pounds, short, (2nd escape)
George Townly, William Maugridge Philadelphia City PA joiner 7/2/1741, English 24 carpenter
    2 pounds, short, (3rd escape)
Joseph Townsend, Joseph Taylor Kent DE 6/9/1763, 23 bricklayer
    2 pounds, 5'10",
Edward Townshend, William Pancoost Burlington NJ 9/11/1740, English 30
    7 days, Thursday, 2 pounds, tall,
William Townsing, James Walkera Anne Arundel MD ironworks 7/27/1769, 20 C
    11 days, Sunday, 5 pounds, 5'6",

Daniel Toy, Abraham Lord Salem NJ 12/25/1750, Irish 26
   11 days, Sunday, 3 pounds, middle,
Elijah Toy, Isaac Fish Gloucester NJ 10/28/1795, 19 A
   20 days, Thursday, 1 dollar, 5'9",
James Tracy, John Roberts Salem NJ 5/9/1751, Irish 28
   1 pound,
Laughlin Tracy, Robert Boyle Chester PA tanner 9/3/1747, Irish 22
   4 days, Sunday, 1.5 pistoles, 6', (lately arrived)
Laughlin Tracy, Robert Boyle Chester PA tanner 7/7/1748, Irish 23 (2nd escape)
   3 days, Monday, 2 pounds, 6',
Isaac Trailer, John Burr Burlington NJ 3/8/1739, English (ran before)
   11 days, Sunday, 6 pounds, (arrived 2 years ago)
William Trainer, John Huithwohl Lancaster PA 1/8/1794, Irish-American 19 L
   13 days, Thursday, 6 dollars, 5'9",
Philip Traner, William Moore New York NY ship captain 10/27/1763, Irish
   2 pounds, 5'7", (ran from ship)
James Trapwell, George Brown Bucks PA 6/14/1775, English 32
   10 days, Monday, 5 dollars, (arrived 2 years ago)
Francis Trasey, Abel Harris Salem NJ 2/22/1775, American 30 L
   16 days, Tuesday, 3 pounds, 5'9-10",
John Christian Travatt, David Bush Philadelphia PA 6/28/1739, German
   4 days, Sunday, 2 pounds, middle, (arrived last fall)
Simon Trayner, Alexander McIntosh Kent MD 12/18/1766, Irish 26 L
   19 days, Saturday, 1 pistole, 5'8",
James Treasey, Samuel Kirkpatrick Lancaster PA 10/26/1774, Irish blacksmith
   2 pounds, 5'3",
Christiana Treasury, Benjamin Sharpless Chester PA 11/29/1750, German 21
   11 days, Sunday, 2 pounds, middle,
John Treeball, Joseph Mitchell Philadelphia City PA merchant 7/6/1769, English 36 mason
   2 days, Tuesday, 6 dollars, 5'6", (arrived last fall)
Thomas Trenter, Isaac Trimble Chester PA 6/9/1773, 18 A
   10 days, Monday, 3 pounds, (has relations in Baltimore)
Andrew Tress, George Gibson Lancaster PA 9/6/1750, English 25
   3 pounds,
Nicholas Trewick, Robert Cooke St Mary's MD 5/16/1745, 40 miner C
   44 days, Tuesday, 1000 pounds tobacco, short,
John Trinder, Benjamin Howell Chester PA 1/22/1754, English 35
   9 days, Tuesday, 1.5 pounds, tall,
James Trot, James Breading Cecil MD 2/12/1756, Irish 20 sailor
   9 days, Tuesday, 2 pistoles, 5'6",
James Trot, James Breading Cecil MD 5/13/1756, Irish 20 sailor (2nd escape)
   4 days, Sunday, 5'6",
John Trow, Veachel Davis Frederick MD 10/14/1756, 35 carpenter
   20 days, Friday, 4 pistoles, 5'3",
John Troy, John Fitzgarrard Chester PA 8/19/1762, American L
   2 pounds, 5'5",
John Truman, George Moore Lancaster PA 8/3/1774, Irish 25
   22 days, Wednesday, 8 dollars, 5'3",
John Trusdel, Matthew Kelley Bucks PA 10/11/1770, Irish 24 weaver
   5'8-9", (arrived 2 years ago)
Richard Trusted, John Nicholson Philadelphia City PA gunsmith 1/24/1776, English 21 gunstocker
   5 days, Saturday, 8 dollars, 5'5-6",
William Tub, John Williams Philadelphia City PA tailor 7/12/1739, 20 tailor
   4 days, Sunday, 1.5 pounds, short,
Henry Tuchness, Isaac Dawson Philadelphia City PA 8/6/1747, A
   4 days, Sunday, 2.5 pounds, 5'10",
Richard Tucker, Isaac Horner 7/30/1761, English 18
   2 pounds, 5'4",
William Tucker, Samuel Read Philadelphia City PA baker 6/29/1749, Irish 17
   4 days, Sunday, 3 pounds, short,
Walter Tudor, William Lawrence Chester PA 9/26/1751, Welsh 30
   2 pounds, tall,
Thomas Tuff, Joseph Husband Baltimore MD 9/29/1773, Irish
   2 pounds, 5'6",
William Tugh, William Ramsey Kent MD 4/17/1760, sawyer
   2 pistoles, 5'8",

Tobias Tuite, William Cox Baltimore MD 5/29/1766, Irish 24 carpenter
 10 days, Monday, 3 pounds, 5'7",
Tobias Tuite, James Webster Baltimore MD ironworks 7/10/1766, Irish 24 carpenter (2nd escape)
 18 days, Sunday, 3 pounds, 5'6-7",
William Tully, William Brown Philadelphia City PA baker 11/9/1774, English 17
 2 days, Tuesday, 1.5 pounds, short, (arrived 19 months ago)
William Tully, William Brown Philadelphia City PA baker 8/7/1776, English 19 (2nd escape)
 10 days, Monday, 1 pound,
James Tumblety, John Bigham Lancaster PA 1/17/1771, mason A
 15 days, Wednesday, 3 pounds, 5'8",
Patrick Tumney, Charles Reed Chester PA 3/29/1775, Irish 20 miller
 9 days, Tuesday, 4 dollars, 5'8-9", (arrived 18 months ago)
Patrick Tumney, Charles Reed Chester PA 8/13/1777, Irish 22 miller (2nd escape)
 4 days, Sunday, 5'8-9",
John Tunmer, William Lux Baltimore MD 5/3/1764, English 22 C
 11 days, Sunday, 7.5 pounds,
John Tupin, John Bleakly New Castle DE 9/1/1763, French 23
 13 days, Friday, 1.5 pounds, 5'2",
Edward Turner, Alexander Kennedy Philadelphia City PA 9/22/1757, sailor A
 5'5",
James Turner, John Cook Chester PA 4/27/1774, Irish 21
 10 days, Monday, 3 pounds, 5'6-7",
John Turner, Edward McFarland Berks PA ironworks 12/18/1750, Irish 21
 19 days, Saturday, 5 pounds, 5',
John Turner, John Jaquet New Castle DE 8/31/1774, Irish 22
 57 days, Wednesday, 10 pounds, 5'7-8",
John Turner, Robert Dryburgh 3/8/1764, American 19 A
 0.03 pounds, 5'3",
Robert Turner, James McDonold Lancaster PA 4/29/1742, Irish
 10 days, Monday, 3 pounds, 6',
Samuel Turner, Michael Earle Cecil MD 4/30/1752, English 21
 13 days, Friday, 3 pistoles, (arrived 2 years ago)
Nicholas Tussing, Joseph Fearpe Lancaster PA 7/5/1770, German 19
 4 days, Sunday, 3 pounds, 5'5",
John Tutle, Thomas Stectham Queen Anne's MD 4/30/1772, English 19 chimneysweep
 14 days, Thursday, 5 pounds, 5'3",
John Tutton, Hugh Lownes Delaware PA 5/21/1794, 16 A
 10 dollars,
Samuel Tutton, Benjamin Poultney 10/16/1776, English 17
 7 days, Thursday, 1 pound, 5'2-3",
Leonard Tweed, William Jones Chester PA 9/19/1765, English 20
 21 days, Thursday, 2 pounds, 5'3",
Joseph Tygert, Henry Moliere Philadelphia PA 3/21/1792, 18 A
 91 days, Tuesday, 1 dollars, 4',
Matthias Tyle, James Bayard Cecil MD 12/18/1744, German 30
 25 days, Sunday, 2 pounds, middle,
Edward Tyler, Richard Brookbank Philadelphia City PA baker 8/9/1750, English 24
 7 days, Thursday, 3 pounds, 5'8",
John Tyler, James Brendly Philadelphia City PA 6/18/1730, 22 hatter
 3 days, Monday, 2 pounds, middle,
William Tyler, John Towsend Chester PA 9/1/1768, English 30 barber
 11 days, Sunday, 3 pounds, 5'6-7", (use to the sea)
John Henry Unclebock, George Adam Widner Berks PA 1/19/1758, toymaker
 9 days, Tuesday, 3 pounds, 6',
James Underhill, Alexander Martin Philadelphia City PA ship captain 12/12/1747, Irish
 2 pounds, (ran from ship which came from Barbados)
John Underhill, Anthony Wayne Chester PA 4/23/1752, 23
 4 days, Sunday, 2 pounds,
Dorothy Underwood, Felix Donnally Lancaster PA gaolkeeper 8/2/1764,
 37 days, Tuesday, 2 pounds,
Daniel Unthank, Aquila Price Baltimore MD 11/11/1772, 20 C
 5 pounds, 5'8-9",
Andrew Ure, Robert Aitken Philadelphia City PA 11/2/1774, Scot bookbinder
 3 days, Monday, 5 dollars, 5'5",
Andrew Urquhart, Jonas Supplef Philadelphia PA 8/28/1776, Scot 20
 15 days, Wednesday, 12 dollars, 5'7", (arrived last Oct.)

Michael Urviler, Henry Henritzy Montgomery PA 3/12/1788, American 18 hatter A
    9 days, Monday, 16 dollars, 5'8-9",
Michael Vachen, Robert Boyle Chester PA tanner 8/25/1743, Irish 26
    2 pounds, short,
Emanuel Vaeda, Roger Clark Cumberland PA 11/8/1764,
    1 pound, 5',
Charles Valaney, William Murray Gloucester NJ 8/7/1766, Irish 21
    9 days, Tuesday, 2 pounds, 5'8",
Cornelius Van De Beck, Jacob Fry Philadelphia City PA 12/18/1793, German 24 baker
    3 days, Sunday, 5 pounds, 5'2", (lately arrived)
Samuel Vandergrift, John Jenkins Lancaster PA 6/29/1774, American 7 L
    9 days, Tuesday,
Joanna Vandersteen, Davis Bevan Chester PA 6/1/1774, German
    3 days, Monday, 4 dollars,
Frederick Vandyke, Edward Hill Philadelphia PA 11/9/1749, German 29 sawyer
    8 days, Wednesday, 1 pound, short,
Frederick Vandyke, John Jacques New Castle DE 7/19/1750, German 30 sawyer (2nd escape)
    16 days, Tuesday, 1.5 pounds, middle,
Abraham Vanpelt, Michael Trump Philadelphia PA 5/8/1776, 19 shoemaker A
    10 days, Monday, 0.03 pounds, 5'6-7",
Christian Van Phul, Jacob Eckfelt Philadelphia City PA 8/7/1793, German-American 18 blacksmith A
    3 days, Sunday, 10 dollars, 5'2",
Breace Vansandt, Robert Worrell Philadelphia PA 5/2/1792, 19 blacksmith A
    17 days, Sunday, 5 pounds, 5'7-8",
James Van Winkle, David Ogden Essex NJ 12/5/1765, 26
    25 days, Sunday, 5 pounds, 5'10", (father lives nearby)
Jacob Varnam, Samuel Cheesman Philadelphia City PA 6/4/1761, 20 shoemaker A
    8 days, Wednesday, 5 pounds, 5'8",
Michael Vaughan, Robert Boyle Chester PA tanner 9/3/1747, Irish 30
    4 days, Sunday, 1.5 pistoles, 5',
Thomas Vaughan, James Shields Chester PA 9/2/1742, Irish 23
    4 days, Sunday, 2 pounds, middle,
William Vepon, Anthony Lee Philadelphia City PA 6/6/1745, 50
    2 days, Tuesday, 1.5 pounds, short,
Catherine Vernon, William Baxter Philadelphia City PA 2/8/1744, German
    0 days, Thursday, 2 pounds,
William Vickers, Isaac Perkins Kent MD 7/16/1772, American 40 soldier L
    26 days, Saturday, 5'9-10",
George Vickle, John Van Lasche Chester PA 6/27/1765, German 20
    5 pounds, 6', (has 2 years 4 months left to serve)
Francis Vigoe, John Metcalfe Baltimore MD 5/14/1752, German shoemaker
    32 days, Sunday, 5 pounds, (has a women with child)
Francis Villaneuve, Archibald McElroy Philadelphia City PA 7/6/1774, French perukemaker
    4 days, Sunday, 4 dollars, 5'3-4",
William Voice, Thomas Chrisholm Baltimore MD 8/31/1769, Welsh 45 plaisterer C
    10 days, Monday, 2 pounds, 5'10",
James Vomable, Alexander Lawson Baltimore MD ironworks 5/29/1746, Irish weaver
    8 days, Wednesday, 3 pounds, 5'2",
Curtis Wade, Robert Maplet Chester PA 7/30/1783, 17 A
    3 pounds, short,
William Wadsworth, Gawes Burrows Philadelphia City PA ship captain 8/21/1755, A
    11 days, Sunday, 1.5 pounds, 5'3",
Henry Waggoner, William Criag Philadelphia PA 9/27/1786, German 19
    8 days, Tuesday, 7 dollars, 5'7", (arrived 1 year ago)
William Waigh, William Hamilton York PA 5/27/1762, (ran before) A
    23 days, Tuesday, 5 pistoles, 5'10",
Joseph Wail, Richard Miller Salem NJ 1/4/1792, 14
    0.03 pounds, 4',
Anne Wainrite, Francis Mines New Castle DE 10/8/1747,
    4 pounds, short,
John Wakefield, William Buckland Anne Arundel MD 4/20/1774, 40 plaisterer
    18 days, Sunday, 5 pounds, 5'8-9",
William Waldron, Thomas Johnson Baltimore MD 1/20/1757, 27 C
    18 days, Sunday, 1.5 pounds, 5'5",
Michael Wale, Benjamin Hooton 10/20/1773, Irish 17
    1 pound, 5'3-4",

Henry Walkens, William Smith New Castle DE 12/5/1754, Irish
    11 days, Sunday, 1.5 pounds, middle,
Daniel Walker, Richard Backhouse Bucks PA ironworks 4/9/1788, American 26 L
    3 days, Sunday, 2 pounds,
Edward Walker, Robert Barnes Philadelphia PA 2/4/1752, English 21 tailor
    3 days, Monday, 4 pounds,
Edward Walker, Robert Walker Philadelphia City PA chairmaker 8/20/1764, English 60
    80 days, Monday, 3 pounds, 5'6",
Edward Walker, Joseph Lukens Montgomery PA 2/10/1790, 18 blacksmith A
    8 days, Tuesday, 4 dollars, 5'9",
James Walker, John Hustin New Castle DE 5/2/1765, Irish
    8 days, Wednesday, 1.5 pounds, 5'6",
James Walker, John Baldwin Chester PA 8/13/1767, Irish (2nd escape)
    3 days, Monday, 3 pounds, 5'5-6", (arrived 2.5 years ago)
James Walker, John Baldwin Chester PA 7/21/1768, Irish (3rd escape)
    17 days, Monday, 3 pounds, 5'5", (arrived 3 years ago)
John Walker, James Harrison Cecil MD 5/27/1756, 40 C
    3 pistoles, 5'9",
Joseph Walker, Joshua Woolston Bucks PA 12/22/1784, 14 A
    12 days, Friday, 4 dollars,
Matthias Walker, Peter Imlay Monmouth NJ miller 11/19/1761, American 15 L
    23 days, Tuesday, 1 pound,
Matthias Walker, Peter Imlay Monmouth NJ miller 11/27/1766, American 20 (2nd escape) L
    2 pounds, 5'9",
Michael Walker, John Garrett Philadelphia PA 7/5/1753, Irish 25
    8 days, Wednesday, 1.5 pounds, middle, (use to the sea)
Robert Walker, John Kelly Lancaster PA 11/21/1751, Irish 20
    44 days, Tuesday, 6', (arrived 9 years ago)
Robert Walker, Captain Crymer Baltimore MD ship captain 8/18/1763, English 44 C
    10 days, Monday, 1 pistole, 5'10",
Thomas Walker, William Ellis Cecil MD 10/2/1746, Irish C
    12 days, Saturday, 1.5 pounds, (lately arrived)
Francis Walkinson, Charles Carroll Baltimore MD ironworks 9/12/1754, English 21
    12 days, Saturday, 3 pounds, middle, (arrived this summer)
Charles Wall, Charles Writelock New Castle DE 9/7/1774, Irish 19 tanner
    18 days, Sunday, 5 pounds, 5'4",
Edward Wall, William Cox Baltimore MD 8/29/1771, Irish
    10 days, Monday, 5 pounds, 6',
James Wall, Henry Sietz Philadelphia PA 4/27/1769, Irish 16
    11 days, Sunday, 2 pounds, 5',
Joseph Wall, Thomas Rickets Cecil MD 4/12/1745, 20
    9 days, Tuesday, 1.5 pounds, middle,
Joseph Wall, Henry Smith Philadelphia PA 6/23/1743,
    10 days, Monday, 5 pounds, middle,
Patrick Wall, Obadiah Elliot New Castle DE 10/10/1754, Irish
    21 days, Thursday, 2 pounds, 5'8", (arrived 3 months ago)
Patrick Wall, William Bird Philadelphia PA 7/18/1751, Irish 21 sailor
    5 days, Saturday, 1.5 pounds, short, (lately arrived)
Patrick Wall, William Bird Philadelphia PA 9/12/1751, Irish 21 sailor (2nd escape)
    4 days, Sunday, 3 pounds, 5'8",
William Wall, Samuel Thompson New Castle DE 5/12/1743, Irish shoemaker
    8 days, Wednesday, 1 pound,
Edward Wallace, Thomas Witherspoon York PA 2/26/1756, weaver
    last April, 2 pounds, 5'10",
James Wallace, Robert Finney Chester PA doctor 1/13/1773, 25
    16 days, Tuesday, 3 dollars, 5'9-10",
John Wallace, James Brandon Cumberland PA 9/4/1755, English 20
    14 days, Thursday, 2 pounds, 5'5",
John Wallace, George Norris Hunterdon NJ 5/29/1755, Irish 16
    3 pounds, short,
Mary Wallace, John Wilkerson York PA ironworks 10/6/1763,
    24 days, Monday, 2 pounds,
Robert Wallace, Curtis Grubb Lancaster PA ironworks 4/21/1773, 20
    34 days, Friday, 2 pounds, 5'10",
William Wallace, Robert Finney Chester PA doctor 1/13/1773, 15
    16 days, Tuesday, 3 dollars,

Aaron Wallen, Joseph Burr Jr Northampton PA 4/30/1794, 20
    24 days, Sunday, 3 pounds, 5'8-9",
John Waller, George Lonberger Philadelphia City PA 12/15/1763, silversmith
    5 pounds, 5'6",
Thomas Walling, Andrew Hertzog Philadelphia City PA 4/21/1779 A
    9 days, Tuesday, 8 dollars,
Andrew Walls, James McCrea Lancaster PA 10/16/1755, Irish 24 weaver
    2 pounds, 5'9", (lately arrived)
Joseph Waln, James Kiemer Chester PA 6/21/1744, English 20
    5 days, Saturday, 2 pounds, middle,
Richard Walton, Joshua Jones Philadelphia PA 10/5/1774, English 20
    11 days, Sunday, 3 pounds, 5'4", (arrived last spring)
Thomas Walton, Edward Stevenson Frederick MD 5/28/1767, English C
    14 days, Thursday, 5 pounds, 5'8",
Martin Walts, Peter Waggoner Philadelphia City PA 1/19/1769, 23 A
    11 days, Sunday, 1 dollar, 5'7",
John Wamsley, Daniel Williams Philadelphia PA 10/15/1747, 23
    9 days, Tuesday, short,
John Wamsley, Benjamin Morgan Philadelphia PA 11/1/1750, Irish 24
    4 days, Sunday, 1 pound, short,
Frederick Wandle, Joseph Williams Chester PA 6/20/1754, German 20
    3 days, Monday, 3 pounds, 5'8",
William Warburton, Richard Gresham Kent MD 7/31/1766, English wheelwright C
    5 pounds,
Barnet Ward, George Emlen Philadelphia City PA 7/3/1746, German 24
    4 days, Sunday, 2 pounds,
Francis Ward, Joseph Reynolds Frederick MD 4/14/1768, English stocking-weaver C
    16 days, Tuesday, 5 pounds, 5'6",
James Ward, John Hanly Chester PA 8/16/1750, Irish 23 L
    3 days, Monday, 4 pistoles, middle,
John Ward, Daniel Surrell Queen Anne's MD 7/17/1760, English 50 mason C
    28 days, Thursday, 3 pounds, 5'6",
John Ward, Charles Carroll Baltimore MD ironworks 5/13/1756, English 27 C
    11 days, Sunday, 4 pistoles,
Lawrence Ward, George Brown Baltimore MD 7/11/1745, Irish
    4 pounds, short,
Luke Ward, John Crawford Bucks PA 7/4/1765, Irish 13 (2nd escape)
    21 days, Thursday, 4 dollars,
Luke Ward, John Crawford Bucks PA 3/7/1765, Irish 13
    7 days, Thursday, 3 dollars,
Owen Ward, Thomas Ustick Essex NJ 6/26/1735, Irish 23 husbandman
    8 days, Wednesday, 2 pounds,
Thomas Ward, Nathan Garrett Chester PA 3/28/1771, English 33 mason
    8 dollars, 5'6-7",
William Ward, James Brooks, Frederick MD 5/21/1772, 22 C
    47 days, Saturday, 20 pounds, 5'8",
Thomas Warde, George Emlen Philadelphia City PA 7/3/1746, English 19
    4 days, Sunday, 2 pounds, short,
Rosanna Wardner, Joseph Chambers York PA 1/1/1767, Scot 23
    5 pounds, 5'4",
Henry Wardrop, Edward Realy Philadelphia City PA 1/14/1752, Scot 24 ship-commander
    3 days, Monday, 1 pound, 6'3",
Thomas Warner, John Willmott Baltimore MD 7/15/1756, gardener C
    33 days, Sunday, 5 pounds, 5'9",
John Warren, David Ridgway Burlington NJ 5/28/1772, American 17 A
    4 days, Sunday, 6 dollars,
John Warren, George Norris Hunterdon NJ 11/25/1772, American 18 (2nd escape) A
    10 days, Monday, 1.5 pounds, 5'5",
John Warren, George Norris Hunterdon NJ 1/13/1773, American 18 (3rd escape) A
    10 days, Monday, 6 dollars, 5'6",
William Warren, Thomas Harrison Philadelphia City PA 5/31/1775, English 24 tailor
    9 days, Tuesday, 5'5",
William Warricker, John Hood Anne Arundel MD 9/20/1770, English 25 C
    18 days, Sunday, 10 pounds, 5'3", (arrived July 1770)
John Wason, Joseph Holdstock Philadelphia City PA 7/16/1772, Irish 13 soldier A
    10 days, Monday, 1 pound, (came to New York with the 26th regiment),

John Wason, Joseph Holdstock Philadelphia City PA 9/8/1773, Irish 14 soldier (2nd escape) A
    3 days, Monday, 1 pound, 4',
George Wass, David Cloyd Chester PA 4/16/1777, German 20
    24 days, Monday, 6 dollars,
William Waters, Thomas Hughes Gloucester VA pastor 6/15/1738, 20 joiner C
    51 days, Tuesday, 1 pistole, (arrived last March)
Catherine Waterson, James Gibbons Lancaster PA innkeeper 10/5/1769, Irish 19
    14 days, Thursday, 4 dollars,
John Watkins, Jacob Dietrick Gloucester NJ 6/30/1773, Irish 36
    17 days, Monday, 5 pounds, 5'8",
Peter Watkins, Andrew Campbell Orange VA 6/17/1742, American L
    1.5 pistoles,
Francis Watkinson, Charles Carroll Baltimore MD ironworks 5/13/1756, English 27 C
    11 days, Sunday, 4 pistoles,
Ann Watson, Thomas Dowman Philadelphia City PA 1/17/1776, English
    2 days, Tuesday, 1 dollar, 5',
Hugh Watson, Nathan Rigbie Baltimore MD 5/3/1739, tinker
    9 days, Tuesday, 1.5 pounds,
James Watson, William Graham Philadelphia City PA innkeeper 6/1/1769, Scot 23 clockmaker
    4 days, Sunday, 6 dollars, 5'6-7", (arrived last fall)
James Watson, Adam Krebs Philadelphia City PA 6/29/1774, Irish 19
    17 days, Monday, 5 pounds, 5'5",
John Watson, John Fouts Lancaster PA 9/12/1765, English 30 cooper
    16 days, Tuesday, 2 pounds, 5'9",
John Watson, John Sibbald NY 9/3/1761, 19 sailor A
    18 days, Sunday, 10 dollars,
Peter Watson, Joseph Harrison Gloucester NJ 10/9/1760, 19
    5 days, Saturday, 4 pistoles, 5'6",
Richard Watson, John Wily Philadelphia PA 11/16/1749, Irish 18
    8 days, Wedneday, 2 pounds, middle,
Samuel Watson, John Thomson York PA 6/1/1774, Irish 22 gaol sale L
    17 days, Monday, 5 pounds,
Thomas Watson, Charles Ridgely Jr Baltimore MD ironworks 9/26/1765, English 25 C
    58 days, Tuesday, 4 pounds, 5'8",
William Watson, William McColloch Lancaster PA 7/3/1766, English
    25 days, Sunday, 6 dollars, 5'4-5",
William Watson, Archibald Mustard Cumberland PA 4/20/1796, 15
    42 days, Wednesday, 20 dollars,
Adam Watt, Thomas Lyell Burlington NJ 4/14/1773, Irish 21
    9 days, Tuesday, 1.5 pounds, 5'7",
William Watt, Joseph Furtad Queen Anne's MD 4/12/1775, English 23 miller
    11 days, Sunday, 10 dollars, 5'8",
William Watters, Allen Gillespie New Castle DE 3/29/1770, 25 shoemaker
    20 days, Friday, 50 dollars, 5'8", (arrived some time ago)
John Watts, Benjamin Taylor Chester PA 9/7/1769, English 18
    7 days, Thursday, 1.5 pounds,
William Watts, David Bell Augusta VA 8/16/1770, Scot 25 C
    39 days, Sunday, 5 pounds, 5'10",
William Wayborn, Abraham Kintzing Philadelphia PA 12/7/1774, English 20
    17 days, Monday, 6 dollars,
Joseph Waytes, John Garriques Philadelphia City PA 7/12/1753, 18 cooper
    2 pounds,
Timothy Wbaland, William Ellis Cecil MD 10/2/1746, Irish C
    12 days, Saturday, 1.5 pounds, (lately arrived)
Connerd Wead, George Kastner Philadelphia PA 6/21/1744, German 30
    4 days, Sunday, 2 pounds, middle,
Hugh Wear, Patrick Carrigan Philadelphia City PA 9/9/1731, 22 spinner
    4 days, Sunday, 1.5 pounds,
William Weare, Joseph Gibbons Chester PA 11/17/1763, Irish 23
    4 days, Sunday, 2 pounds, short,
Joseph Weaver, Walter Comly Philadelphia PA 8/24/1749, English 24
    3 days, Monday, 2 pounds, middle,
Joseph Weaver, Walter Comly Philadelphia PA 3/19/1751, English 26 (2nd escape)
    2 days, Tuesday, 2 pounds,
Joseph Weaver, Walter Comly Philadelphia PA 4/16/1752, English 27 (3rd escape)
    5 days, Saturday, 3 pounds, middle,

Philip Weaver, William Marshall New Castle DE 5/1/1776, German 28
    42 days, Thursday, 1.5 pounds,
John Webb, Joseph Bolton 1/10/1771, American 22 L
    8 days, Wednesday, 6 dollars, 5'9-10",
Samuel Webb, William Slade Baltimore MD 1/13/1763, English C
    32 days, Sunday, 2 pounds, 5',
William Webb, James Baxter Cecil MD 9/5/1754, English sailor
    4 days, Sunday, 2 pounds, (ran from ship)
Benjamin Webber, Benjamin Kirby Queen Anne's MD 5/25/1769, English weaver
    16 days, Tuesday, 4 pounds,
Thomas Webber, Randle Mitchell 2/25/1752, English 21
    3 pounds, 5'9",
William Webster, William Reynolds Anne Arundel MD 11/15/1775, English 23 hatter
    11 days, Sunday, 5 pounds, 5'8-9",
Christiana Weeks, John Chevalier Philadelphia City PA 10/19/1774, English
    2 days, Tuesday, 2 dollars, (arrived last July)
John Weigkel, William Lawrence Gloucester NJ 6/23/1773, German 30 soldier
    6 days, Friday, 5 pounds, 6',
Christopher Weigner, Robert Ritchie Chester PA 11/3/1763, Swedish 26 sailor
    1 pound, 5'6", (lately arrived)
Samuel Weilding, Charles Brown Queen Anne's MD 5/13/1742, English 28 tailor
    37 days, Tuesday, 2.5 pounds, short,
Jacob Weimer, Thomas Dutton Chester PA 11/9/1774, German 20
    15 days, Wednesday, 4 pounds, 5'9", (arrived 3 years ago)
Peter Weisdorf, Charles Read Burlington NJ ironworks 5/28/1772, German 36
    April, 1 pound, 5'8-9",
David Welch, Edward Hanson Baltimore MD 11/9/1769, Irish 26 cooper
    11 days, Sunday, 5 pounds, 5'10",
David Welch, Richard Strode Chester PA 6/21/1786, Irish
    9 days, Monday, 10 dollars, 5'6-7",
James Welch, Joseph Talbott Chester PA 8/24/1738, Irish 23
    4 days, Sunday, 3 pounds,
James Welch, Joseph Talbott Chester PA 10/19/1738, Irish 23 (2nd escape)
    4 days, Sunday, 2 pound,
James Welch, Charles O'Haro York PA 4/21/1768, Irish 23 carpenter
    8 pounds, 5'6",
John Welch, Arthur McIlveen Gloucester NJ 12/5/1751, Irish 25 weaver
    3 days, Monday, 1 pound, 5'6",
John Welch, John Brown Lancaster PA 4/20/1749, Irish 21 shoemaker
    9 days, Tuesday, 3 pounds, 6',
Morris Welch, Hugh Clark New Castle DE 8/23/1750,
    2 pounds, short,
Thomas Welch, Joseph Ellis Gloucester NJ 4/20/1749, Irish 18
    7 days, Thursday, 5 pounds,
Thomas Welch, James Edwards Gloucester NJ 6/3/1756, Irish 25 (2nd escape)
    7 days, Thursday, 1 pound, 5'6",
Thomas Welch, James Baxter Cecil MD ironworks 8/30/1739, English C
    11 days, Sunday, 2 pounds, tall,
William Welch, James Anderson Lancaster PA 11/15/1750, 25 L
    9 days, Tuesday, 5'8",
Alexander Weldon, James Coleman Bucks PA 1/13/1796, 19 A
    25 days, Saturday, 0.03 pounds, 5'8",
Patrick Weldon, Edward Pancoast Burlington NJ 3/4/1756, Irish 19 sailor
    20 days, Friday, 3 pounds,
John Weller, John Sutherland Fredericksburg VA 4/19/1759, 36 gardener C
    38 days, Monday,
Abraham Wells, Robert Shewell Bucks PA cooper 1/25/1732, 18 A
    11 days, Sunday, 2 pounds, middle,
Susannah Wells, Thomas Downing New Castle DE 12/4/1740, English 28
    30 days, Tuesday, 1.25 pounds,
George Welsby, John Clark Bucks PA 3/13/1730,
    5 days, Saturday, 1 pound,
Henry Welsh, William Montgomery Chester PA 6/10/1762, Irish 18
    9 days, Tuesday, 3 pounds, 5'6",
James Welsh, Conrad Hook Lancaster PA 12/28/1769, Irish 17 weaver
    25 days, Sunday, 5 pounds, 5',

Margaret Welsh, Sarah Hopkins Lancaster PA 4/19/1770, Irish 22
   9 days, Tuesday, 1.5 pounds, 5'2",
Margaret Welsh, Sarah Hopkins Lancaster PA 3/28/1771, Irish 23 (2nd escape)
   8 days, Wednesday, 3 dollars, 5'2-3",
Mary Welsh, Archibald Little New Castle DE 10/25/1750, Irish 25
   20 days, Friday, 3 pounds,
Morris Welsh, James Wilson Chester PA 10/8/1767, Irish-American 10 A
   11 days, Sunday, 0.75 pounds,
Nicholas Welsh, Archibald Little New Castle DE 10/25/1750, Irish 40
   20 days, Friday, 3 pounds, middle,
Robert Welsh, Joseph Gavin Philadelphia City PA shoemaker 9/25/1755, Scot
   1.5 pounds, 5',
Sarah Welsh, William Adams Philadelphia City PA 7/7/1784, Irish 36
   10 dollars, (lately arrived)
Walter Welsh, Robert Jamison Bucks PA 2/11/1755, Irish 18
   6 days, Friday, 2 pounds, 5'4",
Thomas Wenn, William Crosthwaite Philadelphia City PA perukemaker 3/12/1740, 40 barber
   9 days, Tuesday, 2 pounds, middle,
Thomas Wenn, William Crosthwaite Philadelphia City PA perukemaker 1/8/1741, 41 barber (2nd esc)
   5 days, Saturday, 2 pounds, middle,
Anna Rosina Wenseling, John Zell Philadelphia PA 10/16/1776, German 30
   4 days, Sunday, 8 dollars, (arrived 2 years ago)
John Wensill, Daniel Kinbord Lancaster PA 11/7/1771,
   2 pounds, 5'2",
Sion Wentworth, John Veneman Chester PA 5/28/1747, American 25 L
   4 days, Sunday, 5 pistoles, 5'6",
Amos West, James Caruthers Gloucester NJ 6/25/1794, 19 A
   1 dollar,
John West, James Wharton Philadelphia City PA 8/15/1771, English 15
   11 days, Sunday, 2 pounds,
Philip West, Samuel Coulter Cumberland PA 9/20/1775, German 27
   61 days, Saturday, 20 dollars, 5'7-8",
William Westburn, Joseph Harvey Bucks PA 3/1/1775, American L
   10 days, Monday, 2.5 pounds, 5'4",
Ezra Westcot, Zachariah Lawrence NJ 2/25/1795, 14 tailor A
   0.5 dollars, short,
James Westcott, Thomas Wilkinson Queen Anne's MD 1/6/1730,
   9 days, Tuesday, 2 pounds,
Stephen Westcott, Thomas Wright Queen Anne's MD 1/6/1730,
   9 days, Tuesday, 2 pounds,
Madlin Westley, Robert Gelton Boston MA 3/16/1747, Welsh 25
   65 days, Tuesday, 1 pound, short,
Edward Westward, James Few New Castle DE 3/13/1753, English blacksmith
   1 day, Wednesday, 1.5 pounds, 6',
Benjamin Wetherby, William Reeve Cumberland NJ 8/13/1794, 19 A
   10 days, Sunday, 6 dollars, short,
Thomas Wetherby, John Wood Cumberland NJ 2/11/1789, 23
   16 days, Monday, 8 dollars, 5'7-8",
Isaac Wetheridge, John Senhouse Anne Arundel MD 6/16/1743, English 30 shoemaker C
   30 days, Tuesday, 3 pounds, short,
Mathias Wexell, William Halloway Philadelphia PA 3/10/1779, German 20
   6 days, Thursday, 8 dollars in silver, 5'7",
John Weyant, Henry Damood Lancaster PA 1/3/1749, German 20
   25 days, Sunday, 2.5 pounds,
Luke Whalen, William Herlan Chester PA 6/18/1752, Irish 30 miller
   4 days, Sunday, 2 pounds, middle,
William Whaly, Abraham Kintzing Philadelphia PA 8/2/1775, English 30
   18 days, Sunday, 10 dollars, 5'6-7",
Robert Wharton, John Davis Queen Anne's MD 6/27/1754, English 35
   38 days, Monday, 2.5 pounds,
Edward Whealen, George Ashman Jr Baltimore MD 7/10/1760, C
   5 days, Saturday, 5 pounds, short,
Daniel Whealon, William Parks Williamsburg VA 12/31/1745, Irish blacksmith C
   25 days, Sunday, 6 pistoles, 5'9",
Michael Whealon, Curtis Trenchard Salem NJ 1/20/1773, Irish
   189 days, Wednesday, 4 pounds, 5'6-7",

Thomas Wheatley, Aquila Price Baltimore MD 11/11/1772, 27 C
   5 pounds, 5'8-9",
Maurice Wheeler, Paul Koul Hunterdon NJ 1/19/1744, Irish 21
   9 days, Tuesday, 2 pounds, short, (has been fishing off Newfoundland)
John Whellen, Joseph James Chester PA 6/27/1745, Irish
   9 days, Tueday, 3 pounds, tall,
Michael Whilan, William Young Salem NJ 8/1/1771, Irish
   5 pounds, 5'6-7",
Margaret Whilley, James White Philadelphia City PA 9/6/1753, Irish 18
   7 days, Thursday, 1 pound,
Francis Whistle, John Patton Berks PA ironworks 6/17/1762, English 23 L
   9 days, Tuesday, 3 pounds, 5'4",
Francis Whistle, Mark Bird Berks PA ironworks 3/31/1763, English 24 (2nd escape) L
   27 days, Friday, 5 pounds, 5'2",
Francis Whistle, Mark Bird Berks PA ironworks 11/13/1766, English 28 (3rd escape) L
   15 days, Wednesday, 5 pounds, 5'1-2",
Ann White, James No Name Chester PA 5/31/1759, 23 workhouse sale L
   80 days, Monday, 1 pistole,
Christopher White, Samuel Potts Lancaster PA ironworks 6/14/1764, 19
   4 days, Sunday, 3 pounds, 5'4",
Christopher White, Thomas Beach Anne Arundel MD 9/24/1767, Irish 30 C
   3 pounds, 6',
Daniel White, Hercules Coutts Kent MD 10/23/1760, English 25 gardener
   end of Aug., 7 PA pounds, 5'10",
Elizabeth White, Michael Bright Berks PA 7/28/1773, Irish 25
   24 days, Monday, 0.75 pounds,
Garret White, John Hart Philadelphia City PA 9/17/1730, 22
   3 days, Monday, 2 pounds, short,
John White, Philip Ward Lancaster PA 6/18/1747, English 40
   1.5 pounds, middle,
John White, Thomas Shoemaker 4/26/1733, English 30
   4 days, Sunday, 3 pounds, middle,
John White, John Wells Philadelphia PA 7/17/1755, 18
   53 days, Sunday, 2 pounds, 5'9",
John White, Godfrey Cline Lancaster PA 7/18/1771, Irish 18
   10 days, Monday, 2 pounds, 5'2-3",
John White, Curtis Lewis Chester PA 5/17/1770, English 21 L
   5 days, Saturday, 3 pounds, 5'4-5",
John White, Curtis Lewis Chester PA 3/10/1773, English 24 (2nd escape) L
   10 days, Monday, 0.08 pounds, 5'4",
John White, James Sheward Chester PA 8/17/1774, English 25 (3rd escape) L
   3 days, Monday, 2.5 pounds, 5'5-6",
Joseph White, Walter Lilly Jr Chester PA 1/14/1795, 18 blacksmith A
   10 days, Sunday, 8 dollars, 5'7-8",
Mary White, Robert Alexander Lancaster PA 9/22/1763, 25
   11 days, Sunday, 2.5 pounds,
Michael White, Henry Baker Cecil MD 12/5/1754, Irish 28 tailor
   3 pounds, 5'8",
Michael White, Henry Baker Cecil MD 6/26/1755, Irish 29 tailor (2nd escape)
   2 pistoles, tall,
Patrick White, John Clark New Castle DE 8/29/1751, Irish 23
   17 days, Monday, 2 pounds, 5'9",
Patrick White, James Duncan Chester PA 1/28/1755, Irish 22
   4 days, Sunday, 2 pounds, middle,
Patrick White, Henry Smith Berks PA ironworks 5/4/1769, Irish 23 gaol sale L
   17 days, Monday, 5 pounds, 5'5-6",
Richard White, John Ford Morris NJ 7/8/1742, Irish 30 ditcher
   14 days, Thursday, 2 pounds, short,
Thomas White, Peter Saunders Philadelphia City PA shoemaker 10/6/1737, Irish 18
   3 days, Monday, 1 pound, tall,
William White, William Keyl Chester PA 11/14/1754, Irish 20 tailor
   16 days, Tuesday, 1 pound, 5'6",
John Whitecraft, William Sharp Burlington NJ 1/30/1788, 19 A
   2 days, Monday, 3 pounds,
Daniel Whitefield, William Edwards Baltimore MD 11/23/1769, C
   23 days, Tuesday, 5 pounds, short,

Edward Whitehead, Ellis Davis Chester PA 7/23/1741, 30 fuller
　　6 days, Friday, 2 pounds, middle,
Jacob Whitehead, John Bringhurst Philadelphia PA 10/30/1776, English carver
　　14 days, Thursday, 4 dollars,
Robert Whitehead, John Burroughs Hunterdon NJ 4/12/1753, English
　　28 days, Thursday, 2 pounds, 5', (whipped and branded as a thief in Trenton)
Robert Whorton, John Davis Queen Anne's MD 9/19/1754, English 35 (ran before)
　　31 days, Monday, 2 pounds,
Richard Wickly, William Bonar Baltimore MD 5/26/1768, English
　　11 days, Sunday, 3 pounds, 5'9-10",
James Wickrey, Swan Boon Chester PA 6/8/1749, American 28 L
　　2 pounds,
John Wicks, Duncan MacKenzie Philadelphia City PA 10/8/1730,
　　3 days, Monday, 1 pound, short,
William Wieldon, John Blackwood Philadelphia PA 5/20/1762, English
　　12 days, Saturday, 2 pounds, 5'4",
John Wife, John Jones Lancaster PA sheriff 8/30/1750, English
　　1 pound,
James Wiggins, Samuel Thompson Gloucester NJ 6/19/1776, 17 A
　　23 days, Tuesday, 4 dollars, 4'9",
Samuel Wiggins, John Lewis Cecil MD 7/22/1756, American 12 L
　　7 days, Thursday, 2 pounds,
William Wighman, James McClure Chester PA 8/17/1774, Irish
　　5 dollars, (arrived 4 weeks ago)
John Wiglay, George Lee Westmoreland VA 10/26/1749, English farmer (ran before)
　　66 days, Monday, 2 pistoles, 5'10", (arrived 1 year ago)
Thomas Wigley, William Kay Philadelphia City PA 2/23/1785, 23
　　100 dollars, 5'6",
John Wilcocks, Edward Stevenson Frederick MD 5/28/1767, English 20 C
　　14 days, Thursday, 5 pounds, 6',
John Wilcocks, Daniel Hughes Frederick MD ironworks 10/5/1774, English 27 (2nd escape) C
　　16 days, Tuesday, 3 pounds, 5'10",
Joseph Wilcocks, Orr Glenholme Philadelphia City PA merchant 6/19/1766, Irish 30 nailer
　　12 days, Saturday, 1.5 pounds, 5'7", (ran from ship)
Robert Wilcox, William Bennet Baltimore MD 5/15/1755, C
　　17 days, Monday, 1 pistole, 5'10",
Thomas Wildeer, Samuel Hastings Philadelphia City PA shipwright 2/7/1740, Irish 25
　　4 days, Sunday, 2 pounds, middle,
William Wiley, Zachariah Nieman Philadelphia PA 8/1/1771, Irish 19
　　4 days, Sunday, 2 pounds, 5'3-4",
Nicholas Wilhelm, Rudolph Miller Dauphin PA 11/30/1785, German 27 cooper
　　14 days, Wednesday, 3 pounds, 5'8-9",
Thomas Wilkens, Samuel Beall Jr Frederick MD ironworks 5/19/1768, English 26 carpenter
　　54 days, Saturday, 5 pounds, 5'3-4", (arrived last fall)
John Wilkins, Flora Dorsey Baltimore MD 4/18/1765, 25
　　11 days, Sunday, 2 pounds,
Joseph Wilkins, Joseph Bullock Philadelphia City PA 7/26/1775, English 14
　　9 days, Tuesday, 1 pound,
Briant Wilkinson, Daniel McCarthy Philadelphia City PA ship captain 11/20/1755, English 22
　　3 days, Monday, 2 pounds, middle, (ran from ship)
John Wilkinson, Thomas Harris Queen Anne's MD 7/1/1756, Scot shoemaker
　　mid-May, 5 pounds, 5'10",
Thomas Wilkinson, Isaac Rettinghouse Hunterdon NJ 5/21/1767, Irish 19
　　8 days, Wednesday, 4 dollars,
Thomas Wilkinson, William Kerlin Chester PA 8/30/1770, Irish 20 gaol sale L
　　2 pounds, middle,
Thomas Wilkinson, William Kerlin Chester PA 1/16/1772, Irish 22 (2nd escape) L
　　20 days, Friday, 2 pounds, 5'8",
William Wilkinson, Joseph Mitchell 11/20/1755, English 19
　　2.5 pounds,
William Wilkison, John Barclay Lancaster PA 7/6/1749, 20
　　3 pounds, short,
James Wilks, Patrick Rock Harford MD 5/1/1776, English 24 C
　　260 days, Tuesday, 20 dollars, 5'5",
Thomas Wilks, Patrick Creagh MD 12/30/1742, 40 brickmaker C
　　25 days, Sunday, 3 pounds, (arrived last Sept.)

Joseph Willard, William Parker 11/6/1746, 19 blacksmith A
  8 days, Wednesday, 2 pounds,
Thomas Willdear, Samuel Hastings Philadelphia City PA shipwright 6/14/1739, Irish
  3 days, Monday, 1.5 pounds, middle,
Peggy William, Charles Woolfall Philadelphia City PA 8/11/1763, English
  3 pounds, (arrived last spring)
Richard William, Nathaniel Water Anne Arundel MD 12/7/1758, English 23 hatter C
  36 days, Wednesday, 10 pounds, 5'8",
William William, Robert Anderson Kent MD ship captain 7/8/1731, Welsh blacksmith
  3 pounds, middle,
David Williams, Thomas Sands Queen Anne's MD 10/9/1755, Welsh
  37 days, Tuesday, 2 pounds, 5'6",
David Williams, James Cochran New Castle DE 3/10/1768, English 25
  8 days, Wednesday, 6 dollars, short,
Edward Williams, William Hooper Queen Anne's MD 5/20/1742, English 30
  11 days, Sunday, 2 Maryland pounds, 6',
Edward Williams, William Young Jr Baltimore MD 7/28/1773, English 37 cooper C
  17 days, Monday, 2 pounds, (arrived 4 weeks ago)
Edward Williams, William Young Jr Baltimore MD 8/25/1773, English 37 cooper (2nd escape) C
  10 days, Monday, 3 pounds, 5'10",
Elisabeth Williams, Samuel Mendenhall Chester PA 2/14/1771, Welsh 24
  36 days, Wednesday, 0.5 pounds, middle,
Francis Williams, James Templeton Philadelphia City PA ship captain 11/21/1745, Welsh
  3 days, Monday, 5'9", (ran from ship)
George Williams, Cornelius Hains New Castle DE 10/10/1771, German
  7 days, Thursday, 4 dollars, 5'1-2",
George Williams, William MacCubbin Jr Anne Arundel MD 9/17/1767, (his 2nd transportation) C
  32 days, Sunday, 3 pounds, 5'7",
Hance Williams, Owen Evans Philadelphia PA 2/5/1756, German 19
  12 days, Saturday, 1 pound, short,
Hugh Williams, Samuel Read Philadelphia City PA baker 5/18/1749, Irish 19
  4 days, Sunday, 5 pounds,
James Williams, John Carsson Lancaster PA 9/26/1751, 40 cooper
  32 days, Sunday, 3 pounds, 5'10",
Jane Williams, John Faries New Castle DE 10/5/1769, 18
  7 days, Thursday, 2 pounds,
John Williams, Isaac Pearson Burlington NJ 9/1/1737, English 37 clockmaker
  6 days, Friday, 1.5 pounds, short,
John Williams, David Potts Philadelphia PA 5/27/1731, 17
  10 days, Monday, 2 pounds,
John Williams, William Harris Philadelphia City PA ship captain 12/6/1733, English
  2 pounds, (ran from ship Vigor from Bristol)
John Williams, William Craig 7/28/1757, Welsh 37 tailor
  2 days, Tuesday, 1.5 pounds, (was in the army)
John Williams, Samuel Cheesman Philadelphia City PA 1/2/1766, 21 shoemaker
  6 days, Friday, 3 pounds, 5',
John Williams, Robert Armstrong Chester PA 12/1/1768, English 40 sailor
  9 days, Tuesday, 4 pounds, 5'4", (use to the sea)
John Williams, Samuel Burrough Gloucester NJ 4/26/1770, English 41 sailor (2nd escape)
  7 days, Thursday, 8 dollars, 5'5",
John Williams, John Brinton Chester PA 5/30/1771, Welsh 38
  2 days, Tuesday, 2 pounds, 5'5-6",
John Williams, John Brinton Chester PA 5/28/1772, Welsh 39 (2nd escape)
  23 days, Tuesday, 4 dollars, 5'5-6",
John Williams, John Bolton Kent MD merchant 5/8/1766, Welsh 25
  21 days, Thursday, 10 pounds, 5'8",
John Williams, Jeremiah Sheredine Baltimore MD ironworks 9/5/1765, English 30 C
  18 days, Sunday, 10 pounds, 5',
John Williams, Hugh Conn Prince George MD 6/27/1745, Welsh tinker C
  67 days, Sunday, 1.5 pounds, middle, (arrived Jan. 16, 1744)
John Williams, Robert Roberts Kent MD 11/3/1763, English 38 C
  2 pounds, (arrived this summer)
John Williams, Charles Carroll Baltimore MD ironworks 6/21/1753, English 30 farmer C
  19 days, Saturday, 4 pistoles, middle,
Lewelin Williams, Thomas Bates Philadelphia PA 5/9/1745, Welsh 20
  4 days, Sunday, 2.5 pounds, short,

Lewellin Williams, Thomas Bowen Chester PA 2/24/1757, Welsh 35
    14 days, Thursday, 1.5 pounds, middle,
Margaret Williams, Edmund Bacon Philadelphia City PA 4/27/1769, English
    12 days, Saturday, 1 pound, 5'2-3",
Margaret Williams, Hugh Conn Prince George MD 6/27/1745, Welsh C
    67 days, Sunday, 1.5 pounds, short, (arrived Jan. 16, 1744)
Mary Williams, Edward Eaton Philadelphia PA 8/14/1776, 17
    10 days, Monday, 0.03 pounds, short,
Matthew Williams, William Keeper Baltimore MD 5/16/1751, English 25
    5 pounds, short,
Mose Williams, Samuel Shivers Gloucester NJ 9/26/1745, Irish-Indian L
    11 days, Sunday, 1 pound,
Owen Williams, Enoch Evans Burlington NJ 2/8/1775, Welsh 18
    7 days, Thursday, 8 dollars, (lately arrived)
Rice Williams, Andrew Work Lancaster PA 11/29/1770, Welsh 25
    3 pounds, 5'9",
Robert Williams, Joshua Owings Baltimore MD 2/16/1769, English 45 C
    10 days, Monday, 7 pounds, 5'6",
Samuel Williams, William Scot Philadelphia City PA tailor 10/23/1740, English
    11 days, Sunday, 3 pounds,
Thomas Williams, John Kirkpatrick Cecil MD 7/29/1756, Irish 20
    10 days, Monday, 2 pounds, 5'5",
Thomas Williams, Peter Imlay Monmouth NJ miller 6/9/1768, Welsh 18
    32 days, Sunday, 3 pounds, 5'3-4",
Thomas Williams, William Fullerton Lancaster PA 7/23/1772, Welsh 20
    2 pounds, 5'7-8", (arrived 1 year and 8 months ago)
Thomas Williams, Valentine Vannolt Philadelphia PA 4/23/1772, Irish soldier hired L
    6 days, Friday, 2 pounds, 5'5",
William Williams, Joseph Williams Philadelphia PA 5/7/1741, Welsh 50
    2 pounds,
William Williams, James Forsyth Cumberland PA 5/9/1765, Irish baker
    2 pounds, 5'6",
William Williams, Jacob Starn Sussex NJ ironworks 5/21/1767, English 45 school teacher
    1.5 pounds, 5'6",
William Williams, Jacob Hetherling Chester PA 12/22/1773, English 19
    5 pounds, 5'3",
William Williams, Richard Gibbs Salem NJ 4/13/1796, 32
    10 days, Sunday, 10 dollars, 6'2",
William Williams, Conrad Alster Philadelphia City PA 7/29/1772, Irish 17 A
    1.5 pounds, 5'5",
William Williams, James Dobbins Philadelphia City PA 5/5/1748, sailor L
    21 days, Thursday, 4 pistoles,
William Williams, Thomas Harrison Anne Arundel MD ironworks 7/27/1769, 30 C
    11 days, Sunday, 5 pounds, 5'6",
Nathaniel Willis, William Hopkins Cecil MD 12/10/1741, Irish 20
    9 days, Tuesday, 2 pounds, middle,
Robert Willis, John Jones Philadelphia City PA 10/8/1730, shoemaker
    3 days, Monday, 1 pound, short,
William Willis, Daniel Bacon Burlington NJ 1/18/1732, 23
    3 days, Monday, 5 pounds, middle,
John Willson, Henry Stevens Kent DE 8/19/1762, 17
    15 days, Wednesday, 3 pounds, (father lives nearby)
Peter Willy, Abraham Emmit Chester PA 4/2/1741, Irish 20 glover
    last summer, 1 pound,
John Wilmoth, William Temple Chester PA 6/28/1775, 30 sadler L
    8 dollars, 5'8-9",
John Wilskicls, John Andrew Messerschmids Philadelphia City PA 11/15/1770, 17 A
    4 dollars, (relatives live nearby)
Albert Wilson, George Henhold Gloucester NJ 12/1/1773, 20 wheelwright A
    3 days, Monday, 3 pounds, 5'10",
Ann Wilson, William Reynolds Chester PA 11/16/1758, English 35
    59 days, Monday, 1 pound,
Ann Wilson, James Braddock Talbot MD 11/8/1775, 45 C
    18 days, Sunday, 2 pounds, 5'2",
Edward Wilson, Edward Woodward Chester PA 6/14/1744, Irish 17
    1.5 pounds, short,

Elizabeth Wilson, Alexander Rutherford Philadelphia City PA shoemaker 1/22/1767, 30
    10 days, Monday, 2 pounds, 5'3-4",
Hugh Wilson, Harmon Yeats New Castle DE 1/14/1768, Irish 30
    16 days, Tuesday, 5 pounds, 5'3-4",
Hugh Wilson, Isaac Atlee Lancaster PA 8/31/1791, Irish 17
    23 days, Monday, 4 dollars, 5'6",
Hugh Wilson, Stephen Love Montgomery PA 7/11/1787, Irish 17
    10 days, Sunday, 3 pounds, 5'6",
Hugh Wilson, Stephen Love Montgomery PA 8/27/1788, Irish 18 (2nd escape)
    8 dollars, 5'6-7",
Hugh Wilson, Stephen Love Montgomery PA 11/14/1792, Irish 22 (3rd escape)
    9 days, Monday, 5'6",
Jeremiah Wilson, John Caldwell Chester PA 6/14/1764, Irish 35
    6 days, Friday, 6 dollars, 5'8",
Jeremy Wilson, Henry Stiegal Berks PA ironworks 5/9/1765, Irish 38
    17 days, Monday, 2 pistoles,
John Wilson, Benjamin Fred Chester PA 4/16/1747, 21
    29 days, Wednesday, 1.5 pounds, middle,
John Wilson, Thomas Allsree New Castle DE 6/6/1745, Irish 20
    15 days, Wednesday, 2 pounds, middle,
John Wilson, Christian Marshall 6/30/1763, Irish 26
    10 days, Monday, 1.5 pounds, short, (lately arrived, ran from ship)
John Wilson, Stephen Onion Baltimore MD ironworks 7/29/1762, Irish 25
    3 pounds, short,
John Wilson, William Denney Chester PA 1/19/1769, Irish 23 weaver
    11 days, Sunday, 2 pounds, 5'6-7", (arrived 5 months ago)
John Wilson, Noah Wheaton Cumberland NJ 9/27/1775, English
    3 pounds, 5'5-6",
John Wilson, Stephen Onion Baltimore MD ironworks 6/20/1745, Irish 27 C
    9 days, Tuesday, 5 pounds, 6',
John Wilson, Stephen Onion Baltimore MD ironworks 4/2/1747, Irish 29 (2nd escape) C
    9 days, Tuesday, 5 pounds, 6',
Joseph Wilson, James Hapnalt Chester PA 8/30/1770, 21
    11 days, Sunday, 6 dollars, 5'4",
Joseph Wilson, Thomas Lewis New Castle DE 1/2/1753, American sadler L
    23 days, Tuesday, 2 pounds, middle,
Lewis Wilson, Thomas Smith Philadelphia City PA ship captain 12/2/1742, Welsh 22 joiner
    2 pounds, short, (ran from ship)
Mary Wilson, Christopher Smith merchant 1/27/1729, English mantuamaker
    1 pound,
Robert Wilson, Benjamin Davis Philadelphia City PA 11/15/1770, Irish 25
    6 dollars, 5'8-10",
Sarah Wilson, Edward Moon New Castle DE 3/10/1768,
    21 days, Thursday, 0.75 pounds, short,
Sarah Wilson, Peter January Philadelphia City PA 6/27/1765, 15 (ran before) A
    6 days, Friday, 1 pound, 5',
Thomas Wilson, John Drummond Kent MD 7/9/1741, Scot
    one month ago, 2 pounds, short,
Thomas Wilson, George Gray Philadelphia City PA brewer 6/25/1752, English 36
    4 days, Sunday, 10 pounds, 5'7",
Thomas Wilson, Navel Win Hunterdon NJ 9/29/1768, Irish 20 wool comber
    16 days, Tuesday, 4 pounds, 5'9", (had run away from the navy)
William Wilson, Benjamin Inskeep Gloucester NJ 1/17/1771, Irish 30
    473 days, Sunday, 7 pounds, 4'6",
William Wilson, Joshua McDowell Chester PA 7/26/1764, English L
    6 pounds, 5'10",
Peter Wilt, Jacob Arden New York NY butcher 3/10/1763, 18 A
    17 days, Monday, 20 dollars,
Thomas Wiltshire, George Aston Chester PA 7/4/1734, English
    7 days, Thursday, 2 pounds, short,
Daniel Winekar, Jacob Levan Jr Berks PA 9/20/1764, 24 weaver
    2 pounds,
Thomas Winey, William Fitzhugh Westmoreland VA 8/31/1749, C
    17 days, Monday, 5 pounds, 5'7",
Richard Wingham, William Streper Philadelphia PA 11/27/1755, English 21
    17 days, Monday, 2 pounds, 5'9",

Barney Winn, John Brown Chester PA 3/23/1774, Irish
    10 days, Monday, 2 pounds, 6',
Jane Winsant, Jeremiah Smith New Castle DE 12/20/1764, 28 L
    20 days, Friday, 2 pounds,
John Winsley, Robert Lamborn Chester PA 5/18/1774, 33 L
    3 dollars, 5'6-7", (arrived 14 years ago)
John Winssly, Daniel Kinfort Lancaster PA 5/2/1771,
    1 pound, 5'3",
William Winter, William Beatry Lancaster PA 6/20/1754, Irish 20
    7 days, Thursday, 2 pounds, 5'6",
James Winterbottom, George Beatho Philadelphia City PA 6/20/1771, English 17 chimneysweep
    44 days, Tuesday, 2 pounds, 4'6",
James Winterbottom, George Beatho Philadelphia City PA 12/26/1771, English 19 chimsweep (2nd esc)
    12 days, Saturday, 2.5 pounds,
James Winterbottom, George Beatho Philadelphia City PA 6/4/1772, English 17 chimsweep (3rd esc)
    5 days, Saturday, 2 pounds, 4'9",
James Winterbottom, James Lattimer New Castle DE 3/1/1775, Irish 24
    6 dollars, 5'6",
Peter Wisely, David Cheston Kent MD 8/26/1742, Irish
    29 days, Wednesday, 2 pounds, middle, (was a servant 2.5 years ago)
Jacob Wiseman, Isaac Perkins Frederick VA 6/12/1755, 19
    19 days, Saturday, 2 pistoles, middle,
Robert Wisenden, Thomas Flemming Fairfax VA 7/25/1751, 28 carpenter
    24 days, Monday, 5 pistoles, 5'7", (arrived last Dec.)
Joseph Wissen, John MacKelfresh Frederick MD 9/8/1773, C
    2.5 pounds, 5'10",
William Wistburn, Joseph Harvey Bucks PA 6/14/1775,
    17 days, Monday, 2 pounds,
Jacob Witlock, Andrew Miller Salem NJ 7/16/1794, German 18 nailer A
    26 days, Friday, 4 dollars, 5', (relatives live nearby)
Henry Witmore, Edward Stevenson Frederick MD 3/12/1772,
    4 pounds, 5'4-5",
Caril Witt, Peter Conrad Philadelphia PA 9/12/1745, German 35 blacksmith
    2 days, Tuesday, 2 pounds, middle,
Moses Witten, Cornelius Quick Hunterdon NJ 4/16/1752, American 22 L
    4 days, Sunday, 3 pounds, middle,
Michael Woldridge, James Payne Philadelphia City PA cooper 5/1/1746, 18
    4 days, Sunday, 1 pound, middle,
Nicholas Wolf, John Hackett Union NJ ironworks 9/27/1764, German 27 carter
    16 days, Tuesday, 3 pistoles, 5'6",
Henry Wolff, Jacob Bauman Philadelphia PA 9/29/1743, German 18
    4 days, Sunday, 2 pounds,
No Name Woman, Roger Connor Lancaster PA 8/3/1769, Irish 20
    15 crowns, short,
No Name Woman, Daniel Few New Castle DE 4/1/1756, American 30 L
    17 days, Monday, 1 pound,
Abraham Wood, Jacob Lewis Philadelphia PA carpenter 1/17/1749, 19 A
    4 days, Sunday, 3 pounds, tall,
David Wood, Thomas James Lancaster PA 4/10/1746, 23 millwright
    26 days, Saturday, 6 pounds, short,
George Owen Wood, William Blair Cumberland PA 5/14/1777, 20 A
    10 days, Monday, 12 dollars, 5'5",
James Wood, Charles Ridgely Jr Baltimore MD ironworks 7/23/1752, 23 blacksmith
    13 days, Friday, 2.5 pounds, short,
James Wood, Joseph Hudson Chester PA 6/13/1754, Irish 26 weaver
    3 days, Monday, 2 pounds, 6'2",
John Wood, Isaac Norris Philadelphia City PA merchant 10/28/1731, English 22 carpenter
    9 days, Tuesday, 2 pounds, (arrived from Bristol in 1730)
John Wood, W. Worthington Jr Baltimore MD 1/1/1745, wheelwright
    76 days, Wednesday, 10 pounds, tall,
John Wood, Archibald Ritchie VA 3/21/1765, English 45 sailor
    6 days, Friday, 5 pounds, (arrived last summer)
John Wood, Francis Smith Burlington NJ 7/26/1739, English 40 L
    3 days, Monday, 2 pounds, (arrived 10 years ago)
Patrick Wood, James Bruce Chester PA 6/21/1770, Irish 35
    6 days, Friday, 8 dollars, 5'8", (arrived 4 years ago)

Robert Wood, Charles Porter Baltimore MD 9/6/1750,
   46 days, Sunday, 8 pounds, short,
Samuel Wood, William Harris Philadelphia City PA ship captain 12/6/1733, English
   2 pounds, (ran from ship Vigor from Bristol)
Thomas Wood, John Smith Baltimore MD 12/26/1752, English 19
   5'5",
Thomas Wood, Samuel Smith Chester PA 12/19/1754, English 21 (2nd escape)
   12 days, Saturday, 1.5 pounds,
William Wood, Thomas Postgate Salem NJ 7/19/1733, 18
   37 days, Tuesday,
Thomas Woodcock, Charles Carroll Baltimore MD ironworks 5/13/1756, English 30 C
   11 days, Sunday, 4 pistoles, 5'8",
Thomas Woodcock, Charles Carroll Baltimore MD ironworks 4/3/1760, English 34 (2nd escape) C
   10 days, Monday, 5 pounds, 5'8",
Peter Woodford, Uriah Paul Gloucester NJ 2/13/1772, 21
   28 days, Thursday, 16 dollars, 5'7-8",
George Woods, James Ager Baltimore MD 4/26/1764, English
   17 days, Monday, 2 pounds, 5'9",
Glowd Woods, Thomas Cummings Chester PA shoemaker 6/12/1740, Irish (man)
   3 days, Monday, 1 pound, middle,
James Woods, John Smith Chester PA 11/22/1753, Irish 23
   3 days, Monday, 2 pounds, 5'4",
Mark Woods, Esther Lowdon Philadelphia City PA 9/17/1730, 24 bricklayer
   3 days, Monday, 2 pounds,
Rebecca Wooley, George Lee Westmoreland VA 10/26/1749, Irish (pregnant)
   66 days, Monday, 1 pistole, (arrived 2 years ago)
Robert Wooley, William Pennell Chester PA 8/30/1759, American L
   11 days, Sunday, 1.5 pounds, 5'10",
Joseph Woore, Joseph Flowers Philadelphia City PA joiner 10/8/1730,
   3 days, Monday, 1 pound, short,
Joseph Woore, Samuel Auston Philadelphia City PA 10/6/1737, 34 joiner
   1.5 pounds,
William Worley, Ely Dorsey Anne Arundel MD 7/2/1761, American L
   15 days, Wednesday, 10 pistoles, 5'8",
John Wort, Arnold Bombarger Lancaster PA 11/23/1774, tailor A
   3 days, Monday, 6 dollars, 5'3-4",
James Worthington, Richard Gill Philadelphia City PA 4/24/1746, English carpenter
   (no other information)
George Wortman, William Clarke Hunterdon NJ 11/11/1772, German 20
   5 pounds, 5'6-7",
George David Wortz, Christian Wirtz 6/22/1785, German 22 butcher
   3 days, Sunday, 10 dollars, (arrived last fall)
George David Wortz, Richard Backhouse Bucks PA ironworks 10/12/1785, German 22 butcher
   15 days, Tuesday, 5 pounds, (2nd escape)
Elias Wright, James Eddy Philadelphia City PA 8/9/1764, 15
   1 pound, 4'6",
Henry Wright, George Peirce Chester PA 10/25/1775, 25
   9 days, Tuesday, 8 pounds, 5'7",
John Wright, Jacob Lemmon New Castle DE 7/31/1766, English weaver
   1.5 pounds,
John Wright, Jacob Lemmon New Castle DE 9/18/1766, English weaver (2nd escape)
   1 pound, 5'7-8", (lately arrived)
John Wright, Peter McKinley 2/3/1773, 50 tailor
   7 days, Thursday, 6 dollars, 5'5-6",
Joseph Wright, John Howard Anne Arundel MD 5/15/1760, English 40 C
   12 days, Saturday, 2 pounds, short
William Wright, Obidiah Hireton Burlington NJ 8/12/1742, 24
   1.5 pounds, middle,
William Wright, Joseph Nicholson Gloucester NJ 6/11/1772,
   6 days, Friday, 1.5 pounds, 5'1",
Leonard Yanawine, Samuel Flower Chester PA ironworks 4/10/1755, German wheelwright
   64 days, Wednesday, 2 pounds,
Daniel Yare, Hannah Whigam Chester PA 8/15/1754, German
   1 day, Wednesday, 2 pounds, 5'8",
James Yates, Cornealius Van Horne Monmouth NJ 4/27/1738, English school teacher
   11 days, Sunday, 2.5 pounds, short,

Susannah Yates, John Pearce Duvall VA 7/27/1769, English 37 C
    37 days, Tuesday, 2 pounds, middle,
Daniel Yaw, John Smith Chester PA 10/23/1755, German 33
    10 days, Monday, 2 pounds, 5'6",
Jacob Yaw, John Wagoner Philadelphia PA tanner 10/31/1781, 17 A
    24 days, Sunday, 0.03 pounds,
William Yeates, James Valens Philadelphia PA 9/20/1775, Irish 23
    12 days, Saturday, 1 pound, 5'10-11", (lately arrived)
James Yeats, Thomas Pristley Philadelphia City PA 8/6/1747, English 18 A
    4 days, Sunday, 2 pounds,
Jacob Yerb, Jonathan Hunter Chester PA 6/12/1776, English 30
    14 days, Thursday, 2 pounds, 5'9",
Henry Yongken, Daniel Fulmer Bucks PA 5/23/1792, 19 tanner A
    43 days, Tuesday, 8 dollars, 5'7",
David Young, William Davison Philadelphia City PA 6/12/1746,
    3 pounds, 5'10",
Elizabeth Young, William White York PA 6/14/1775, (pregnant)
    25 days, Sunday, 3 pounds, short,
Isaac Young, Aaron Musgrove Chester PA 9/28/1758, Irish 25
    8 days, Wednesday, 1.5 pounds, 5'6",
John Young, Daniel McPherson Lancaster PA 7/31/1766, 25
    11 days, Sunday, 5 pounds, 5'6",
John Young, Lewellyn Davis Chester PA 12/19/1792, Irish 16
    2 days, Monday, 3 dollars, 5', (arrived last Sept.)
John Young, John Fitzwater Philadelphia PA 3/26/1788, German 40 cooper
    8 days, Tuesday, 4 dollars, 5'5",
John Young, James Westbay Lancaster PA 3/17/1768, American 20 L
    3 pounds, 6',
Mary Young, John Hall Philadelphia City PA cooper 1/4/1759, Irish 19
    4 days, Sunday, 2 pounds,
Moses Young, John Betts Bucks PA 3/28/1787, 19 A
    15 days, Tuesday, 2 dollars,
Simon Young, Robert Evans 6/16/1784, Irish cabinetmaker
    3.3 pounds, 5'6",
Thomas Young, John McFarland Lancaster PA 6/14/1775, English 20
    11 days, Sunday, 5'7-8",
William Young, George Lindenburger Baltimore MD 9/20/1764, 23 miller A
    17 days, Monday, 5 pounds,
Elias Younken, Hance Lambson Salem NJ 9/20/1764, German 18
    11 days, Sunday, 2 pounds,
John Zaps, William Eachus Jr Chester PA 4/29/1789, German 25
    16 days, Monday, 6 dollars, 5'3", (arrived 1 year 9 months ago)
Christopher Zechan, Jacob Metzger Lancaster PA 9/12/1781, 19 A
    0.5 dollars, 5'6",
Peter Zeigensoss, Henry Geissinger Northampton PA 11/27/1766, German 21 blacksmith A
    11 days, Sunday, 3 pounds,
Jacob Zeigler, Thomas Mendenhall Lancaster PA 10/12/1774, 18 A
    11 days, Sunday, 4 dollars, 5'7-8",
John Leonard Zembes, Joseph Carter Bucks PA 4/25/1754, German pinmaker
    4 days, Sunday, 2 pounds, middle,
George Zieger, Jacob Miller Berks PA 1/20/1763, German 23
    5 years ago, 5 pounds, (thought he enlisted but instead he ran away)
Bernard Zimmerman, Johannes Harpell Philadelphia PA 8/15/1754, German 17
    7 days, Thursday, 4 pounds, tall,
George Zundel, Francis Kruk Berks PA 4/12/1770, German 26 butcher
    5 pounds, 5',

www.ingramcontent.com/pod-product-compliance
Lightning Source LLC
Chambersburg PA
CBHW051743230426
43670CB00012B/2137